Catching Ourselves in the Act

Complex Adaptive Systems

John H. Holland, Christopher Langton, and Stewart W. Wilson, advisors

Adaptation in Natural and Artificial Systems: An Introductory Analysis with Applications to Biology, Control, and Artificial Intelligence, John H. Holland

Toward a Practice of Autonomous Systems: Proceedings of the First European Conference on Artificial Life, edited by Francisco J. Varela and Paul Bourgine

Genetic Programming: On the Programming of Computers by Means of Natural Selection, John R. Koza

From Animals to Animats 2: Proceedings of the Second International Conference on Simulation of Adaptive Behavior, edited by Jean-Arcady Meyer, Herbert L. Roitblat, and Stewart W. Wilson

Intelligent Behavior in Animals and Robots, David McFarland and Thomas Bösser

Advances in Genetic Programming, edited by Kenneth E. Kinnear, Jr.

Genetic Programming II: Automatic Discovery of Reusable Programs, John R. Koza

Turtles, Termites, and Traffic James: Explorations in Massively Parallel Microworlds, Mitchel Resnick

From Animals to Animats 3: Proceedings of the Third International Conference on Simulation of Adaptive Behavior, edited by Dave Cliff, Philip Husbands, Jean-Arcady Meyer, and Stewart W. Wilson

Artificial Life IV: Proceedings of the Fourth International Workshop on the Synthesis and Simulation of Living Systems, edited by Rodney A. Brooks and Pattie Maes

Comparative Approaches to Cognitive Science, edited by Herbert L. Roitblat and Jean-Arcady Meyer

Artificial Life: An Overview, edited by Christopher G. Langton

Evolutionary Programming IV: Proceedings of the Fourth Annual Conference on Evolutionary Programming, edited by John R. McDonnell, Robert G. Reynolds, and David B. Fogel

An Introduction to Genetic Algorithms, Melanie Mitchell

Catching Ourselves in the Act: Situated Activity, Interactive Emergence, Evolution, and Human Thought, Horst Hendriks-Jansen

Catching Ourselves in the Act

Situated Activity, Interactive Emergence, Evolution, and Human Thought

Horst Hendriks-Jansen

A Bradford Book
The MIT Press
Cambridge, Massachusetts
London, England

This book was set in Palatino by the Maple-Vail Book Manufacturing Group.
Printed and bound in the United States of America.

Library of Congress Cataloging-in-Publication Data

Hendriks-Jansen, Horst.
  Catching ourselves in the act : situated activity, interactive
emergence, evolution, and human thought / Horst Hendriks-Jansen.
     p.   cm — (Complex adaptive systems)
  "A Bradford book."
  Includes bibliographical references and index.
  ISBN 0-262-08246-2 (hc : alk. paper)
  1. Intentionalism. 2. Philosophy of mind. 3. Philosophical
anthropology. 4. Cognitive science. 5. Artificial intelligence.
I. Title. II. Series.
BF619.5.H46   1996
150—dc20   96-972
                                                    CIP

For Fotini and in memory of Phil Hooper

Contents

Preface

This book is an attempt to provide a scientific basis for what Bruner (1990) has called the contextual revolution in psychology, sociology, and the philosophy of mind. The new paradigm tries to construct dynamic, microanalytic descriptions of the ways in which language and culture help to shape, constrain, and sustain human action. A special terminology has sprung up to clarify this approach and to differentiate it from more traditional models of the mind. Rather than issuing fully specified from people's heads or existing in some preregistered form "out there," meaning is said to be "constructed" or "negotiated" in interactions between persons and to be "constitutive" of their standard practices with artifacts and tools. Such notions are difficult to accept for a positivist scientific tradition. Much of the literature of the contextual revolution reads more like literary criticism than hard science to someone coming from artificial intelligence or cognitive psychology. On the other hand, it is becoming increasingly clear that the holy grail of the latter tradition—a coherent computational model of the mind that actually works in real-life situations—is not likely to be achieved.

Human beings can be said to live in a natural environment of meaning. One of the great difficulties for any theory of human intelligence is to explain how we are bootstrapped into that world as infants and children. How do the correct correspondences become established between the representations in our heads and states of the world, or, alternatively, how do we acquire our situated skills of interaction and meaning construction? Much of this book is dedicated to that problem and to the proposition that good explanations of development and learning may provide the link between the insights of the contextual approach and the scientifically more acceptable methods of ethology and situated robotics.

Such a link requires a comprehensive and flexible theory of behavior: a descriptive framework that will rescue behavior from behaviorism and provide conceptual tools to analyze its structure. Artificial intelligence and cybernetics have tended to formalize behavior as a directed arc or step function from a starting position to a goal—a trajectory fully controlled and fully specified by the internal mechanisms of the creature that performs the action. This severely limits the descriptive range of the resulting models, and it means that intentional behavior can only be explained top-down, in terms of "intentional icons" imported into the agent's head. It thus becomes a category totally different from reflexive behavior and the fixed action patterns of ethology, precluding any possibility that an explanatory link can be forged between them. The notion of interactive emergence introduced in this book is intended to break that deadlock. It suggests that there *is* a way of catching ourselves in the act and that it involves species-typical activity patterns adapted to an intentional world.

When I arrived at the School of Cognitive and Computing Sciences at Sussex University in 1987, I felt strongly that there was something wrong with the traditional AI view of human intelligence. I tried to express that conviction by stressing the individuality of each person's mental and physical abilities and the way those abilities grow out of a personal history of situated, embodied experience. Margaret Boden made me see that this was not enough. She heightened my awareness of the formal requirements of a scientific explanation and alerted me to the philosophical and psychological implications of my ideas. Because of her wide reading in many related disciplines, she was able to direct me to the relevant sources and save me again and again from traveling up blind alleys that had already been explored. I thank her as well as Aaron Sloman and Andy Clark for helping me to sort out my ideas. (Of course, they should not be blamed for the conclusions at which I arrived under their guidance.) I also thank Phil Agre for alerting me to the literature of ethnomethodology and conversational analysis during the year he spent at COGS.

But even after I had become reasonably clear about what I was doing, the explanatory framework I had set up as an alternative to the computational model of the mind appeared to lack a bottom stop, in the way that traditional AI has always been able to use the universal Turing machine as its bottom stop. It was my discovery of recent work by Rodney Brooks and his colleagues at MIT, and in particular a robot built by Maja Mataric, that provided me with concrete evidence that I was not merely waving my arms or coining suggestive metaphors. This work was drawn to my attention by Dave Cliff, Inman Harvey, and Phil Husbands, who also gave valuable feedback and moral support when I needed it most. The multidisciplinary atmosphere of COGS and the free-for-all Alergic meetings organized by Inman, Phil, and Dave have provided a near-perfect environment for situated, interactive learning. Finally, I thank Margaret Boden, Rodney Brooks, Phil Husbands, and Inman Harvey for reading various drafts of the manuscript and giving me their comments.

Chapter 1

Situated Robotics, Natural Selection, and Cultural Scaffolding: The Ingredients of a Historical Explanation

1.1 Meeting the Challenge of a New Paradigm

The new disciplines of artificial life and situated robotics have called into question some of the basic principles of cognitive science and traditional AI (artificial intelligence). Decomposition by function, the conceptualization of an autonomous agent as an input-output model, the separation of central processes from peripheral processes, and the principle of formal task definition have all come under attack. If these criticisms are taken seriously, as I believe they should be, they call for a fundamental reappraisal of the computational paradigm.

Unfortunately, the new disciplines have failed to produce a coherent alternative framework. This is partly due to the persistence of old habits from traditional AI, but its more basic cause is a lack of clarity about the theoretical implications of the emerging paradigm. The problems of implementation are even more complex than those in traditional AI and thus tend to demand most of the researchers' attention, obscuring the nature of what their artifacts imply about computer-based explanation in general. The domain of study has shifted dramatically from the higher reaches of human problem solving to the rudimentary behavior of some of the "lowest" forms of life. There is a danger that Alife (artificial life) and autonomous agent research will turn into computational disciplines specializing in slime molds and six-legged insects.

A more realistic view of the complexities involved in such apparently mundane behavior as recognizing a face or negotiating a route through a cluttered room has caused most of the researchers working in Alife to defer the study of mental phenomena to some distant date in the future. The assumption is that the human brain, since it is the product of millions of years of evolution, will probably require hundreds of years to reconstruct from behavior modules or to re-evolve by artificial means, and until such a model is produced, there is little sense in worrying about the way it works. According to this view, situated robotics provides the only principled method for creating artificial intelligence, but it will not have anything to say about human intelligence for quite some time.* I agree that we shall have a long time to wait for a genuine replication of human intelligence (as opposed to systems that mimic rational choice within some formally specified task domain), but I believe that the new paradigm has much to tell us now about the nature of an explanation.

Two important though little-discussed questions inherent in the traditional approach have been brought to the surface. The first concerns the role that natural selection can, and perhaps ought to, play in an explanation of human behavior. The second concerns the nature of explanatory models. Are the computer-based models produced by AI models of the mind or models of the brain, or perhaps neither? If neither, what are they models of? The two questions are related, and the new disciplines I refer to point to answers that have been implicit in artificial intelligence from the start but have been obscured by the search for explanatory entities based on definitions of computation and various programming techniques.

1.2 Symbol Processing as a Scientific Theory of Human and Animal Behavior

In the next four chapters I shall argue that cognitive science, conceived as a legitimization of folk psychology and the intentional stance through computer-based models, has so far failed to provide a satisfactory scientific explanation of human and animal behavior. Explanations of this type (irrespective of whether they use classical or connectionist architectures) depend on internal representations derived top down from an analysis of full-blown symbolic behavior. This strategy has not succeeded in identifying defensible "natural kinds," and it might be based on a misconception about the role that explanatory models have traditionally played in science.

My argument will require me to examine in some detail a variety of philosophical systems developed in support of the traditional approach. It will also involve a certain amount of discussion of problems in the philosophy of science. Finally, it will be necessary to bring out the underlying complexities of the modern synthesis combining the theory of natural selection and Mendelian genetics, which are frequently ignored by the advocates of an evolutionary explanation. At times it may appear that the discussion has strayed very far from the main concerns of Alife, but it should be remembered that my ultimate

---

*However, see Brooks and Stein (1993). I was unaware of the COG program, which has been getting underway during the past year at the MIT Artificial Intelligence Lab, until this book was almost completed. As far as I can tell, its aims and methods for building a humanoid robot are in general agreement with the explanatory strategies I propose.

aim is to show that the new paradigm can serve as a coherent explanatory strategy for human as well as animal behavior, and not just as an engineering tool to produce interesting or useful artifacts.

The use of models as explanatory devices is central to AI. The earliest, and probably the most influential, example of this approach is seen in the work of Newell and Simon (Newell and Simon 1961, 1972; 1976; Newell 1973; Ericsson and Simon 1980; Vera and Simon 1993). In chapter 2 I shall examine the persistent claim made by these authors that computational models can, and in many cases already do, provide uncontroversial and principled scientific explanations of psychological phenomena. I shall argue that unlike, for example, the empirical laws that explain the diverse properties of matter in physics, computational explanations have not resulted in anything that resembles a unifying calculus and that the main reason for this failure must be sought in the impossibility of constructing a computationally based analogical model of psychological phenomena.

The experimental laws of cognitive psychology are not laws about behavior but formal task descriptions that implicitly assume a computational framework of discrete operations and states. The computational model dictates the style in which the laws are to be framed; it does not "fall out" as a unifying theory from independently formulated empirical laws. The model derives its validity not from properties of the creature or its behavior but from a formal method of description devised for mathematical proofs.

I shall argue that the deductive approach to scientific explanation implicitly assumed by Newell and Simon is not conducive to an understanding of human and animal behavior. An alternative, genetic (Nagel 1961) or historical (Sloman 1978) approach needs to be adopted. The ultimate warranty for explanations of this type is Darwin's theory of natural selection. Explanatory entities derive their claim to the status of natural kind not from some functional role that may be deduced by taking a design stance but from actual stages in the creature's development. Models of situated activity using autonomous robots can be used to test such hypotheses. These models must be seen as models of behavior rather than models of brains or minds. However, a better understanding of the detailed structure of behavior as it emerges from interactions with the creature's species-typical environment is more likely to lead to an understanding of its neural and mental concomitants than functional decomposition inspired by the notion that natural creatures are designed like machines.

Whatever model may turn out to be the most appropriate, there appears to be a growing consensus in cognitive science that natural selection represents our best hope for naturalizing the model's explanatory entities. The alternative strategy for naturalizing content is through some form of hard reductionism, correlating mental phenomena with specific events in the neurophysiological substrate. Few cognitive scientists now subscribe to that approach, and I shall refer to it only in passing.

In chapter 3, I discuss Dennett's proposal (Dennett 1969) that the theory of natural selection be called upon to imbue the internal representations posited by the symbol-processing paradigm in AI with the intentionality that appears to characterize symbols in human thought. This challenge was taken up by, among others, Dretske (1986, 1988), Sterelny (1990), and Millikan (1984), but I conclude that none of these authors has ultimately succeeded in bridging the gap. Internal representations cannot be "naturalized" by an appeal to natural selection. Any attempt to do so needs to resort to an overly simplified view of genetic transmission and to ignore the complex processes involved in ontogeny, as well as the way in which early development and learning emerge from species-typical interactions with a creature's ecological and cultural environment. I shall examine, in particular, the work of Millikan (1984), who has been most radical and consistent in exploring this line of philosophical investigation. I conclude that her proposal that language and thought must be seen as biological categories cannot be sustained, but that her notion of history of use provides a valuable starting point for a historical explanation of behavior.

In chapter 4, I examine the claim that connectionist networks, by virtue of distributed representation that results in the emergence of soft-edged symbols from low-level features, can be used to ground the symbols of the symbol-processing paradigm in terms of pure sensory categories isolated by psychophysical investigation. I argue that this idea rests on a confusion of two different views of connectionism, which I call the analytic and the synthetic views. The analytic view (e.g., Minsky and Papert 1969) encourages hopes of grounding the symbols of a classic symbol system directly in nonsymbolic, low-level features. The synthetic view (e.g., Smolensky 1988) provides grounds for believing that the symbols of connectionist networks have similarities with the symbols "in people's minds."

A failure to be clear about the different sources of meaning in the two conceptualizations can lead to the belief that connectionist networks, by their very nature, can provide an explanation for symbolic thinking in humans. In fact, as I try to show by a close examination of two seminal papers by Smolensky (1988) and Harnad (1990), the gap between the two is impossible to bridge. Intentional objects cannot emerge from pure sensory categories simply by the combinatorial virtues of connectionist networks, and the "subsymbols" of existing connectionist systems are not subsymbolic in any true sense but merely features derived by top-down analysis in accordance with some existing conception of the subject matter they are meant to represent.

In his exposition of the connectionist approach to explanation, Smolensky (1988) compares the relation between the subsymbolic and the symbolic levels to the relation between the level of colliding gas molecules and the level of temperature, pressure, and volume in the theory of thermodynamics. This analogy is misleading. If Maxwell and Boltzman had followed Smolensky's approach to the "semantics" of their problem, they would have tried to analyze the notions of temperature, pressure, and volume and framed their theories in terms of features that define the meanings of these terms. Smolensky's "atoms of meaning" will not work as explanatory entities for human behavior, because they are merely a redescription of the units used in folk psychology and in the symbolic paradigm for which he is trying to provide a deeper explanation. The revolutionary impact of the molecular theory of thermodynamics, the characteristic that gave it its explanatory force, was the fact that the underlying entities and their dynamic relationship bear no obvious resemblance to the higher level of temperature, pressure, and volume they were called on to explain.

In chapter 5, I argue that scientific explanation often requires such a leap in the dark. The key ingredient in this type of explanation is the analogical model. A well-known object or artifact is used as an explanatory device for some natural phenomenon that is not well understood. There is no a priori reason that the model needs to be a machine, but many of the most fruitful explanatory models in science have been mechanical models. Cognitive science can be seen as a culmination of this tradition. However, I argue in chapter 5 that, with Turing's introduction of the effective procedure and his proof that all such procedures may be reduced to permutations of the three basic operations of a universal Turing machine, the computer forfeits its role as a fruitful source of analogies.

Analogical models are not constructed; they are found. Their function is not to provide a copy or simulation of the original but to act as a kind of mirror that brings out illuminating features of the phenomenon we are trying to understand. As Hesse (1966, 1980) points out, drawing an analogy must begin with a holistic, unanalyzed perception of similarity between the *explicandum* and the *explicans*. Once that holistic similarity has been seen, the structural and causal relations of the model can be used to delineate the structural and causal relations of the phenomenon for which it provides the analogy. This means that analogical models are fruitful sources of explanatory kinds. An analogical model of the mind or brain would be a mechanism that exhibits behavior similar to that of an animal or human being but was not specifically designed for that purpose, so that its internal structure could provide unexpected insights into the subtending mechanisms of naturally occurring behavior. I conclude that this type of model is beyond the reach of science; a different explanatory strategy will be required.

It might be said that cognitive science represents a coming together of two ideas that have made it impossible to discover a helpful explanatory entity for the phenomena of mind. One strand holds that we are the product of evolution, the other that the mind is in some sense like a computer and therefore ought to be conceptualized as a general-purpose machine that runs particular bits of software to perform specific tasks. There is nothing intrinsic to this machine, nothing inherent in the explanation of its mechanism, that relates it to the world. If its congruence with the world is to be explained, additional explanatory entities, in the form of programs and internal representations, need to be introduced. The question then becomes how these programs and internal representations can be legitimized, tied in to the rest of science: "naturalized" or "grounded."

This is the conundrum faced in various ways by Dennett (1969), Dretske (1986), Sterelny (1990), Millikan (1984), Harnad (1989), Smolensky (1988), and others. But the puzzle is an artificial one. It stems, I shall argue, from an imposition of the wrong natural kinds, which appear to be required because the brain is conceived as a stand-alone, all-purpose mechanism whose essential operations may be specified without reference to the circumstances under which they evolved. This all-purpose mechanism encourages formal task description. Anything that can be formalized in terms of a task description may be run on a computer. But neither that fact, nor the logic of the program that is written to implement it, nor the type of virtual machine on which it is run confers compelling explanatory force. As Heil (1981) points out, we may grant that what a person does or learns is describable in a certain way without assuming that the person has, in some sense, internalized that description.

In chapter 6, I argue that explanations of human behavior are inextricably bound up with an understanding of their historical emergence through evolution and learning. Although much of cognitive philosophy depends on natural selection to link computational concepts to the rest of science, there has been little discussion of how such a link might be defended on biological grounds. References to evolution tend to be notional and abstract, treating the process as a kind of heuristic, and amounting to the claim that mental structures, as well as external form, may be "designed" by a selective process. The fact that such a process can operate only indirectly on neural structure through its behavioral consequences, and the questions this raises about how those consequences should be conceptualized and related back to neural structure, are rarely mentioned.

Any appeal to Darwin's theory must be tempered by a clear understanding that evolution is not a rational designer. Optimal solutions in evolutionary terms might be difficult to recognize as efficient solutions in design terms. Natural selection often hijacks organs or patterns of behavior that originally emerged for a quite different "purpose." Traits may be selected because they are genetically linked to other, completely unrelated but reproductively advantageous traits, even though they themselves do not confer any selective advantage. The conditions under which a particular trait was selected in the past may no longer obtain in the creature's existing environmental niche. An understanding of evolutionary solutions requires a historical approach to explanation, coupled with an awareness of the complex interactions between the logic of genetic reproduction and the pressures of an ever-changing environment.

These complexities of the evolutionary process make it extremely difficult to use top-down analysis or functional decomposition to identify the explanatory entities for a behavioral or morphological trait resulting from natural selection. In particular, they render highly problematic a justification of internal representations based on "proper function" along the lines attempted by Millikan (1984). What is required is a strategy that suspends generic classification in terms of purpose or function as long as possible and focuses on patterns of behavior as they occur under natural conditions. Ethologists have shown that there are ways of linking species-typical activity patterns to the environment through natural selection, but this requires careful observation of an animal in situ, imaginative reconstruction of possible alternatives to the behavior being studied (or their isolation in related species if these can be found), and a keen sense of the ambiguities inherent in the notion of optimality.

The early experiences of Lorenz (1937) provide an instructive example. In studying the behavior of mother ducks in the presence of their offspring, he naturally subsumed the various activity patterns he observed under the general heading of parenting behavior. For the purpose of descriptive classification, there was clearly nothing wrong with this. But it carried with it the implication (at first not explicitly recognized) that there exists somewhere in the mother duck a common denominator for these different patterns of behavior—an internal representation of some kind corresponding to the duckling "out there," which could serve as an explanatory locus for the various activity patterns. In fact, as Lorenz subsequently discovered, the different activities that together make up parenting behavior are all triggered by quite different stimuli. The only point at which these activities can be said to intersect is on the duckling "out there." The concept of parenting behavior was thus a helpful descriptive classification in that it focused attention on certain activity patterns by supporting them with an evolutionary rationale, but it proved to be seriously misleading as a guide to the most fruitful natural kinds for an explanation of the subtending mechanism.

I therefore conclude that functional decomposition and natural selection do not mix. "Why is it there?" is a better question to ask than, "How would a rationally designed artifact perform that task?" but it still is not the right question. Natural selection warrants only one question, and that is, "How did it come to be there?" This implies that teleological, as well as deductive, explanations (Nagel 1961) need to be shelved. The only appropriate explanation for a piece of behavior resulting from natural selection is an explanation in terms of its historical emergence within a succession of species-typical environments. Only this type of explanation offers any hope of isolating the natural kinds of interactively emergent activity.

1.3 *The Basic Ingredients of an Alternative Approach*

The explanatory entities of a historical or genetic explanation are the successive stages in the development of a phenomenon, trait, or event. As Nagel (1961) pointed out, one of the difficulties with this type of explanation is the problem of deciding which specific occurrences, out of a more or less continuous historical line, deserve to be singled out as particularly significant and therefore worthy of being designated its "natural kinds." In chapter 7, I argue that, for historical explanations of behavior, a principled choice can in fact be made, based on a slightly modified version of Millikan's (1984) notion of history of use. In support of my argument, I draw on recent research with autonomous robots, concentrating in particular on a wall-following and navigating robot by Mataric (Mataric 1991a, 1991b, 1992; Mataric and Brooks 1990).

The fundamental principle involved is that of interactive emergence. Patterns of activity whose high-level structure cannot be reduced to specific sequences of movements may emerge from the interactions between simple reflexes and the particular environment to which they are adapted. In the case of Mataric's robot, the independent operation of four low-level reflexes within an office environment results in the emergent activity of wall following. There are no explicit instructions inside the robot that tell it to follow walls. No formal definition of walls is required to produce its behavior. The emergent behavior of the system as a whole is the result of various autonomous activities interacting with each other and with the environment, and not of a centralized system making decisions based on internally represented courses of action or goals. The robot is therefore unlikely to follow a particular wall in exactly the same way on different occasions. Its route will depend on its approach in a specific instance, on noise in its sensor readings, and on the numerous unspecified contingencies of a dynamic environment. But it can be relied on to follow the wall every time.

Such patterns of activity can result in the emergence of dynamic features with temporal extent that correspond only very indirectly to features in the world. The wall-following behavior of Mataric's robot facilitates navigation by landmarks. Landmarks come into being as the result of the robot's structured activity within a particular environment. This structured activity allows the robot to detect correlations between its sensory input and its own movements and permits the classification of landmarks into types. Landmarks have extension over time. It may be said that the robot chops the routes it has traveled into segments of activity rather than placing signposts along the way. Navigation becomes a matter not so much of traveling from one landmark to another but of slipping from the behavior specified by one landmark into the behavior specified by the next. This is possible only because of the robot's structured, low-level activity of wall following, which results in the emergence of reliable correlations between its sensor readings and its movements.

Such a configuration, if found in a naturally occurring creature, would confer the status of "natural kind" on the lower level of activity, since it would clearly establish a history of use for that activity in the creature's evolutionary past. The fact that the creature displayed landmark detection and navigational behavior that depends so crucially on the existence of wall following would constitute evidence that wall following must have been a stable element in the creature's behavioral repertoire for a considerable part of its evolutionary history. In a historical account of the evolution of the creature's behavior, the emergence of wall following would stand out as a significant occurrence in a more or less continuous sequence of changes.

It is important to stress that the natural kinds of this type of explanation come into existence only as the result of the creature's situated activity. They are not entities that can be reduced to events inside the creature's head; neither can they be defined by classifying its environment. Interactive, situated behavior cannot be explained in terms of a deductive or generative law. It requires a historical explanation because there can be no rules to predict the sorts of behavior that might emerge. It is impossible to define an "implements relation" (Horswill

1992) relating environment, behavior, and the underlying mechanisms of the organism, because none of the elements in such an equation is susceptible of prior classification. There is no shortcut for deriving the sequence of events in a historical process.

The alternative approach to model building I shall propose accepts that computational models are deliberately designed to mimic human or animal behavior and concludes from this that such models must be seen as models of behavior rather than models of the brain or mind. Computer hardware and programming techniques enable the model builder to construct autonomous creatures that behave in intelligent, flexible, well-adapted ways under natural conditions. They provide powerful (and perhaps indispensable) tools for building such creatures, but they can play no role as explanatory kinds. The hardware and software used in such models carry no explanatory burden; it is the interrelationships between the robot's activity patterns and its "natural" environment that constitute the explanation.

Fruitful hypotheses for such models are most likely to come from the observation of naturally evolved behavior, in its natural surroundings, supplemented by controlled experiments in the same natural habitat, and comparisons with the behavior of related species. (See Webb 1993, 1994 and Webb and Smithers 1992 for a particularly elegant example.) In chapters 11 to 14, I examine the orienting attitudes and classic concepts of ethology and argue that species-typical activity patterns may be isolated in this way. The approach pioneered by Lorenz (1939) and Tinbergen (1951), and subsequently developed by Hinde (1970, 1982), Barlow (1968), and Baerends (1976) among others, imposes principled constraints on historical explanations. Critiques of the classic concepts of ethology made by Schneirla (1966) and Lehrman (1970) serve to sharpen those concepts and bring them into line with the insights gained from autonomous agent research.

Species-typical activity patterns must be thought of as emergent phenomena in three different senses of the word. They have emerged in the species through natural selection, they emerge in the individual by a process of maturation and/or learning, and they emerge at the time of execution from interactions between the creature's low-level activities and its species-typical environment. Within the framework of autonomous agent research, this makes better sense than the blueprint model espoused by early ethology.

Artificially built models serve to confirm hypotheses about the interactive causes of such emergent behavior. They can be seen as "existence proofs," each of which contributes to delineating further a space of behavioral possibilities (Sloman 1978). It is only by accumulating such natural kinds of behavior that the space of possibilities can be explored, since there can be no deductive or generative rules for behavior, no competence theories from which a range of specific "performances" may be derived. This alternative conception has always been inherent in the notion of a computational model, but it has been obscured by more traditional ideas about the use of models in scientific explanation and by the imposition of a dualist framework encouraging explanations in terms of causal mechanisms situated within the creature's head.

1.4 Can Situated Activity and Interactive Emergence Explain the Intentional Behavior of Human Beings?

In traditional cognitive science, intentionality is conceptualized in causal and informational terms as arising from the rule-governed manipulation of internal representations. Minds are seen as syntactic or semantic engines that derive their intentionality from symbolic structures physically embodied in the brains that "run" them. The folk taxonomy of propositional attitudes is assumed to be mirrored in the underlying mechanism of syntactic relations, and the natural kinds to describe these mechanisms are derived by conceptual analysis from the descriptive terms of folk psychology.

The alternative account I shall put forward in the final chapters of this book suggests that the intentional behavior and contentful thoughts of adult human beings are emergent phenomena that require a historical explanation. The details of such an account are only just beginning to become apparent. Chapters 15 through 18 are therefore presented as a rough sketch rather than a fully worked-out theory. As I have pointed out already, one of the main contentions of this book will be that a grand, unified theory of human behavior is in any case ruled out. Historical explanations depend on painstaking identification of species-typical behaviors in situ and on using such singularities to delineate the space of possibilities.

Our intentional descriptions of the activities of young infants and other animals can usually be shown to be mistaken. They ascribe an "aboutness" to such activities that is not supported by the operations of the underlying mechanisms. The fixed action patterns and orienting mechanisms that subtend a mother duck's behavior toward her duckling require no internal representation of the duckling, the mechanisms that subtend wall following by Mataric's robot do not refer to walls, and the focusing mechanisms that cause a young infant's gaze to center on his mother's face are not *about* the mother (Johnson 1993b). But an adequate explanation of the behavior and thoughts of adult human beings *does* require a reference to the things they are about (real or counterfactual), because the underlying mechanisms that subtend this behavior have been shaped interactively by the objects, properties, and relations picked out by our language and culture.

The key components in this type of explanation are species-typical activity patterns and cultural scaffolding. In chapters 15 and 16, I present evidence from the recent literature of developmental psychology that human infants, observed in their natural setting, perform activity patterns that are far more complex and far more varied than had previously been supposed (see, in particular, Bullowa 1979a; Kaye 1982; Papousek and Papousek 1977; Schaffer 1977a; Thelen 1981; Trevarthen 1977; von Hofsten 1984). Many of these activity patterns would seem to be unique to human infants, and they appear to have been selected for their power to attract and hold the attention of adults. Their performance requires no inborn knowledge of the world. They can be shown to result from the interactions of simple reflexes and motor programs with a mother who is biologically primed to respond to her infant's species-typical behavior as though it were intentional and purposeful.

The explanatory entities of psychology have tended to be static entities like beliefs, desires, memories, and mental states. These new discoveries suggest that meaning emerges in dynamic interactions. More sophisticated recording and sampling techniques, allied to the orienting attitudes of ethology, have revealed the importance of temporal patterning in the establishment and maintenance of mother-infant exchanges. It has begun to be realized that the main "function" of many of the early activity patterns is the establishment of an interactively emergent, typically human scaffolding of mother-infant dialogue. Many of the patterns performed in early infancy do not survive into adult behavior. They seem merely to serve this bootstrapping role to launch the infant into an environment of adults who think in intentional terms, communicate through language, and manipulate tools and artifacts.

The notion of interactive emergence that I develop in this book is not merely a different way of talking about epigenesis. The concept of epigenesis has recently gained favor as a description of the processes of ontogeny and maturation (see Carey and Gelman 1991; Johnson 1993a; Boden 1994.) The term was probably introduced into psychology by Piaget, but its use in biology goes back to early nineteenth-century controversies, when it was deployed in opposition to the doctrine of preformation. Preformationists held that the adult already exists, preformed, in the egg or sperm; the supporters of epigenesis proposed that the embryo somehow develops from undifferentiated tissue. It will be obvious that this argument has long been won by the latter.

The biological concept of epigenesis is helpful in that it stresses that ontogeny should not be conceptualized as a process of constructing a creature from a genetic blueprint. In its contemporary form, it is generally felt to have the following implications:

1. The development of the mature creature proceeds in stages.
2. Each stage builds on the results of the previous stage.
3. The genetic instructions do not specify the shapes of these stages or the final form of the creature but merely tell cells what to do when they find themselves in specific chemical environments or at specific locations.

In psychology, the concept of epigenesis can provide insights into the emergence of behavioral processes, but it also tends to bring with it a number of related notions that can obscure the nature of those processes. It suggests that new forms of behavior are created from less mature forms by a process that resembles cell differentiation in the embryo. This implies that behavioral development should be seen as a series of specializations and bifurcations of the coarser, simpler, and less finely tuned elements of early infant behavior into the more detailed, better coordinated, more perfectly adapted acts performed by adults.

The model I shall argue for is subtly but radically different. It posits that early forms of activity, resulting from interactions between subcortically mediated reflexes or motor patterns and the species-typical environment by which they were selected, provide a dynamic context for the emergence of more advanced forms of behavior. Immature behavior patterns are perfectly adapted to the stage of development during which they emerge and to the task of setting up such interactive contexts. They are not imperfect versions of adult behavior. It can often be shown that a more mature form of behavior would make it impossible for the creature to respond in a developmentally fruitful way. The process of behavioral development is therefore not so much constrained as facilitated. It is best described in terms of possibilities that open up as the result of new dynamic contexts that become available through the creature's activities in conjunction with its species-typical environment.

The notion of an act—a physical act, a speech act, or an act of thought—is central to folk psychological explanation. I argue in chapter 17 that this notion cannot provide natural kinds for an explanation of human activity and that the underlying mechanisms can be discovered only through a historical understanding of how we learn to perceive our own and other people's behavior in terms of acts. Acts are best conceptualized as parts of our own and other people's situated behavior that we learn to articulate through the use of language. (It follows that nonhuman animals and very young babies do not perform "acts.")

A species-typical capacity to produce a variety of language-like sounds, which matures gradually during the first year and is spontaneously exercised by the infant, supplies the vocal responses around which the mother can shape primitive dialogues. Simultaneously, ritualized games involving cultural artifacts and toys impose a primitive form of systematicity on the infant's behavior (Bruner 1976). The environment of the young child is predominantly a cultural one. It provides material scaffolding that promotes groupings of activity patterns around objects designed for specific functions and purposes. The species-typical reflex of reach-and-grasp (Trevarthen 1977; von Hofsten 1984) is gradually transformed within the interactive context of mother-infant dialogue into pointing (Bruner 1976), which enables the mother to attach linguistic labels to the behavioral groupings that have become established.

Concepts, in this view, do not correspond to specific internal states or structures within the creatures who use them. They must be equated with the ability to use a skill: that of deploying the concept in a convincing range of relevant situations. Internally, such a skill may be sustained by a variety of disjunct computational states that need to have nothing in common from the point of view of physics, neuroscience, or even computational psychology. They are held together purely by the fact that, together, they enable an agent to "negotiate some macrolevel domain which interests us in virtue of our daily life" (Clark 1993, p. 203).

Task descriptions, rules, plans, and belief-desire psychology do not describe the underlying mechanisms of our behavior, but they do provide valuable aids and resources, enabling us to transmit forms of activity, "debug" our own behavior, attend to aspects that do not seem naturally relevant but help to keep our behavior on the right track, and hold ourselves and other people responsible for our actions. Public culture provides the indispensable scaffolding for the interactive emergence of our uniquely human activity patterns. The stories we tell ourselves about our own behavior may not be good science, but the quality of such stories is all important, because they are what make us human.

1.5 Traveling through the Book by Different Routes

In this book I draw on a variety of disciplines to construct my argument. Not all of these will be of equal interest to all readers, and although the argument ultimately depends on all of them, it can be approached from different angles. Chapter 2 discusses the philosophy of science and various types of scientific explanation. Chapter 3 is concerned with the philosophy of mind as it relates to computational explanations. Chapters 4 and 5 examine the theoretical implications of connectionist and classical AI. Chapter 6 is a discussion of natural selection and how it relates to functionality. My purpose in these early chapters is to draw attention to the limitations and methodological problems of the computational approach and to establish that an alternative explanation is both possible and necessary.

The construction of this alternative explanation begins in chapter 7. Chapters 7 through 10 present a technical discussion of the new field of situated robotics. Chapters 11 through 14 are devoted to ethology and make a case for the orienting attitudes of this discipline, which is currently out of fashion. Chapters 15 through 17 discuss the early development of human behavior and thought, and chapter 18 drives home the argument and concludes with some speculations about future developments.

The basic elements of an activity-based explanation of mind can be picked out of chapters 7, 10, and 15 through 18, but to be convinced, readers probably will need to read chapter 2 on scientific explanations, chapter 6 on natural selection, and chapters 11 and 12 on the methods and explanatory entities of ethology.

Chapter 2
Computers, Models, and Theories

2.1 The Search for a Unifying Calculus in Computational Psychology

The claim that a computational framework can provide us with a genuine scientific theory of mental phenomena has probably been made most explicitly and consistently by A. Newell and H. A. Simon. Over the past thirty-five years, they have collaborated with a succession of authors to reiterate this claim in a variety of contexts and guises. Simon's latest, and perhaps most vociferous, assertion of the claim occurs in the spring 1993 issue of *Cognitive Science,* devoted to a discussion of situated action:

> Cognitive psychology is an empirical science, aimed at explaining the behavior of thinking human beings. It makes statements whose implications can be tested, more or less accurately, with the help of empirical evidence. In the case of those theories that are based on the physical symbol-system hypothesis, the statements of the theories are generally encapsulated in computer programs, and the implications of these statements are obtained by running the programs in the same task environments as those of human subjects in psychological experiments, or human beings observed in natural situations—there are numerous examples of both. (Vera and Simon 1993, p. 118)

To Simon and his coauthor, the case for computer-based theories of human behavior has long been made. Doubts concerning the scientific legitimacy of such theories cause them to respond with evident exasperation:

> We find preposterous, in the light of the accumulated evidence, Agre's (1993) view that "nobody has described a system capable of intelligent action at all—and that nothing of the sort is going to happen soon" (p. 69). This is wishful (or rueful) thinking, like the regret one might feel because astronauts have already reached the moon, removing that achievement from the list of possible

feats of discovery. Computer programs exhibiting the kind of behavior that is called intelligent when exhibited by humans have
been around since the 1950s. (This is quite different from a claim
that all aspects of intelligence have been explained. Physics is not
over yet either.) (Vera and Simon 1993, p. 85)

In chapter 5, I shall discuss the nature and implications of the sorts
of programs to which Vera and Simon refer. In this chapter I concentrate on the issue of what might count as a genuine scientific explanation of human behavior, and on the role computers can play in
providing such explanations. It should be clear from the paragraphs I
have quoted that Simon and his collaborators do not merely see computers and their programs as devices to mimic or simulate certain aspects of intelligent behavior. To them, the computer-based models
produced by thirty-five years of research in AI represent scientific theories explaining how human beings perform the tasks that the programs
are designed to accomplish, in the same way that molecular theories explain the behavior of gases, liquids, and solids in physics. The
constituents of these programs are seen as explanatory entities
corresponding to the natural kinds of human behavior:

> The symbolic theories assert that there are also symbol structures
> (essentially changing patterns of neurons and neuronal relations)
> in the human brain that have a one-to-one relation to the sym-
> bolic structures . . . in the corresponding program. (Vera and Si-
> mon 1993, p. 120).

> The high degree of isomorphism . . . , far from being a cause for
> concern, represent(s) the beauty and the triumph of the physical
> symbol-system hypothesis, setting the stage for empirical dem-
> onstrations that the theory does predict and explain the data. . . .
> Isomorphism is not conflation: just plain, old-fashioned fit of the-
> ory to data. (Vera and Simon 1993, p. 121)

Programs and symbolic representations are thus seen as the "abstract calculus" and the "theoretical terms" (Nagel 1961) of a theory in
the classic mold, whose validity may be tested by empirical means. To
what extent are these notions justified? On what grounds (apart from
the fact that some of the simulations work under strictly controlled
conditions) do Simon and his colleagues base their claim that a computational perspective allows one to pick out the natural kinds of human
and animal behavior?

There are at least four possible ways to approach the elucidation of
mental phenomena using computers and computational techniques.

1. Assert that the fact that computers exist and that they run programs that are transferable between different hardware configurations proves the viability of a "software" model of the mind—an explanation that is reductionist in accepting a physical substrate for mind but not reductionist in the "hard" sense of requiring one-to-one correspondence between the psychological and neurophysiological levels. There are many variations on this approach, ranging from appeals to Turing's definition of an effective procedure and the functional architecture of specific virtual machines to appeals to the properties of physical symbol systems and of various computational languages and programming devices, such as list processing and production systems. All of these variations have in common a conviction that the characteristics of the computational approach provide sufficient basis for a scientific theory of the mind, since they demonstrate the possibility of a physical instantiation of mental phenomena.

2. View the computer as an input-output device and construct programs whose outputs are related to inputs in the same way that the "outputs" of human beings are related to "inputs." This encourages the idea that *programs* constitute a form of explanation. Since they enable the computer to mimic the input-output behavior of human subjects, the underlying mechanisms of the human subjects must correspond at some level of description (so the argument goes) to the formal processes instantiated by the programs. Failure of the programs to mimic human behavior in every detail can always be rectified by modifications, which would then have to be interpreted as alterations to the theory.

3. Analyze human behavior and formulate principled theories to explain it (preferably covering a broad class of behaviors), and then convert such theories into algorithms and programs that can be implemented on a computer. In this approach, neither the hardware nor the program, nor even the language in which it is written, constitutes an integral part of the theory, which exists prior to implementation. The implementation merely serves to test the soundness of the theory. Failure of the program to mimic human behavior may be due to a simple programming mistake, in which case it can be corrected without affecting the theory. But if the inadequacy of the implementation can be traced to a deeper cause, then the explanatory cascade needs to be started again at the highest level of computational theory. Ad hoc changes to programs made to improve their performance are considered scientifically unsound by this approach.

These three approaches all depend, in different ways on the nature of computation as defined by Turing (1936), McCulloch and Pitts (1943), and subsequent authors. In the first approach the software-hardware dichotomy and characteristics of Turing machines, operating systems, programming languages, and computational formalisms are used as explanatory devices in their own right. In the second approach, specific programs and data structures provide the constituents of an explanation. Explanations of the third type, though they do not make reference to computational notions or techniques at the level of theory, assume that explanations must be computational in nature. I shall argue for a fourth approach, which uses the computer as a tool for model building but does not draw on its formal characteristics or method of operation as a source for explanatory kinds:

> 4. Like the second approach, this one is ad hoc in the sense in which Marr (1977, 1982) criticized most of the programs of traditional AI (including those of Newell and Simon) for being ad hoc. Modifications are made to the programs as and when they are needed to correct deviations from the desired behavior. On the other hand, it resembles the third approach (which describes the methodology Marr himself advocated), in that theory precedes implementation and does not depend on the computational mechanisms and programming devices that are used to test it. This apparent paradox is, I hope to show, a paradox only for computational explanations. If the explanatory kinds of the theory are not computational entities that play a part in the programs, modifications to those programs need not raise questions concerning the scientific status of the theory. The type of model I shall propose is not a computational model of the mind; it is a model of situated behavior that uses computation as a model-building tool. In chapters 7, 8, 9, and 10 and the final chapters of this book, I shall argue for the scientific legitimacy of such a model and show how it resolves the explanation-imitation dispute that has haunted AI.

The approach taken by Newell and Simon and their succession of coauthors straddles the first two approaches. At various times, they have claimed that the human mind should be characterized as an information processing system (IPS) with specific storage and processing capabilities, running a production system that operates on internal representations described as a physical symbol system. They have also claimed special explanatory powers for list processing and, of course, for specific programs written to perform tasks like playing tic tac toe or number scrabble, and solving problems in symbolic logic (Newell and Simon 1972, 1976; Vera and Simon 1993).

As Newell and Simon (1972) make clear, specific programs embodying theories about human problem solving in particular task domains serve to prevent an information processing model of the human mind from degenerating into a mere metaphor:

> Something ceases to be a metaphor when detailed calculations can be made from it. . . . With a model of an information processing system, it becomes meaningful to try to represent in some detail a particular man at work on a particular task. Such a representation is no metaphor, but a precise symbolic model on the basis of which pertinent specific aspects of the man's problem solving behavior can be calculated. (Newell and Simon 1972, p. 5)

The particular theories confirm and constrain the computational framework, much as the diverse empirical laws of classical physics provide confirmation for a more abstract molecular theory of matter. However, in order to confirm the overall explanatory framework and justify its choice of natural kinds, the particular theories and their task domains must in some sense be representative of human behavior as a whole, so that explanations in these areas may with some justification be taken to provide insight into mental processes in general and the overall functional architecture of the mind. Unfortunately, as Newell and Simon (1972) make quite clear, all their theories are derived from a deliberately restricted investigative base:

> The present study is concerned with the performance of intelligent adults in our own culture. The tasks discussed are short (half-hour), moderately difficult problems of a symbolic nature. . . . The study is concerned with the integrated activities that constitute problem-solving. It is not centrally concerned with perception, motor skill, or what are called personality variables. The study is concerned primarily with performance, only a little with learning, not at all with development, or differences related to age. (pp. 2, 4)

These restrictions on the scope of the studies, coupled with the far-reaching conclusions that Newell and Simon have drawn from them, imply a host of tacit assumptions, among them the following:

1. That our understanding of human thinking can be furthered by a theory of problem solving—that is, that problem solving should be seen as an explanatory kind for psychology.

2. That a theory of problem solving may be derived from studying the performance of mature human beings of our own culture on specific tasks like chess, symbolic logic, and cryptarithmetic, all of which involve a clearly circumscribed task domain, comprising a finite set of objects, properties, and situations whose meanings are implicitly defined by the rules that characterize the domain.

3. That the essential ingredients, or defining characteristics, of intelligent behavior may be separated out from perception and motor skill by conceptualizing contact with the world as mediated by a set of "interfaces" that produce and accept the symbolic representations required by the problem solver. "Thinking" becomes an activity separate from perceiving and acting.

4. That the functional architecture and basic processes that explain intelligent behavior are discoverable without reference to evolution, ontogeny, or learning. The underlying mechanisms involved in the performance of a mature chess player receive an explanation that is independent of the player's temperament, personal history, or exposure to past games: the explanatory framework is derived purely from an analysis of the relevant task domain.

Newell and Simon's theories concerning particular examples of problem solving in fully specified task domains are meant to confirm and constrain the basic explanatory framework, which posits that human beings are information processing systems with certain capacities and limitations. Thus, the nature and form of the mind is ultimately inferred from the analysis of formal task domains, interpreted in computational terms. Is this an adequate basis for a psychological theory?

Newell and Simon themselves remark that if one factors out motivation and emotion and assumes that behavior can be analyzed in terms of tasks or problems, then a study of behavior "would appear rather more suitable for investigating the structure of task-environments than the nature of behaving organisms" (Newell and Simon 1972, p. 53). They point out that the science of economics does precisely this by positing an "economic man" who is motivated to maximize utility and always is able to discover and execute the optimal course of action, allowing the theorist to predict his behavior from an analysis of the available choices. (I shall have more to say about economic models and their inability to provide clues to underlying mechanisms in chapters 3, 6, and 9.)

However, Newell and Simon insist that, unlike the approach taken by economists, their computational theories of human problem solving must be seen as genuine psychological theories. By studying the discrepancies between the actual behavior of a particular subject on a particular task and the optimal behavior indicated by rational task analysis, they claim to be providing not a theory of the task environment but a scientific theory of human rationality:

> 1. To the extent that the behavior is precisely what is called for by the situation, it will give us information about the task environment. By observing the behavior of a grandmaster over a chess board, we gain information about the structure of the problem space associated with the game of chess.
> 2. To the extent that the behavior departs from perfect rationality, we gain information about the psychology of the subject, about the nature of the internal mechanisms that are limiting his performance. (Newell and Simon 1972, p. 55)

This is a strange idea. It would seem to imply that there can be no computational explanation of the chess-playing behavior of the grandmaster, since his performance conforms precisely to the optimal strategy dictated by the task environment and contains no mistakes that allow us to infer the nature of the underlying mechanisms. If this were true, and if computational explanations are all that Vera and Simon (1993) claim they are, it would put a severe limitation on our understanding of human behavior. (However, see de Groot 1966.)

Newell and Simon's logic is sound. Their argument has brought out one of the implications of the design stance, about which I shall have much to say in later chapters of this book. It views adaptedness not as the outcome of historical processes of evolution, ontogeny, and learning but as a collection of functional answers to formal problems posed by the environment. Evolution, as well as the organism itself, is assumed to confront these problems in the same way that a rational designer might confront them. This means that, in order to formulate explanations of a creature's behavior, one does not really need to study the creature itself. A comprehensive understanding of its various task environments and the problems they pose should be sufficient to explain its behavior.

But where is one to find the natural kinds for such an explanation? A psychological theory that takes task analysis as its starting point is stuck with the explanatory entities of the task domain. Newell and Simon believe that a genuine psychological theory must have something to say about what goes on inside the creature and that this requires explanatory entities referring to the underlying mechanisms. These entities, in cognitive science and AI, take the form of functional architectures and computational formalisms, which again do not require one to study the creature itself. Hence the only way in which the creature can enter into the equation is by not living up to the optimal solutions for its ecological niche or task domains. Psychological factors are reduced to questions of processing speed and constraints on the storage capacity of long- and short-term memory.

Newell and Simon's "hard" approach to cognitive explanation has often been criticized from within the field (Marr 1982, pp. 347, 348; Hofstadter 1985; Boden 1988, pp. 153–169; Clark 1989, pp. 9–17). My aim in this chapter is not to beat a dead horse (though, clearly, the editors of *Cognitive Science* believe there is life in the old steed yet). What I am attempting to bring out is the indebtedness of Newell and Simon's model to a particular view of scientific explanation that I believe underlies traditional AI and connectionism and continues to be implicitly held by most of the research community working on autonomous robots and artificial life. I have concentrated on the writings of Newell and Simon and their collaborators because they provide the clearest expression of this view.

Newell and Simon's "theories" more closely resemble what Nagel (1961) calls experimental laws. Experimental laws relate entities that are observable, in the sense that each descriptive term has a meaning that can be fixed by overt observational or laboratory procedures. The essence of a fruitful scientific theory, as Nagel defines it, is its ability to explain a variety of experimental laws at a deeper level. No reference is made in the formulation of the theory to specific empirical concepts. The theoretical entities that occur in the theory itself may receive different interpretations in the context of the diverse experimental laws. The theory ties the various interpretations of the theoretical entities together; it implies that the different phenomena described by the laws are in fact manifestations of the same underlying processes and entities.

This is quite different from an abstract formalism that can receive diverse interpretations that have nothing to do with each other. The law for thermal expansion has the same mathematical form as the law for freely falling bodies, but clearly no one believes that the two phenomena derive from a common underlying cause. An abstract calculus, by itself, does not constitute a theory. Nor do the rules of correspondence relating the theoretical entities to the observable phenomena of experimental laws suffice to turn it into a theory. What ties together the diverse experimental laws is the third constituent of a scientific theory of this kind: a model that provides a semantics for the abstract calculus.

The parallels with Newell and Simon's conception of cognitive explanation should be obvious. They account, I believe, for their persistent conviction that the programs of traditional AI provide empirical evidence to support an information processing model of the human mind. The software is seen as the abstract calculus, the information processing system plays the role of the model, and the various theories of problem solving derived in specific task domains are taken to be empirical laws whose correlations between inputs and outputs confirm the theory.

As I have tried to show, however, things are not as neat as they may appear at first sight. First, computational theories result not in a single, unifying calculus but in a proliferation of programs to suit the various task domains. Any correspondence between the programs in these diverse problem-solving environments is purely coincidental, like that between the equations for thermal expansion and free fall. Nor can the formal definition of a universal Turing machine be taken as the unifying calculus, since it can be used to explain any process at all, providing the process can be rephrased as an effective procedure. (I shall return to these questions in greater detail in chapter 5.)

Even more important, the experimental laws are not laws about behavior but formal descriptions of specific task environments that implicitly assume a computational framework. The computational model dictates the style in which the laws are to be framed; it does not provide a unifying theory for independently formulated empirical laws. The model derives its validity not from properties of the creature or its behavior but from a formal method of task description devised for mathematical proofs. Despite the superficial similarities, Newell and Simon's conception of computer-based explanation does not match Nagel's (1961) prescription for a scientific theory of this type. Fortunately, it is not the only type of theory acceptable to science.

2.2 Alternative Types of Scientific Explanation

Nagel (1961) distinguishes four types of scientific explanation:

> 1. Deductive explanation, in which the *explicandum* is a logically necessary consequence of the explanatory premises, which must contain a set of initial conditions and a general law.
> 2. Probabilistic explanation, in which the explanatory premises do not formally imply the *explicandum* but make it probable.
> 3. Functional or teleological explanations, in which a thing or event is explained in terms of the function it performs in some larger whole, or the role it plays in bringing something about.
> 4. Genetic explanations, which I shall discuss in greater detail below.

One of the central arguments of this book is that the first three types of explanation, applied to human and animal behavior, run into the problem of isolating defensible "natural kinds." As Nagel (1961) says, "The development of comprehensive theoretical systems seems to be possible only after a preliminary classification of kinds has been achieved, and the history of science repeatedly confirms the view that the noting and mutual ordering of various kinds—a stage of inquiry often called 'natural history'—is a prerequisite for the discovery of more commonly recognized types of laws and for the construction of far-reaching theories" (p. 31).

Deductive explanations have proved extremely successful in the physical sciences and are therefore often taken to be the paradigm for all explanation in science. Their use in the behavioral sciences has proved less illuminating. The search for universal laws has thrown up candidate principles like the stimulus-response arc and the TOTE loop (Miller, Galanter, and Pribram 1960), which, I shall argue in later chapters, do not provide adequate descriptions for even the most primitive forms of situated behavior. The explanatory entities in such explanations tend to be abstractions for which there is little warranty beyond the confines of a Skinner box or a computer-based simulation.

Probabilistic explanations have been called "actuarial" explanations in clinical psychology (Meehl 1954), where they play an important role, and they are also used extensively in behavioral ecology (Maynard Smith 1978; McFarland 1989) and in the new discipline of artificial life (Meyer and Wilson 1991; Varela and Bourgine 1992; Cliff et al. 1994). I shall argue that the statistical methods used in such explanations, though helpful in isolating and predicting abstract categories of behavior like "recidivism" or the "dove and hawk strategies," can be misleading if they are used as pointers to the nature of the underlying mechanisms of an individual creature's behavior.

Teleological explanation has often been taken as the hallmark of the behavioral sciences. Much of the dispute surrounding the scientific explanation of behavior has centered on the legitimacy of such notions as energy-directed-toward-a-goal and function defined as purpose (Boden 1972; Lorenz 1937; McDougall 1932, 1936; Millikan 1984; Wright 1973). As Nagel (1961) points out, such explanations take the form of statements asserting that an entity exists "for the sake of" the proper functioning of some larger whole or that an event occurs "in order that" some other event may take place.

One of the important claims of cognitive science has been that such locutions can be given concrete, nonvitalistic interpretations in computational terms. Functional decomposition, hierarchies of processes or "agents" (Minsky 1987) and, above all, the formalization of purposive activity as negative feedback have been put forward as credible scientific alternatives to the now-discredited vitalistic interpretation of such apparently irreducibly teleological phenomena (Rosenblueth, Wiener, and Bigelow 1943; Miller, Galanter, and Pribram 1960; Boden 1972; Dawkins 1976b). A large part of my argument will be devoted to an examination of these claims, and of the legitimacy of the explanatory kinds that are used in the explanations that have resulted. I shall argue that functions derived from functional decomposition are difficult to defend on the grounds of natural selection and that the explanatory entities derived from formal task descriptions cannot be "grounded" in the way that Dennett (1969) proposed.

The final category listed by Nagel (1961) was genetic explanation.* "The task of genetic explanations is to set out the sequence of major events through which some earlier system has been transformed into a later one. The explanatory premises of such explanations will therefore necessarily contain a large number of singular statements about past events in the system under inquiry" (p. 25). Nagel points out that obviously not every past event in the career of the system can be mentioned in the premises and that consequently a selective process is implied, which involves (often tacit) assumptions about what sorts of events are considered important to its development. He then draws attention to the role of intraspecies and cross-species comparisons of traits in evolutionary biology as an example of how such assumptions can be formulated and supported.

Genetic explanations are different from deductive, probabilistic, and teleological ones because the explanatory premises take the form of a historical sequence of events. The *explicandum* cannot be shown to follow from some general law that, given certain initial conditions at time t_0, will inevitably produce the thing or event that we are trying to explain at time t_1. It cannot even be shown to follow with a certain degree of probability from such a law. Nor can it be explained as necessary in order to bring about some other state or event or as a functional component of some larger whole. What is proposed in this type of explanation is that the thing or event can be shown to have come about as the final stage in some historical process consisting of singular events.

An important element in this notion is that genetic explanation depends on the actual occurrences of the events in the explanatory sequence. There is no single law that constrains these occurrences. It

---

*The term *genetic* in this context does not imply any connection with genes but harks back to the term's earlier meaning of "pertaining to or having reference to origin."

would be impossible to predict the event E_t, given the event E_0 at some previous time. It is not even possible to explain by some general principle in retrospect how the particular form taken by E_t followed from the occurrence of E_0. However, given the occurrence of all the states between E_0 and E_t, it becomes clear how the latter issued from the former.

This emphasis on actual occurrences recalls Sloman's (1978) definition of a historical science. Sloman divides the task of extending our knowledge and understanding of the world into two main categories. The first involves extending our knowledge of what sorts of things are possible and what sorts of things are impossible in the world. The second involves extending our knowledge about specific objects, events, and processes that actually occur in particular places and at particular times. This he calls historical knowledge.

Sloman's notion of historical does not include Nagel's (1961) idea of an explanation provided by a sequence of occurrences. The ultimate purpose of the dichotomy he sets up is to make intelligible the notion of a competence theory that can serve as a generative formalism for a range of possibilities. To this end, Sloman wants to divorce the notion of what is possible from both the notion of what is conceivable and the notion of what actually exists. In chapters 3 and 5, I shall have more to say about competence theories and the difficulties of grounding generative processes and keeping at bay the importunate facts of performance.

What I want to emphasize at this point is the insight, common to both Nagel (1961) and Sloman (1978), that in some types of explanation actual occurrences serve as the *explicans*, rather than causal, or probabilistic, or even generative laws. The classic example of this type of science is evolutionary biology. Like all other historical explanations, natural selection confers no predictive power. It is generally agreed that the theory does not provide a causal or probabilistic law to predict the emergence of particular traits, and despite occasional protestations to the contrary (Brian Goodwin, personal communication) there is as yet no sign of a generative law that will perform such a function. This has led some authors (notably Popper 1963) to question the scientific credentials of Darwin's theory. However, the theory has withstood the test of time and proved highly successful in providing a great diversity of historical explanations, not only of morphological traits but of behavioral entities as well. I shall discuss in later chapters how ethology and natural selection combine to provide a principled way of carving up the continuous stream of a creature's behavior that permits the isolation of temporally extended activity patterns and facilitates intraspecies and cross-species comparisons. This has allowed definitive answers to be given to questions concerning creatures' taxonomies, where the evidence based on morphological traits had been unclear (Mayr 1958).

2.3 Interactive Emergence

The notion of emergence has been used in different senses. Nagel (1961) distinguishes two main categories of usage. The first amounts to a thesis about the hierarchical organization of entities and processes. It maintains that the properties at higher levels of organization are not predictable from properties at lower levels. As Nagel points out, there is nothing unusual about such a situation in science. The observation can be said to hold even for phenomena whose explanations are generally considered to be reductive in the hard sense. The gross properties of water, like wetness, cannot be deduced from the properties of molecules because molecular theory does not include statements about such properties.

The second sense in which the notion of emergence is frequently used is a historical one. This draws attention to the fact that simple traits and forms of organization give rise, in the course of evolution, to more complex and irreducibly novel traits and structures. As Nagel (1961) points out, "the question whether a property, process or mode of behavior is a case of emergent evolution is a straightforward empirical problem and can be resolved at least in principle by recourse to historical inquiry" (p. 375). He warns that such a strategy will run into two main difficulties: the poverty of historical evidence (fossil records can provide only indirect information about activity patterns that are now extinct but may have contributed to the emergent evolution of a creature's current behavior) and what exactly should count as a genuine property or trait of the creature. It is to this problem that much of my argument will be addressed: the difficulty of isolating defensible and explanatorily fruitful kinds for a historical explanation of behavior.

Put simply, the question is this: The form or nature of a species-typical trait or character emerges gradually over many generations. Because of the complexities of genetic transmission and ontogeny, as well as a continually changing environment exerting conflicting selective pressures, evolution of the trait is unlikely to proceed in a straight line. If the explanation is to be a historical one, how do we decide which of the intermediate stages warrant the status of explanatory kind? At what point can we even begin to talk about the historical emergence of the trait in question, given that it is only in retrospect, when we can see that it confers certain advantages, that it really becomes a trait?

In order to answer these questions, I shall introduce a third type of emergence, different from the two types discussed by Nagel (1961), which I call "interactive emergence." I shall also introduce a modified version of Millikan's (1984) notion of history of use that circumvents the need for the complicated ontology and extreme position on function she is forced to adopt. In chapters 4, 6, 7, 8, 9, and 10, and in my subsequent discussions of ethology, early childhood, and the interactive emergence of intentionality, I shall argue on empirical and conceptual grounds that all behavior is situated activity, and all situated activity results from interactive emergence. Behavior cannot be adequately described in terms of events that take place inside a creature's head. It cannot be explained by rules that formalize neural activity or mental activity, for it comes into existence only when the creature interacts with its species-typical environment. (This is true of human beings as much as of insects, though their species-typical environment is to a large extent composed of cultural artifacts.)

Species-typical emergent behavior results in perceptual environments that cannot be reduced to task domains preregistered into the objects, properties, and situations apparent to an objective observer. The *Umwelt* (von Uexkull 1934) of a wall-following robot (Mataric 1992, discussed in chapter 7) presents possibilities for "solving the problems" of navigation that are quite different from the solutions suggested by the task domain of a map reader. Emergence thus becomes important as an explanatory principle because of use. It is because the emergent phenomena open up possibilities for behavior that did not exist prior to their emergence that an interactive explanation is essential.

To sum up, a historical explanation of the type I am proposing looks for naturally occurring patterns of activity and their interdependencies. It investigates these patterns through unintrusive observation and controlled experimentation in the creature's natural environment. Explanatory hypotheses are then formulated within a historical framework. The ultimate warranty for such explanations is Darwin's theory of natural selection; the explanatory entities that are posited derive their claim to the status of natural kind not from some functional role that may be deduced by taking a design stance but from actual stages in the creature's development. Interactive emergence, coupled with historical explanation, solves the problem of natural kinds.

Models of situated activity using autonomous robots can in principle be used to test such hypotheses. These should be seen as models of behavior rather than models of brains or minds. They can lay no claim to being design specs for mental components or structures, in the sense that computational psychology has always claimed to provide design specs. However, a better understanding of the structure of behavior must, I shall argue in this book, precede any attempt to make sense of its neurophysiological or psychological substrate. It could be said that cognitive science, and psychology in general, have tried to construct theories and laws without going through the necessary stage of behavioral taxonomy, which, as Nagel (1961) points out, generally precedes theory construction in science.

Chapter 3

Internal Representation and Natural Selection: Epistemological and Ontological Strains in the Cognitive Approach

3.1 Dennett's Formulation of the Problem

In 1969 Daniel Dennett published a book entitled *Content and Consciousness* in which he laid down the key strands of the cognitive story. As Dennett announced in his preface, it was an ambitious attempt to tackle the fundamental questions that other philosophers had recently preferred to leave untouched: "What is the relation between a man's mental life and the events in his brain? How are our commonplace observations about thinking, believing, seeing and feeling pain to be mapped on to the discoveries of cybernetics and neurophysiology?" (p. ix). The assumption was, as the rest of the book made clear, that the second question simply provided a more cogent rephrasing of the first—that the underlying mechanisms in the brain could be explained by the recent advances in computer science and neurophysiology and that the difficulty lay not so much in constructing a satisfactory mechanistic theory for the functional level that underlies our mental activity but in reconciling our stubborn habit of thinking in intentional terms to this firm causal basis. In the book, Dennett ultimately contrived to bridge the gap between intentionality and causal mechanism by invoking natural selection, although, interestingly enough, he did not mention that fact in the outline he gave in his preface.

Dennett's argument, as I read it, went like this (in the next three paragraphs, all proposals, questions, and answers are Dennett's, not mine):

1. Propose that mental terms are nonreferential (in the way that the word *sake* is nonreferential in the sentence, "He did it for his wife's sake") and that, consequently, it neither makes sense nor is necessary to equate them with extensional terms—but insist nonetheless that some explanation of mental phenomena must be found that accords with the rest of physical science. (*Question:* Why bother about mental phenomena at all? *Answer:* We need them because we have no other way of making sense of human

and animal behavior. Behaviorism cannot provide a coherent explanation of goal directedness or of the generalization of learning. The rat does not learn a sequence of skeletal movements, as
can be shown by inhibiting these; it learns where the food is. But
because of his self-imposed ban on intentional terms, the behaviorist is not allowed to say that the rat *knows* where the food is.
Dennett holds out the hope that one day we shall grow out of
this primitive need for mental terms, but he does not explain how
this could happen, since he admits that even if we knew the complete story in terms of synapses and action potentials, this would
still not tell us *what* the rat was doing.)

2. Introduce the notions of internal representation and information structure, which provide the possibility, in principle, of producing a scientific reduction of intentional expressions to
extensional expressions about internal states. (*Question:* Why
venture into this area of subpersonal analysis, which philosophers like Wittgenstein and Quine have shown to be a mine field
of semantic confusion? *Answer:* If animal behavior is goal directed, then the animal must somehow hold that goal in its head
and be able to apply it with a considerable degree of flexibility to
different external situations. We have little idea of what actually
goes on in the head, but we do have computer programs that
exhibit similar goal-directed behavior. Computer science has
taught us to describe their activity in terms of internal states and
information structures. As long as we are careful not to introduce
intentional terms into this subpersonal level, it can provide us, by
analogy, with a coherent way of talking about the links between
afferent and efferent impulses in animals and humans that behaviorism had to ignore.) However, there is one big problem: it
is clear that the computer's internal states derive their intentionality from the person who writes the programs. Where do animals and humans get *their* intentionality?

3. Introduce natural selection. The species that survive are those
with afferent impulses connected to efferent impulses in ways
that help them survive. Discrimination of afferents according to
their significance just *is* the production of appropriate efferent
effects in differential response to afferents. This is not the epistemological point that, as behaviorists, we cannot tell whether the
organism's brain has discriminated the stimulus as having significance until the organism manifests this in its behavior. It is
"the logical or conceptual point that *it makes no sense* to suppose
that the discrimination of stimuli *by their significance* can occur
solely on the afferent side of the brain" (Dennett 1969, p. 74). One

can ascribe content to a neural event, state, or structure only when it is a link in a demonstrably appropriate chain between the afferent and the efferent.

By this train of arguments, Dennett set the scene for the second half of his book, which had the purpose of demystifying consciousness. He was clearly determined to dethrone consciousness from the central position of decision maker and voluntary agent that it had occupied in folk psychology. He declares that our everyday notion of consciousness is hopelessly confused and, against the advice of his philosophical mentors, introduces new terms of his own, first to separate intentional uses of consciousness (being conscious *of* and conscious *that*) from non-intentional uses (being just plain conscious), and then to separate, within the intentional uses, the consciousness that is open to introspection (which he calls "awareness1") from the consciousness that is effective in directing behavior ("awareness2").

Dennett believes that awareness1 (which he says has caused most of the confusion) is merely a matter of signals crossing some internal awareness line. He does not believe that it plays any part in directing behavior. What it amounts to is that the signal has become the content of the input state of the creature's speech center. Consequently, only creatures that can speak can have awareness1, and the only thing they can do with such a signal is either to say it or not to say it. Of the real mental activity, which performs the work in directing behavior, we know nothing at all. Intentional actions are not willed. The verb *to will* is a hoax.

The appeal of Dennett's proposal is obvious. It holds out the promise that modern science will finally be able to undercut the dualism that has plagued Western philosophy since Descartes. By a combination of computer science and natural selection, mental phenomena will be brought into the explanatory framework that has proved so spectacularly successful in providing theories of the physical world. Dennett's book was important because it brought into focus and pulled together a number of ideas that had been hanging in the air: that the discoveries of control theory and cybernetics had once more made it scientifically and philosophically respectable to talk about the internal mechanisms that subtend behavior; that these internal mechanisms might be disconnected from introspection and appeals to conscious willing and believing; that folk psychology was a kind of theory with considerable predictive power but might be misleading in its causal explanations of what actually goes on in the mind; and, finally, that the mind is in some sense a product of natural selection and that this may point to a legitimate scientific grounding for mental phenomena.

Dennett's book was valuable, and I believe that the task he set cognitive science is the correct one, but I also think that it played an important part in sending cognitive science off on the wrong tack. His argument is based on a number of tacit assumptions that have become embedded in the subsequent literature of cognitive philosophy but I believe are open to question:

1. That animal behavior can and should be described as goal directed and that this is the only alternative to the ultimately sterile explanatory framework of behaviorist psychology. Dennett does not unpack that notion or defend its use in a biological and evolutionary context. He does not discuss its roots in the theory of servo-mechanisms and automatic control systems, nor does he elucidate the uneasy relation between teleological explanations and physical explanations in terms of set points, *Sollwerts,* and internal representations. He takes goal directedness as an unproblematic, given fact of nature.

2. That goal directedness and generalization of learning (the fact that the rat learns to find the food rather than to perform specific movements) can be explained only in terms of internal representations that play a causal and functional role in the animal's behavior. During the next twenty years, Dennett was to work out in greater detail his instrumentalist view of the relation between the intentional terms of folk psychology and the explanatory framework he had borrowed from computer science. He continued to believe that intentional talk could never be reduced to neurophysiological equivalents and that content or meaning could not play a straightforward causal role, but he was more and more impressed by the predictive power of the "intentional stance" and came to advocate "intentional systems theory" as a medium for drawing up "design specs" for the human and animal mind. The intentional stance, according to Dennett, picks out the true categories of competence; it is the correct way to organize the task of model building before doing the detailed implementation in terms of search trees, data structures, and evaluation algorithms (Dennett 1978, 1981, 1983).

3. Arguably the most important assumption Dennett made was that, ultimately, some link would be found between the explanatory categories picked out by the design stance and the entities involved in natural selection—a link that would serve to naturalize the categories of competence theories and prove that the explanation of mental phenomena these theories propose is in accord with the rest of physical science. Again, Dennett did not

discuss this link in detail, nor did he try to back up his belief, though he has attempted to do so more recently (Dennett 1983).
4. A model of the human mind derived through the application of Dennett's intentional systems theory will inevitably be couched in terms of the "objects," "properties," and "situations" of folk psychology, no matter how much these may have been cleaned up by conceptual analysis. Its categories will be established by top-down analysis, not by working bottom up from the underlying mechanisms. Competence theories presuppose an "explanatory cascade" (Clark 1990), leading from computational theory down to hardware implementation, that needs to be taken on faith. They assume that the task domains that can be picked out at the level of Dennett's intentional systems theory correspond to legitimate domains in the underlying mechanism.

The aim of this book is to show that none of these assumptions is warranted by our knowledge of the facts. In chapter 6, I shall argue that there are serious problems with the concept of goal directedness as applied to the underlying mechanisms of animal behavior and that, in essence, it is an attempt to "naturalize" teleological explanations that will not work. In this chapter I shall attempt to show that internal representation is not necessary, or even tenable, in an explanation of behavior grounded through natural selection. We are made in such a way that we have a good chance of surviving in the world. Our behavior, or disposition to behave in certain ways, or to learn to behave in certain ways, was selected by conditions prevailing in the world. This must mean that it is somehow "in tune" with the world—that in a sense the behavior can be said to incorporate knowledge of the world. On the other hand, we have our theories of the world, including those that may be loosely described as "naive physics" and "folk psychology." However, this does not give us any reason to suppose that the categories picked out by those theories are in any way built into us; that the "knowledge of the world" incorporated in our behavior has the same form as our theories; that the behavior is mediated by internal representations of our explicit categories; or even that those categories refer to some objective truth concerning the real structure of the world.

The rat does not learn a sequence of muscle movements; it learns where the food is. Well, maybe. Lorenz (1937) assumed at first that, in order to explain the mother duck's pattern of activity in the presence of her offspring, it could best be described as parenting behavior, with the implication that the duck knew who her offspring was. He decided in the end that each of the different activities that made up this behavior was triggered by a different sign stimulus and that the locus of all these stimuli existed only in the duckling "out there." The mother duck could not be said to have any internal representation of her offspring. An internal representation of the duckling, if it exists at all, can exist only in the experimenter's mind—in the part of his mind that is consciously engaged in constructing theories about parenting behavior, and not necessarily in the part that mediates his own untheoretical behavior in relation to ducklings—and this, as Dennett implies, is largely a matter of language.

A theory that is serious about grounding mental phenomena through natural selection must start from behavior. It is only on behavior, or interaction with the world, that natural selection can work. Ethology has shown that animal behavior does not necessarily require internal representations of objects, properties, and situations. On the other hand, human behavior most certainly can be mediated by such categories. We do act in conformance with our theories *some of the time*—when we allow consciousness, in Dennett's sense of awareness1, to play a part in our actions. A top-down approach to mental model building, in which internal representations of conceptual categories are taken to play a causal role in the mechanisms that subtend behavior, means that the naturalization of content through natural selection can be achieved only at the expense of consciousness. Consciousness must be relegated to the role of impotent observer or figment of the imagination. As Millikan (1984) writes, "What consciousness consists in from a naturalist's point of view, if it consists in *anything* from a naturalist's point of view, I have nothing to say about. It is the *intentionality* of human purposes that, I suggest, allows of a naturalist account" (p. 48). Thus, a clean break is achieved between intentionality and consciousness. This seems counterintuitive, but it is necessary if Millikan's project for naturalizing mental phenomena is to succeed. As the literature on cognitive dissonance and the attribution process (Zimbardo 1969; Nisbett and Wilson 1977; Storms and Nisbett 1970) and research with commissurotomy patients (Springer and Deutch 1981) has made clear, there is good reason to doubt the reliability of introspection. Our conscious explanations of our own behavior often prove to be highly imaginative confabulations, which can be shown to bear little relation to the real physical or psychological causes of that behavior. However, there is also ample proof, if such proof were really needed, that our conscious attitudes to things make a difference to the way we act in their presence, that to a certain degree we can modify our prejudices or fears by conscious reasoning, and that this will make a difference to our subsequent behavior. A model of the human mind that denies consciousness (whatever it may be) *any* role in shaping behavior does not look like a very convincing model of the human mind.

To sum up the argument so far, I agree with Dennett's conclusion as to what will ultimately be required to tie in mental phenomena to the rest of science, but I have reservations about the strategy he mapped out in *Content and Consciousness* for accomplishing that feat*. "What is the relation between a man's mental life and the events in his brain" does not inevitably equate to "How are our commonplace observations about thinking, believing, seeing and feeling pain to be mapped onto the discoveries of cybernetics and neurophysiology?" There might be alternative models, based on explanatory frameworks that are quite different from those posited by control theory and computer science.

But whichever model may turn out to be most appropriate and fruitful, there appears to be less and less doubt that natural selection provides the best hope for naturalizing that model's explanatory entities. The alternative strategy for naturalizing content is through some form of "hard" reductionism, correlating mental phenomena with specific events in the neurophysiological substrate. Few cognitive scientists would now subscribe to that approach, and I shall refer to it only in passing. A convincing model to explain human behavior must accord with the known facts of neurophysiology, but the model need not refer to those facts, and as I explain in later chapters, it may prove to be an advantage if it does not.

Dennett pointed us in the right direction when he appealed to evolution as a way of naturalizing mental phenomena. Unfortunately, he also insisted that Darwin's theory should be pressed into service to ground entities derived from computer science. Ever since his book came out, cognitive philosophy has tried to square these two (in my view irreconcilable) notions. In the remainder of this chapter, I shall try to bring into sharper focus some of the tensions implicit in Dennett's proposal by examining the work of various authors who have tried to resolve them.

3.2 Attempts to Reconcile Internal Representation and Natural Selection

I shall discuss briefly the work of Dretske (1986, 1988) and Sterelny (1990), before passing on to Millikan (1984, 1986, 1989), who has contributed the most thorough and radical attempt to achieve this reconciliation.

---

*As I discuss in the final chapter of this book, Dennett has elaborated his theory of consciousness in recent years (see, e.g., Dennett 1984, 1988, and particularly 1991). But his position on the role played by natural selection in shaping intentional behavior and his belief in the validity of the "design stance" as derived from that role do not appear to have changed.

Dretske follows Dennett much of the way. Like Dennett, he assumes that an adequate theory of the mind must be a representational theory and that its representations need to be naturalized in some way that accords with the rest of science. Like Dennett, he believes that the correct strategy for achieving such a link is by an appeal to natural selection. But he is more inclined to face up to the detailed problems inherent in supporting a causal-informational account with an evolutionary grounding.

Dretske (1988) distinguishes among three basic types of representation. Type I representations are symbols used by human beings. They lack what Dretske calls intrinsic representational power. Their meaning is dictated by convention, and they will perform their function only if the users stick to that convention. Type II representations are what Dretske calls "natural" signs. They derive their representational power not from us but from the way they are objectively related to the conditions they specify. Thus, according to Dretske, the number of rings in a tree is not merely correlated to the age of the tree; it actually represents and even means the age of that tree.

This is a peculiar notion, but it is essential to Dretske's argument. He is progressing from the conventional idea of representation to a type of representation that is both natural and intrinsic to the system. The implication is that there exist conditions in nature—objective, observer-independent facts—that can be said to serve as natural indicators of other facts because there is a lawful dependency between the indicator and the thing it indicates, and that this warrants describing those conditions as natural representations.

Dretske's definition of a natural representation begs a number of questions. It is certainly not the function of tree rings to indicate the age of a tree, nor, presumably, did they indicate such a thing until human beings learned to interpret them. Tree rings are the result of variations in growth rate over the seasons. They have no natural function and no natural "users" of their representational potential.

Type III representations in Dretske's classification do have natural users. They are used by the system of which they form a part: "Natural systems of representation, systems of Type III, are ones which have *their own* intrinsic indicator functions, functions that derive from the way the indicators are developed and used *by the system of which they are a part*" (Dretske 1988, p. 62). Dretske has thus arrived at a notion of representation that might be used for the purpose of naturalizing the symbols of a physical symbol system as defined in classical AI. Like Millikan (1984), Dretske compares the function of such representations to the functions of physical organs like the heart: "Can there be a serious question about whether, in the same sense in which it is the heart's function to pump blood, it is, say, the task of the nocturnal moth's auditory system to detect the whereabouts and movements of its arch-enemy, the bat?" (Dretske 1988, p. 63).

I shall have a lot to say in later chapters about the problems involved in ascribing natural functions to particular parts of a creature's anatomy. In the discussion on Sterelny that follows, I shall also examine the difference between using an evolutionary account in support of a functional description of a mechanism (like the moth's auditory system) and using it in support of internal representations produced by such a mechanism. Millikan (1984) is able to sidestep many of these questions by making a clean break with causal and informational accounts. Dretske is not prepared to go that far. For him, natural function is not merely a normative concept. He feels it is necessary to spell out the details of the causal links that might enable an internal representation to perform that function.

The best way to understand the differences between their two positions is to compare their approaches to misrepresentation (Dretske 1986; Millikan, 1989). How is it possible for an organism to get things wrong, given that it is a product of evolution that needs to reflect states of the world accurately in order to survive? Dretske maintains that if we do not have an answer to this question, we cannot understand the nature of human beliefs, for clearly these are often wrong. As I shall discuss in the next section, Millikan's account refers to the "normal conditions" for the representation's "proper function," determined by its "history of use." Her explanation is normative and historical rather than causal and informational. She is not interested in the mechanistic details of how misrepresentation might be implemented. Dretske attempts an intricate causal account of correlations between an internal representation and its object-in-the-world, showing how such a correlation might have come about and where it might go wrong.

He begins by defining a sense of "natural meaning," which he calls meaning(n) and is based on Type II representation. Flowing water "means(n)" that there is a slope. Meaning(n) is not susceptible of misrepresentation. If the cause is not present, the sign means nothing at all. However, when a gas gauge malfunctions and indicates that the tank is half full when in fact it is empty, we say that it misrepresents the state of the tank. Misrepresentation helps to clarify our conception of a different sense of meaning. Let us call this sense of meaning meaning(f)—functionally derived meaning. (It is the function of the gauge to indicate correctly the state of the tank.)

This concept, says Dretske, will help us to naturalize meaning and misrepresentation only if function can be defined in some natural way, without reference to an observer's interpretative purposes. Hence the appeal to natural selection. Information gathering is required for the satisfaction of certain biological needs. It depends on the use of internal representations that must track states of the world. Our photoreceptors had better register something that corresponds to what is out there (meaning(n) indicating the presence of a relevant world state). Then what the various states of these receptors mean(f) will depend both on what the photoreceptors register and the function of these states in the organism's internal economy.

Does this provide a framework for naturalizing misrepresentation? To clarify that point, Dretske uses the example of a species of bacteria that live in the Northern Hemisphere and avoid toxic, oxygen-rich water near the surface of the sea by means of internal magnets called magnetosomes. Since these magnets always point toward the north pole, they function, under normal conditions, as infallible indicators that are totally independent of the condition it is their function to indicate. However, the magnetosome can obviously be fooled by a magnet. Is this, Dretske asks, a primitive form of misrepresentation? Only if you accept that the function of the magnetosome is to indicate the whereabouts of oxygen-free water. But why describe its function in this way? Why not say that its function is to indicate the direction of geomagnetic north, or simply of magnetic north? If I need vitamin C, my perceptual system should not be automatically credited with recognizing objects as containing vitamin C, just because it supplies me with the information required to satisfy that need. Representing things internally as lemons and oranges will do quite nicely.

The determination of a system's function must take account of how the system actually performs that function. The magnetosome is a magnetotactic sensor, not a chemotactic one, and if we choose to describe the function of the sensor in this more modest way, we no longer have an example of a system with misrepresentational powers. It requires more complexity to get genuine misrepresentation.

Dretske advises us to imagine a system that has more than one way of detecting the presence of a toxic substance F. The representation of F may be triggered by any one of the alternative stimuli. It does not stand in a one-to-one relation with a specific proximal stimulus. In other words, it becomes legitimate to say that its function is to signal the distal cause, rather than the proximal stimuli, and that it misrepresents this distal cause when one of the mechanisms is fooled.

Or does it? It is still possible to object, Dretske concedes, that the representation has a disjunctive proximal cause (either f_1 or f_2 or f_3). But now take an organism that can learn by association. A conditioned stimulus can come to stand for the presence of F. What the representation means(n) will depend on the individual's learning history. There is no time-invariant meaning(n) for the representation, no proximal stimulus that, over time, we could take to be its function to indicate. So if we want a time-invariant function for the cognitive mechanism, we must think of it not as indicating the nature of the proximal or even the distal stimulus but as indicating the condition F for which the various stimuli are signs. At this level you do have a genuine capacity for misrepresentation.

Dretske's argument is a perfect example of the tensions between functional concepts borrowed from computer science and the attempt to naturalize meaning through natural selection. The basic problem lies in his determination to naturalize a sense of function that cannot in fact be naturalized. I shall discuss this problem in much greater detail in chapter 6, but since the naturalization of what Dretske calls meaning(f) is the cornerstone of his analysis, it is essential to say a few words about it now.

Is it the function of the magnetosome that exists in the oxygen-shy bacterium to point to geomagnetic north or to indicate the presence of oxygen-free water? Clearly, from an ecological point of view, its function is to ensure that the bacterium keeps heading toward oxygen-free water. What worries Dretske briefly, before he mistakenly dismisses the worry, is that a functional analysis in terms of an internal representation passed on by the magnetosome to the efferent components of the bacterium seems to produce a different story.

If we view the bacterium as we might view a product of engineering design and assume that it works by passing internal representations from one component to another, then the conclusion must be that it is the function of this particular internal representation to signal geomagnetic north. And it is this internal representation, together with the functional role assigned to it by this type of causal-informational account, that Dretske must naturalize if he is to accomplish Dennett's program of squaring computational analyses with natural selection. Dretske pretends that the discrepancy he has uncovered is in fact a boon—that it provides a starting point from which he can build to a full-blown naturalization of misrepresentation. Here, in my opinion, he is evading the issue.

What Dretske has told us in effect is this: I need to naturalize meaning(f) to show that organisms can have internal representations with functional meanings in the same way as the representations produced by the gas gauge have functional meanings. The functional meanings of naturally occurring internal representations must not be assigned by human observers or designers; they need to be derived from natural selection. Let us take as an example the bacterium with the magnetosome. I find that I have problems identifying the causally and

informationally defined meaning(f) of the internal representation produced by the magnetosome with the natural condition that it seems to
be its ecological function to indicate. But rather than doubting the fact
that I have found an example of naturalized meaning(f), I will take this
as a hopeful sign that it is possible for internal representations to be
derived through natural selection and also to misrepresent the condition they were designed to indicate. (He then goes on to admit that
this is not, after all, a genuine instance of misrepresentation but forgets
to explain the discrepancy between the two notions of function.)

Mistakes, false beliefs, elaborate, mythical theories about how to behave to make the crops grow or what causes the sun to rise every
morning and go down every evening are indeed a salient feature of
human thought. Much of our conceptual baggage seems quite useless,
or even detrimental, from a straightforward survival point of view. If
these concepts are translated into internal representations, which then
need to be naturalized by an appeal to natural selection, the task begins
to seem quite daunting. Dennett has consistently skirted this problem,
and, as we shall see, Millikan contrives to avoid it by not resorting to
causal mechanisms at all, but Dretske feels uncomfortable with such a
solution.

Computer science tells a causal-informational story. Dretske believes
that his acceptance of the representational theory of mind commits him
to deploying internal representations in that way. In order to ground
meaning by a causal chain that might have come about through natural selection, he posits meaning(n) and meaning(f) and increasing degrees of complexity to prove that it is possible for an internal
representation that is a product of evolution to represent some state of
the world falsely. But Dretske's argument from complexity is unconvincing. It cannot establish a natural correlation between an internal
representation and its object-in-the-world rather than between that internal representation and a more proximal stimulus.

It is this problem that chiefly exercises Sterelny (1990). He discusses
various causal relations that have been suggested and notes that all
run into the problem of referential ambiguity. The causal chain that is
assumed to link the mental representation to its object-in-the-world
turns out to be long and complicated regarding both the formation of
concepts and particular instances of their use. Why is my concept of a
tiger a concept of tigers rather than of mammals, or tigers-in-zoos, or
even of keeping-tigers-in-zoos? A causal account of concept formation
must make clear how concepts are generalized beyond the stimulus set
encountered by the subject but generalized only to the proper degree.

On the other hand, what defines the stimulus set implicated in a
particular instance of representational use? As Sterelny points out, the

causal chain posited by this type of explanation stretches back through a sequence of representational stages "inside the head," to the retinal image of a tiger, to a structure of ambient light the tiger produces, to various tiger surfaces, and finally to the tiger as object-in-the-world. Why isn't my concept of tiger a concept of tigerish retinal projections, or of a certain configuration of ambient light? What legitimizes the link between my internal representation of a tiger and tigers-in-the-world?

Sterelny notes that authors like Dretske and Millikan have appealed to natural selection to solve these problems. Our perceptual systems are designed to maintain a constancy between percept and the perceived world, even across a great variety of proximal stimuli. The stable correlation is between object and concept, not between the concept and its sensory intermediaries. Sterelny objects that this is fine for simple, isolated, and presumably innate structures like the frog's fly detector or the bacterium's magnetosome but that it will not work for propositional attitudes.

Most human beliefs, he argues, have not been around long enough to be the products of a selective process. Few of them can be innate. An adaptionist grounding of internal representation requires that an evolutionary rationale be found for the causal link between every instance of representation and the corresponding object-in-the-world. But certain beliefs may simply be side effects of something else. Most concepts do not even have a clearly identifiable behavioral consequence that could have caused them to be selected for.

Can it really be the natural function of some neural states to indicate the presence of kitchen utensils or playing cards? As I shall discuss later in this chapter, Millikan's answer to this question involves an elaborate analysis of language. Dretske's answer is to say that the representational powers developed to perform a specific biological function need not remain restricted to that function: "In order to identify its natural predator, an organism might develop color, shape and movement detectors of considerable discriminative power. Equipped, then, with this capacity for differentiating various colors, shapes and movements, the organism acquires, as a fringe benefit so to speak, the ability to identify (and, hence, misidentify) things for which it has no biological need" (Dretske 1986, p. 29). The details of how the outputs of such modular detectors might become detached from their original function and turn into separate representations in their own right (which could then be combined with other "features" to build up representations of cultural artifacts) are not discussed by Dretske. It is one thing to say that the ability to distinguish colors might confer selective advantage but quite a different matter to provide a plausible account of how the possession of internal representations corresponding to such features might have come about through natural selection working on a creature's behavior. One of the main arguments of this book will be that appeals to natural selection must provide plausible historical accounts, even if the precise details of such accounts may have become difficult to unravel.

Sterelny concludes that it is possible to give a teleological explanation for a cognitive mechanism but not for the products of that mechanism. Our beliefs and desires relating to playing cards are the products of a general-purpose system, and because of that they interact. It is not possible to define the content of such beliefs by building up from representations of naturalized features. To a large extent, the referent of a particular concept is determined by its relation to other concepts.

This interdependence of conceptual referents threatens to make the causation of behavior holistic, and Sterelny wishes to steer clear of a purely holistic account of content. He argues that it would make causation utterly idiosyncratic. No mental state would ever be tokened more than once. It would never be true that different people, or the same person at different times, acted the same way for the same reasons. There would be no true intentional generalizations, and generalization, allowing taxonomy, is the first requirement for a scientific explanation.

Sterelny's own solution involves a basic set of input modules that are innately specified, providing a semantic foundation of primitive concepts. This enables him to avoid the problems of holism. (A causal explanation of the concepts produced by such modules does not require reference to other concepts, and the concepts produced by the modules will not be idiosyncratic but species specific.) It also, in Sterelny's opinion, avoids most of the teleological pitfalls he signposted earlier in his discussion. Sterelny further posits that modular representation must extend beyond representations of such basic features as shape and color. There are likely to be modules for the recognition of faces and phonemes, for instance. The candidates for modular representation are features that were biologically important to our ancestors and are also reliably detectable by a special-purpose mechanism. All such modules represent objective features of the world, because that is what they were selected for.

He argues that this deflects any attempt to equate his system with traditional concept empiricism. The properties represented by his modules are not sensory properties, as posited in classical empiricism, but properties of the world that those modules have been specifically selected to represent. He further defends his proposal by claiming that his nonbase concepts do not need to be defined in terms of the base concepts. Many of them will "depend in part on causal links between concept and referent. I am not looking for definitions of the nonbase concepts, so I need not worry about the fact that there are no such definitions" (Sterelny 1990, p. 140).

In view of the difficulties in specifying causal links (to which he has repeatedly drawn attention), it is not clear why Sterelny believes that he has now provided a satisfactory solution to his problem. His innate modules have a superficial appeal, but they will not buy him the causal explanation he is after. Perceptual modules became popular as a result of Marr's (1982) successes with low-level vision. Marr's reliance on environmental constraints that had been hard-wired into our perceptual system through natural selection enabled him to formulate computational explanations for some of the early stages of visual processing in human beings. However, as I have tried to show (Hendriks-Jansen 1990), this explanatory strategy did not enable Marr to bridge the intentionality gap.

Calling something a face-recognition module begs the question of how such a feat is actually accomplished. Sterelny makes vague references to Marr's final stage, involving a hierarchy of "generalized cones" that need to be matched to candidate objects in a "2.5-D sketch" for the purposes of recognition, but he wisely refrains from going into too much detail. This part of Marr's proposal has never been made to work, though a number of researchers, including Rodney Brooks (1981), have tried. (A "toy" connectionist system proposed by Hinton 1981 as an alternative to Marr's model has, as far as I know, never been convincingly implemented.)

I have argued (1990) that any attempt to build up to full-blown, viewpoint-independent, context-free internal representations of objects-in-the-world from a retinal projection is doomed to failure. Appeals to low-level perceptual modules in support of a causal-informational account of internal representation require solutions to the segmentation problem, the two-dimensional to three-dimensional conversion problem, the problem of indexing some sort of "library of shapes," and the problem of what to do with the internal representation once it has been "retrieved."

Dretske and Sterelny are both interested in a causal account of internal representation. They both, in different ways, resort to natural selection to support these accounts. Their attempts have highlighted the difficulties inherent in such an approach. Dretske has brought into focus the problem of providing a definition of function that is independent of interpretation by an observer and the problem of linking such a definition to objects-in-the-world rather than proximal stimuli. Sterelny has stressed the problem of constructing causal links between high-level content and objective features or properties, particularly if natural selection is used to legitimize such links. I have argued that neither author has succeeded in providing a satisfactory solution to these problems.

Their arguments touch on a number of issues I shall discuss at greater length in later chapters. It is certainly true, as Sterelny stresses, that a principled taxonomy must underpin theory construction in science. On the other hand, as the example from Lorenz that I quoted shows, the underlying mechanisms of behavior can easily be obscured by a too rigid adherence to what might appear to be a natural kind for behavior (in that case "parenting behavior") but turns out, on closer inspection, not to have a unifying internal cause.

Sterelny makes reference to the theories of inclusive fitness and evolutionarily stable strategies. His aim in doing so is to demonstrate that even in such relatively hard sciences as population genetics and behavioral ecology, reference to functions, goals, and purposes must underpin classification. Behavior patterns on their own cannot provide a taxonomy or an explanation. I shall argue that the theories to which he refers cannot provide clues to underlying mechanisms. Such theories take what Meehl (1954), in a somewhat different context, called the "actuarial approach": they abstract away from concrete, individual behavior and treat it as a statistical phenomenon.

Actuarial predictions are useful for predicting the occurrence of generalized, heterogeneous, folk psychologically inspired classes of outcome or behavior, like "academic success," "recidivism," "altruism," or a "dove strategy." In behavioral ecology, predictive theories of this type use notions of cost and benefit, by analogy with the economic notion of utility, but linked to the Darwinian concept of fitness. In chapters 6 and 9, I shall discuss at length the inherent difficulties of making such a connection. In the present context, it is necessary merely to stress again that the explanatory entities in these theories are statistical entities. There are many different ways to land back in prison, and countless individual manifestations of a dove strategy.

The danger is that, having resorted to statistically defined categories of behavior like the dove strategy, the scientist will be tempted, as Sterelny occasionally appears to be, to project these actuarial notions back into the animal—in other words, to assume that the individual creature is actually following or using a dove strategy, implemented by some internal mechanism that would correspond to that description.

Natural selection does not *design* behavior; it merely works as a selective filter on the behavioral consequences of genetic mutation and recombination that emerge as a result of ontogeny. It would be very surprising if those processes had produced an internal mechanism that mirrors our rational procedures of functional analysis and planning.

3.3 Millikan's Definition of Proper Function

Millikan's approach to the task laid down by Dennett is, by Dennett's own account, the most thorough and radical that has yet been attempted. She is determined to wrest content from the grip of what she calls "meaning rationalism": all philosophy that pretends that introspection or a priori knowledge can lead to any truth at all: "Intentionality is not harbored within consciousness, nor can consciousness, in the guise of a priori reflection, provide an affidavit for the genuine intentionality of seeming thoughts" (Millikan 1984, p. 12). Millikan is prepared to face all the epistemological and ontological consequences of such a position, and she succeeds in avoiding some of the traps that have ensnared other practitioners of cognitive philosophy. Her tightly reasoned argument is an attempt to provide a naturalist correspondence theory without getting bogged down in causal or informational accounts of mental content. From Quine and the later Wittgenstein, we know that a pure correspondence theory will not work. There are any number of possible mappings for a given sign. If a correspondence theory is to work, it must tell what is different or special about the mappings that map representations onto the things they represent. This specialness must be natural rather than logical, and the theory must be a coherent part of the rest of science.

The question is: What defines certain circumstances as those that fix the semantic content of a particular mental state, so that, if that mental state occurred under different circumstances, it would count as a misrepresentation? A more basic question that needs to be answered first is what makes something a representation. Not every state of a system represents its normal causes. A red face, though it may be a natural sign of recent exertion or of an excessively heated room, does not represent the exercise or the hot room that caused it. (Millikan's analysis departs at this point from Dretske's, which sought to elevate such natural signs to a primitive form of representation.) So what sort of states do constitute representations? One possible answer is, "states whose function it is to represent or detect things in the world." But then, says Millikan, we need to define "detect" and "represent." How does one naturalize notions like "detect" and "represent"?

Millikan's solution to both questions posed in the previous paragraph is to concentrate on the consumption of the representation rather than its production. It is the part of the system that uses the representation that determines that it *is* a representation and also determines its content. In addition, she shifts the focus of attention away from what it is the job of the representation to get the consumer to do to what she calls the "normal conditions" for its "proper function."

The "proper function" of a wild seed is to develop into a particular species of plant. Statistically this may not happen very often; the "normal conditions" for it to happen may be satisfied only rarely. Nevertheless, it makes sense to think of its proper function only as developing into a plant, since that is why it evolved into the seed we see today. Function, in Millikan's explanatory scheme, is defined historically, in terms of an entity's contribution to the survival of the species that contains it. The proper function of the seed, together with the normal conditions under which it operates, define its "meaning". Similarly, the tail splash of the beaver "means" danger, because only when the splash actually signals danger does the instinctive reaction of the other beavers to take cover serve any purpose. That the splash corresponds to danger is a normal condition for proper functioning of the other beavers' instinctive reaction to the splash. It is not necessary to assume that most representations are true. Many biological devices perform their proper function not on average but just often enough to ensure their survival through natural selection.

Instead of concentrating on what it is the representation's job to get the consumer to do (which leads to the problem that there is no such thing as the proper response, or even a range of functionally appropriate responses, to what perception tells us), we look to the normal conditions for proper functioning to define the representation's meaning. This bypasses all causal and informational accounts of mental content. Take the bacteria with magnetosomes. It does not matter, for their consumer part, how the pull comes about; for them it represents a pull toward oxygen-free water. What is represented by the magnetosome is not proximal but distal. Nor is the bacterium performing an inference from the proximal stimulus (the magnetic field) to the existence of the represented. For the consumer part of the bacterium, the pull of the magnetosome represents oxygen-free water because that is its proper function under normal conditions for its operation.

The great advantage of Millikan's radical proposal is that it makes a clean break with causal and informational theories of content and locates meaning squarely outside the head. She has taken the final strand in Dennett's story and elevated it to the sole and true arbiter of intentionality. Of course, Dennett occasionally appears to do something similar in his later writings (1978, 1981, 1983), when he backs up the legitimacy of his intentional stance by appeals to natural selection. But there is a crucial difference between the two authors.

Natural selection, for Millikan, confers true intentionality. Proper function under normal conditions just *is* intentionality, and there is nothing more to be said about it. To Dennett, the intentional description derived from natural selection is merely a temporary expedient, a rough design sketch that picks out the areas of competence that require further explanation. Minds are in fact syntactic engines that merely display all the hallmarks of intentionality, and the ultimate explanation is to be found in a causal-informational account. The intentionality derived from natural selection does not provide a satisfactory explanation as far as Dennett is concerned, just as it did not provide an explanation for Dretske or Sterelny. True explanation can come only from looking into the creature's head. Millikan (1984), because of her radical stance, does not believe that intentionality can be found in the creature's head:

> Analogy with the "functions" that computers have begs the question of course, since what counts as a computer's "functions" are just what it has been designed in accordance with *some person's explicit intentions* to do. Insofar as some functionalists have probably had design via evolution in mind as delineating what counts as a brain's "functions," they have not faced the fact that this entails that such "functions" are determined by a thing's history, hence that if intentionality is determined by "function" intentionality does not reside in a mechanism but in its history. (p. 339)

This leads Millikan to the extreme, almost mystical naturalist position that if by some cosmic accident, a perfect clone of a given person were to coalesce spontaneously, this clone would have no beliefs, no intentions, no ideas, not even a heart or a liver—despite the fact that it would have the same collection of cells, the same neural networks, and perhaps even the same state of consciousness as the original person—because its history would not have allowed these things to be established through proper function.

Millikan's notion of proper function focuses on one of the crucial differences between function as derived from functional analysis and function as grounded in natural selection. The function of a particular component of a machine may be inferred from the role it plays in the overall mechanism, together with the purpose of the machine as a whole. There is no need to appeal to a legitimizing functional history, because we know that the machine was designed from a functional perspective in the first place. Its maker analyzed the tasks he wanted his machine to perform, conceived of a rational division into parts linked by causal chains that would achieve this performance, and since a rational observer will tend to think in similar terms, the components and their functions will readily disclose themselves to functional analysis.

Functional analysis of living creatures assumes that they are constructed in much the same way: that nature designed them with a purpose and that their components or traits represent solutions to problems posed by the environment, or by a rational subdivision of the tasks performed by the organism as a whole. This assumption will be examined in greater detail in chapter 6, where I shall argue that it conceals a host of insoluble problems.

Millikan's definition of proper function tries to come to terms with some of these problems. If intentionality is to be grounded in function, and function is to be grounded in natural selection, it must be shown that the function in question is completely independent of an observer's interpretation. The organism's trait or part must have a particular function not because we interpret it that way or, obviously, because some designer deliberately designed it to behave that way, but for an objective reason that can be derived wholly from natural selection.

This is the explanatory task performed by "history of use" in Millikan's scheme. The function of a trait or organ depends on the role it has played in the course of its evolutionary history, ensuring its survival. It has itself survived because of its contribution to the survival of the organism of which it forms a part. That contribution, and the way it was accomplished, define its proper function.

This concludes my discussion of the basic elements of Millikan's normative theory. I shall proceed shortly to discuss her development of these ideas into a full-blown "biological" theory of language, but it may be appropriate at this point to say a few words about the relation of Millikan's notions of proper function and history of use to what are currently accepted as the scientific facts of natural selection and genetic transmission. (I discuss these matters in more detail in chapter 6.)

The processes involved are not as simple or clearly defined as Millikan's theory assumes—and almost certainly requires. Traits can survive because of all sorts of complex reasons. A particular trait's genotype (if it is permissible to speak of a genotype's corresponding to a trait) may "hitchhike" on a chromosome that carries another genotype that confers high survival value, and thus be transmitted though it performs no "proper function" whatsoever. A disadvantageous trait may survive as a result of stochastic perturbations in the gene pool called "genetic drift," which can swamp the effects of natural selection. Some traits appear as the result of complex interactions between various genes, which can "turn each other on and off" in ways that bear little relation to their "survival value."

As a consequence of these and many other complications, it would be very difficult indeed to disentangle the contribution made to the survival of some creature by a hypothetical internal representation in terms of its "use" to the creature as a whole. Evolution is an undirected, opportunistic process. Natural selection continuously employs structures and behaviors that are already in place for new adaptations to a changing environment. If history of use is to be taken seriously (as I believe it must be), then all the false starts and changes of use that went into producing the current "intentional icon" should be taken into account in defining its current meaning. What is more, by Millikan's criterion, we are not really entitled to appeal to the proper function of a trait displayed by the present generation of animals until it has been passed on to their descendants, for only then will its proper function in this generation have been established.

This is not a demand for logical proof of Millikan's empirical theory. I believe that logically Millikan's thesis is correct. History of use—a specific, clearly identifiable contribution to survival and reproductive success in past generations—is the only way to establish the function of a trait on evolutionary grounds. However, I do not see how this can possibly be done for internal representations. As will become clear in chapter 7, Millikan's notion can be given substance within a different explanatory framework, but only if the explanatory entities prescribed by cognitive science are given up.

Despite these problems, Millikan's theory remains the most interesting and thorough attempt to ground a representational theory of mind in natural selection. For this reason, it is worth continuing with the analysis and examining all the epistemological and ontological consequences of such a position, which only Millikan seems prepared to face.

Millikan's (1984) main concern is the naturalization of "language devices" without recourse to the intentions, beliefs, or desires of the people who use them. In her view, words and sentences are biological categories in their own right. The meaning of a term is wholly determined by its history of use. The notions of direct proper function and normal conditions are defined using the idea of a reproductively established family. In first-order reproductively established families, the members are direct copies of one another with respect to one or more "reproductively established properties" (properties conducive to survival).

Sentences and words are examples. They are copied through use and survive because they perform a proper function, which is to promote cooperation between the speaker and the listener. They do not depend for their meanings on the speaker's intentions or purposes. Having a belief or intention requires that one represents the act to be performed. Normal speaking is more like walking, which is purposive and intentional, though one does not act from explicit intentions to put one foot in front of the other. Similarly, speaking does not involve the speaker's thinking of her beliefs and intentions, or of those held by the person she is talking to. In this severely anti-Grician view of language use, the intentionality of language devices might be said to precede the beliefs and intentions of the people who use them.

Millikan is trying to establish that intentionality comes first and can be defined objectively; it does not even require internal representations. The bee's waggle dance and the beaver's splash are "intentional icons" in the same way as sentences are. Internal representations are a special type of intentional icon. They are distinguished by the fact that when they perform their proper function, their referents are identified. Bees do not know what their dances are about; they just respond to them appropriately. But human beings *do* know what their thoughts are about.

The public term is like a tool, whose use is objectively defined. It has been designed to perform that function by its history as a public term, during which it has survived and proliferated by successfully eliciting cooperative behavior between speakers and interpreters. Each individual user needs to develop the know-how, the ability to use the term. This means translating it into an inner program that allows her to iterate the term in the context of inner sentences. There are internal programs that iterate the term from dictionary-type definitions (explicit intentions), and others that iterate it working directly from perceptual data (implicit intentions). Implicit intentions are discrete perceptual abilities rather than "stimulus meanings," since perception is an active process, involving attention and, in the case of vision, focusing, movement of the head, and hand-eye coordination.

To save us having to test the validity of each individual term or sentence by trial and error in the real world, we have, says Millikan, an in-built "consistency tester." She draws an analogy between this consistency tester and our ability to focus our vision. Infants must have an innate inclination to bring an object that appears in front of their eyes into focus, and an innate skill that enables them to do so. In the same way, human beings have an in-built inclination to focus their concepts, and the mechanism for doing so is the consistency tester. We generate a variety of internal sentences containing the term, run them through the consistency tester, and in that way bring the corresponding concept into focus. The consistency tester is thus a focusing device for inner terms, just as vision is a focusing device for objects-in-the-world. Knowing how to focus on unities in nature is a skill that was put into us by natural selection, since we evolved to deal with the structure of the world.

Millikan assumes that language, science, naive physics, and folk psychology carve up the world in the same way as do the abilities that underlie our concepts, and that all correspond to predefined, objective states of affairs in the world because our concept-forming mechanisms are adapted to deal with these. Her commitment to a rigorous naturalization of intentional icons does not allow her to fudge this issue:

> If language has its powers because it maps the world, then the identity or selfsameness of the significant variables of the affairs it maps must be an objective or thought-independent selfsameness—one that explains rather than being explained by the operations of language and thought. There must be objectively selfsame world affairs that different sentence-tokens can map, objectively selfsame subject variants *in re* for subjects of sentences to map, and objectively selfsame predicate variants *in re* for predicates of sentences to map. A realist view needs support from a compatible ontology. (Millikan 1984, p. 239)

In other words, underpinning the theory as a whole, there has to be the assumption of a world that is preregistered into objects and properties. Millikan herself occasionally seems uncomfortable with this. In order to explain an object's identity over time, she invokes what she calls a "subessence" of the object. Since, as a result of natural conservation laws, certain properties of an object will persist over time, there must be something that *has* these properties. This is its subessence. It is not the collection of properties; it *exhibits* those properties. But unfortunately different properties of a particular object will persist over different intervals of time. This means that any enduring object must have more than one subessence associated with it:

> The principle of strict identity over time is not strong enough by itself to divide up the world into a determinate set of enduring objects. Or, more accurately, it divides the ongoing world into chunks that are far too numerous, overlapping, and criss-crossing to try to keep track of. So a great deal of room is left for decision on our part as to how to divide the world into sensible-sized and sensibly unified temporally extended wholes to be recognized and honored with common and/or proper names. (Millikan 1984, p. 293)

This ontology of subessences that do not quite line up with our concepts, so that we still need to deploy some sort of theory in order to decide which of the subessences should be combined to make up an object, begins to seem like the worst of all possible worlds. However, we should be grateful to Millikan for having followed through her argument to its final conclusions. She, more than any of the other philosophers who have taken up the challenge laid down in Dennett's

Content and Consciousness, has brought out the internal contradictions in trying to ground a representational theory of mind through natural selection. There are passages in her book that make one wonder why she does not give up the enterprise altogether and adopt the even more radical approach that appears to be indicated by her logic: that of abandoning the notion that intentional icons and internal representations must constitute the basic entities for an understanding of the mind:

> A great deal of what a person does "automatically" or "with the mind on other things" may be done by systems that produce very complex prearranged patterns of behavior that are not put together or prescribed step by step on the spot but simply "run off." It seems likely that the development of higher-order control is, largely, the development of systems that can start and stop and use pieces of the complicated performances of lower-level systems as appropriate and in some cases "train" or "program" them appropriately. (Millikan 1984, p. 68)

> For example, there is no question that my ability to identify a substance—any substance—depends upon the fact that that substance has certain characteristic properties that affect me in lawful ways. It does not follow that I must employ *concepts* of those properties in order to identify that substance. In fact, I do not have the slightest idea what properties it is of paint enamel vs. porcelain enamel that allow me to tell the one substance from the other by tapping these with my teeth, but that's how I tell nonetheless. (Ibid., p. 315)

These are insights that point to a mode of explanation that does not start from formal task definitions and folk psychological concepts but builds up from situated patterns of activity and interactive perceptuo-motor skills. My argument will be that only a theory whose natural kinds can adequately describe the skills referred to in these quotations can accomplish Dennett's project of naturalizing human behavior through natural selection. I shall conclude this chapter by discussing the work of an author who does not appeal to natural selection but whose analysis of the "grounding problem" inherent in computational models provides a useful perspective on the questions that Millikan has raised.

3.4 Task Domains and Skill Domains

In a paper entitled "The Connectionist Construction of Concepts" (1990), Adrian Cussins suggests that it might be possible to build up from what he calls the "S-domain" of situated skills to the full-blown symbol-processing model envisaged by classical AI. Cussins's declared aim is to "reinstate experience in psychology," just as the cognitive revolution reinstated representation. He wants to hold on to internal representations as the basic explanatory entities of the model but proposes a grounding for such entities in viewpoint-dependent perceptuomotor skills.

Cussins reminds us that the essence of a theory in cognitive science is the explanatory relation it sets up between computational artifacts and psychological categories and that this relation is embodied in the theory's concept of internal representation. Representations are physical objects that have two kinds of properties: the properties of the representational vehicle, which affect the computational functioning of the model, and the properties of the representational content, which affect the psychological explanations that can be derived from the model. It is the theory's concept of representation that ties together these two sets of properties and thus establishes the connection between computational functioning and psychological explanation.

Cussins's proposal involves what he calls the construction of cognitive properties out of noncognitive ones. It is never made entirely clear how he believes this can be done. Ultimately, as his title implies, Cussins relies on connectionism to do the work for him, but his account of the constructionist alternative to reductionism, eliminativism, and "explanatory dispensability" is presented solely in terms of analogies and metaphors. He talks of "finding one's way in the world" and "making a map by walking different routes," concluding that his theory requires "psycho-computational transformations defined over non-conceptual contents which have the effect of reducing the perspective-dependence of the contents."

To provide a foundation for this explanatory scheme, Cussins needs to give substance to the notion of nonconceptual content. He points out that the traditional view of conceptual content depends on the notion of a task domain: a bounded domain of the world that is taken as already registered into objects, properties, and situations and is assumed to be independent of the agent's viewpoint. In order to have determinate truth conditions, the content of a cognitive state must be capable of being specified with reference to such a task domain. This kind of content Cussins calls "alpha-content." An organism that is capable of grasping such content needs to "know" the corresponding task domain; it must possess the concepts in terms of which the task domain is structured. In other words, concept-based activity necessarily takes place in an idealized world—an abstraction from reality that is assumed to correspond to the "real" world and consists of objects,

properties, and relations. It must be a closed world, since all its constituents are exhaustively prespecified, and behavior that is described in
terms of these constituents does not make reference to the subject's
viewpoint. An explanation of behavior in conceptual terms grants the
subject a God-like view of his domain of action, allowing him to plan
his behavior in an objective way.

But, says Cussins, there is a large class of cognitive states (such as
those involved in perception and action) that crucially involve a particular point of view. Such states can be conceptually specified only from
within the point of view. Doesn't this close them off to science, since it
is impossible for an objective observer to share the experience of the
perceiving or acting subject? Cussins replies that a scientific explanation is ruled out only if we insist on a conceptual structure for their
content. Viewpoint dependence does not rule out a principled nonconceptual structure. The problem is how to make sense of such a notion.
In order to do this, he introduces the idea of an S-domain: a substrate
corresponding to the system's perceptuomotor abilities. These are not
represented by the system itself: "An intelligent agent does not need
to have concepts of its S-domain, so if *beta-content* can be canonically
specified by reference to the objects and properties of the S-domain,
we will have motivated a kind of content which is specified by means
of concepts that the system or organism need not have" (Cussins 1990,
p. 394).

What are these "objects" and "properties" of the S-domain, and what
are these "concepts" that the organism need not have but that can be
used to "motivate beta-content"? As we saw, Millikan said something
quite similar about perception and activity: that it may involve properties without employing concepts of those properties. The question is
whether it continues to be meaningful or helpful to think of activity
and perception in terms of concepts and content. "The experiential
content of perception is specified in terms of certain fundamental skills
which the organism possesses" (Cussins 1990, p. 396). "The 'syntax'
and the 'semantics' of non-conceptual content are not explanatorily
independent so they are not, strictly speaking, syntax and semantics"
(Cussins 1990, p. 401). In that case, why not forget about syntax, semantics, and content and try to build a psychological explanation
based directly on situated perceptuomotor activity? Categories borrowed from linguistics are unlikely to provide an adequate description
of Cussins's S-domain.

In the traditional symbol processing model, Cussins reminds us, reasoning is placed at the center of the explanatory scheme; perception
and activity are relegated to the periphery. A theory based on nonconceptual content would place perception and activity at the center and

make reasoning the more peripheral concern. As will be discussed later in this book, a similar ambition inspires the research program of Rodney Brooks and his colleagues (Brooks 1986a, 1986b, 1991b). The difference is that these researchers have abandoned any pretense that autonomous behavior can be conceptualized or implemented by using task definitions framed in terms of concepts. Cussins wants to hold out for a dual explanatory framework. He is loath to give up the symbols of classic symbol processing entirely, because he assumes that a cognitive theory must rest on an explanatory account involving the "relation between computational artifacts and psychological explanation."

Cussins deplores the fact that, according to conceptual theory, there can be nothing psychological below the explanatory level of concepts, only an implementation theory. The job of interfacing with the world is thus left to neurophysiology, as in Sterelny's (1990) "face-recognition module," or to a normative theory like Millikan's, relying on evolution:

> The more satisfying alternative is to suppose that the explanation of cognition and the explanation of the world are interdependent. If we combine this idea with the idea that we should use a notion of non-conceptual content to provide a construction of our conceptual capacities, the result is a glimpse of non-conceptual psychological explanation: the story of the capacity to think is the story of the *non-conceptual emergence of objectivity.* (Cussins 1990, p. 408)

Unfortunately it *is* only a glimpse that Cussins provides. He has touched on a number of important issues that I shall examine in later chapters in this book. His arguments will be shown to point to the conclusion that a genuine explanation of human and animal behavior requires a reevaluation of the explanatory framework laid down by psychology. The underlying assumption has always been that we must start from a world of objects, properties, and situations and that an explanation of behavior should describe our ways of responding to and interacting with this world. According to that view, all that is really needed to explain the relevant causal mechanisms is a principled analysis of the "folk psychology" and "naive physics" that supply us with our explanatory kinds in the first place. Cussins has drawn attention to some of the problems inherent in this assumption. If we take seriously the fact that perception and motor activity are viewpoint dependent and inextricably situated in a species-typical environment, this traditional framework may turn out to be an encumbrance to explanation.

At times Cussins seems to be saying not only that we acquire our concepts by nonconceptual means but also that their conceptual import and semantic relations are emergent properties of a nonconceptual substrate. This is similar to Smolensky's (1988) suggestion that an adequate explanation of human thought cannot be found at the conceptual level but requires going down to a subconceptual level consisting of subsymbolic entities. Like Smolensky, Cussins seems to believe that connectionism, by its very nature, will provide the explanatory mechanism he is looking for. I shall examine the claims made for the connectionist paradigm in the next chapter and cast doubt on this widely held view that networks offer a panacea for all the ills of symbol processing.

Chapter 4

Connectionism: Its Promise and Limitations as Currently Conceived

4.1 Analytic and Synthetic Connectionism

Not only Cussins but other philosophers as well have thought that connectionist systems represent a distinct improvement on the symbolic implementations of classical AI. Churchland (1989), Clark (1989, 1990, 1993), Dreyfus and Dreyfus (1986a), and even Searle (1991), each in different ways, see distributed representation as a more realistic model, capable of simulating some of the key characteristics of mental phenomena, such as the ability to cope with ambiguity and shades of meaning, the capacity to generalize from particular instances, content-addressable memory, analogical thinking—in short, the general flexibility and "slippability" (Hofstadter 1985) of human thought. Searle (1991) seems surprised by his own conversion: "One of the unexpected consequences of this whole investigation is that I have quite inadvertently arrived at a defense—if that is the right word—of connectionism. . . . Among their other merits, at least some connectionist models show how a system might convert a meaningful input into a meaningful output without any rules, principles, inferences, or other sorts of meaningful phenomena in between" (p. 594).

It is not clear exactly what Searle means by "converting a meaningful input into a meaningful output." He is attracted to the connectionist paradigm because it appears to do away with rules and internal representations that are inferred top down from the meaningful entities of folk psychology to explain unconscious processes. But his talk of meaningful inputs and outputs reopens the very can of worms he has just been trying to close forever. "Meaningful" in whose terms? Those of the observer or those of the organism experiencing the "input" and producing the "output"? Or does Searle hope to "naturalize" meaning in some way as Millikan does, showing that the input and output have meanings of their own, independent of the meanings they may have for the user, and derived from their history of use? Clearly not. For Searle, meaning is inextricably linked with consciousness. But then, to talk of meaningful input being converted into meaningful output without meaningful processes in between is highly confusing. Searle has deliberately deprived himself of any mechanism to confer aspectual shape, which he takes to be the hallmark of meaning, on the input and output linked by his connectionist network. Something must be shown to confer meaning on the input and output (if behavior can indeed be explained in those terms), whether the processes in between are conscious or not. As I shall argue in this chapter, that turns out to be the central question raised by connectionist networks as currently conceived. They have been seen as a solution to what Harnad (1990) calls the "symbol grounding problem."

The symbol grounding problem is the problem of intentionality in a different guise. As conceived by authors like Harnad, it is predicated on the assumption that questions of meaning can be settled by concentrating on what goes on inside the head—that mechanisms in the brain, when properly interpreted, will somehow be shown to provide a direct link between physical entities that have their place in traditional science and fully fledged intentional symbols. Distributed representation, because of its "brainlike" physical structure and its "mindlike" emergent properties, is now felt to be the most promising computational paradigm to accomplish this trick.

I intend to examine Harnad's (1990) proposal in some detail, because I believe it will bring to the surface a number of important questions concerning the nature and ultimate capabilities of connectionist networks. One of the reasons these questions have tended to be obscured is that there are two very different ways of looking at networks, which I shall call the analytic and the synthetic views.

The *analytic* view sees connectionist networks in terms of their powers of abstraction. It looks on them as machines capable of extracting patterns and classificatory rules from raw data that have not been preinterpreted or presegmented in any way. It therefore concentrates on specifying the precise nature of these capabilities in computational terms and on delineating the formal limitations of networks as pattern detectors (McCulloch and Pitts 1943; Minsky and Papert 1969; Marr 1982). The mathematics of this approach tends to be the mathematics of task domains: propositional logic for the "ideas immanent in nervous activity," topology for pattern recognition, and differential operators for the detection of "zero-crossings" in low-level vision.

The *synthetic* approach is more interested in the ability of connectionist networks to mimic the qualities of human thought—in the way that distributed representations of related symbols seem to blend into each other, and the same symbol in different contexts will be represented by overlapping constellations of weights and units (Smolensky 1988; Clark 1989). The apparent abstraction of classificatory rules from the task domain is seen by these authors as an emergent phenomenon, and there is thus no sense in defining the capacities of networks in terms of their abilities to derive such rules. The computational emphasis of this view is on network properties, not on the properties of the task domain. Its mathematics tends to be the mathematics of activation functions, vector spaces, and statistical thermodynamics. There is a clean break, in this approach, between the formalism of the system and any formalism that science may have discovered in the task domain— between the subsymbolic and the symbolic levels, as Smolensky calls them.

It should be stressed that some of the existing "toy" networks can be viewed from both of these perspectives. However, the alternative views suggest potential applications, "real-life" extensions, and explanatory frameworks that are radically different—and a failure to keep them apart can lead to exaggerated claims for the paradigm. The analytic view encourages hopes of grounding the symbols of a classic symbol system directly in low-level features. The synthetic view provides grounds for believing that the symbols of connectionist networks have similarities with the symbols in people's minds. A failure to be clear about the different sources of meaning in the two conceptualizations can lead to the notion that connectionist networks are, by their very nature, explanatory models for symbolic thinking as practiced by human beings.

Most of the connectionist systems that have been built to date are models in which the inputs and outputs are assigned by the programmer following analysis of a particular task domain. The world is conceived in terms of objects, properties, and situations, as it was in the design specs for programs in traditional AI. What has changed is that the programmer no longer imposes explicit internal representations of the objects on the system. Following assignment of a set of features to the input units, she enters a collection of representative examples in terms of these features, and by a process of competitive learning, or through back-propagation of the desired behavior, the network arrives at its own categorization of the task domain.

Connectionist systems do not contain explicitly represented data structures. Nor do they contain rules that are explicitly formulated as production rules or procedures and apply uniformly to all instances of a given class. Any apparent rule following is an emergent phenomenon, to which only the ideal case of the system will normally conform. The system's knowledge is embodied as a superimposition of individual instances of learning, each of which will cause a slight adjustment to the connection weights between the internal units. Recall is not a matter of looking up the required item in accordance with hierarchical class membership criteria; it is more a case of the symbol's being recreated if a sufficient number of the units involved in its representation are brought into play.

The advances in flexibility, pattern completion, analogical linking, and graceful degradation are quite apparent, but is there any justification for the programmers' surprise when their systems turn out to carve up the task domain in ways that are similar to our own? Clearly the "meaning" of the symbols is still derived from the analysis performed by the programmer—from the constraints she imposes through her choice of input and output units and the meanings she assigns to them.

The hope behind the symbol grounding project is that, ultimately, the smaller and smaller "microfeatures" into which the domain is analyzed will somehow link up with "information" at a purely physical level: that meaning will be shown to be grounded in "features" that can be defined strictly in terms of entities recognized by traditional science. If symbol processing in the classical sense can be shown to be "emergent" from microfeatures of that type, then conceptual thought will finally be grounded.

This dream brushes aside Dennett's warning that "it makes no sense to suppose that the discrimination of stimuli by their significance can occur solely on the afferent side of the brain" (Dennett 1969, p. 74). It brushes aside Sterelny's, Dretske's, and Millikan's worries about the ability of living organisms to achieve the correct correspondence between internal representations and their objects in the world, rather than between internal representations and their proximal stimuli or sense impressions. It assumes that meaning is in some way "data driven" and that connectionism will unlock the secret of how this is done. What is more, it assumes that the meanings that distributed representations will acquire from features defined in purely physical terms are capable of being imported into the symbol processor that would be needed for full-blown conceptual thought.

There are at least two distinct versions of this dream. In one, the bottom-level entities are the connections and electrochemical events of neurophysiology; in the other, they are the "primary sensations" of psychophysics. The first is what Sejnowski, Koch, and Churchland (1988) call a "realistic brain model"; the second is Harnad's (1990) solution, which I will discuss at greater length in the next section.

Realistic brain models hold some promise for the modeling of very simple insect behavior, such as that of the horseshoe crab (Barlow 1990) or the hoverfly (Cliff 1990, 1991). However, there is little hope that they will ever provide an explanation, even at this level of behavior, without reference to the ecological niche in which the creature evolved and the environment with which its nervous system interacts. It is not even possible to guess at the "meaning" of neurophysiological events without knowing everything about the creature's habits and physical characteristics, the speed at which it moves, and the manner in which it deploys its receptors and effectors. The problem becomes far greater if the behavior one is trying to model is that of a human being. Even Sejnowski, Koch, and Churchland (1988) admit that a model of the human mind conceived in "realistic brain" terms has little chance of ever serving as an explanation. Its complexity and lack of intelligibility would rival that of the brain itself, and it would certainly not explain what the nervous system was doing. The level of explanation required to make sense of human behavior will need to accord with the neurophysiological facts as far as they are known, but it will have to deal in entities that make some contact with what the person is doing. There is little prospect that a connectionist network that models neural structure and activity can ever make contact with intentional behavior. But what about a model of the other type—a connectionist model that grounds symbolic activity in primary sensations?

4.2 Harnad's Model of Symbol Grounding

Harnad (1990) begins by laying down a formal definition of the classic symbol system, based on the work of Newell and Simon, Fodor, Pylyshyn, and the more successful programs of traditional AI. The possibility of generating intelligent behavior through symbol manipulation has, he says, been empirically demonstrated by such programs. The general impression he leaves is that symbol systems of the traditional kind can explain the high-level complexities of human behavior and that the main criticism that has been leveled against them is Searle's (1980) objection that the symbols do not possess intrinsic meaning. Thus, although Harnad finally concludes that symbol grounding needs to proceed bottom up, his operational thinking is basically top down. He concedes that it is not possible to have a "free-floating" symbol system of the classic variety, met halfway by a bottom-up approach of the kind he proposes—that this conception is "hopelessly modular"— but on the other hand he appears to believe that classic symbols constitute a natural kind for psychological explanation:

> Semantic interpretability must be coupled with explicit representation ... syntactic manipulability ..., and systematicity ... in order to be symbolic. None of these criteria is arbitrary, and as far as I can tell, if you weaken them, you lose the grip on what looks like a natural category and you sever the links with the

> formal theory of computation, leaving a sense of "symbolic" that
> is merely unexplicated metaphor (and probably differs from
> speaker to speaker). Hence it is only this formal sense of "sym-
> bolic" and "symbol system" that will be considered in this discus-
> sion of the grounding of symbol systems. (Harnad 1990, p. 337)

The nature of symbols is thus wholly defined by their formal properties within the classic framework. The way they interact with each
other and mediate behavior is also defined by that framework. But
the framework is seen to be incapable of conferring "meaning": the
meanings of the symbols will need to come from some other source.
Harnad rejects the notion that symbols acquire meaning fortuitously
(because the semantics just happen to mirror the syntax), and he is also
unhappy with the idea that they get their meaning through convention. His aim is to show that the symbols of classical AI can derive
semantic content from "low-level discrimination and identification of
perceptual inputs." Symbol grounding, Harnad realizes, is not a trivial
matter of hooking up a self-contained symbolic module to the senses.
There is a real problem of explaining how the symbol manipulator is
able to pick out the objects, events, and states of affairs in the world
that correspond to its symbols. He believes he can solve this problem
by apportioning it between two fundamental capacities of the human
mind: the ability to *discriminate* and the ability to *identify*. Harnad con-
tends that these are separate operations, which are performed sequentially and require independent explanations.

Discrimination is "relative judgment." It is our ability to tell things
apart and judge their degree of similarity. Harnad believes there is experimental evidence that this can be accomplished without semantic
criteria for comparison. Discrimination occurs prior to the introduction
of features or meaning of any kind. Our ability to discriminate depends
on low-level, data-driven mechanisms that form "iconic representations" of our inputs. These are "analog transforms of the projections of
distal objects on our sensory surfaces". For a representation of horses,
they would be analogs of the many different shapes that horses cast
on our retinas. Harnad admits there might be problems with figure-
ground discrimination, smoothing, size constancy, and shape constancy but insists that these do not invalidate the basic principle.

The other component of his symbol-grounding scheme—the ability
to identify—cannot, he concedes, be accomplished by representational
icons. We would need too many of them, and they would tend to blend
into each other and become confused. For this purpose, icons must be
reduced to "those *invariant features* of the sensory projection that reliably distinguish a member of one category from any nonmembers with

which it could be confused." (Harnad 1990, p. 342) This produces a second type of internal representation, which Harnad sometimes calls a "category-specific feature detector" and other times a "categorical representation." The representations may be innate, or they may be learned through experience. They are not symbolic. There is, says Harnad, no problem about their connection to objects-in-the-world. It is a purely causal connection, based on the relation between distal objects, proximal sensory projections, and the "acquired internal changes that result from a history of behavioral interactions with them."

He admits that no mechanism has yet been found to explain how such categorical representations are formed and that it has even been claimed that there are no invariant features in the sensory projection—that the intersection of all the projections of a category like "horse" is empty. But he is certain that this conclusion must be false:

> In my view, the reason intersections have not been found is because no one has yet looked for them properly. Introspection certainly isn't the way to look, and general pattern learning algorithms such as connectionism are relatively new; their inductive power remains to be tested. In addition, a careful distinction has not been made between pure sensory categories (which I claim must have invariants, otherwise we could not successfully identify them as we do) and higher-order categories that are *grounded* in sensory categories;. . . . (Harnad 1990, p. 344 fn.)

It requires only a cursory examination of vision research in classical AI (e.g., Guzman 1969; Kosslyn 1975; Ullman 1980, 1984; Waltz 1972; Winston 1975; Marr 1982) to realize that Harnad's model glosses over some of the most difficult problems associated with this approach. There is little evidence that he has taken on board the hard-won realizations concerning the need for a principled computational theory and a system of internal representation based on well-defined primitives that were formulated by Marr (1982). Like Sterelny (1990), Harnad relies on a vague notion of low-level perceptual modules to produce his "iconic representations." He brushes aside the worrying persistence of all the problems that Marr's model of object recognition brought to the surface: the problem of deciding what parts of a retinal projection are meaningfully related *before* meaning is assigned, the problem of converting two-dimensional projections into three-dimensional representations of "objects" with the necessary variety and flexibility, the inevitable need for a "library" of such objects to support the process of "identifying," or template matching, as it has usually been called.

To sum up, Harnad's scheme posits three levels of internal representation: iconic representations, categorical representations, and symbolic representations. At times his iconic representations appear to be phenomena of short-term memory, temporarily created by sensory projections and used to compare contiguous inputs in space or time. But at other times he describes them as permanent entities that may be retrieved from long-term memory whenever required (Harnad 1987, p. 551). If this is the case, we are talking about some form of template matching. By Harnad's own admission, it would mean holding in memory a distinct iconic representation, not only for every "object," but for every one of its possible variations "in size, form and color, . . . position, surroundings and time of day" (Harnad 1987 p. 551). Potentially, the number of templates corresponding to each object would be infinite.

Harnad's first level of representation has other problems. As I have argued (1990), discrimination without identification is a practical impossibility because of the segmentation problem. There simply is no getting away from the fact that isolating a given area of the sensory projection as worthy of special attention presupposes identifying it as a meaningful entity first. Various ingenious proposals have been made (Ullman 1984) to suggest that this process could be "data driven"— that areas of particular interest could be picked out from a retinal projection purely on the grounds of low-level properties of that projection itself, but as Marr (1982) pointed out, areas that are of potential semantic interest do not necessarily correspond to areas that are prominent in the image.

So why does Harnad involve himself in this clearly signposted circularity? Why is he so determined to separate discrimination from identification, which not only makes segmentation an insoluble problem but also means that he has to introduce viewpoint-specific templates to isolate the different projections of a putative object-in-the-world? The answer lies in the presuppositions of the symbol-grounding idea itself and in the area of experimental research on which Harnad implicitly bases his model, a branch of psychophysics called categorical perception (Harnad 1987).

Psychophysics tries to investigate subjective sensations within a scientific framework. Absolute judgments concerning the magnitude of sensory stimulation are known to be very poor. In the nineteenth century, Ernst Heinrich Weber and Gustav Fechner developed the method of "just-perceptible differences" to get around this problem. It seemed for a while that their method had produced a genuine scientific unit, but that claim has since been discredited. The method itself nevertheless remains one of the cornerstones of psychophysics, and it clearly is the basis for the experiments in categorical perception. Its claim (which remains controversial, as a variety of papers in Harnad's book make clear) is that there are natural boundaries in the perceptual continua of color, musical pitch, and stop consonants, causing the difference between two stimuli that straddle such a boundary to be perceived as greater than the (physically equal) difference between two stimuli that fall within a bounded range: "Categorical perception occurs when the continuous, variable, and confusable stimulation that reaches the sense organs is sorted out by the mind into discrete, distinct categories whose members somehow come to resemble one another more than they resemble members of other categories" (Harnad 1987, p. ix). It would therefore seem that the boundaries of perceptual categories can be established purely on the basis of discrimination. There is no need for an appeal to absolute judgment concerning category membership. In a sense the boundary exists prior to and independent of the description of the category. It is "data driven," though there appears to be some uncertainty to what extent the boundaries are innate and to what extent they are learned. Harnad's insistence on the separate operations of discrimination and identification can thus be seen as a bid to predicate his symbol grounding scheme on the experimental results of categorical perception, which appear to hold out the promise of breaking the deadlock I have described.

The question is whether this assumption is valid, or whether it is merely an artifact of a particular investigative approach. To begin with, the phenomenon appears to be restricted to only a very few modes of perception. The papers in Harnad's book discuss categorical perception of color, musical pitch, and stop consonants. They have nothing to say about taste, smell, discriminations of texture through touch, or categorization of loudness. It is noteworthy that in the areas that are discussed, we possess clear and distinct category labels, while the labels for the other perceptual modes are far less plentiful and notoriously vague. Harnad might say that this proves his point: that categorical perception is precisely the mechanism that provides us with those labels, the implication being that in smell and taste there are somehow less distinct low-level boundaries. However, even if we restrict ourselves to color, the question of whether our discriminations are achieved bottom up or top down (or whether such descriptions fail to reflect the underlying mechanism altogether) is not as clear as Harnad would like us to believe.

It has been shown (Bruner 1951) that judgment of color can be altered by association of the color with different objects. This effect is strongest when the objective color of the presented image is gray, and it can be overridden by brighter colors, but there is little doubt that expectations about an object's color play an important part in our subjective sensations.

The experiments conducted by Land (1977, 1986) with "color Mondrians" also cast doubt on the notion of absolute color categories linked to invariant low-level features. Land proved conclusively that his subjects' judgment of the color of a particular square on the Mondrian was not determined by the intensities of light in the three basic retinal wave bands that were coming from that square. A far more complicated mechanism is required, involving saccadic movements of the eyes across the entire Mondrian and pair-wise comparison of intensities in all three wavelengths at a large number of boundaries—and even this "retinex" model has been shown to break down under certain circumstances (Grossberg and Todorovic 1988).

Perception of color thus turns out to be a "cognitively penetrable" (Pylyshyn 1984) and highly active process. Harnad's experimental evidence does not establish a conclusive case for the possibility of deriving "pure sensory categories" on a presemantic, strictly causal, data-driven basis.

But even if it did establish such a case, could the results of categorical perception carry the entire weight of Harnad's scheme for symbol grounding? Harnad has taken the terms *feature* and *discrimination* as they are used within the context of experimental research into categorical perception and extended them to a much wider context, where they no longer apply in such a straightforward manner. Within the experiments he draws on, visual or aural "features" correspond to quantitative parameters of stimulation. "Discrimination" is a simple matter of reporting at what points quantitative change leads to a perceived change in quality. When he applies the terms to his model for symbol grounding, they are made to serve a much wider purpose. "Feature" can mean "having more than one leg"; "discrimination" covers the ability to tell mushrooms from toadstools. The whole weight of Harnad's argument rests on the supposed facts of categorical perception, but he implies that the same principles apply all the way up to the most abstract levels of categorization: "Abstract CP remains to be investigated, but it is certainly possible in principle. Moreover, in the present model it will be hypothesized that the feature extraction required to form categories in the first place necessarily involves abstraction" (Harnad 1987, p. 549).

Given its tightly circumscribed legitimizing definition within the context of a particular investigative approach, it is difficult to see what "abstract" categorical perception might mean. We have examined some of the practical problems involved in enlisting categorical perception to explain anything but the restricted phenomena to which it is applied in psychophysics. These are technical problems that have been clearly signposted by thirty years of AI research into object recognition. Harnad's belief that a straightforward causal chain can be set up between the categories of primal sensation isolated by his colleagues' experiments and top-level symbols as used in classical AI has little support from the successes and failures of that research.

There is, however, another side to the notion of symbol grounding. It concerns the assumption made by Harnad (and implied by all such attempts) that the sole difference between the symbols of traditional AI and the symbols used in human thought is their lack of grounding. In other words, symbol grounding is predicated on the notion that Fodor and Pylyshyn's (1988) criteria for a true symbol system exhaustively and accurately describe the way that symbols work in human thought—that these criteria constitute a definition for a natural kind and that the only missing ingredient in classic systems is the link to the real world that symbol grounding would provide.

In order to throw doubt on that assumption, I shall list a number of objections and alternative criteria that I believe ought to be taken into account. This list does not pretend to be an alternative formal definition. It is merely meant to draw attention to some of the qualities that "real-life" symbols seem to possess and that no amount of symbol grounding could ever add to a classic system. I shall phrase my discussion in connectionist terms, though I intend to show in later chapters that only an activity-based model can solve some of the problems that are brought out.

4.3 What Do We Mean by "Symbols"?

It seems important to differentiate between signs and symbols. *Signs* are proxies for the objects, properties, or events they signify. There is a straightforward, one-to-one relationship between a sign and its referent. *Symbols* are not straightforward proxies for objects. If the concept of a symbol is to serve any purpose in explaining human thought, it must take on board this distinction. Symbols lead the subject to *conceive* of their objects. If a symbol can be said to "signify" anything, it would be the occurrence of an act of conception. The symbol is reactivated—or iterated by means of an internal program, as Millikan puts it—every time it occurs in the person's thoughts.

The meaning of a symbol cannot be reduced to the "shapes" of sensory projections, no matter how wide an interpretation is put on the term *shape*. As Pylyshyn (1984) points out, "Organisms can respond selectively to properties of the environment that are not specifiable physically, such properties as being beautiful, being a sentence of English, or being a chair or a shoe. These properties are not properties involved in physical laws. They are not *projectable properties*" (p. 15).

Quite apart from this question of whether all relevant features can be reduced to physically specifiable entities, the notion that a symbol can be built up, or causally derived, or picked out, or logically defined in terms of a collection of fixed low-level features has probably done more to confuse the issue than to explain it. What constitutes a "feature" is to a large extent determined by context.

Shanon (1988) gives the example of a newborn baby who is examined by aunts on both sides of the family. Each aunt will find in the baby's face features that are similar to those observed in some relative on her own side. Similarity is first postulated, and then the features are discovered. What stands out as a feature for one aunt may be totally invisible to another, because it is distributed and diluted among the alternative constellation of features she has imposed from her different point of view.

It may be objected that this example is about a conscious process and that the features that the aunts discovered had already been isolated by the underlying cognitive mechanism prior to their conscious selection in the search for likeness. However, I believe this objection largely misses the point. Symbol grounding, as conceived in Harnad's system and others like it, is seen as a bottom-up, data-driven process determined by predefined, low-level features. Shanon's aunts were clearly not data driven in that sense. At the very least, their selection of the data was skewed by their perceptual experiences with other members of their respective families and their desire to claim the new baby for their side.

But more than that, it would be impossible to define an exhaustive set of "primitives" from which all family resemblances seen by all possible aunts could be constructed. What Shanon's aunts actually "saw" was in the nature of a metaphor: the "features" they picked out in the baby's face were brought into prominence—isolated from the background, possibly even imposed on the baby's face—because the face as a whole was conceived as a visual metaphor for their respective families.

There have been attempts (notably by Way 1991) to explain metaphor in terms of shifting hierarchies of predefined features. I shall return to the problems raised by Way's system in a later chapter. For the present purposes, it is sufficient to point out that her feature-based explanation of metaphor requires her to posit a series of "masks" that alter the inheritance links between features to take account of variations in context. This inevitably requires an even higher-level mechanism to decide which mask is appropriate in a particular situation, and as far as I can see, there would be no end to the meta-masks or meta-hierarchies involved.

The problem with hierarchical systems like Way's is twofold: they are committed to hard-edged, predefined "atoms of meaning," and their hierarchical structure imposes the relations between these atoms top down. A type hierarchy can be constructed only from a specific point of view. It presupposes a task domain, preregistered into objects, properties, and situations that are exhaustively defined in terms of the permissible features.

No predefined set of atomic features (even if one accepts "nonprojectable" ones) is ever likely to encompass all of the metaphoric senses that human beings can generate and grasp for a given term. The notion of a truth rule (Fodor 1978a) to define the extension of a term denies the phenomenon of metaphor, which is inextricably bound up with context. Context cannot be separated from "inner meaning," in the way that, for instance, Hofstadter (1980, chap. 6) tried to do. As Smolensky (1988) says in explaining the context dependence of symbols in highly distributed connectionist networks, "the context alters the structure of the symbol . . . in the subsymbolic paradigm the context of a symbol is manifest *inside* it" (p. 17).

The notion of context needs to be expanded and clarified if it is to serve a useful purpose in an explanation of symbolic thinking. When we talk about the context of a term, we are referring to more than the way it is semantically embedded in a particular sentence (and we are emphatically not employing it in Harnad's sense, which is derived from Claude Shannon's mathematical theory of information): what we are talking about is the particular, concrete instance in which the term is iterated.

For each individual, there will typically have been many such instances in the past, and they will have occurred in a large variety of circumstances, both internal and external to the individual. (For example, the person may have been in a good or bad mood, might have just won the lottery or had a stomachache, and her experience with the term may have involved listening to it being repeated ad nauseam by a boring politician, or having had it whispered into her ear by a boyfriend in the transports of ecstasy. The point is that any term is likely to crop up in any combination of circumstances.)

Although some selection undoubtedly goes on, many of these attendant circumstances will have been laid down as part of the internal structure of the symbol for that particular individual. Thus, in

Smolensky's Parallel Distributed Processing terms, the activity vector for "coffee" would have a different structure not only according to whether it referred to coffee in a cup or coffee in a can; it would also have a different structure according to whether you were drinking coffee after a satisfying meal, or putting a cup of coffee to your lips at the very instant that you learned that someone very dear to you had died.

In the latter case, the "paradigmatic" activity vector for coffee would no doubt be permanently skewed. This single instance would have a disproportionate effect on the connections that all instances of coffee have in common. The taste of coffee would have taken on a very special meaning for you, and if you were a poet, you might be driven to express that meaning in a new metaphoric use of the term *coffee*. If you were a good poet, this new metaphoric use might actually gain general acceptance, and your particular experience with the term *coffee* would have become part of its universal connotation. Coffee would have become blacker and more bitter for everyone. And the reason it would have done so would be because your poem had caused other people to share your paradigmatic experience: to iterate the term in a personal context similar to your own.

In fact, this would appear to be the only way that private meanings can be lined up with public meanings. Infants learn the public meanings of terms through iterating them in shared experiences with their parents. Such a conception of the acquisition of language requires that there is a sense of context that predates articulation in terms of symbols: that meaningful interactions with adults take place prior to the acquisition of the terms they help to define. Bateson (1975), Brazelton (1979), Bullowa (1979b), Kaye (1979, 1982), Papousek and Papousek (1977), Schaffer (1977b), Trevarthen (1977, 1979), and Tronick, Als, and Adamson (1979), among others, have begun to show that this is in fact the case. Careful observation of very young infants has revealed that they naturally engage in complex interactions with their mothers. Species-typical activity patterns performed spontaneously by the infant are interpreted as meaningful acts by the parent and incorporated into an interactively emergent dialogue of gestures and expressions. Elaborate games with well-defined patterns in space and time are established by the sixth month, whereas an awareness of objects as permanent and separate entities does not come until somewhat later. Trevarthen speculates that without these initial patterns of interaction, infants could not possibly take their first steps in understanding the world. The "pragmatics" of meaningful conversation precede any explicit "content," and as I shall argue in chapters 15 to 18, they provide the necessary scaffolding for the emergence of symbols.

4.4 Smolensky's "Proper Treatment"

The conception of a symbol I have tentatively sketched out is at variance with the notion that has traditionally been used in AI. It is meant to suggest that the qualities Harnad picked out (following Newell and Simon 1976 and Fodor and Pylyshyn 1988) as the defining characteristics for a natural kind of human thought—systematicity, explicit representation, and syntactic manipulability—are not fundamental aspects of the phenomenon. They may be characteristic of human discourse at certain levels, but this need not imply that they define the underlying mechanisms. Systematicity, explicit representation, and syntactic rules could be emergent properties of a system built on different principles altogether. In my opinion, that is the most important insight to come out of recent work with connectionist networks, and it is the central argument of Smolensky's (1988) paper, which sets out what I have called the synthetic approach to connectionism.

Smolensky makes much of the fact that since the birth of cognitive science, language has provided the dominant theoretical model. The von Neumann machine is eminently suited to executing rules expressed in formal language—rules that are modeled on those we consciously deploy to manipulate and describe explicit task domains. Smolensky argues that this is not an adequate model to describe the intuitive knowledge of a physics expert, or the processes involved in animal behavior and human perception, or the largely unconscious mechanisms that enable us to ride a bicycle and drive a car.

He suggests that the "programs" that are responsible for such skilled behavior run on a different "virtual machine," which he calls the *intuitive processor*. He dismisses the notion that these programs take the form of linguistically formulated rules referring to the entities we use in task descriptions. The operations of the intuitive processor can be formalized only at a "subsymbolic" level, "in between" the neural and symbolic levels. The correct way to describe it is in terms of a connectionist network, and the most appropriate formalism for doing so is the state vector, which represents the activity at a particular moment in time of all the processors that make up the network. The equations governing how the state vector changes over time are formalized in the system's activation evolution equation, and the model as a whole should be viewed as a dynamical system, since it can be adequately conceptualized only in terms of its evolving state vector rather than static units of meaning.

The question is whether such a framework offers a genuine alternative to the language model it seeks to displace (though not, as

Smolensky hastens to add, entirely to displace). At the beginning of his paper, Smolensky cautions that he does not intend to defend the scientific adequacy of his approach. His aim is merely to provide a proper framework for theoretical discussions about connectionism. However, he insists that his "subsymbolic paradigm" challenges both the syntactic and semantic role of language in traditional cognitive models of the mind. Despite his initial disclaimer, Smolensky clearly believes that the subsymbolic paradigm constitutes an alternative scientific model for what Cussins (1990) called the S-domain of human behavior and thought. Like Cussins, Smolensky suggests that an adequate explanation of human behavior can be given only in subsymbolic and nonsymbolic terms and that symbolic thinking must be grounded in operations that are not symbolic in themselves.

In Cussins's paper, the mechanism of grounding, as well as the precise nature of the subsymbolic level, were only hinted at through analogies. He spoke of "finding one's way in the world" and making a map of the terrain by traversing it along a variety of routes. But Cussins also declared that what was needed were "psycho-computational transformations defined over non-conceptual contents which have the effect of reducing the perspective dependence of the contents" (Cussins 1990, p. 426). These notions hint at a number of ways in which connectionism, as defined in Smolensky's paper, might help to do the job.

As I shall argue more fully in later chapters, dynamical systems theory by itself does not provide an explanation. It requires that the essential explanatory entities of a system be picked out by some other means. The explanatory entities of Smolensky's paradigm are, as the name implies, subsymbols—entities that lie below the symbolic level and can be apportioned among the various units of a connectionist network. These subsymbols, and their embodiment in a connectionist system, may be said to constitute the vehicles of "nonconceptual content" that Cussins required.

Are Smolensky's subsymbols truly nonconceptual? Are they viewpoint dependent? Can they be thought of as the products of "finding one's way in the world"? In a certain sense, the answer to all of these questions is yes. Smolensky's discussion of the internal representation of coffee will serve as an example. It is built up from superimposed representations of coffee in various concrete situations or contexts: coffee-in-a-cup, coffee-in-a-can, coffee-on-a-tree, coffee-being-drunk-by-a-man. The abstract symbol for coffee emerges from the intersection of all these representations. In a sense perspective-independent content has been shown to emerge from separate perspective-dependent instances. However, these perspective-dependent instances are in fact derived top down from the task domain they are supposed to ground.

They have no separate ontological or epistemological status, and therefore provide no added explanatory force. They are as much an artifact of the language model as the formal symbols of traditional AI. An examination of the connectionist models that have been produced to date will show that they all tend to suffer from this problem*.

Smolensky recognizes the problem. He asks what sort of subconceptual features the units in the intuitive processor represent and admits that, at the moment, there are no systematic or general answers to this question. He then goes on to discuss the various top-down methods that have been used to generate explanatory entities for existing models: "Representational features are borrowed from existing theoretical analyses of the domain and adapted (generally in somewhat ad hoc ways) to meet the needs of connectionist modeling" (Smolensky 1988, p. 8). Alternatively, the networks themselves are seen as an instrument for identifying "principles of subconceptual representation for the various problem domains." In other words, a set of examples is entered (presumably in terms of a collection of predefined input parameters), and their "correct" categorization is fed back into the system during training; once the system has learned to categorize fresh examples adequately, the "meanings" of the hidden units are determined and taken as clues to these underlying principles of representation. It seems unrealistic to expect anything in the nature of a scientific explanation to emerge from such strategies.

A third approach Smolensky puts forward is to start with a mass of data on human performance. At first glance, this might seem to be the most promising strategy of all. Since the strength of connectionist networks is their ability to abstract rulelike behavior from a multitude of concrete examples, one might hope that by superimposing a representative selection of real-life instances of human performance, one could produce a network that would not merely be able to reproduce these training instances but would behave in a credible manner in new situations as well, and also give clues to the underlying structure and dynamics.

---

*An exception are connectionist networks that serve as control systems for autonomous robots by linking sensor inputs to motor outputs (Cliff, Husbands, and Harvey 1993; Husbands and Harvey 1992; Harvey, Husbands, and Cliff 1993; and Pfeifer and Verschure 1992). Produced through situated learning or evolution by genetic algorithm, such networks do incorporate nonconceptual "knowledge" of a specific environment, which may be said to result from the robot's "finding its way in the world." However, their authors make no claims that these systems (as currently conceived) could provide a grounding for some higher level of symbolic thinking. I shall discuss in chapters 8 and 15 how networks of this type may contribute to an explanation of the interactive emergence of meaning in humans.

Unfortunately, any selection of data on human performance necessarily presupposes some theory about the fundamental nature of, and
the significant constituent elements of, that performance. Smolensky
cites multidimensional scaling as used by Shepard, "which allows data
on human judgments of the similarity between pairs of items in some
set to be turned into vectors for representing those items" (Smolensky
1988, p. 8).

I have already discussed the problems of trying to disentangle similarity and features. The methodology Smolensky here advocates is
predicated on what Nelson (1974) calls the "abstraction model" of concept formation. According to this theory, a concept is built up through
an abstraction of the features that different instances have in common.
Nelson points out that very young children perform poorly at the task
of concept formation under experimental conditions that, from the
point of view of the abstraction model, should be ideal. On the other
hand, they clearly are quite good at developing concepts under "natural" conditions, which impose almost insurmountable obstacles when
viewed in terms of that model. (Savage-Rumbaugh 1991 has recently
provided evidence that the same may be true of Bonobo or pygmy
chimpanzees.)

The world of young children is composed of complex, dynamic
events. The abstraction model presupposes that the child first extracts
simple, static features from this dynamic perceptual array and then
recombines them to form concepts that serve to make sense of that
array. No one has ever been able to suggest a comprehensible way of
doing this, and in view of the poor performance of infants under
"ideal" conditions, as well as the logical problems I have pointed out,
this model seems to have little going for it.

I shall discuss these problems at greater length in my final chapters.
The point here is that the use of multidimensional scaling, as advocated by Smolensky, inevitably imposes the abstraction model on any
system that is built in terms of the results. The theoretical stance inherent in the data would define the dynamics of the resultant connectionist model, and it seems unlikely that these dynamics would
provide a useful description of the underlying processes that subtend
the human performance to which the method was applied.

There is no such thing as theoretically neutral data. Any hope that
connectionist networks might prove capable of abstracting a model of
human behavior from a sufficiently large body of performance data is
based on a mistaken assumption concerning the nature of scientific
models. It assumes that such models are derived by some form of "induction" from raw data—that the scientific process consists of first
gathering a large body of "facts," and then deriving a theory from this

by staring at it long enough, until the significant "regularities" begin to fall out of their own accord.

As Popper (1963), Kuhn (1970), Hesse (1980), Wilkes (1989), and many other philosophers of science have pointed out, the history of scientific discovery does not confirm this interpretation. More often than not, the genesis of a new theory is a complete change in the accepted notion of what constitutes a "fact." Theory depends crucially on what is seen as a "natural kind"—on what the prevailing scientific opinion considers a fruitful and legitimate explanatory entity. Smolensky (1988) often seems to believe that connectionism has provided such a shift in the nature of explanatory entities:

> Unlike symbolic explanations, subsymbolic explanations rely crucially on a semantic ("dimensional") shift that accompanies the shift from the conceptual to the subconceptual level.
> The overall dispositions of cognitive systems are explained in the subsymbolic paradigm as approximate higher-level regularities that emerge from quantitative laws operating at a more fundamental level with different semantics. This is the kind of reduction familiar in natural science, exemplified by the explanation of the laws of thermodynamics through a reduction to mechanics that involves shifting the dimension from thermal semantics to molecular semantics. (p. 11)

The question is, what are those lower-level "semantics" in the subsymbolic paradigm? In the molecular theory of thermodynamics, the explanatory units at the underlying level are clearly defined. They constitute a hypothesis about the nature of matter that ultimately could be tested. The revolutionary aspect of this hypothesis, and the characteristic that gave it its explanatory power, was the fact that the underlying entities bore no obvious resemblance to the higher level of temperature, pressure, and volume they were called on to explain. If Maxwell and Boltzman had followed Smolensky's approach to the "semantics" of their problem, they would have tried to analyze temperature, pressure, and volume and to define these phenomena in terms of their characteristic features.

Smolensky appeals to statistical thermodynamics because the mathematics of his own harmony theory resembles the mathematics Maxwell and Boltzman used. But he has not been able to identify explanatorily fruitful "molecules" for his theory. His "atoms of meaning" will not work as explanatory entities for human behavior, because they are merely a restatement of the atoms used in folk psychology and in the symbolic paradigm for which he is trying to provide a deeper explanation. I shall argue in chapter 9 that this is a weakness not only of Smolensky's analysis but of all appeals to dynamical systems theory, which assume that dynamic equations, by their very nature, can provide an explanation of cognition.

Toward the end of his paper, Smolensky (1988) attempts a different escape from the problem. He asks what distinguishes a cognitive system from a purely physical one (given that the dynamics of both can be described by the mathematics of statistical mechanics) and answers that cognitive systems maintain a large number of goal conditions under a wide variety of environmental conditions: "The issue of complexity is critical here. A river (or a thermostat) only fails to be a cognitive dynamical system because it cannot satisfy a *large* range of goals under a *wide* range of conditions. Complexity is largely what distinguishes the dynamical systems studied in the subsymbolic paradigm from those traditionally studied in physics" (p. 15). In this passage, Smolensky expresses a hope that runs through much of cognitive science and AI: that sheer complexity will ultimately perform the trick of bridging the gap between the entities recognized by traditional science and intentional behavior. In chapter 3, I discussed some of the pitfalls of taking goal directedness as a defining characteristic of intentionality, and I shall discuss its role in scientific explanation in the chapter that follows. At this point I suggest that a reliance on complexity as the distinguishing mark of a cognitive system can be seen as an attempt to evade the need for adequate explanatory entities. What Smolensky seems to imply in the passage just quoted is that complexity is not just a necessary but also a sufficient condition for moving from an explanation of thermostats to an explanation of cognitive systems. Perhaps this will ultimately be shown to be the case, but only if a natural kind can be found that, together with the dynamical equations, provides a satisfactory and unifying explanation for both types of system.

Another way of obtaining the true measure of Smolensky's problem is by examining his somewhat ambiguous attitude to what (following Sejnowski, Koch, and Churchland 1988) I have called "realistic brain models." I have mentioned already that he tries to distance his subsymbolic paradigm from the "semantics" of neurophysiology. On the other hand, he seems to hope that the models constructed in that paradigm will "one day be shown to be some reasonable higher-level approximation to the neural system supporting that process" (Smolensky 1988, p. 9). What Smolensky (1988) means by a higher-level approximation becomes clear from the following passage: "Our information about the nervous system tends to describe its structure, not its dynamic behavior. Subsymbolic systems are dynamical systems with certain kinds of differential equations governing their dynamics. If we knew which dynamical variables in the neural system for some cognitive task were the critical ones for performing that task, and what the 'equations of motion' were for those variables, we could use that information to build neurally faithful cognitive models" (p. 10). Again, Smolensky shows his faith in the power of dynamical equations as a comprehensive explanatory device. What prevents us from bridging the explanatory gap between neurophysiology and the performance of cognitive tasks, he appears to be saying, is our ignorance of neural dynamics. If these were discovered, the subconceptual level could be collapsed onto the neural level, and the subsymbolic paradigm would provide a methodology for building models of the brain that would also be explanatory models of the mind. The dynamic variables of the neural system would provide the building blocks for such a model and thus turn out to be adequate explanatory entities for a model of cognitive behavior. In order to throw doubt on this belief and try to get a sense of what is really required of such a model, I shall look in some detail at an actual case from neurophysiology.

4.5 The Curious Case of the Horseshoe Crab

The horseshoe crab (Limulus polyphemus) has one of the most extensively studied nervous systems in nature. It has been a favorite of neurophysiologists for over fifty years. Its visual system, in particular, has received almost continuous attention since H. Keffer Hartline began to study it in 1926. One of the reasons for its popularity is that the eye of the horseshoe crab contains photoreceptor clusters, called ommatidia, that are a hundred times larger than the rods and cones of the human eye. Their size makes them far easier to isolate and also enables neurophysiologists to determine their connections to other nerve cells. There are only one thousand ommatidia in a Limulus eye, which explains the other reason for its popularity. It was thought for many years that the eye of the horseshoe crab was an extremely simple and primitive mechanism. In fact, the consensus of opinion among neurophysiologists involved in its study was that the Limulus eye had been fully understood. And in a certain sense it had. As Barlow (1990) explains, "The horseshoe crab's eye is one of the few networks of neural cells whose connections and behavior have been modeled exactly. The equations that describe its response to static images have been known for about 30 years, those describing the response to moving images for nearly 20" (p. 70). In other words, here was a case where the dynamical neural equations for a realistic brain model were all available—or so it seemed until Barlow suggested to two of his students that they try to record the neural responses from the Limulus eye without (as had always been done in the past) removing it from the animal. The students discovered that the eye's receptivity varied on a daily cycle. Its sensitivity turned out to be controlled by an internal clock, using a number of highly complex mechanisms, the existence of which had previously not been suspected. These mechanisms included changing the aperture of each ommatidium, causing the photosensitive region of the ommatidium to fold into itself, weakening the lateral inhibitions in the retina, which, in stronger light, enhance contrast discrimination, increasing the sensitivity of individual photocells, and reducing their level of random noise at the same time (a feat previously considered impossible in a biological system).

It thus became clear that the neural dynamics that had been taken as proved beyond question for almost twenty years were in fact an artifact of a particular experimental approach. On the assumption that visual processing was entirely bottom up, researchers had designed their experiments in such a way that the model became self-fulfilling. Of course, the dynamical equations that had been discovered were in some sense correct. They simply described a system that was quite different from that of the actual *Limulus* eye. They described a system of "data-driven" processes using *Limulus* ommatidia and neural connections as its components or "modules." A slight shift of perspective revealed a very different picture and brought into focus a multitude of previously invisible facts. And there were further surprises to come.

The discovery of the *Limulus* eye's daily variation in sensitivity renewed interest in a question that had never received a satisfactory answer and had largely been ignored: no one really knew what the horseshoe crab's eye was for. *Limulus* does not appear to use its eyes to find food, and there do not appear to be any predators it needs to avoid. Since it had now been established that night vision was in some way extremely important to it (the eyes can become a million times more sensitive at night than they are during the day), Barlow began to investigate the animal's nocturnal behavior in the field. Having eliminated food detection and predator avoidance, the most likely candidate was mating. Every spring, horseshoe crabs migrate from deep water to protected beaches along the east coast of North America. They mate during the night at high tide, building shallow underwater nests near the water's edge. By an ingenious set of experiments, Barlow proved that the male crab does indeed use its vision to find a mate. When its wanderings across the ocean floor bring it to within about a meter of a female (or a cement casting of one), it will turn and head in the female's direction. Black castings of females sighted in this way evoked the entire pattern of mating behavior.

Armed with this new information, Barlow and some students programmed a connection machine to model the horseshoe crab retina and then fed it simulated images from an underwater camera. They found that "the simulation indicates that the eye's combination of spatial and temporal responses may be optimized for detecting objects the size of another *Limulus* moving across the field of view at rates a horseshoe crab would be likely to travel. (To the eye of a moving crab, stationary objects appear to be in motion, so the male detects castings of females as well as it would detect the real thing.)" (Barlow 1990, p. 71).

I believe the following tentative conclusions should be drawn from this story:

1. Although the visual system of the horseshoe crab had been studied for sixty years, and its neurophysiology seemed to have been fully understood, nobody had any idea what the *Limulus* eye was actually doing.

2. The only way to understand what the eye was doing was to study its' performing its function in situ. What is more, the only way to make sense of what the eye was really doing was by understanding what the horseshoe crab was doing when it made use of the eye.

3. An abstract definition of what the crab was doing ("mating behavior," or "perception of a mate") would not have provided the appropriate clues to the real nature of the eye. It was only within the context of its movements and its mating activity in the particular environment to which it was adapted that an explanation could be found.

4. Is it helpful to think of the behavior of the horseshoe crab in terms of internal representations? It would require, as Barlow's discoveries made clear, an internal representation of "objects-the-size-of-another-*Limulus*-moving-across-the-field-of-view-at-rates-a-horseshoe-crab-would-be-likely-to-travel." This is not an internal representation corresponding to an objective entity. It is more like Gibson's (1979) notion of an invariant. The crab does not distinguish between movement of the object itself and movement caused by its own displacement. The entity to which it responds comes into being only through the crab's own behavior in particular circumstances.

5. Note also the use of the terms *optimized* and *responds much more strongly* in the quotation from Barlow. We have a network that shows graceful degradation; it is not an on-off system that depends on specific hard criteria. But the "prototype" that causes it to respond most strongly is the invariant of the crablike profile moving across the retina at a crablike speed.

6. Barlow seems to tend to the view that this whole complex mechanism, with its one thousand ommatidia and its intricate, endogenously controlled processes to give it a million-fold increase in sensitivity at night, came about "merely" to enable the male crab to catch sight of a female from a distance of about one meter in almost total darkness (the time of day when mating takes place), and thereby set off the sequence of activities involved in mating. The horseshoe crab's eye chiefly makes sense in the context of one particular bit of behavior: it serves to detect what ethologists call the "sign stimulus" that triggers the "fixed action pattern" of mating.

These concepts will be discussed more fully in chapters 11 through 14. What I want to stress at this point is that it would not help in the search for an explanation to conceptualize the *Limulus* eye as an information-processing system. This might tempt the investigator into viewing its behavior in terms of first principles borrowed from Boolean algebra or topology. It might tempt him to suppose that, in order to be able to detect a moving crab, it is first necessary to be able to detect a stationary one and then to be able to compare successive images on the retina to determine its movements. But in order to be able to pick out a stationary mate, *Limulus* would clearly need to contain mechanisms that identify boundaries; then compute "closure," "convexity," and "connectedness"; and finally, its nervous system would have to be capable of inferring size constancy from the lawful variations in the retinal projection of a female *Limulus* at different distances.

Boolean algebra and topology have their uses in describing the logic and analytical power of low-level artificial cell assemblies. They hold out little hope of providing an explanation of even so "simple" a natural mechanism as the *Limulus* eye. The *Limulus* eye was not built on abstract first principles; it evolved through incremental changes that turned out to confer advantage under certain environmental conditions. It cannot be understood without reference to those conditions and to *Limulus's* situated activity within them. An explanation of the eye is an explanation in terms of the sign stimulus and the fixed action pattern in whose service it evolved. An explanation of the *Limulus* eye requires an explanatory entity that describes the eye's acting within that context. Viewing the *Limulus* eye in terms of abstract first principles both complicates and oversimplifies the matter. In fact, the *Limulus* eye is not simple at all. For what it does, its one thousand ommatidia and one hundred thousand neural connections and fivefold mechanism to increase nighttime sensitivity may seem like overkill.

No rational designer would design such a mechanism from first principles. It took the invention of the connection machine to make it possible to construct a neural model of this level of complexity. As Barlow (1990) says, "In theory, a comparison between the response of cells in the Limulus eye and in the model to the same image could significantly advance the goal of understanding what information the eye must transmit for the brain to see. In practice, until recently such a computation from the equations for individual ommatidia taxed even the largest and fastest computers. Only with the advent of massively parallel computers has a network containing 1000 elements and tens of thousands of connections become tractable" (p. 70).

Notice that Barlow continues to talk in terms of "information" transmitted from the eye "for the brain to see." This can be treated as a kind of scientific shorthand. No doubt Barlow realizes that it is unhelpful to describe the brain as "seeing" anything, let alone "information." Perhaps it is worth asking whether it is helpful to think of the crab as seeing anything and whether the concept of "information"—whose tight mathematical definition by Shannon (Shannon and Weaver 1949) within the context of electronic communication channels has tempted many cognitive scientists into believing that a similarly tight definition can be provided for its more general use—has not been a greater source of confusion than it has been a help. The horseshoe crab has a physiological mechanism (presumably innate) that makes it change course under certain environmental conditions to commence mating behavior. One part of this mechanism is the surprisingly intricate neural wiring of the eye. Other parts are the surface characteristics of the ommatidia and the pattern of movement of the crab before it turns. The physiological mechanism can be described only as the sum of those parts, as well as the environmental conditions under which it was adapted to work.

Barlow's model works in the sense that it responds most strongly at its output terminals to images that resemble the natural sign stimulus described above. As far as I know, it has not been tested in a model crab under natural conditions. No doubt quite a lot of fine-tuning would be required to produce behavior like that of a male horseshoe crab. But even if it could be made to work under those conditions, would it constitute an explanation? Would it, that is, provide us with an explanatory model, in the sense that Maxwell's equations together with the molecular theory of gases provided an explanatory model for the gas laws, or Bohr's model provided an explanatory model of the atom? I do not believe that it would, and I think that any impression to the contrary rests on a confusion of levels.

4.6 The Limitations of an Input-Output Model

This is not just Smolensky's point about symbols, subsymbols, and neurons. I am suggesting that an explanatory model of a living organism cannot be an input-output model. It cannot be a model that rests on functional decomposition into perception, central processing, and motor responses. Apart from the fact that, as Dennett (1969) cautioned, "it makes no sense to suppose that the discrimination of stimuli by their significance can occur solely on the afferent side of the brain" (p. 74), the "stimuli" in question owe their very existence and their operational characteristics to the situated activity of the organism within its ecological niche. Their "significance" cannot be described without reference to that activity and that ecological niche; it is impossible to characterize in terms of the properties of incoming stimuli alone.

I am not disputing that realistic brain models like Barlow's are valuable contributions to science; however, by themselves, they do not provide a scientific explanation. In the case of the horseshoe crab, the problem is not acute. By providing some additional information about its mating habits, its speed of locomotion, and the appearance of the female crab, it is possible to make the neural model serve the purpose of an explanation. The real problems begin when the same organism has ten or twenty such patterns, or even hundreds, or many thousands, as is undoubtedly the case with human beings.

For too long, it has been assumed that an explanation of the underlying mechanisms of behavior, to be a scientific explanation, must take a Cartesian view of "inside" and "outside" and therefore worry about the "transformations" from purely physical events into meaningful "stimuli," and after processing, back into the efferent "signals" that trigger motor neurons. Connectionism is no exception. The methodology and mathematics of network theory may give reasons to suppose that a new explanatory level has been achieved (statistics or dynamical systems theory instead of symbol processing), but ultimately the paradigm still rests on an input-output model, and it therefore needs to incorporate a theory about the nature of its inputs and outputs, as well as the internal representations in between. I have argued in this chapter that all it has been able to come up with to date are redescriptions of the symbolic level it purports to replace.

In the next chapter I shall examine some of the fundamental issues of the computational approach that has played such a crucial role over the past forty years in lending new credibility to an input-output model of the human mind.

Chapter 5

Scientific Explanation of Behavior:
The Approach Through Formal Task Definition

5.1 Grounding Scientific Paradigms

Over the past forty or fifty years, the philosophy of science and the philosophy of mind have become ever more closely entangled. Churchland (1989) draws attention to this fact by saying that problems in the philosophy of mind are gradually being reconstructed as problems in the philosophy of science; Wilkes (1989) concludes that an examination of what is meant by explanation in psychology leads one to question what should count as "realism" in this particular science, which might deepen our understanding of realism in the physical sciences. Explanation, says Boden (1962), is describing one thing in terms of something else. The secret of an illuminating and helpful explanation is that the *explicans* and the *explicandum* should neither be identical nor so completely dissimilar that no connection or analogy between the two can be grasped. It is this act of grasping the connection, of seeing the analogy, that most clearly pinpoints the intersection between the philosophy of science and the philosophy of mind.

The key element in most types of scientific theory identified by Nagel (1961) is the model that provides a semantics for the abstract calculus. It is this model that ties together diverse experimental laws so that apparently quite different surface phenomena are seen to be manifestations of the same underlying processes and entities. Thomas Kuhn (1970) examined the peculiar power of such models to make sense of the world by imposing a unifying perspective on the practitioners of a science: "all models have similar functions. Among other things, they supply the group with preferred or permissible analogies and metaphors. By doing so, they help to determine what will be accepted as an explanation" (p. 184).

The question then arises: What underpins or defines such a model? In what terms can *it* be described or explained? How should we view this underlying framework that determines the preferred and permissible analogies? Kuhn admits that he does not have an answer to these questions: "In a sense that I am unable to explicate further, the proponents of competing paradigms practice their trades in different worlds" (p. 150). He discusses how, once a new model or paradigm has become established, the only way such a model can be internalized by a student is through working a sufficient number of "exemplars": paradigmatic problems or experiments that will give her a sense of what is "correct" and what is not. After solving enough of these, the student will be able to view any future problem as similar to the ones she has mastered already. But again, the question arises: similar in what sense? What determines the basis of this similarity? Kuhn seems to imply that this is the wrong question to ask: "I am claiming that the explication will not, by its nature, answer the question, 'Similar with respect to what'? That question is a request for a rule, in this case for the criteria by which particular situations are grouped into similarity sets, and I am arguing that the temptation to seek criteria (or at least a full set) should be resisted in this case" (p. 192).

It becomes clear at this point that Kuhn is no longer in the business of explaining the nature of scientific theories but is trying to come to grips with the psychological processes involved in *doing* science. He has begun by tracking the emergence of some of the key concepts in Western science and the way these were supplanted by radically different concepts. In each case where a new paradigm emerged, its acceptance involved a completely new way of seeing things, to the extent that proponents of the new theory find it difficult to talk to fellow scientists who continue to uphold the theory that preceded it. As Kuhn points out, the two camps are in a sense speaking a different language. The same words may even be used for quite different things without scientists' explicit awareness that such is the case.

These observations led Kuhn to the conviction that a change in scientific paradigms resembles the perceptual shifts that occur when we look at certain trick figures, such as the Necker cube or the vase that may also be seen as two symmetrically opposed profiles. An explanation of such perceptual shifts clearly falls within the province of cognitive psychology, but Kuhn appears to step back from an explanation of scientific practice in these terms. Although he is certain that the basis of similarity cannot be found in rules or explicit criteria that can be formulated in the language of the particular problem domain itself, he seems to hold on to the idea that if a coherent explanation is to be found at all, it can come only from a deeper understanding of such domains or the way they are internally represented in the mind of a scientist. This forces him to throw up his hands and admit that science appears to be somewhat of a mystery.

What seems to be required, given the distance that Kuhn has traveled already, is an explanation of the mechanisms that underlie the student's ability to see similarity. There is no a priori reason that these mechanisms should depend on similarities in the problems themselves or in the domain prescribed by a particular scientific theory. Kuhn is right in rejecting rules and criteria as the explanation for similarity, but it is to be hoped that he is wrong in his conclusion that no coherent explanation exists at all; if that were the case, there would be no principled grounding for analogical thinking, and as my earlier reference to Boden (1962) makes clear, this might have dire consequences for our understanding of science.

One does not have to subscribe wholeheartedly to Kuhn's analysis of the history of science to accept the central role of analogy and models in the scientific process (for a more detailed discussion of that role, see Hesse 1966, 1980), or to doubt the adequacy of the classic empiricist prescription of observation followed by hypothesis, followed by testing and confirmation. All theories are underdetermined by the data that are supposed to provide their proof, and classical empiricism has never succeeded in supplying a formal definition for the notion of induction on which it ultimately rests. A psychological component in the theory of science seems unavoidable.

Science is explanation. To explain is to "remove puzzlement" (Wilkes 1989) and "increase intelligibility" (Boden 1962)—to describe one thing in terms of something else. The secret of an illuminating and helpful explanation is that the *explicans* and the *explicandum* should neither be identical nor so completely dissimilar that no connection or analogy between them can be grasped. But before this can happen, there needs to be agreement on the phenomena that require an explanation and on what will count as similarity.

At this point an understanding of the scientific method merges with an understanding of mental processes. As Kuhn observed, what is involved is more akin to visual perception than to logical reasoning, and the change from one paradigm to another acts like a perceptual shift. Phenomena that were barely noticed before suddenly achieve salience, and others that previously stood out seem to have melted into the background. Analogies that could not be drawn within the domain of the previous model suddenly become obvious and highly illuminating. In Cussins's (1990) words, the new paradigm has set up a new task domain with its own preregistered objects, properties, and relations that may be quite different from the objects, properties, and relations of the previous task domain. And ultimately, these conceptual entities will need to be "constructed out of" (Cussins's words) something else. A psychological explanation will need to be provided in terms of the

S-domain of perceptual and motor skills—in terms of viewpoint-establishing, situated processes that explain how we find our way in the physical world as well as in the world of scientific models.

I shall return to these questions in chapter 16 and argue that a nonregressive explanation of analogy and metaphor requires a historical approach. It is only by explaining how an infant is "bootstrapped" into a world of meaning that we can hope to explain what ultimately underpins a plausible and illuminating scientific model. Such an explanation involves an understanding of the role played by successive layers of interaction between species-typical activity patterns and a cultural environment of artifacts and language. Traditional AI has tried to bypass this developmental process. As a result, cognitive science has tended to equate meaning with explicit definitions and formal rules relating public terms. In the remainder of this chapter, I shall examine some of the tacit presuppositions and classic exemplars of this model. My examination lays no claim to being exhaustive. It is intended to pinpoint some of the key ideas and show their inadequacy to the task of providing a genuine psychological explanation. Above all, it is meant to support my conclusion that a theory of human behavior that ignores the interactive emergence of meaning cannot hope to ground its explanatory terms by an appeal to natural selection.

5.2 Turing's Time-and-Motion Study of a Mathematician at Work

The traditional view of models in AI is that they must be functioning systems that mimic the outward manifestations of the mental phenomena we are trying to explain. We are faced with a bewildering variety of human and animal behavior. We would like to discover what produces it, how the underlying mechanisms work, and what natural laws, if any, they obey. We hope that if we can build a machine that reproduces the behavior, then, because we fully understand the rules or causal links of our model, we shall have discovered the rules or causal links that underlie the activities of naturally evolved creatures. At the very least, we hope that we shall have discovered a set of explanatory entities that are in some sense isomorphic to the entities that subtend natural intelligence.

In historical terms, this is a conflation of two quite different ideas: on the one hand, the notion of a model as a scaled-down copy of the original, made to show how the full-scale version will look, or to remind people of the real thing they were unable to afford or carry with them, and on the other hand, the explanatory device of using existing machines as analogies for phenomena that were less easy to understand. For the greater part of their history in thought, explanatory models have been mechanical models. The prevailing technology has provided analogies for the processes that underlie the behavior of stars, plants, hearts, the organs of perception, and finally, minds. This worked well so long as machines were relatively simple and, above all, built for a specific purpose. A pump performs a single, clearly defined function: it makes it possible to conceptualize pumping action and its results. It enabled Harvey to conceive of the heart in such terms and to discover the circulation of the blood. This convenient method of finding analogies for biological processes, however, was seriously undermined by the invention of the computer.

The computer was not conceived as a machine to perform a specific function. Its functional parameters, as laid down by Turing (1936), were not derived from real-world requirements or constraints. On the contrary, they derive from an attempt to delete all reference to reality, so that the resulting processes can apply in all possible worlds. To put it in a way made familiar by computational theory, the computer is a universal machine. Any process whatsoever may be run on it, providing the process can be formulated as an effective procedure. As a result, the computer becomes analogically inert.

Of course, this has long been recognized in cognitive science. The realization is embodied in the notion of a virtual machine. It is not the underlying operations at machine level that provide the illuminating analogies, so the argument goes, but the structure of the virtual machine that runs on top of it: the types of processes and data structures that are defined at this level and the particular programs that are designed to simulate behavior. Essentially, the computer has liberated us from the tedious necessity of building a new machine for each new function or process.

Nevertheless, this still leaves a major difference between the analogies drawn from mechanical models in the past and the analogies provided by AI systems. In order that something may be compared to something else in an illuminating and fruitful way, it needs to be something quite different (though not *too* different, as Boden 1962 pointed out). Until Harvey drew his analogy between the heart and a pump, it had never occurred to anyone that there was a resemblance between them. The pump had been invented without any reference to hearts. It had become a part of the common furniture of the world, as familiar as rocks and houses, with the difference that it was a functioning object and that its effect and operation were well understood. This was what made Harvey's insight so fruitful.

AI systems, on the other hand, are deliberately *designed* as models. They are in fact models of the scaled-down copy type, which happen also to be functional. In the eighteenth and nineteenth centuries, clockwork automata were sometimes used for a similar purpose; they were seen as possible explanations for the underlying mechanisms of animal and human behavior. But the analogy there was ultimately one with clockwork, not with the specific copies of animals and human beings. What seemed illuminating at the time was that the behavior could be produced by systems of cogwheels and eccentric cams and mechanical linkages. It was the mechanism of the automaton that provided the fruitful analogy. With computers, as we have seen, the mechanism is metaphorically inert. It is the purposely designed system running on top that is supposed to provide the analogy. One consequence has been a periodic unease in the AI community, expressed, for instance, in Marr's (1977) accusation that most AI programs were merely ad hoc redescriptions of the phenomena they were trying to explain, and in the argument between Fodor (1978b) and Johnson-Laird (1978) about the role of canonical representation in computational linguistics.

The fact is that despite frequent denials involving reference to virtual machines and to computational rather than implementational levels of description, AI ultimately does draw on analogies derived from the mechanism of the computer itself. Turing's original design specs have left their mark. They have saddled us with the notions of "effective procedure" and "mental state," both of which are central to cognitive science. Where did these notions come from? What supports the widely accepted claim that they are not only descriptive of but somehow basic to human—and possibly also animal—intelligence?

Turing's (1936) purpose was to provide an answer to Hilbert's Third Question: Could it be shown that there exists a definite method that might in principle be applied to any mathematical assertion to produce a correct decision as to whether that assertion was true? His proof was the culmination of a line of thought that had started in ancient Greece and had been pursued with increasing vigor in the nineteenth century. This was the attempt to reduce mathematics to its most basic elements: to show that all of its propositions and theorems could be derived from a small set of irreducible axioms by logically consistent rules.

By the late nineteenth century, mathematicians had largely succeeded in freeing their subject from any dependency on the physical world. Terms like *line, point,* and *natural number* were now taken to derive their meanings from the context in which they occurred. This meant that formal definitions had to be found to replace the appeal to self-evident truth based on observation. Russell and Whitehead had made their attempt to legitimize basic mathematical concepts by using Fregean logic. The formalist school, led by Hilbert, concentrated on examining the formal properties of the resulting system rather than worrying about the ultimate nature of mathematical truths. The propositional calculus provided a set of rules that would be true in all conceivable worlds, since its statements were context free. Hilbert hoped that it might be possible to prove the consistency of formal number theory by using only the propositional calculus added to some basic numerical reasoning. It was this hope that was ultimately shattered by Turing's proof.

Turing's main problem was to define a context-free notion of computability. His attack on the problem led through a definition of computable numbers, but he subsequently broadened its application to various classes of functions and, in an appendix to his paper, proved that his notion of computability was equivalent to Alonzo Church's formal definition of effective procedure. It has since been shown that every alternative definition that has ever been proposed is in fact equivalent to the one at which Turing arrived in terms of his notional machine.

An effective procedure for solving a given problem may be thought of as a set of rules that tell us, step by step, precisely how to behave in order to arrive at a solution. But such a definition runs into the problem of correct interpretation. It begs the question of how exactly the rules are to be specified and what is to ensure that they will always be understood in the way they were intended. Turing's solution was to specify, together with the rules, a detailed, self-contained mechanism to interpret them: a stripped-down language of symbols in which any rules could be expressed and a simple, universal machine that could interpret and execute instructions written in that language.

At this time, Turing did not believe that mathematicians' minds actually worked in that way. His concern was with a formal definition of the task, not with the way it was actually performed by human beings. Only later, when his design specs had been turned into functioning machines, did Turing himself become convinced that this way of implementing the task was also the way it must be implemented in real-life mathematicians.

Considering the abstract nature of the question to which it was addressed, it may be thought surprising that Turing's proof, involving the visualization of an actual machine, was so readily accepted. The read, write, and erase operations, to say nothing of the infinite tape, seem totally extraneous to the subject. It was a bit like saying that in order to arrive at a formal definition of physical work, one should reduce it to a set of basic operations performed on and regulated by an infinite, moving belt conveying partially finished products. And, of course, this was a concept very much in the air at the time. As far as I know, the similarities between Turing's universal machine and the assembly line in manufacturing have never been pointed out, but I believe they are unmistakable and may be very important to our understanding of the basic concepts involved.

Industrial psychologists like F. W. Taylor working at the beginning of this century were given the task of speeding up production and increasing managerial control over the manufacturing process. In order that management would be in a position to dictate entirely what items were produced at what time, it was necessary to reduce dependency on specialized skills possessed only by certain craftsmen. In order to speed up production, it was necessary to introduce a means of comparing the time taken to perform various tasks, as well as a regulating mechanism to ensure that workers performed them at the optimum rate.

Time-and-motion studies succeeded to a considerable extent in solving these problems. Psychologists broke down manufacturing operations into their constituent movements. They were able to formulate "canonical representations" for the processes involved and to get workers to perform these processes in the way they had been respecified. The main elements in forcing through this change were the assembly line and the deskilling of work through a deliberate redesign of products to suit a fragmented production process. Skill was transferred from the human craftsman to the organization of the assembly line and the logical design of the product. No one pretended that the quality or nature of mass-produced objects was the same as that of an artifact produced by a craftsman, but the results were cheap and had the advantage of being easily changed to follow fashion.

Consciously or unconsciously, I suggest, Turing drew on this new process of manufacturing for the principles of his notional computing machine. As far as I know, there is no documentary evidence to support my claim, but the similarities are too striking to be fortuitous. Assembly line production is context free. The assembly line is a universal machine that will perform any task that can be specified as an explicit process. Production is regulated by the infinite conveyor belt, and following each operation, the results are deposited back onto the belt before the next operation is performed on them. There is a basic repertoire of simple operations, which permits a canonical representation of every task in terms of a "language of work."

If my contention is correct, then Turing's proof is a particularly striking example of the use of analogy in science. The current mathematical formalisms, such as the propositional calculus, did not provide a way of formalizing process; they were essentially declarative formalisms. To arrive at a context-free notion of computability, Turing had to reach outside his subject altogether and draw on a mechanism that was familiar and well understood by most of his contemporaries. If it was possible to divorce physical work from specialized skills as well as from any reference to particular products and use a mechanical device as an aid to its formal definition, then perhaps it was possible to do the same for mathematical reasoning. Again, it should be stressed that Turing did not intend his machine to be a model of a mathematician's thought processes. His aim was to formalize the tasks involved in mathematical proof, just as the pioneers of mass production set out to formalize manufacturing tasks. It would not have occurred to these industrial psychologists to claim that they were simulating the behavior of a craftsman, since they were well aware how drastically the products had had to be redesigned to allow them to be manufactured on an assembly line.

The concept of the assembly line proved analogically fruitful to Turing, but the concept of an effective procedure is analogically inert when applied to psychological explanation. Process has been reduced to an abstract formalism, which renders it context free and universal but also devoid of explanatory force. The same holds true of the notion of mental state, or as Turing called it, the machine's "m-configuration." This notion was required for two different reasons. In the first place, the assembly line on which I am suggesting that Turing drew for his analogy has the character of a dialogue. Traditional craft is a dialogue with the material and the artifact that is being shaped; assembly line production is a dialogue with the conveyor belt, which makes the same request and demands the same response again and again of each particular worker. Dialogue is an essential aspect of the formalism. It permits the abstract specification of the task and its tight control of the production process. Turing took the further step of compressing the entire workforce, with their separate, prespecified sequence of operations, into a single machine. In order to do this, he needed to force the machine to change at each step, and the only way this could be accomplished was by enriching the nature of the dialogue. It was not just a matter of the machine's changing the product on the tape; the symbols on the tape also had to be capable of changing the state of the machine so as to prepare it for its next operation.

The step-by-step nature of symbolic interaction with the tape dictated a corresponding step-by-step notion of mental change. Turing seems to have had some doubts that his readers would be prepared to accept this idea, because he advises them at one point to think of the m-configurations as notes jotted down on a piece of paper, in the way that a human mathematician might leave himself a note if he were called away in the middle of his proof. As Minsky (1972) pointed out, the notion of mental state is essentially a device for giving a personal history to a machine that does not have any. But what I should like to emphasize at this point is that the step-by-step view of mental processing, which ultimately leads to the reification of mental states as internal representations, is derived from the nature of the dialogue imposed by Turing's mathematical assembly line. Normal interaction with the world imposes no such structure. Tasks are not cut up into predefined chunks. Our dialogues with the natural environment and our interior monologues are not necessarily constrained by this type of formalism.

Like the effective procedure, the notion of mental state is analogically inert, because it is merely a device to allow mental tasks to be reformulated in systematic terms. The fact that it might be an interesting exercise to show that formal systems can be constructed that hold true in all possible worlds—even the fact that human beings are capable of constructing such systems and devising proofs concerning their internal consistency and formal adequacy—does not imply that human behavior, including, as a very special case, mathematicians' mental behavior, is subtended by such systems. In fact, it seems highly unlikely that evolution should have produced a formal calculating machine that can cope with all possible worlds, when all that was needed was a creature well integrated with this particular world. This is not to say that an adequate explanatory model may not finally be implemented on a computer; it is merely to say that the basic concepts underlying the operation of a computer do not provide fruitful analogies for an explanation of human behavior and that cognitive science should be wary of all notions derived from these concepts. What is required is an explanation of symbolic activity, not a logical redescription of it or an abstract specification of its rules based on task descriptions.

5.3 Newell and Simon's Physical Symbol System

In 1973, Newell gave a talk entitled, "You Can't Play 20 Questions with Nature and Win" (Newell 1973), in which he drew attention to a peculiarity of current research in psychology. Psychology, as Newell saw it, lacked a unifying principle—a way of "putting it all together," a framework to give meaning to the proliferation of experimental results. It had degenerated into a series of unrelated experiments, each of which might be methodologically correct and of undoubted interest in its own terms but which never seemed to add up to anything more than an explanation of specific, narrowly defined phenomena. Newell was addressing an audience of AI programmers and cognitive psychologists concerned with visual information processing. He assumed that this audience agreed that the human mind should be viewed as

an information processing system, and his dissatisfaction with the up-
shot of their research implied that this conceptual framework had not
provided the necessary unifying factor. Newell's solution to psychology's malaise took the form of three suggestions:

1. He urged his audience "to construct complete processing
models rather than the partial ones we do now" (Newell 1973, p.
300). What he meant was that programmers should adopt a single, unifying control principle for all aspects of mental behavior.
His candidate for the most promising control structure to explain
the operations of the human mind was the production system.
2. He proposed that cognitive psychology concentrate on the
analysis of complex tasks involving a diversity of perceptual and
mental skills rather than on isolated phenomena. His candidate
for this sort of task—"a genuine slab of human behavior" (p.
303)—was the game of chess.
3. He suggested that there ought to be a single program that
could be used to perform all tasks: "This single system (this
model of the human information processor) would have to take
the instructions for each, as well as carry out the task. For it must
truly be a single system in order to provide the integration that
we seek" (p. 305). Again, Newell points to production systems as
the best hope for such a system.

The message of Newell's talk might be summed up as follows: computer science and AI are basically on the right track. The information
processing model constitutes our only hope for a scientific explanation
of intelligent behavior. There is a slight problem—computational models do not appear to add up to anything resembling a unified theory of
the mind—but this should not cause us to question the fundamental
principles of the computational paradigm. Perhaps the Turing machine
and the information processing model are not quite enough. What is
required is the addition of a standard control system and a single programming framework, as well as analyses of "genuine slabs of human
behavior" like chess.

In chapter 2, I examined the underlying assumptions that inspire
Newell and Simon's persistent claims that the computational framework has provided genuine scientific theories of mental phenomena. I
discussed the mutual dependence between specific programs simulating the performance of formally defined tasks and the general information processing model of the mind. I quoted Newell and Simon to the
effect that such specific programs prevent an information processing
theory of the mind from degenerating into a mere metaphor. I then
pointed out the similarities between Newell and Simon's conception

and the structure of classic theories in physics but listed a number of discrepancies between the two types of theory.

In particular, I drew attention to the difficulties of deriving theoretical entities for a psychological explanation from a design view that thinks in terms of problems and tasks. I concluded that Newell and Simon's information processing model is not a model in the sense formulated by Nagel (1961): it does not provide a semantics for psychology that is capable of unifying the experimental data treated by diverse empirical laws that are implemented as task-specific programs. Newell's (1973) complaint about the state of the discipline bears out my contention, but his three suggestions do not hold out any promise of solving the problem. Uniform control systems; larger, more complex formal tasks; a single program capable of processing the instructions required to implement all empirically established phenomena: none of these computational "fixes" can improve on the universal Turing machine as a source for the semantics of a psychological model. In chapter 2 I concluded that a theory of the type that Newell and Simon have in mind is beyond the reach of psychology. The study of behavior demands a different approach, which I called a "historical" or "genetic" explanation. Before I go on to discuss that approach, I want to examine the scientific status of yet another highly influential concept Newell and Simon introduced.

In their 1975 ACM Turing Award lecture, Newell and Simon declared that one of the fundamental contributions to knowledge made by computer science had been "to explain, at a rather basic level, what symbols are" (Newell and Simon 1976, p. 114). This lecture, and a subsequent paper by Newell (1980), may be seen as attempts to establish the status of "natural kind" for their notion of a physical symbol system.

As Nagel (1961), Kuhn (1970), Wilkes (1989), and other historians and philosophers of science have pointed out, one does not get very far in science without defining natural kinds. Before illuminating analogies can be drawn, there needs to be agreement as to which phenomena require an explanation and which are merely unimportant side effects. There also needs to be agreement as to what shall count as a valid explanatory entity. Natural kinds, says Wilkes (1989), may be thought of as crutches for scientific advance: explanatory entities that pick out the nodes in nature capable of being related by general laws.

As we have seen, an acceptance of the importance of such entities is perfectly compatible with skepticism about whether natural kinds are in any sense basic to the furniture of the world. "Naturalness" may be glossed in terms of the likelihood that the entities chosen will generate fruitful laws and generalizations. "Atom" is a natural kind because it acts as a node in various scientific laws. The concept of 'jealousy' can be applied and understood in a variety of contexts as well, but this is not because we have laws or theories in which jealousy plays a pivotal role but merely because we have learned to use it appropriately. The main thrust of Wilkes's paper is this: "To put the point very bluntly, the science of psychology yet needs to work out which of its *explananda* and *explanantia* are more like force, mass, energy, gold, donkeys and molecules, and which are more like carpets, ashtrays, fences, editions of Hamlet, and ornaments" (pp. 203–204).

It is clear from their lecture that Newell and Simon (1976) believe they *have* discovered a psychological entity that is more like force or atom than like carpet or ashtray. They begin by drawing attention to an important fact about explanatory entities: that these do not need to be defined exhaustively before they can inspire fruitful generalizations. They write: "All sciences characterize the essential nature of the systems they study. These characterizations are invariably qualitative in nature, for they set the terms in which more detailed knowledge can be developed. Their essence can often be captured in very short, very general statements. One might judge these general laws, due to their limited specificity, as making relatively little contribution to the sum of science, were it not for the historical evidence that show them to be results of the greatest importance" (p. 115). They go on to give some examples of such "laws of qualitative structure": the cell theory in biology, the theory of plate tectonics in geology, the germ theory of disease, and the corpuscular theory of matter. Initially such theories derive their explanatory force from the mere fact of hypothesizing an underlying entity that gives structure to the phenomena under investigation. It is not essential that the nature of this entity be well understood, and there is no need to assume that it takes the same form in all its manifestations.

In due course, Newell and Simon point out, the underlying entities will tend to be described in greater detail. Once researchers have a notion of what to look for, new examples will be found, and the different manifestations will be analyzed, taxonomized, and quantified. Quantitative theories will then be formulated, and these will tend to "assimilate all the general structure in the original qualitative hypothesis" (p. 115). A prime example of this type of development is the history of the atom in scientific explanation. But with cells, tectonic plates, and germs, "the variety of structure is so great that the underlying qualitative principle remains distinct, and its contribution to the total theory clearly discernible" (p. 115).

What Newell and Simon are trying to do is to establish the scientific credentials of their own candidate for a natural kind. Physical symbol systems differ in their shape, size, and structure. It is impossible to formulate quantitative laws that will categorize and define them. However, Newell and Simon contend, this should not disqualify physical symbol systems from being accepted as a natural kind of psychology, because similar objections may be raised against cells, germs, and tectonic plates, and these have all proved extremely useful in scientific explanation.

I see no reason to dispute that contention. It is echoed in a remark made by Pylyshyn (1984) to the effect that all science designates complex things by simple names in order to enable it to frame elegant and revealing laws. The question is whether the physical symbol system provides us with the means to do this: whether it is capable of revealing explanatory structure in psychological phenomena and of providing the unifying framework that Newell (1973) called for.

In the previous chapter I discussed Harnad's (1990) attempt to ground the symbols of a physical symbol system. I argued that Harnad's strategy could not work for two important reasons. First, it is impossible to construct a convincing explanatory link between primary sensations and "symbols" conceived in Newell and Simon's terms. And second, their conception of a "symbol" does not provide an adequate description of the role performed by linguistic, pictorial, and musical symbols in human thought.

Newell and Simon have not in fact "explained what symbols are"— at least not if they are using the term *symbol* in its generally accepted sense. As we saw in the previous chapter, symbolic activity has a character quite different from the formal operations that may be performed on the constituents of a physical symbol system. Part of the job of a fruitful natural kind in psychology would be to explain symbolic activity in human beings rather than to provide a formal redescription of subjects' verbal reports on their mental activities.

In a revealing passage, Newell and Simon (1976) return to their analogy with the germ theory of disease and remind us that its basic method of confirmation has been to "identify a disease; then look for a germ" (p. 118). They imply that the strategy they advocate for computational psychology is exactly the same: identify a task domain, then look for a physical symbol system. Unfortunately, the investigative cytologist has a number of crucial advantages in her quest for new germs over the computational psychologist in search of naturally occurring physical symbol systems.

To begin with, she starts from a consensus as to what constitutes an infectious disease: a well-defined natural kind that allows her to taxonomize the phenomena at the highest level of her explanatory scheme. As Wilkes (1989) discovered by consulting a variety of textbooks, the behavioral sciences have not been able to arrive at a similar consensus concerning the nature of the phenomena they are meant to explain.

Agreement about the appropriate natural kind at the highest level, based on the fact that it has proved its worth as an explanatory category in the past, gives the cytologist the confidence to look for a unitary cause at some lower level. And this is her second advantage over Newell and Simon's computational psychologist: she is clear about the type of entity she is looking for and knows it is different in kind from the disease it causes. It would not occur to her to try to construct a description of a germ in terms of the concepts her patients use to describe their symptoms. She may infer some of the germ's habits and characteristics (life cycle, latency period, rate of proliferation) from the nature of the disease, and—by analogy with germs that are already known to cause similar diseases—formulate hypotheses concerning the structure of the microorganism she is trying to identify, but a cytologist would never commit the error of importing concepts or processes from patients' reports into the level of microbiological explanation.

In a joint paper with Ericsson (Ericsson and Simon 1980), Simon presents a detailed justification of his reliance on verbal protocols in constructing psychological models. This paper was written in response to the excitement generated by recent investigations of the attribution process (see, for instance, Storms and Nisbett 1970 and Nisbett and Wilson 1977), the results of which seemed to indicate that people have very little insight into the real causes of their behavior and will spontaneously confabulate spurious causes to fill in the gaps.

Simon and Ericsson defend their methodology by an appeal to correct procedure. The questions put by the experimenter should match the nature of the cognitive processes that are being investigated. It should be made clear that what is required from the subject is a report of those processes rather than comparative evaluations or value judgments. Verbal reports should be collected concurrently with visible behavior, allowing the information to be cross-checked and enabling the subject to retrieve his version of events from short-term memory rather than having to drag it back from long-term memory, which is less reliable. For the same reason, the questions should not require a subject to explain why she behaved differently from other occasions, nor should she be asked if she would have behaved differently if the conditions were altered. It is questions like these, Simon and Ericsson imply, that induce the subject to confabulate extraneous causes for her behavior.

The assumption behind these strictures is that Nisbett and her colleagues, by using flawed experimental procedure, have somehow muddied the data. Evidence of confabulation is seen as an argument against the ability of computational psychologists to extract the correct symbolic model; it is not assumed to call into question the role of symbolic models in explanation. This reduces the problem of descriptive levels to a question of conscious versus unconscious processes. Since Newell and Simon have often accused their critics of confusing "symbolic" with "conscious," I want to make clear that the issue of conscious access is not relevant to this discussion.

What is at stake is the validity of explanations couched in folk psychological terms (however much those terms may have been cleaned up by conceptual analysis). The sort of confabulation uncovered by Nisbett and his colleagues (and, even more strikingly, by the experiments with commissurotomy patients reported in Springer and Deutch 1981) demonstrates the powerful tendency of human beings to assign intentional and meaningful interpretations to their own and other people's behavior. This tendency, and the way it is put into effect, clearly require an explanation. The practice of folk psychology is one of the phenomena that a science of psychology will have to explain.

Protocols are descriptions of the causes of behavior in folk psychological terms. Whether those descriptions are "correct," in the sense that they correspond to a rational task analysis given the constraints and goals pertaining at the time, does not really matter to the problem we are discussing. Perhaps Simon and Ericsson have developed better ways of getting their patients to report correctly on their symptoms, but we are still talking the language of symptoms, not that of germs. Explanation is a form of description, but it has to be something more than redescription. An important element in what makes infectious disease a convincing explanatory category is that lower-level explanatory entities have been isolated that correlate reliably with instances of that category, and that this level of description can be characterized in terms that make no reference to the language of symptoms or patients' reports.

In the final section of their paper Newell and Simon (1976) introduce a "second law of qualitative structure," which states that physical symbol systems "accomplish" intelligent action by solving problems and that the way they do this is through heuristic search: "Knowing that physical symbol systems provide the matrix for intelligent action does not tell us how they accomplish this. Our second example of a law of qualitative structure in computer science addresses this latter question, asserting that symbol systems solve problems by using the process of heuristic search" (p. 120). Does heuristic search add anything to computational explanation that might reveal physical symbol systems to be a convincing natural kind? Again, the answer to that question has to be negative. Heuristic search is merely another programming technique, which can be used to simulate process control in a refinery or an optimization of stock market investments as readily as intelligent behavior. There are several different varieties of heuristic search, but they do not correlate reliably with categories of mental phenomena. They are varieties of abstract procedure, and for the purposes of psychological explanation these procedures are analogically inert, just as the Turing machine, list processing, and production systems are.

At the end of their paper, Newell and Simon become entangled in the problem we have encountered a number of times already: heuristic search requires a move generator for problems, which in turn requires a space of symbol structures in which problem situations, including the initial and goal situations, can be represented. But what determines the choice of problem space? Newell and Simon have realized that this can be all important. Some problems that take enormous amounts of processing when expressed in terms of one representation pretty much "fall out" of an alternative representation: "Perhaps, however, in posing this problem we are not escaping from search processes. We have simply displaced the search from a space of possible problem solutions to a space of possible representations. In any event, the whole process of moving from one representation to another, and of discovering and evaluating representations, is largely unexplored territory in the domain of problem-solving research. The laws of qualitative structure governing representations remain to be discovered" (Newell and Simon 1976, p. 125). And assuming they are, then what about the laws of qualitative structure governing the representations of representations, and those governing the representations of representations of representations? Newell and Simon have run up against the problem of context. Their explanatory framework is tied to explicitly formulated problem representations, defined in terms of the objects, properties, and relations reported by their experimental subjects and imported into the programs on which computational explanation depends. A higher-level mechanism to determine which task representation might be appropriate to a specific context can be described only in terms of those same objects, properties, and relations. Not only problem solving itself, but also context and meta-context need to be explicitly defined in what are ultimately folk psychological terms. There is no way out of this explanatory loop, except by a true metaphorical leap into an explanatory level described in terms of entities that are different in kind.

Newell and Simon have sharpened our appreciation of the problem. They have clarified that no definition of process in terms of computational mechanisms can ever perform the requisite explanatory leap. Computational mechanisms are metaphorically inert. They define universal processes and therefore give us no purchase on the specific nature of *mental* processes.

5.4 Marr's Concept of Internal Representation

Marr's (1982) notion of internal representation is probably the most successful attempt to break this deadlock. Marr was one of the first to see that computational mechanisms could not by themselves carry the weight of a scientific explanation of mental phenomena. This led him to conclude that, in an information processing view of the mind, internal representations must share much of the burden; they should be accorded a more active role in explanation than that of mere tokens in a computational process. A computational theory, as Marr saw it, must begin by defining the problem in terms of *what* is being computed and *why*, and the way it can do this is by positing the appropriate internal representations: "A representation is a formal system for making explicit certain entities or types of information, together with a specification of how the system does this" (Marr 1982, p. 20). Marr's notion of "making explicit" is not the generally accepted one. It has nothing to do with "being available to consciousness." Marr repeatedly warned computer scientists against tackling conscious phenomena. Unlike Newell and Simon, he was keenly aware that even such apparently straightforward activities as mental arithmetic are likely to be subtended by mechanisms that are entirely different in kind from the surface rules they appear to follow.

Making explicit, in Marr's terms, is a process of selection, of extracting form from apparent chaos, or rather, since his research was concerned with the phenomenon of object recognition, of recovering shapes that are underdetermined by the raw data contained in a retinal projection. The specification of how a system does this requires a set of "primitives": elementary units of the sort of information that needs to be made explicit. And herein lies the active role of representation in Marr's theory. The primitives of a representation determine its "scope"—what can and cannot be represented by the particular representation—and they also ground the computational theory in the real world, since the nature of these primitives has been determined by the creature's evolution in its natural environment. They represent the constraints imposed on the computation by the animal's ecological niche. Everything that cannot be made explicit in terms of these primitives will be lost in the description that results after the representation has been applied. Mental representations are therefore not inert tokens that get pushed around by computational processes; they are not simply data structures to be modified and transformed as required by these processes. In a very real sense it is the system of representation that defines the computational processes.

Marr clearly felt that by introducing this concept, he had liberated explanation in AI from its dependence on computational mechanisms. Process was no longer an abstraction, defined in terms of the Turing machine, or heuristic search, or production systems; it could be defined as transformation from one internal representation into another, characterized by the primitives of the successive representations. Internal representations were no longer computational artifacts, such as Newell and Simon's property lists or Minsky's frames; they were true explanatory entities defining what was being computed and why, because they had been shaped by natural selection to make explicit only certain aspects of the available information.

At first sight, Marr seems to have bridged the gap I discussed in chapter 3. His concept of internal representation appears to offer a genuine possibility of reconciling computational explanation with natural selection. However, since Marr is wedded to an information-processing view of explanation, he must continue to think in terms of solutions to problems. This involves him in two major assumptions that had already been sign-posted by Dennett (1969):

1. That evolution has worked as a rational designer to find optimal solutions (from an engineering point of view) to the problems posed by the creature's ecological niche. This in turn presumes that the ecological niche, as it can be observed today, has been around long enough to constitute the determining factor and that the intricacies of morphogenesis and genetic transmission and the history of successive adaptations have not imposed their own logic.
2. That the "problem" posed by the environment can be unambiguously determined. The example of the horseshoe crab given in the previous chapter makes it clear that this is not a trivial matter. How do we decide what the computational problems really are? Does it make sense to talk about a "problem" of motor control or the "problem" of object recognition, as Marr did?

When Marr laid down that a computational theory should specify what needs to be computed and why before going on to specify how, he did not appear to realize that, by adopting a problem-solving approach, he had already constrained his possibilities concerning what and why by making the most fundamental assumption of all concerning how. Marr's internal representations have a ring of truth when he restricts himself to low-level vision where neurophysiological clues are relatively easy to interpret. But when he proceeds to higher stages involving the more abstract problems of object recognition, the primitives and form-matching processes of his internal representation for shape begin to take on the character of arm waving. As I have tried to show (Hendriks-Jansen 1990), Marr's object-recognition stage simply does not work. Nobody has been able to implement anything like it on a computer, and it is singularly unconvincing as a scientific explanation.

Introducing natural constraints into solutions to problems defined in computational terms does not guarantee that the resulting explanatory entities will be illuminating natural kinds for a psychological explanation. The formal definition dictates the character of the explanatory entities, even if the programmer manages to avoid the obvious pitfalls of "mimicry" that Marr criticized in Newell and Simon and Minsky. Nature does not solve problems; it produces creatures by the undirected, opportunistic process of natural selection. To discover natural kinds that accord with an evolutionary account, it is necessary to examine the historical contingencies of that process. I shall develop this argument further in the next section and put it onto a more formal basis in the chapter that follows.

5.5 Chomsky and Competence Theories

Competence theories assume that explanatorily fruitful "problems" can be defined for a wide range of mental phenomena, including some aspects of intentional behavior. The distinction between competence and performance was introduced by Chomsky in the early 1960s, but Marr felt that Chomsky's theory of deep structure and syntactical transformation was one of the few genuinely computational theories that had been proposed before his own theory of vision. There is a broad equivalence between Chomsky's definition of a competence theory and the computational level of what Marr called a Type 1 theory. A competence theory, says Boden (1988), provides a means of separating the forms that are logically possible from those that are logically ruled out. It may be seen as a logical mechanism for generating the class of lawful structures in a particular domain. Not all of these need occur in practice, and the constraints imposed by performance may sometimes obscure surface manifestations, thus making competence theories unhelpful as predictive tools, but the test of a useful scientific theory is not necessarily its predictive power (see also Sloman 1978). A competence theory reveals the underlying patterns and similarities in apparently diverse surface phenomena: "To know a language, I am assuming, is to be in a certain *mental state,* which persists as a relatively steady component of transitory mental states. . . . I further assume that to be in such a mental state is to have a certain mental structure consisting of a system of rules and principles that generate and relate mental representations of various types" (Chomsky 1980, p. 5). Chomsky adds that notions like "mental state," "mental representation," and "mental computation" should be taken as abstract characterizations of certain physical mechanisms that yet remain largely unknown and that his use of such terms as explanatory devices must be judged in the light of their success in providing insight and explanation.

Although he has never shown any interest in implementing his linguistic theories on a computer, Chomsky was profoundly influenced by the concept of the finite state machine and Claude Shannon's (Shannon and Weaver 1949) mathematical theory of communication. In *Syntactic Structures* (Chomsky 1957), he adopted this mathematical framework to effect his escape from the behaviorist tradition of Bloomfield and Harris in which he had been educated. He was able to show that a language like English could not be generated by a finite state grammar and introduced a top-down generator of phrase structure supplemented by syntactic transformations. Over the next few years, Chomsky became more and more convinced of the essential modularity of syntax and the (to him) inescapable conclusion that the grammatical faculty in humans must be innate.

Syntactic competence is seen as a product of natural selection that is potentially present in every individual at birth. It is a solution, which can be specified in terms of logical rules, to a problem posed by one of the peculiarities of the human environment. Chomsky suggests it should be conceptualized as an organ, analogous to an arm or the heart. Its development in each individual has to be seen as a process of maturation triggered by the appropriate environmental conditions rather than as a product of learning. It functions in accordance with certain predefined principles that are embodied in "mental structure," and this mental structure must ultimately reside in neurophysiological structure.

Chomsky (1980) admits that some patients whose left hemispheres (the supposed seat of the language faculty) have been surgically removed in infancy seem to develop normal language, but, he insists, on closer inspection, these people will be found to display abnormalities that go undetected in everyday life. What these patients have done, Chomsky (1980) posits, is use what he calls the "conceptual system" as a substitute for the proper language faculty: "Conceivably, further research may show that while the conceptual system is intact, certain elements of the language system are not, and that language use, while superficially normal, involves rather different mechanisms" (p. 7).

The question that inevitably arises is this: if these alternative mechanisms are capable of language production to a degree of competence that makes the "abnormality" undetectable in day-to-day life, what does this tell us about the need for a specialized language faculty and the notion of modularity? As Lakoff (1980) points out in his commentary on Chomsky's paper, research by Chomsky's own followers has increasingly revealed that it is difficult to maintain the principal assumption of modularity: that syntax and phonological discrimination are independent from meaning:

> What we found was that meaning and use (communicative function) affected virtually every rule of syntax. In order to keep the central modularity assumption—the independence of syntax—Chomsky has progressively redefined and narrowed the domain of syntax so that rules that were traditionally part of syntax ... were redefined as being in "semantics"—that is in a different module. Only by the constant redefinition and narrowing of the facts for which the syntactic module is supposed to account has Chomsky been able to maintain modularity. (p. 23)

Chomsky replies that Lakoff's reading of the changes in his position is based on a misunderstanding of his more recent technical work. I do not have the linguistic competence (in the professional sense of the word) to form a judgment about this, but the question I posed above still stands: if learning through the deployment of a conceptual system in the context of meaningful interchange can produce syntactic competence (in the everyday sense of the word) without recourse to Chomsky's language faculty, then why would evolution have bothered to produce a specialized language faculty in the first place? Is natural selection so pedantic that it insists on a fully fledged formal competence (in Chomsky's technical sense of the word) that conforms in all respects to his notions of deep structure and transformational rules? This question is not merely rhetorical. Its point is to cast doubt on the assumption that formal systems of rules, or mental structures embodying such rules, could ever be the result of a process of natural selection: to question whether it is possible to discover natural kinds that have an evolutionary justification by a formal analysis of a predefined task domain in terms of logical principles.

To say that a mental faculty is innate implies, among other things, that the faculty has been produced by natural selection. Natural selection is a process by which variations resulting from genetic differences are acted on by the natural environment. In the case of "mental structure," the only way the environment can have this effect is through differences in behavior resulting from the changes in mental structure.

The morphology of the brain cannot have selective repercussions in any other way.

A mutation in neural structure may result in a new pattern of behavior. Its chances of survival will be increased if the behavior confers reproductive advantage of some sort. But in order that this may happen, the new structure must also match the other structures that are already in place and mesh with the creature's existing sensory apparatus. A neural structure that confers the capacity for hand-eye coordination is of little use to a snail. It will not be able to grow arms fast enough to allow it to make use of its valuable neurological capacity. Indeed, this particular mutation is more likely to cause disturbances to patterns of behavior that are useful to the snail in its current ecological niche and will therefore be eliminated by natural selection before its time has come. Changes need to be incremental and congruent with existing morphology as well as existing behavior to stand a chance of survival.

How would a syntactic engine of the type Chomsky proposes have come into being by such an incremental process? What specific instances of verbal behavior, caused by subtending changes in neural structure, could result in the emergence of a language faculty as Chomsky defines it? It is possible to imagine incremental steps in, for instance, the development of a hand from a fin, each step conferring sufficient advantage to warrant its' being selected for. But Chomsky's language faculty, like all other formally defined systems, has an all-or-nothing character. One would find it difficult to construct a partially generative grammar, and there does not seem to be any possibility of a progression from a finite state grammar to a phrase structure grammar without syntactic transformations to a phrase structure grammar with syntactic transformations. In any case, would it be possible to point to specific behavioral consequences of such notional formalisms that might be said to have survival value?*

Chomsky purposely isolates the definition of his language faculty from performance, and he has little hope that a theory of performance will ever be formulated. He is not really interested in the speaker's surface abilities or skills. But it is only through these abilities and skills that natural selection could have produced its effects. The introduction

---

*Chomsky himself has consistently resisted demands to provide an evolutionary rationale for his language acquisition device and has even suggested that its existence may be incompatible with modern Darwinian theory. In chapter 16, I discuss Chomsky's position on this question in somewhat more detail and describe an attempt by Pinker and Bloom (1990) to provide an evolutionary explanation for an innate language faculty. Like Pinker and Bloom, I believe that such an explanation is required by Chomsky's theory, but unlike those authors, I do not believe it could ever be produced.

of a competence theory has forced Chomsky into extreme positions on modularity and maturation versus learning, but it also precludes a satisfactory explanation of how the innate faculty he requires could have come into being.

Competence theories and Type 1 computational theories have the all-or-nothing character of design solutions to formally defined problems. Naturally occurring creatures are, of necessity, the result of a long series of "kludges," superimposed without plan or purpose one on top of the other, but conferring, in their time, some slight reproductive advantage. The solutions of nature are ad hoc to a degree that not even the worst AI programs attacked by Marr (1982) were ad hoc, but the fact that they survived confers on them an authority that has proved elusive to artificial simulation.

5.6 Conclusion

We have examined a number of key attempts in AI to arrive at an explanation of mental phenomena through formal task definition. All of these theories have ultimately been grounded in the classic approach Turing defined. They start out from the assumption that the underlying mechanisms are best explained as formal processes defined in computational terms over internal representations. They therefore assume not merely that it is possible to simulate the outward manifestations of mental phenomena on a universal Turing machine but also that Turing's method of proof, and the programming tools it subsequently inspired, are necessary and sufficient ingredients for a scientific explanation of these phenomena. This assumption, however, has not been productive of illuminating analogies or natural kinds, the essential ingredients of explanation in science.

When a computer is used for real-world, real-time performance of a task, appropriate sensors and effectors are connected to the general-purpose central processor. Software is written to provide the interfaces between these purpose-designed links to the external world and the general-purpose central processing unit (CPU). In the case of the human brain, the sensors, effectors, and central processor all evolved in tandem, and they evolved because, together, they enabled the creature to engage in particular types of behavior. It could be said that the central processor is merely an extension of the sensors and a regulator for certain patterns of activity. Its structure was determined by the nature of the tasks it performed in the course of its evolution. Taken in isolation, without reference to the characteristics and operational modes of the senses and effectors—without reference to the creature's morphology and degrees of movement and its particular ecological niche—

taken as a separate entity, the brain is not susceptible of explanation at all.

This is an entirely different point from the one that is often made about the independence of software and hardware in a computer: that it would be very difficult to infer, from an examination at the electronic level, what a functioning computer was actually doing. Because the CPU of a digital computer was designed as a general-purpose machine, it is possible to examine one in isolation and determine exactly how it works. Determination of its mode of operation does not require reference to specific tasks. It is an entity whose meaning is contained in itself. Its natural kinds are the natural kinds of a general purpose machine: internal states and basic read, write, and arithmetic operations. The natural kinds of programs running on computers can similarly be defined without reference to extraneous events or circumstances; they are data structures, more sophisticated logical and mathematical operations, and various means of altering the sequence of processing.

Formal task definition reduces all process to context-independent problem solving in terms of such data structures and explicitly formulated operations. The same data structures and operations may be used to simulate weather patterns or control a refinery. This universality renders the computer metaphorically inert. Previous explanatory models drew analogies with machines whose use was well established and widely understood. The act of drawing an analogy between mental functioning and the operations of such machines could be productive of natural kinds. Since the machines had been designed for an altogether different and quite specific purpose and had become part of the familiar furniture of the everyday world, they had become a rich source of semantics, which, as Nagel (1961) points out, is essential if an explanatory model is to be more than just an abstract calculus. Explanatory models in AI are purposely designed to mimic the behavior they are meant to explain and therefore do not bring into the explanation such well-established, extraneous sources of meaning. They are devoid of explanatory power for psychology because they do not produce new explanatory entities on a different level of explanation; they can only redescribe. As Heil (1981) points out, we may grant that what a person learns is describable in a certain way without assuming that the person has, in some sense, internalized the description.

Chapter 6

Scientific Explanation of Behavior: The Logic of Evolution and Learning

6.1 Liberating Behavior from Behaviorist Explanations

In this chapter I shall argue that human, as well as animal, behavior requires an evolutionary explanation and that this sort of explanation is predicated on an explanatory logic different from that of functional decomposition, conceptual analysis, or formal task description. Evolutionary, or historical (Sloman 1978), or genetic (Nagel 1961) explanation relates what a creature can do to how it is done by examining the process by which the behavior emerged through evolution and learning in specific environmental circumstances. It assumes that a snapshot approach that isolates the behavior from its historical and environmental contexts cannot succeed in the areas it addresses.

The logic of evolution requires that we look closely at patterns of behavior rather than framing computational solutions in terms of formal entities "in the head," or trying to derive an understanding of what the system is doing by detailed examination of the neurophysiological substrate. Natural selection can affect that substrate only by working on differences in behavior. The crux of the argument presented here is that decomposition by activity provides our only explanatory access to the level of neurophysiology, and therefore constitutes the "natural" explanatory level between that substrate and folk psychology.

The term *behavior* tends to set alarm bells ringing in cognitive science. There is an almost instinctive tendency to associate any mention of behavior with behaviorism. Cognitive science is committed to the belief that the human mind is more than a stimulus-response engine—that it is capable of discrimination, problem solving, planning, and goal-directed activity. The aim of cognitive science has been to reinstate mental processes, and it has assumed that, in order to make people take mental processes seriously, it was necessary to make them take mental terms seriously as legitimate explanatory entities in science.

Computer science appeared to offer a ready-made solution. Programs manipulate data structures that can be equated with mental terms, and thus can be conceptualized as "symbols." These symbols can be made to interact, combine, pass through transformations, and have causal dependencies. Yet they are implemented in a purely physical substrate. Computers provide a perfect example of a physical system in which output is related to input in a far more complicated way than could ever be expressed as a stimulus-response pattern. Programmed appropriately, they can respond selectively and conditionally to well-defined (or, in the case of connectionist systems, even not-so-well-defined) categories. We saw in the previous chapters, however, that this conception has run into serious problems.

Fortunately, there does not seem to be any a priori reason that the research program that cognitive science has followed until now must be the only one that can achieve its aim. It is quite possible to take seriously the existence of mental phenomena—to reject the behaviorist ban on "looking inside" and share the conviction of traditional cognitivists that neither classical nor operant conditioning can provide adequate explanations of the full range of human behavior—without at the same time accepting that, in order to explain mental phenomena, it is necessary to use mental terms assigned to data structures in a computer program. What is needed is an explanation of intentional behavior, not a restatement in different terms that it *is* intentional. Such an explanation does not have to use intentional terms as explanatory entities; in fact, it is probably better that it does not.

The explanation of the gas laws did not come from a conceptual analysis of the notions of temperature, pressure, and volume. There is no conceptual link between those notions and the explanatory level of atoms and their impact velocities. The entities at the lower level are completely different from those at the level they are meant to explain, but somehow the explanation "feels right" because the entities can be related to the rest of science and we can imagine how atoms would speed up if the temperature rises, and how the pressure would increase when those atoms collide with greater and greater force. There is a relation between the two levels that can be grasped intuitively, though their entities are so different. The analogy is between fundamentally distinct conceptual levels, but there are parallels between them, grounded in prescientific physical experience, which permits it to work as an analogy. This sort of rapport does not appear to exist between, for instance, the intentional level of human behavior and the level of neurophysiology.

Before the gas laws could be explained at the atomic level, they had to be formulated at a higher level as laws. Temperature, pressure, and volume had to be identified as the significant parameters, whose relation required an explanation at a lower level. But there is little agreement in the behavioral sciences about what the significant top-level parameters of mental phenomena should be. Each discipline and school of thought has its own favorite candidates and its own prescriptions for the best methods of isolating parameters that need to be explained. There are statistical methods that accord the status of a natural kind to notions derived by factor analysis from large samples of self-ratings on a series of ten-point scales (see, for instance, Brody 1988). There are the almost mythological entities posited by the various schools of psychoanalysis, whose existence is self-evident to the practitioners of the particular school, since almost any evidence can be reinterpreted to count as a verification. There are abstract notions like economic or rational man, which have to be accepted as a priori entities for entire systems of explanation to work.

One of the many things wrong with behaviorist methodology was its cavalier approach to this problem of what is to be classed as a significant top-level entity. The stimulus and response classes in a Skinner box have no ethological or evolutionary justification. They exist only under laboratory conditions and are largely defined by a decision on the part of the experimenter as to what shall be considered to fit a chosen category of behavior and will therefore constitute a condition for reinforcement. Both a lever pressed down by the creature's paw or by an accidental swipe of its tail count as the same act of lever pressing. There is no attempt to relate the animal's patterns of behavior to its repertoire of activities in the natural world, and there is an unspoken assumption that the explanation of behavior must be seen in terms of associations between objective, atomic stimuli, and specific motor outputs. What we get is not so much a scientific explanation as a deployment of animals in the service of an experimental design. The laboratory situation is arranged in such a way that the animal can act only as an input-output device to verify the theory.

It might be said that behaviorism was not primarily interested in behavior. It was interested in establishing the validity of classical or operant conditioning as explanatory devices, in order to demonstrate that psychology could do without introspection and consciousness. An interest in behavior for its own sake, leading to its study under natural conditions, reentered animal psychology with the work of the classic ethologists von Uexkull (1934), Lorenz (1935, 1937, 1939), and Tinbergen (Lorenz and Tinbergen 1938). It was based on patient observation rather than on attempts to elicit predefined responses. It tried to make sense of the data in an evolutionary context but to withhold judgment for as long as possible concerning aims and final causes. These pioneers made a genuine attempt to isolate top-level explanatory entities. Some of their most basic assumptions have since been discarded, but the attention to patterns of behavior, and the renewed interest in field studies and natural selection, have become established features of mainstream animal psychology.

Although cognitive philosophy depends crucially on natural selection to link computational concepts to the rest of science, there is little discussion about the details of how such a link might be established. References to evolution tend to be notional and abstract, amounting to a claim that mental structures, as well as external form, may be "designed" by a selective process. The fact that such a process can operate only indirectly on neural structure through its behavioral consequences, and the questions this raises about how those consequences should be conceptualized and related back to mental structure, are rarely mentioned. Perhaps this is because the whole subject seems too daunting. It is one thing to observe the nesting behavior of a greylag goose and succeed in isolating certain fixed patterns of behavior and the occasions of their onset; it is quite another thing to perform the same sort of feat with human beings. How do we discover behavioral units that make evolutionary sense? Can it possibly help to talk in terms of fixed action patterns and sign stimuli when describing intentional behavior? If not, what are the elements in human behavior that can be traced to natural selection? Is it possible to isolate such units at all? Where and how should we begin?

6.2 Functions, Goals, and Purposes

One way of extracting explanatory entities for a complex system is to apply the principle of functional decomposition. This strategy is much favored in AI. Minsky (1987) provides an extreme example. Minsky's "natural kinds" for human behavior (which he calls "agents") include BUILD, FETCH, THIRST, WARMTH, ANGER, MORE, ARCH, THING, EVENT, and SELF-IDEAL, as well as agents to recognize faces, move muscle groups, and distinguish the sounds of words. This is functional decomposition run riot. Minsky justifies his strategy by saying that agents that turn out to be redundant to the final explanation, or just plain "wrong," can always be eliminated after they have served the purpose of sharpening our understanding. This recalls Wilkes's (1989) remark that natural kinds may be seen as crutches for theory construction. But the arbitrary proliferation of entities and processes in Minsky's account, rather than holding out a promise of understanding, ends up being a powerful argument for a more principled approach. Functional decomposition, if it is to be helpful as an explanatory method, needs to proceed from some unifying rationale. There must be a reason that the system is decomposed in one particular way rather than another.

Minsky appears to believe that any concept that is used in folk psychology may be converted into an "agent." He unquestioningly assumes that folk psychology, or "common sense," decomposes behavior in a principled way that brings out lawful relations. As Wilkes (1989) pointed out, common sense is not concerned with whether its explanatory entities are capable of being related by theories or laws; it merely tries to make behavior intelligible. Much of folk psychological explanation is post hoc, and it often seems that any "story" will do, as long as it makes behavior seem "meaningful" (Zimbardo 1969; Storms and Nisbett 1970; Nisbett and Wilson 1977; Springer and Deutch 1981).

Sloman (1978) stresses that if conceptual terms from folk psychology are to be used as pointers to behavioral entities, then it is important to be absolutely clear about their descriptive function. He advocates conceptual analysis to determine whether a term in everyday use describes a state, a process, a disposition, or an ability. This addresses one of the problems with Minsky's (1987) approach, but it still assumes that folk psychological terms, suitably "cleaned up" and reduced to formal task descriptions, can provide a principled decomposition into functional units, and—assuming we are committed to Dennett's program of "naturalization"—that these elements can be given an evolutionary rationale.

One of the problems with functional discussions of naturally occurring behavior is that they tend to conflate function (in the sense of what role a behavioral entity performs in the larger system) with either purpose (in the teleological sense of why it is there or what end it serves) or goal (in the sense of what the behavior itself or the system as a whole is trying to achieve during the process of operation). I shall try to unravel some of these senses of function and determine how they relate to evolutionary theory.

Nagel (1961) lumps together functional and teleological explanations into a single category. Such explanations, he says, take the form of statements that assert that an entity exists "for the sake of" the proper functioning of some larger whole or that a particular event occurs "in order that" some other event may take place: "Teleological explanations focus attention on the culminations and end products of specific processes, and in particular upon the contributions of various parts of a system to the maintenance of its global properties or modes of behavior. . . . Nonteleological explanations, on the other hand, direct attention precisely to the conditions under which specified processes are initiated or persist, and to the factors upon which the continued manifestations of certain inclusive traits of a system are contingent" (pp. 421–422). Nagel thus claims that the difference between teleological and nonteleological explanations is merely one of emphasis, and he goes on to show how teleological explanations in biology may be converted into nonteleological explanations without loss of content. His method is to conceptualize an organism as a dynamical system that is "directionally organized."

I shall discuss dynamical systems and their role in explanations of behavior in more detail in chapters 9 and 13. For now, it is sufficient to point out that Nagel's account describes living organisms as "goal directed," but dispenses with the need for negative feedback from a formally specified "goal." The explanatory mechanism he invokes makes no reference to an end state or property; it merely refers to the conditions under which the system persists in its characteristic organization and behavior. "Goal directedness" becomes a consequence of a "dynamical law" or "evolution equation," which ensures that whenever one parameter is altered, the other parameters will also change to maintain the system's "directional organization." This is one of the hallmarks of dynamical systems theory, which makes it an interesting alternative to computational explanations featuring negative feedback and internally represented goals.

Wright (1973) objects to Nagel's equation of function and goal directedness. He points out that even when goal-directed behavior has a function, that function may be quite different from the achievement of its goal. His example is a species of plankton that moves up and down during the course of a day. The goal of this behavior (i.e., the operant parameter for its goal-directed mechanism) is keeping the intensity of the light that reaches the creature relatively constant, but its function is to ensure that the creature has an adequate supply of oxygen. We have encountered similar arguments in Dretske's (1986) and Millikan's (1986) use of the magnetosome. Wright's conclusion is that functional decomposition must depend on a notion of design and that design by natural selection is no different from design in engineering. A piece of behavior may prove to be useful to a creature by accident, but if we consider it its function to be useful in that way, then its performance cannot be an accident. Functional ascriptions are intrinsically explanatory. The entity or behavior is assumed to be there *because* it performs the particular function: "We can say that the natural function of something—say an organ in an organism—is the reason the organ is there by invoking natural selection" (Wright 1973, p. 361).

Wright's conclusion provides the starting point for Millikan's (1984) definition of "proper function" based on "history of use." Essentially, the position may be summed up as follows: Function is defined not by causal or informational mechanisms but by history of use. The function of a naturally occurring trait can be distinguished from the trait's other, "accidental" consequences by the fact that the trait owes its survival through natural selection to this particular consequence.

Boorse (1976) invokes a historical argument against this definition of function. He points out that when Harvey discovered that the function of the heart was to ensure the circulation of the blood, natural selection had not been thought of: "Functional statements do often provide an answer to the question 'Why is X there?' . . . There is, however, another sort of explanation using function statements that has an equal claim to the name. This sort answers the question 'How does S work?' where S is the goal-directed system in which X appears" (Boorse 1976, p. 374). Boorse concludes that it would be better to abandon attempts to ground functional explanations through natural selection and accept that functional statements in biology do not carry evolutionary content at all.

This view is endorsed by Cummins (1975), who gives a succinct definition of functional analysis as it has traditionally been used in biology: "The biologically significant capacities of an entire organism are explained by analyzing the organism into a number of 'systems'— the circulatory system, the digestive system, the nervous system, etc.— each of which has its characteristic capacities. These capacities are in turn analyzed into capacities of component organs and structures. Ideally, the strategy is pressed until the analyzing capacities are amenable to the instantiating strategy" (p. 403). By the "instantiating strategy," Cummins means a reduction to the level of physics. R. Dawkins (1986), who calls this approach "hierarchical reductionism," expresses the same idea: "We explain the behavior of a component at any given level in terms of interactions between sub-components whose own internal organization, for the moment, is taken for granted. We peel our way down the hierarchy, until we reach units so simple that, for everyday purposes, we no longer feel the need to ask questions about them. Rightly or wrongly for instance, most of us are happy about the properties of rigid rods of iron, and we are prepared to use them as units of explanation of more complex machines that contain them" (p. 12). Philosophers of science thus appear to range themselves into two broad camps with respect to functional explanations in biology.

On one side are those who argue that the correct question to ask in order to isolate and justify a natural kind of behavior is, "Why is it there?" These philosophers equate function with purpose but not with causal explanations or goals. They believe it is possible to decompose a living system in such a way that the various parts can receive confirmation from the theory of natural selection without requiring causal links to explain them. The behavior of a part may have many consequences, but it will be shown to have survived because one of those consequences conferred selective advantage on the creature as a whole, and it is this particular consequence that defines its function.

On the other side are those who have seen that functional decomposition, as an explanatory strategy, predates Darwin's theory. These philosophers tend to equate function with causal links or goal directedness rather than with purpose. They believe that the correct questions to ask are: "How does the system work, and what sorts of constituent activities and parts would it require to get a machine to work in that way?" Practical research in artificial intelligence largely follows this strategy, and it therefore describes the view of functional decomposition that is tacitly assumed in the discipline. Minsky's *The Society of Mind* (1987) is a prime example.

As we have seen, however, there have been periodic doubts as to the legitimacy of the representational systems and computational mechanisms produced by this method. These have resulted in appeals to natural selection by cognitive philosophers and in Marr's (1982) call for principled computational solutions based on an understanding of the relevant environmental constraints. Natural selection is seen as conferring "proper function" on explanatory entities derived from an engineering or design approach.

I shall argue that Wright (1973) is correct in equating functional decomposition with the notion of design but that Boorse (1976) is correct in his analysis of what the design stance entails. Design of a working artifact proceeds from the assumption that it will be constructed out of functionally defined and causally related parts. There is no reason in principle that the key constituents of a behavioral system resulting from natural selection must coincide with functional modules identified in this way. I shall therefore conclude that functional decomposition and natural selection do not mix. On the other hand, I believe, with Dennett (1969), Wright (1973), and Millikan (1984), that natural selection constitutes our only hope of a principled explanation of behavior. "Why is it there?" is a better question to ask than, "How would a rationally designed artifact do it?" But it is not quite the correct question to ask because it subtly misconstrues the logic of natural selection.

6.3 Why Is It There? Fitness and Survival Value

Functional explanation predates Darwin's theory of natural selection. It is intimately related to the use of machines as explanatory metaphors. The constituent parts of a machine are designed to contribute in clearly defined ways to the overall performance of the system. The reason they are there is that the designer intended them to perform a particular function, which can be specified in terms of their interactions with each other and the performance of the machine as a whole.

Before Darwin, it was possible to think of naturally occurring creatures as purposely designed by God to perform their specific functions. The design view, with its decomposition into functional parts, accorded perfectly with a full-blown teleological explanation. Just as an engineer would purposely fit his machine to a particular job, so God had made every creature to perform its special function, designing the parts in such a way that they each contributed clearly and efficiently to the overall performance. Natural selection removed God from the role of purposeful designer. It also removed the underlying rationale for the design stance as applied to naturally occurring creatures.

A sufficient mechanism for natural selection, as Lewontin (1980) points out, is contained in the following three propositions: (1) There will tend to be slight variations in morphological, physiological, and behavioral traits among members of a species. (2) The variation is partly inherited; offspring resemble their parents more than unrelated individuals. (3) The variants have different numbers of offspring.

The notion of design plays no part in this definition. Genetic recombination and random mutation throw up new variants; natural selection preserves some and eliminates the rest and after a certain number of generations will result in clearly differentiated species. The characteristics of these species cannot be explained by appealing to some predefined aim, nor are they "solutions" to clearly defined "problems." They have simply come about.

Darwin's theory, as embodied in the three propositions, has seemed to many to be nothing more than a tautology. Baldly put, it states that the fittest individuals will leave more offspring in future generations and that relative fitness can be determined from the number of offspring left by different individuals. The notions of adaptation and ecological niche were introduced into this tautology to provide an extraneous explanation for differential fitness. But as Lewontin (1980) points out, they also dilute the explanatory force of Darwin's theory: "By allowing the theorist to postulate various combinations of 'problems' to which manifest traits are optimal 'solutions,' the adaptionist program makes of adaptation a metaphysical postulate, not only incapable of refutation, but necessarily confirmed by every observation" (p. 244). Adaptation reintroduces design by the back door. Some animals are more successful than others because they are better adapted to their environment. Why are they better adapted to their environment? Because they possess certain traits of morphology, physiology, or behavior that give them an advantage over other members of their species. How can we identify these traits? By thinking of them as solutions to specific problems posed by an environmental niche.

Adaptionist accounts suffer from the same sort of problem as folk psychology. Just as the commissurotomy patient can always find a plausible story to square the behavior of his left and right hemispheres and, when attention is drawn to the inconsistencies in his story, instantly produces yet another plausible account (Springer and Deutch 1981), so the adaptionist need never be at a loss for plausible evolutionary stories to fit his explanatory hypothesis. In the absence of hard historical data, it is possible to propose any number of such evolutionary explanations, depending on how one breaks down a creature's ecological niche and adaptive behavior into "problems" and "solutions." Adaptionist stories do not confer authority on a particular combination of such explanatory entities or "natural kinds."

Functional decomposition interprets the question, "Why is it there?" as a request for solutions to formally specifiable problems. The adaptionist version of this strategy assumes that nature poses such problems and that behavioral entities can be specified in terms of solutions. These solutions are seen as the "proper functions" of the traits. The trait is there to solve a particular problem; that is its function in relation to the creature as a whole. But within the context of Darwin's theory, the only *function* of a trait is to increase, via natural selection, the genetic contribution to future generations of the creature that possesses it. It is wrong to use this notion, as even some biologists do, to describe a more specific contribution made by the trait to the survival or reproductive success of an individual. There is an important conceptual difference between the notions of "fitness" and "survival value," and as McFarland (1985) warns, "survival value" is best reserved to describe the advantages of specific characteristics to an individual.

Darwin's theory is about fitness, not about survival value. Fitness is by definition relative fitness. It results from differences in genetic makeup. As M. S. Dawkins (1986) points out, what geneticists mean when they talk about a "gene for" a character is a difference between animals that results from a difference in genotypes. Genes for behavior are therefore properties of populations, and the notion cannot be applied to a single individual.

Isolation of a trait that was favored by natural selection requires detailed knowledge about the historical alternatives. It is dangerous to rely on notional alternatives, because the animals that are postulated in a design exercise of this sort may never have existed, and this withdraws the status of trait from the morphological or behavioral characteristic that has been isolated. Without hard historical alternatives, there can be no differential fitness, no alleles corresponding to alternative phenotypes, and therefore no traits. Evolutionary explanations depend crucially on actual occurrences for their explanatory premises. The problem for evolutionary explanations of behavior is that we have very little evidence of the variants that have become extinct. Behavior leaves no fossils. It may sometimes be inferred from fossils, from footprints, and from the contents of the digestive tract found among a creature's bones, but such indications remain shadowy and imprecise.

Does this mean that natural selection cannot get us any further in isolating explanatory entities for behavior? Ethologists have shown that there are ways of linking behavioral patterns to the environment and natural selection, provided that sufficient care is taken to avoid conceptual and methodological traps. M. S. Dawkins (1986) describes a number of these strategies:

1. Make use of genetic variation that is still available today. There are dark- and light-colored moths. It is known that the difference has a genetic basis. It is possible to restage the effects of natural selection by importing moths from the country into the town and vice versa, and actually watch the badly adapted ones succumb to birds.

2. Use artificially produced variations if no naturally occurring variations are available. Tinbergen created gulls' nests from which the eggshells were not removed and discovered that these attracted predators much more often than nests from which the parent gulls had removed the empty shells. This made it likely that the gulls that lacked "the gene for" eggshell removal had been eliminated by natural selection.

3. Compare related species that live in different habitats. Kittiwakes, a species of gull, nest on steep cliffs. They do not remove empty eggshells from their nests. This is a strong confirmation that eggshell removal in ground nesters is indeed an antipredator adaptation, because all the other potential dangers, such as the shells' harboring disease or injuring chicks, would apply as much to kittiwakes as to other gulls. The only observable difference is that there are no predators on the cliffs that might be attracted by the white insides of the empty shells. Dawkins warns that it is best to apply the comparative method to a wide range of species and be cautious when drawing the conclusion that correlation implies causation.

4. Finally, Dawkins also advocates the design approach. Natural selection, over the course of many years, will have resulted in animals that appear to be designed in certain ways—to have

certain "design features." It may be possible to examine the animals existing today to find out what they appear to be designed to do and then use this information to infer why it was that natural selection favored them and eradicated their rivals. We make a comparison between a real animal and the most effective machine that human beings could design to do the job. The closer the match is between the machine and what the animal does, the more likely it becomes that we have identified the selection pressures operating on the animal.

Note that, in this method, the analogy of the machine is used to make an informed guess about the key environmental pressures. We observe that a particular species of bird has a distinctive beak and conclude that this beak is "designed for" foraging, because we have seen how the bird uses its beak to extract its favorite mollusk from below the surface of mudflats. Our design sense tells us that if we wanted to construct a machine to extract mollusks from mudflats, that is the sort of beak we would give it. We conclude that the reason the bird (and therefore the beak) has survived must be that the struggle for survival with the short-beaked variants that are now extinct was waged in terms of food gathering rather than escaping from predators or attracting mates.

As M. S. Dawkins (1986) points out, this process of deduction depends on two assumptions of optimality. First, a design feature is by definition a characteristic that stands out and whose use is clearly apparent. We would not have noticed the beak, and we would certainly have failed to draw our design conclusions, if it were not so eminently suited to its purpose. Had we been given a brief to design a complete and viable bird, we might have discovered that the shape of the beak spoiled its aerodynamic characteristics, or prevented the bird from getting together with a mate. This would induce us to modify the beak so as to achieve a compromise with other design parameters. But the consequence of that might have been that the beak no longer stood out as so obviously designed for mollusk extraction. An adaptionist who was asked to identify its function might miss that point entirely. This is one of the paradoxes of the design approach. In order for it to be useful in analysis, it has to rely on a rather crude conception of design, because it requires a high degree of feature specialization, if not outright optimization.

On the other hand, we have assumed in our evolutionary explanation of the beak that foraging was indeed the overriding factor for survival—that extracting mollusks acted as the operant design parameter in selecting the long beaks and eliminating the short beaks. We have assumed that, in this particular case, nature chose to concentrate on feeding at the expense of other activities and to produce an optimized feeder on mollusks buried in mudflats. Of course, there might have been all sorts of other reasons that shorter-beaked birds died out. The reason we picked foraging as the operant parameter was that we took a particular design stance dictated by our identification of the beak as a specialized mollusk extractor. What we have in fact done, as M. S. Dawkins (1986) correctly pointed out, is use a "design feature" based on two assumptions of optimality to establish a link between survival value and fitness. This link is extremely tenuous, and the design approach should probably never be used in isolation as an explanatory strategy for naturally occurring behavior.

There are other problems, which Dawkins does not touch on but have been mentioned a number of times in previous chapters. Evolution, assuming we allow ourselves to think of it as a designer, never starts from scratch. This means that even a highly specialized solution must have been arrived at through many stages, some of which might have very little relation to its current function. Natural selection often hijacks organs or patterns of behavior that developed for one purpose to serve some other, quite different purpose. The most effective machine to do a particular job may thus have little resemblance to an animal that performs the same sort of job. An "optimal" solution in evolutionary terms may be difficult to recognize as an efficient solution in design terms.

Up to now we have been concentrating on the selective side of the equation—the problems created for functional decomposition into traits or parts by the complex ways in which natural selection disposes of the results of genetic variations. But there are serious problems on the other side as well. As Cummins (1975) points out, some traits persist simply because they are in the "genetic plan." In a certain type of protozoon, contractile vacuoles serve the purpose of eliminating excess water; in another type they clearly do not serve that purpose, since the animal does not suffer from the "problem" in question. They have remained in the genetic plan because they have not proved to be a serious disadvantage. Their presence cannot be explained by their function.

Genes may be said to have a logic of their own, quite separate from the logic of natural selection. Here, too, changes must be seen as cumulative. The DNA "designers" (mutation and sexual reproduction) never start from scratch. The genetic material inherited by today's animals contains discarded or temporarily filed plans for many previous forms, and these sleeping genes may resurface as unexpected new phenotypes.

Genetic variants relate to their phenotypic expressions in ways that no designer could ever dream up. There is pleiotropism (one gene's influencing many different characteristics, some of which may be highly functional, while others are not), and there are various types of interaction between genes. With complementary genes, neither can produce its phenotype in the absence of the other. In epistasis, one gene masks the effect of another. A modifier gene alters the phenotypic expression of a related gene.

The logic of how a particular creature and its behavior are put together is inextricably bound up with these genetic processes and with the process of ontogeny. I shall discuss the consequences in more detail in the later chapters on ethology, but it should be clear that analytical decomposition by function could lead us badly astray in picking out the relevant explanatory kinds for a creature whose morphological and behavioral characteristics were shaped in this way.

The design specs for a living creature do not have the character of a blueprint from which the creature is built. They do not even contain instructions describing the sequence of processes by which the creature can be built. Evolution and ontogeny are examples of what I have called interactive emergence, in which the environment plays an intimate role at every stage. The logic required to isolate the explanatory entities for a creature that results from such a process is that of a "historical" (Sloman, 1978) or "genetic" (Nagel, 1961) science, rather than an analytical or deductive, or even a teleological, one.

6.4 Historical Explanation and Economic Models

Sloman (1978) characterizes the difference between interpretative and historical science by saying that the first is mainly interested in form, whereas the second focuses on content. He then elaborates on what he means by content, explaining that historical scientists are interested in particular instances rather than in general categories that can be made to fit universal laws.

Nagel (1961) writes that what he calls "genetic" explanation is different from deductive, probabilistic, and teleological explanations because the explanatory premises take the form of a historical sequence of events. The *explicandum* cannot be shown to follow from some general law, which, given a set of initial conditions, will inevitably produce the thing or event we are trying to explain. It cannot even be shown to follow with a specifiable degree of probability from a law of that kind. Nor can it be explained as necessary in order to bring about some other state or event or as a functional component of some larger whole. What is proposed in this type of explanation is that the thing or event can be shown to have come about as the final stage in a historical process consisting of specific occurrences.

Darwin's theory of evolution is the paradigm for historical theories of this kind. Its causes and effects are worked out on the level of specific occurrences: the succession of creatures that make up a genetic line. The general law (if, indeed, it should be called that) deals with variations among individuals that are acted on by the environment and either eliminated or preserved to become the parents of yet further individuals that may differ in particular respects.

Genetic variation and the concept of fitness may also be viewed from a statistical perspective. The rate of change of gene frequencies in a given population can be said to depend on the relative fitness of the competing genotypes. If the fitness of the genotype with the highest rate of increase is designated as 1.00, a competing genotype with a rate of increase that is 85 percent of the highest rate is said to have a relative fitness of .85. The difference of .15 is called the coefficient of selection against the inferior genotype. An advantageous allele will increase in frequency at a rate proportional to the coefficient of selection and the frequencies of both of the competing alleles.

In practice, however, the natural environment is so complex that it is extremely difficult to correlate differences in fitness with specific variants in behavior accurately. Relative fitness can be derived only by comparing the changing frequencies of phenotypes in a substantial population. The differences among species we observe today are the results of events that happened long ago, and we have no means of measuring the changes in actual populations and thus determining the selective pressures of the past.

"Economic" models in behavioral ecology and Alife may be seen as an attempt to get around these problems. They try to specify in detail the various costs and benefits associated with alternative behavioral strategies and to relate these notions to the concept of fitness. It is assumed that the totality of the creature's behavior is the result of rational choice (if it were not, natural selection would have long eliminated it), and this permits the introduction of a common measure called "utility," which can be used to compare the benefit of the various activities to the creature in question.

Natural selection, writes McFarland (1985), has seen to it that there is an optimum balance between the amount of time spent by a brooding bird on incubation and the amount of time she spends on foraging to keep up her strength. This much is beyond dispute. The next step is to point out that there is an obvious relation between different strategies (i.e., different proportions of time spent on the two activities) and reproductive success. Since both behaviors are important to the production of offspring and compete for the bird's time during the period of incubation, there must be a measurable correlation between behavioral strategies and genetic survival. Again, this cannot be disputed.

The crucial question, however, remains: What, in fact, is the nature of that correlation? It will not do to say that it consists of a "gene for foraging" and a "gene for incubation" or even that we are dealing with a gene for more or less time spent on incubation as compared to foraging. Clearly these notions are too abstract to be correlated in any direct way with genetic factors. In order to link the balance between the two activities to genetic transmission, and thus establish a connection between measures of utility and measures of fitness, it is essential to understand in detail how the balance is achieved. That sort of understanding can come only from an examination of the actual activities involved and from a grasp of their operational and evolutionary interdependencies, as well as their interactions with the environment.

The optimal balance identified by a cost-benefit exercise is not an equation that can be traced to the creature's genes. Foraging and incubation are functional categories that cannot be "grounded" through natural selection. As McFarland (1985) himself admits, "Such considerations are purely functional. They specify what animals ought to do to make the best decisions under particular circumstances, but they do not say anything about the mechanisms that animals might employ to attain these objectives" (p. 456).

The fact that cost-benefit bird (an actuarial abstraction like "economic man") necessarily optimizes or maximizes its utility (because utility is by definition that which it optimizes) does not imply that individual birds contain choice mechanisms that work by optimization on entities like foraging and incubation. But the question that interests us is what sort of choice mechanisms (if that is the right word) the creature does contain. We would like natural selection to provide clues about the underlying mechanisms, and given sufficient patience and care and an ethological approach, it can in fact be made to do so. But economic models are not the way.

The application of such models in behavioral ecology results in explanations of behavior that account for observed correlations between certain environmental factors and formally defined classes of behavior by applying a logical calculus like game theory. Such explanations are valuable in their own right. As I shall discuss in chapter 9, computational models may be built that incorporate this logic and produce the desired correlations between input and output. But these are not models of behavior, in the sense of modeling a behaving creature; they remain economic or actuarial models that reproduce statistical correlations. It is a conceptual error to treat the programs used in such models as explanations of the underlying mechanisms that subtend the behavior of individual creatures.

Economic models may be seen as the latest attempt to break the tautology of Darwin's theory. If the utility (the survival value) of formally defined classes of behavior like "foraging" or a "dove strategy" could be related to a statistical treatment of fitness in terms of relative gene frequencies, then the result might be something approaching a deductive or a generative law. It might become possible to formulate hypotheses as to the utility of various alternatives in specific environments and predict the outcome of the evolutionary process.

For most of the behavior we observe today, however, no such link is possible, since the populations and conditions required for statistical analyses cannot be recreated. Nor, given the cumulative nature of evolution and the complexities of genetic processes and ontogeny, is it possible in principle to provide an explanation of this sort, except for the very simplest kinds of behavior. As I shall argue in chapters 7, 8, 9, and 12, behavior is situated activity that results from three processes of interactive emergence. The environment plays an inextricable part in all three processes, and it is not possible to separate out the genetic component and correlate it directly with differences in behavior. This is why a historical science is the only realistic approach to explanation in psychology and why Darwin's theory must remain the tautology it is.

6.5 Situated Patterns of Activity: The Natural Kinds of a Historical Explanation of Intelligent Behavior

If Darwin had felt constrained to produce a predictive or a generative theory, he might not have hit on the theory of natural selection. He would have searched for similar causes having similar effects or for generative rules to explain the emergence of formally defined categories of adaptive traits. His quest for universal categories would have led him to ignore the unexpected variations that became the basis for his explanation of evolution.

Similar habitats do on occasion result in similar forms of life, but this is not a law that can be taken for granted. The particular manifestation of the category can be discovered only after the fact, and even then it requires imaginative observation, comparison with other species, and elaborate restaging of the selective process.

A trait is a trait only because it has been isolated by a particular instance of natural selection. It becomes a trait only after it has been selected and after we have recognized it as an identifiable consequence of natural selection by comparing it with similar traits in related species. (There are schools of systematics that might quibble with the second part of this statement, but they would have to agree with the first.) Traits come in many shapes and sizes, ranging from the morphology of an oyster-catching beak to behavior patterns like nest building. We are prepared to countenance the ad hoc nature of adaptive traits because of the discipline imposed by Darwin's theory. As in folk psychology, it is often a case of trying out one, and if that does not work, trying out another. But we are confident that we know what we are looking for because of the discipline imposed by the theory: a trait must be heritable, it must be susceptible of variation, and some variations must confer selective advantage over others. These are general criteria imposed by Darwin's theory, and they produce a framework that gives credibility to particular instances.

The fundamental logic of natural selection may be conceptualized as "generate and test," but it is generate and test of a very peculiar kind. To begin with, its solution-space cannot be mapped out in explicit terms. No predefined set of parameters exhausts the potential range of phenotypes. Before the primate hand emerged, it would have been difficult to imagine the principle of the opposing thumb and characterize it in functional and operational terms as one of a set of solutions comparable to the prehensile tail of a gibbon and an elephant's trunk. Until the vertebrate eye emerged, seeing, as we understand it, could not be characterized. Nor was there any indication, in the protective cup around the original light-sensitive spot, or the rim that progressively folded over to produce a pinhole to facilitate focusing, of the principle of a lens that provides some of the key parameters for our conception of "seeing." Until the final "solution" emerged, there were no parameters to define where the process was leading.

What is more, the logic of the genetic system that generates candidate solutions knows nothing about the phenotypes that make up the solution space. Not only are the processes of genetic recombination and mutation unaffected by the demands of the environment, the complexities of ontogeny ensure that there is no simple relation between genotypic and phenotypic solutions. The genetic process does not generate solutions to solve problems, but neither does it generate solutions at random: the solutions it generates are determined by the logic of genetic structure and the mutations of which it is capable, and by genetic transmission and the relation of phenotypes to genotypes. As we have seen, this logic can be extremely convoluted.

Nevertheless, the basic mechanism of evolution does resemble generate and test. It has often been suggested that learning should be conceptualized as following the same pattern (Winston 1975; Fodor 1978a; Minsky 1987). Critics of this suggestion (e.g., Churchland 1989; Heil

1981) have tended to concentrate on the fact that its proponents are forced to posit an innate language of thought that allows the system to formulate hypotheses that can be tested against the world. The assumption has always been that the solution space of hypothesis and test that subtends the process of learning must have parameters that correspond to objects, properties, and situations of the real world—that it must be a task domain of concepts and that these concepts must dictate the scope (Marr 1982) of the underlying mechanism.

Natural selection provides an example of a system in which the generator works on entities that have their own logic and are quite different from the entities of the solution space and in which the world is not predefined in terms of objects, properties, and situations but achieves definition from the process itself. (I am talking about the theory of natural selection, whose standpoint allows us to pick out traits, which in turn define ecological niches in the world, not about whether those traits and niches are in any sense basic to the furniture of the world.) Phenotypes are emergent phenomena of a subtending mechanism whose functional components are genotypes. But they are subjected to constant pressure from the environment, which determines what genotypes, or combinations of genotypes, will survive, and thus makes sense of the products of sexual transmission and mutation.

Evolution has all the time in the world, but a creature that learns must do so before it succumbs to a hostile environment. It is therefore unlikely that any type of learning starts from scratch, even if that were feasible in principle. Viewed from a classic cognitive standpoint, the inherited component may be broken down into (1) straight knowledge about the world, (2) inbuilt structures that facilitate the learning of particular things, and (3) inbuilt strategies of development that ensure that certain types of learning are switched on at the right time and place. From a biological standpoint it becomes difficult to maintain a sharp distinction between these three varieties of inherited "knowledge."

As I shall discuss more fully in chapter 12, genetic and environmental forces are inextricably bound together in ontogeny, not as a blueprint and materials but more along the lines of epigenesis. Each step in the development sets the stage for the next, but no step ever dictates the next. Further development can proceed only if the partly completed phenotype has developed appropriately so far, the correct gene products are available, and environmental conditions fall within a certain range. There is no overall plan; it is only the happy coincidence of these different factors at each stage that gives the process as a whole the appearance of being planned—and the reason these factors tend to coincide at the right time is simply that the creature is a product of natural selection. Both learning and maturation are a form of situated activity, and the sharp conceptual distinction between the two made, for instance, by Chomsky (1980), appears to have little basis in biological fact.

This is not merely a quibble about terms. The traditional cognitive view of learning presupposes that it operates on a task domain of objects, properties, and situations. The threefold distinction outlined above makes sense only if the underlying mechanism is viewed as a rule-governed system operating on chunks of knowledge about the real world represented internally as concepts. We saw in chapter 3 how a number of authors have tried but failed to come to grips with the difficulties of positing the inheritance of concepts and of rules that involve the manipulation of concepts. As Sterelny (1990) put it, there is no characteristic behavioral consequence of most concepts that could have caused them to be selected for. If part of the mechanism for learning, and perhaps even a certain kind of "knowledge," is innate, it seems unlikely that its parameters can be adequately specified in terms of an explicitly formulated task domain. The alternative is best described by Gould and Marler (1984):

> We suspect, then, that innate, context-specific behavioral predispositions may play a role in certain stages of trial-and-error learning by providing animals with a degree of adaptive (but by no means absolute) guidance. Songbirds all seem to know to experiment with their syrinxes rather than their wings or feet in order to shape their singing behavior to match the song on which they have imprinted (although even here there is a default program— a crude "innate song" motor program—available. . . .). It is also interesting to note that many cases of quite complex motor learning appear to involve the liberal use of innate behavioral elements. The elaborate shell-harvesting behavior of oyster catchers, learned from the parents over the course of several months (and of which there are two very different forms), is composed almost entirely of innate behavioral gestures which are reordered, coordinated, and directed on the basis of learning. (pp. 65–66)

Human infants, too, are born with certain innate behavioral dispositions (see Trevarthen 1977, 1979 and the various contributors to Bullowa 1979a, Schaffer 1977a, and Johnson 1993a). They seem to "know" how to experiment with their facial muscles in order to elicit responses from their mothers, and the way they do this appears to be controlled by a number of "default motor programs." The muscles and nerves are organized in such a way that a wide repertoire of well-formed expressions is present before the baby could have had an opportunity to learn them from adult exemplars. The mother's expressions of happiness, sadness, or surprise can be imitated. Within the first month of life, an intricate pattern of emotional interactions is established, which allows the mother to begin shaping her child's other behavioral dispositions.

Newborn infants can orient to and track moving objects with their eyes. This had been known for some time, but it was not realized until the late 1970s that, in doing so, they tend to perform reach-and-grasp movements with their hands in which it is possible to detect a well-formed prototype of the movement that an adult makes to take hold of an object. The newborn infant is incapable of modifying this movement to adjust it to the type and size of object, but it constitutes a valuable "hypothesis" that can be shaped through solitary play and interactions with the mother. Trevarthen believes that this basic reach-and-grasp pattern is a necessary prerequisite for the perception of objects and that it also forms an important component in the development of intentional action. There are other patterns for responding to and producing a variety of sounds, which are soon integrated into the affective dialogue with the mother as well.

In all of these instances, it is possible to conceptualize the learning process as generate and test, but the hypotheses produced by the infant are patterns of activity rather than hypotheses about the nature of the world. These patterns have no meaning to the infant; they are not produced as tentative solutions to some problem. It is only through interaction with the mother and the physical environment that they gain any definition or meaning at all. The mother "selects" certain facial expressions, vocalizations, and gestures as being meaningful in particular contexts. The physical environment (in the case of human beings, largely a cultural environment composed of artifacts and tools) selects the appropriate forms of movement to match particular situations. But natural selection has already ensured that the right material is at hand in the form of patterns of activity that are naturally recognized as "meaningful" by the mother and are easily shaped through interaction with the cultural environment.

The details of this process, as far as they can be inferred from recent evidence gathered by developmental psychologists, will be discussed in the final chapters of this book. Before that, it is necessary to address one of the main difficulties in historical or genetic explanations, to which Nagel (1961) drew attention when he first outlined the characteristics of that approach: deciding which specific occurrences, from among a more or less continuous historical line, deserve to be singled out as particularly significant and are therefore worthy of being designated its "natural kinds." It is to this problem that I shall devote the next few chapters, arguing that a principled choice can in fact be made, based on a slightly modified version of Millikan's (1984) notion of history of use. To support my argument, I shall draw on work that has recently been done with autonomous robots and single out one of these robots in particular to serve as an "existence proof" for the feasibility of a historical explanation in terms of situated, interactively emergent patterns of activity.

Chapter 7

Toward a Working Definition of Activity: Recent Developments in AI That Try to Come to Terms with the S-Domain

7.1 The Advantages of an Existence Proof

In the next few chapters, I shall use Mataric's robot (Mataric 1991a, 1991b, 1992; Mataric and Brooks 1990) as a paradigm for autonomous agent research, because it illustrates most clearly the various points I wish to make. The performance of this robot shows how recognizable patterns of activity may emerge from low-level interactions between an autonomous agent and the environment to which it has been adapted and how such behavior can provide the basis for activity of a more abstract nature. This higher level of activity, in Mataric's robot, uses landmarks that are derived from correlations between the robot's movements and its sensory input. They depend for their existence on the lower level of emergent behavior and are not defined in terms of objective features of the world. Landmarks have extension over time. There is no "space" between them. Navigation becomes a matter not so much of traveling from one landmark to another but of slipping from the behavior specified by one landmark into the behavior specified by the next.

These are straightforward, concrete manifestations of ideas that have been mooted by diverse authors (Cussins 1990; Chapman and Agre 1987; Garfinkel, in Heritage 1984) yet often seem problematic because of terminological obscurities. The reductionist bias of the physical sciences, and their tendency to analyze phenomena that have temporal extent in terms of discrete snapshots, have made it difficult to talk coherently and with the necessary precision about interactive emergence. Mataric's robot provides a clear and simple way of doing so. I make no claims for the validity of its activity levels as explanatory entities for naturally occurring behavior, and clearly landmark navigation cannot be seen as a paradigm for all high-level behavior but as a model of behavioral interdependencies and interactive emergence, Mataric's robot has distinct advantages over the computational models proposed by traditional AI.

Mataric's robot did not spring fully formed from Mataric's brain. It grew out of research done over the past ten years at the MIT Artificial

Intelligence Lab under Rodney Brooks, and it was Brooks (1986a, 1986b, 1991a, 1991b, 1992) who laid down most of the key parameters for this type of research. An explanation of Mataric's robot must begin with a discussion of Brooks's main ideas.

7.2 The Concepts and Methodology of Autonomous Agent Research

Brooks believes that the only way to achieve artificial intelligence is through building robots that are viable in a "natural" environment—one that has not been specially constructed or in any way altered to suit the perceptual limitations of the robot. His robots operate in the MIT Artificial Intelligence Lab and are expected to cope with its static furniture as well as its mobile workforce.

Brooks insists that his approach is that of an engineer. Building an autonomous agent, like all other engineering projects, requires that an inherently complex problem be decomposed into more manageable parts. Brooks objects, however, to the decomposition into parts that has been practiced by traditional AI, which sees intelligence as a functional module separate from vision and motor activity, allowing the programmer to assume that his system will receive only the "relevant" details about the environment, conveniently abstracted and converted into the appropriate format by a front-end vision module. Brooks believes that the isolation of relevant details may in fact be the most important part of intelligence. Instead of the decomposition by function for which he criticizes traditional AI, he favors decomposition by activity.

An activity is a pattern of interactions with the world—for example, "avoid running into obstacles," "wander about aimlessly," and "explore interesting-looking areas." Each activity or behavior-producing system directly converts input into action. It functions independent of other activities and decides for itself when to act. It is not called as a subroutine by some central program or monitor, nor does it function as a condition-action pair in a higher-level production system. The activities are individually debugged until they become viable in the natural environment and then superimposed like layers in what Brooks calls a subsumption architecture. In hardware terms, connections from the new layer are tapped into the already existing layers at certain points allowing suppression or inhibition of the activity system below.

The overall behavior of the system is thus a result of various autonomous activities' overriding each other, and not of the system as a whole making a global decision based on centrally held internal representations of the world. Each layer is sensitive only to particular aspects of the environment, and these aspects constitute the "meaning" of the environment for its particular purposes. There is no "meaning" for the system as a whole, except in the interpretation by an observer of its overall behavior. (Recall Lorenz's experiences with the mother duck, from which he eventually concluded that her "parenting behavior," with the duckling as its "object," was *his* interpretation of a number of quite distinct processes triggered by diverse sign stimuli whose only locus of convergence was on the duckling "out there.")

Brooks maintains that his approach is not only truer to evolutionary reality but that it also makes his robots more robust than systems that depend on a centrally located model of the world, since any such model needs to be highly accurate in all its details and radically updated whenever there is a minor change in the agent's circumstances. A further advantage of the subsumption architecture is that intelligence can be built up in bits, with the assurance that lower levels of behavior will not be disturbed by the new additions.

Brooks's systems are not connectionist networks. Each layer consists of a number of finite state machines, all assigned specific tasks. The connections are sparse, and the messages passed from one unit to another can take on only a limited number of well-defined values. Unlike most builders of connectionist networks, Brooks does not expect any revelations from the internal behavior of his systems. There is no hope that underlying internal representations corresponding to some conceptual domain will be revealed by the distribution of weights once the system has settled down. Brooks has accepted that it is the designer's decisions that ultimately determine what the internal activity of the machine will be. But the fixed architecture of his robots also means that they are incapable of learning from examples. Each layer needs to be specifically fine-tuned to do its job, and it remains fixed forever after.

Brooks and his colleagues appear to use the terms *activity module* and *behavior module* interchangeably. Because of its distracting associations with behaviorism, I shall try to avoid the term *behavior* as much as possible and use *situated activity, patterns of activity,* or simply *activity,* but it should be clear that an activity pattern exhibited by one of Brooks's robots as the result of adding a new subsumption layer is not describable as a sequence of particular movements. "Avoid running into obstacles," "wander about aimlessly," and "explore interesting-looking areas" are in fact pieces of behavior in the traditional sense of the word, which emerge from a combination of low-level responses by the robot in interaction with a particular type of environment. I shall discuss these matters in more detail when I examine the work of Mataric later in this chapter, but it is important to realize from the start that autonomous agent research provides a quite simple and straightforward distinction between activity and movement. The difference does not lie in some mysterious intentional ingredient, and it does not require that the agent's activity be directed toward a goal. It is simply due to the fact that a recognizable temporal structure emerges from the interaction of a number of low-level reflexes with a particular environment.

One of the points Brooks stresses repeatedly is the inherent unreliability of sensors. Since his is an engineering approach, he is concerned mainly with the problems associated with artificial sensors. However, the strategies he adopts to cope with these problems have important repercussions for an understanding of naturally evolved organisms. Brooks points out that uncertainty is particularly acute when sensors are used to compile information that goes into building a centrally held model of the world:

> The original readings used to build the existing model were noisy and introduced uncertainties in the representation of the world. The new readings also include noise. Furthermore, if the robot has moved between sensor readings then there is uncertainty in how the coordinate systems of the two (or more) sets of sensor readings are related. . . . If more than one type of sensor is used, there is also the problem of fusing the different classes of data into a single representation.
>
> If there are no models built, the problem of uncertainty is inherently reduced. This alternative is to operate in a tight coupling with the world through a sensing-acting feed-back loop. Instead of relying on inaccurate values returned by noisy sensors, we can rely on the time averaged derivative of these signals as the creature actively changes its state within the world in a way which forces larger changes in the sensor readings than those contributed by noise. (Brooks 1991a, p. 437)

Brooks thus puts forward an engineering rationale for active vision: the conception of vision as a process with temporal extent and mediated by self-induced movement which, I have concluded (1990), offers the only viable escape from the problems inherent in Marr's (1982) theory. Brooks sees active vision as a weapon against sensor noise. By inducing changes of state that are larger than any possible changes due to uncertainties in the sensors' readings, the creature transcends the limitations of its own sensors. But noise can be caused by factors other than unpredictable sensor fluctuations. It is possible to think of everything except the particular signal in which the creature is "interested" as noise. The advantage of the sort of tight coupling with the world Brooks advocates is that the nature of each activity-bound signal can be kept quite simple, and its relation to self-induced movement is therefore unproblematic. By moving in specific, structured ways, the creature selects the information it is interested in. It might be said that it creates a clear and unique signal by its own movement, that it creates an entity with temporal extent that does not exist in the world "out there."

The opportunistic nature of evolution allows us to speculate as to what might happen if new modes of sensing are grafted onto a creature with an already quite intricate repertoire of activities. Again, these matters will be discussed in more detail when I examine Mataric's work later in the chapter, but it should be clear that this opens up a principled way of conceptualizing the notion of a creature's *Umwelt* (von Uexkull 1934). The agent's *Umwelt* can be understood only in the context of its activity patterns, which, at the lowest level, are "boot-strapped" by tight stimulus-action feedback loops, evolved to meet particular environmental constraints.

Although the work of Brooks and his colleagues affords new insights into the creative possibilities of evolution when coupled with interactive movement and sensing, this should not deceive us into viewing his method as a faithful reenactment of the evolutionary process. What Brooks has done is to borrow two key principles from natural evolution and incorporate them into his engineering approach: the idea that each step leading to the creature we can see today must have constituted a creature that was viable in its own right and the idea that new adaptations are grafted opportunistically onto already existing ones, resulting in an end product that may not be as elegantly designed as it would be if an engineer had approached the current requirements from an analytical point of view but that is likely to be more robust and less brittle than such a minimal design.

Until recently (Brooks and Stein 1993), Brooks maintained that he had no particular interest in demonstrating how human intelligence works. What interested him was the engineering problem of constructing autonomous creatures that would be seen by humans as intelligent in their own right. From this perspective, any environment, providing it is not too simple and has not been specifically altered to cater for limitations of the robot, constitutes a "natural" environment. The offices and labs in which Brooks's robots operate are natural in that sense. However, this is clearly not the sort of environment that the human race or any other species evolved in. Similarly, Brooks's layers do not constitute steps in an evolutionary process that would enable a creature to survive in any biological sense. Brooks has played God and defined survival within his chosen environment as the avoidance of collisions, a tendency to wander aimlessly while continuing to avoid collisions, and the inclination to be attracted by interesting-looking spaces while wandering aimlessly and still avoiding collisions. What is missing in all this is the apparent (though ultimately spurious) sense of direction given to the evolutionary process by the competition for limited resources—a direction that does not depend on aims or transcendent purpose but comes about merely through the interaction of genetic variation and the environment.

Brooks's robots are in fact designed, not evolved. They are designed bottom up, in the sense that activity layers are superimposed one on top of the other, and the builder of the robot observes what happens after the addition of each layer, and fine-tunes the resulting system until it exhibits the desired behavior. It might even be said that this fine tuning is similar to natural selection, in the sense that interaction with the environment is the final arbiter of the internal structure. But the objectives of these successive stages in the construction process, the characteristics of the particular activity patterns that the layers are meant to perform, are imposed top down. In the final analysis, Brooks's approach is still based on an objective decomposition of the desired end result, and he has merely substituted decomposition by activity for decomposition by function. This is why the approach is one of design rather than evolution. It is design that borrows ideas from natural selection, seen as a reliable and effective optimization process.

A science that is interested in discovering the underlying mechanisms of the human mind would need to go much further in taking its cues from Darwin's theory. It would need to adopt a historical approach and accept that the past activity patterns on which our present-day behavior is built—the sequence of adaptive kludges that finally resulted in the behavior we observe today—must have left their mark on the underlying mechanisms we are trying to unravel. The insights afforded by Brooks's robots must be supplemented and tempered by an ethological view of natural selection. This sees it not so much as a practical example of an optimization heuristic but more as a spur to close observation of other animals' behavior in their natural habitats, leading to comparative studies of related species, designed to isolate the key activity patterns that may serve us as natural kinds.

The achievement of specific aims through Brooks's design approach requires as much ingenuity as the traditional method, if not more. With each additional layer, the interactions between self-contained activity modules, the resultant interactions with the environment, and the nature of the emergent behavior become more and more difficult to control. There have recently been suggestions (among others, by Brooks himself; Brooks 1992) that genetic algorithms might provide relief from these potentially intractable demands of designing by hand. As a development tool, genetic algorithms may indeed offer important advantages, but the term *genetic* must not deceive us into assuming that they provide a shortcut to scientific explanation. Genetic algorithms require evaluation functions, which, as I shall discuss in the next chapter, constitute the design input to this approach. The need to isolate the defensible natural kinds for human behavior cannot be removed by replacing manual design with design by genetic algorithms.

To sum up, Brooks has rehabilitated activity and shown that there is such a thing as emergent activity. He has demonstrated that quite complicated behavior can result from the simultaneous operation of quite simple reflexes within the constraints of a particular environment. This is different from any notion of emergence mooted in the traditional holistic solutions to the mind-brain problem or in connectionism. Its defining characteristics are temporal extent and the fact that the emergent entities are the result of interactions between the creature and its environment. Brooks's most important contribution, from my point of view, is his rejection of internal representations as the explanatory entities for intelligent behavior and his concentration on the direct implementation of activities or skills.

The question is, as Brooks himself admits, how far this approach can take him. How many layers can be grafted onto the subsumption architecture before the interactions between layers become too complex to understand? Is it possible to produce truly intelligent behavior, involving such skills as object recognition, without the aid of centrally held representations? Can higher-level functions like learning be performed by his fixed topology networks of simple finite state machines? And if not, does it make any sense to turn to Brooks's methods and principles for an explanation of such high-level behavior?

Paradoxically, I suspect that although the answers to some of the first questions may turn out to be "no," research into the behavior of relatively simple autonomous agents can provide some key insights into the best explanation for even the most abstract and symbol-ridden levels of human intelligence. The next step in making out a case for the central role of activity patterns in such an explanation involves a look at the work of Brooks's colleague Maja Mataric.

7.3 An Autonomous Agent That Builds Maps by Finding Its Way in the World

Mataric's navigating robot (Mataric and Brooks 1990; Mataric 1990, 1991a, 1991b, 1992) is based on Brooks's subsumption architecture. It has three distinct layers, each operating independently from the others and receiving its own data from the robot's sensors. The bottom layer produces the robot's basic form of structured activity, which might be called wall following or boundary tracing, the middle layer performs landmark detection, and the top layer does the map learning and navigation. Each of these layers is worth examining in detail.

Mataric's implementation of wall following is an excellent example of emergent activity. It is the result of four independently operating reflexes (each closely coupled with the robot's environment), which Mataric calls STROLL, AVOID, ALIGN, and CORRECT. The main sensors used in these reflexes are sonar range detectors. Her robot has twelve of these detectors, dividing the surrounding 360-degree space into 30-degree wedges. The sonars are not very accurate and have a low refresh rate, and these limitations, in conjunction with the characteristics of the robot's environment, played an important part in determining the characteristics of its boundary-tracing behavior, as well as its navigation system.

The STROLL and AVOID behaviors use the two sonars pointing forward. The space they subtend is imagined to contain a danger zone, which extends up to .3 meter from the robot, and a safe zone lying between .3 and .6 meter. (The dimensions of these zones are dictated by the robot's speed and the range of its sonars.) An object in the danger zone brings into play the robot's STROLL behavior, which causes it to back up if such an obstacle is detected. An object that appears in the safe zone calls into operation the AVOID behavior, which will turn the robot by a fixed angle of 30 degrees (the arc subtended by one sonar) in the direction opposite to that of the sonar that detected it. If the object is detected by both forward-looking sonars simultaneously, the robot will always turn to the left. If no obstacles are detected in either zone, the robot is repeatedly given a target distance, resulting in smooth, continuous motion straight ahead.

The lateral sensors (two on each side) operate with an imaginary "edging distance" of .8 meter. The ALIGN behavior uses these lateral as well as the rear-lateral sonars. If an object is detected by the rear-lateral sonar on one side but not by the two lateral ones, it makes a 30-degree turn in that direction. In other words, if it is heading obliquely away from a nearby surface, it will tend to turn in the direction of that surface so as to run parallel with it. The CORRECT behavior uses the two lateral sensors only. If the rear of the two detects an object within the edging distance and the front sonar does not, the robot will turn 30 degrees in that direction. This prevents it from losing track of a wall that suddenly veers away from it. (It will, of course, keep turning until the two lateral sonars both detect the wall within their edging distance; if it should turn too far, the AVOID behavior will turn it back again.)

The wall-following behavior that results is not a predetermined series of movements; it is an emergent activity pattern with a structure that lies at a level above that of the reflexes that produce it. The robot does not follow a particular wall or traverse a particular corridor in exactly the same way on successive occasions, as is shown by the traces Mataric made of the robot's path. Its route will depend on its approach in that particular instance, on noise in its sensor readings, and on the numerous unspecified contingencies of a dynamic environment. But it can be relied upon to follow the wall each time.

There are no explicit instructions within the robot that tell it to follow walls. The notion of a wall does not have an internal representation inside the robot; no formal description or definition of walls is necessary to produce the behavior. What Mataric has done is to construct an engineering description of walls in terms of the robot's characteristics and limitations and to implement that description as STROLL, AVOID, ALIGN, and CORRECT in combination with the robot's sensorimotor equipment. The only place at which the underlying mechanisms that subtend wall following intersect on a wall is at the wall "out there," and if there is any "representation" of walls, it is only that produced by the robot's actual behavior. Its route is a kind of mapping of the office environment for which it was built, a representation of that environment produced by the activity patterns resulting from its low-level reflexes.

We perceive the robot as following walls; the robot itself has no such aim or purpose, though, of course, it was designed for that purpose. The purpose is not represented within the robot, not used by the robot in the form of some internally represented goal, but because it was designed for that purpose, there can be no objection to saying that the robot is following walls. Its emergent activity was intended by its designer. It is not just an arbitrary interpretation imposed on that activity by us, the observers.

Establishing the legitimacy of a particular description of naturally occurring patterns of activity resulting from evolution is clearly not so simple. We cannot appeal to the designer's aims. The evolved behavior does not merely emerge from lower-level mechanisms; it also emerged in the historical sense from the processes of genetic mutation, sexual reproduction, and environmental selection. Is there any hope of isolating legitimate natural kinds in the behavior of biological creatures? Can there ever be a justification, grounded in natural selection, for preferring one description over any number of others? In the course of this chapter and the ones that follow, I hope to show that there is and can be.

The robot's structured activity produced by low-level reflexes in interaction with the particular environment for which it was built plays a crucial role in Mataric's implementation of the higher levels of landmark detection, map making, and navigation. Mataric accepts that finding one's way in the world, in the sense of being able to retrace one's path and recognize routes that have been traveled before and detect revealing relations between different routes, requires some form of "cognitive map," which may be seen as an internal representation of the environment. She maintains, however, that this does not need to be an analytical or centralized representation.

Her first move away from abstract representations is to propose that the environment be coded in terms of landmarks rather than distances and directions defined in terms of some global coordinate system. A landmark is generally conceived as an internally held representation corresponding to an objective entity in the world that serves as a point of reference. Space is represented as a collection of such landmarks and their relative locations. As long as the creature is always in sight of some landmark and has a record of the sequence of landmarks it passed to get to its present location, it should be able to "tell where it is."

The advantages of landmarks over a more global representation in terms of spatial coordinates is that distances do not need to be precise and directions are determined by the location of landmarks along specific routes. Landmarks are a first attempt at implementing Cussins's (1990) idea of making a map by walking a series of routes. A creature can have only landmarks that are located along the routes it has physically traveled in the past, and their relationship to each other must be defined in terms of those routes or in terms of the creature's efforts in getting from one landmark to another.

Mataric takes this one step further. She is driven to take that step by the problem of sensor noise already mentioned in connection with Brooks's work, but again, I believe that hardware constraints, together with the discipline of having to produce a robot that works in a "natural" environment, result in a solution that is highly revealing in a biological sense.

> Sonar-based models usually perform landmark detection by matching sensory patterns to stored landmark models or signatures. . . . These approaches are "static" in their use of a discrete snapshot of the world based on a single set of sensor data. However, the expected accuracy of any one data point is low, and different sonar signatures are generated in different trials due to sensor error and noise. . . .

We explored an alternative, "dynamic" approach to landmark detection, based on continuously monitoring the robot's sensors and taking advantage of the robot's underlying boundary tracing behavior. The landmark detector looks for features in the world that have physical extensions detectable over time, i.e., it monitors for consistencies in the sensory data as the robot is moving next to objects in the environment. (Mataric 1992, p. 308)

Mataric's landmarks are defined in terms of the robot's own behavior, resulting in sensor readings of a distinctive type, which must persist for a minimum amount of time before achieving the level of confidence required for acceptance as a landmark. The robot must continue heading roughly in the same compass direction for that period, while at the same time the sonars must continue to report approximately the same readings, before a landmark of a particular type is recorded. There are four basic landmark types: left walls (LW), right walls (RW), corridors (C), and long, irregular boundaries (I). Clearly these descriptions refer to objective features in the world, and clearly there has to be some reliable correspondence, in order that the robot may negotiate its office environment successfully, between its landmarks and the distinctive features of that world. However, it would be wrong to conclude that the landmarks are defined in terms of objective features in that world.

The landmarks emerge from the robot's wall-following behavior. It is only the fact that the robot can be relied upon to find and follow walls that gives substance to the four types of landmark chosen by Mataric. A landmark descriptor is a tuple (T,C,L,P), in which T is the landmark type, C is the average compass bearing, L is a rough estimate of the landmark's length (the time for which it persists), and P is a coarse position estimate. (The final element is used exclusively to disambiguate two landmarks that otherwise have the same description, telling the robot whether it has detected a new landmark or come upon an already recorded one from a different direction.) The algorithm to determine the type and bearing uses a running average to eliminate spurious sonar and compass readings. The office environment is tolerant of this approach, since it consists mainly of right angles and straight walls. Wall following, emergent from low-level reflexes, does not result in straight lines, but it does have a recognizable structure at the level of running averages. A creature adapted to a different type of environment would need alternative activity patterns to produce temporally structured inputs that would allow it to cope with the limitations of its sensors.

The landmarks are stored in the nodes of a distributed graph. The structure of this graph reflects the constraints on the robot's low-level behavior. Wall following restricts it to what is essentially a one-dimensional trajectory, with an occasional crossing of its own past route. This can be represented as a straightforward linear list, in which the crossings are handled by jumper links to a switchboard. Each node in the graph is connected to its neighbors. Initially the nodes are all empty, and exploring the environment consists of filling the empty nodes with landmarks discovered along the route.

The first landmark detected in accordance with the algorithms described above is automatically stored in the first node (which is special, since it "knows" that it is the first node). The node is then activated to indicate the robot's current position in the graph. Whenever a subsequent landmark is detected, its type and compass bearing are broadcast to the entire graph. Each node compares that information with its own type and compass bearing. If none of the nodes reports a match, the landmark is assumed to be new and stored in the successor node to the one currently activated. Since the matching is done in parallel, map localization is effectively achieved in constant time, regardless of the size of the graph.

If matches with existing nodes are found, a landmark is considered to be accurately matched only if "expectation" has spread to it from the currently active node in the direction of travel. If the matching node is not the expecting node, its coarse position estimate is compared with that of the robot to see if it has crossed its own path and thus come across one of the nodes it had previously visited in a different context. If that turns out to be the case, a jumper link is added to the graph. Otherwise the landmark is rejected as spurious. In other words, the robot will never store two landmarks with the same description.

The system is made more robust by insisting that landmarks can occur only in the context of its route (which is constrained by its wall-following behavior), as well as by making the landmarks themselves into dynamic, time-averaging entities. Very little information about the environment is actually stored in the graph. There is no accurate representation of the landmarks' locations in Cartesian space. "Facts" like the existence of corners, doorways and other types of convexity and concavity, the nature of furniture, and the characteristics of human beings who cross the robot's path are all taken care of by the autonomy of the low-level reflexes. These facts do not have the power to confuse the higher-level navigation system, since this relies implicitly on the independence and robustness of wall following. There is thus no need to store such facts or to plan for contingencies that might arise as a result of their existence. It is not necessary for the robot to "know" about environmental contingencies that its low-level behavior is adapted to cope with.

It is important to dispel any impression that Mataric's system could just as easily be recast as a top-down hierarchy, in which the job of coping with low-level features is delegated by some top-level agent (in Minsky's 1987 sense) to low-level behavior modules. The low-level behavior produces an autonomous wall-following creature. The higher-level navigation system exists only in terms of the "experiences" of this wall-following creature, and this is why facts like corners are not available to it. It would not be possible to design such a creature top down in terms of a hierarchy of tasks. The way Mataric's system operates is not a matter of a higher-level planner's "calling" lower-level modules as and when they are required; the lower-level reflexes are in continuous operation and decide for themselves when they are required. The robot can "survive" perfectly well in its environment by using low-level behavior alone. This allows it to construct its map by exploring the environment without any plan or goal. Even if the resulting landmark graph might be called a plan for action in its environment, it must be seen as emerging from this autonomous, low-level behavior rather than being imposed on it or directing it.

One consequence is that in a more complex system capable of a variety of behaviors, it would probably be necessary to have separate "cognitive maps" corresponding to each type of activity, with landmarks expressed in terms of the creature's experiences in performing different types of activity at the lowest level.

Mataric's graph is not a distributed representation in the connectionist sense. Information about the landmarks is held within the nodes, not stored in the weights of the links between them. The links in the graph merely indicate topological relations between landmarks and serve to spread activation. Once the map has been constructed, the experimenter can select a goal node. Activation is spread from the goal throughout the map, until it eventually reaches all locations. The spreading activation is graded, growing weaker with every node it passes through, thus indicating the direction of the "shortest path" at each point. This eliminates the need for replanning if the robot strays from the desired path, since it always "knows" the optimal direction to pursue at each landmark, regardless of where it finds itself. (If its present position is not at any landmark, low-level behavior will take over and see that it reaches some point it will recognize as corresponding to a landmark node.)

The landmark information stored in the current node indicates what the robot's behavior should be at that node. Since nodes can be approached only from their neighbors and the low-level wall-following behavior will see to it that the robot is behaving in the same way as it did when that node was first detected, there is little chance of confusion, despite the fact that navigation is achieved without explicit directions.

Mataric's map-making and navigation system takes Brooks's ideas several steps further. The important points, for the purposes of this discussion, are the following:

1. Landmarks come into being as the result of the creature's structured activity within a particular environment. This structured activity allows the robot to detect correlations between its own movement and its sensory input and permits the categorization of landmarks into types.

2. Landmarks have extension over time. The algorithm for detecting them uses a running average that has to be maintained within certain values over a minimum period. There is no "space" between landmarks in the landmark graph. In a sense, the robot's map chops the routes it travels into segments of activity rather than signposting them with positional landmarks. Navigation becomes a matter not so much of traveling from one landmark to another but of slipping from the behavior specified by one landmark into the behavior specified by the next.

3. The notions of path and neighbor thus become very important. They allow spatial information to be encoded in terms of a succession of activity segments. Mataric (1991a) quotes O'Keefe (1989) to the effect that the environment is represented in the rat hippocampus through the way the firing rate of adjacent neurons changes as the animal moves around in the environment, and Foster, Castro, and McNaughton (1989) to the effect that the relationship between two locations is represented by the movements executed in getting from one to the other. Segments of activity stored contiguously (or at least in some way that allows "expectation" to be passed from one to the other) perform a mapping of the environment in terms of traveled paths. The map and the paths do not exist inside the creature in any objective or global sense; they come into existence only when the creature is placed in the environment and allowed to move as dictated by its low-level reflexes and by the instructions in its landmark nodes.

4. Neighbors and well-traveled paths provide context. This context is initially established through wandering about aimlessly (but not randomly, since the wandering has a low-level structure imposed by wall following) and covering as much as possible of

the environment with paths. These paths map the environment in terms of segments of situated activity. Once this has been accomplished, information about the environment is always seen in context, because at any particular instant, the robot will be doing something, and what it is doing is related to its location in the graph and to what it was doing at the previous location and will be doing at the next. No data ever occur out of context, and the context does not require global knowledge about the environment or top-down specification in terms of type hierarchies; it flows naturally from the robot's structured activity in the particular environment, which always ensures that the robot is firmly situated in that environment.

Mataric makes out a strong case for the ethological and neurophysiological validity of her conception. In addition to the evidence from rat studies she cites, there is an extensive literature on landmark navigation in bees (Collett and Cartwright 1983; Cartwright and Collett 1987; Gould 1986), which also largely supports her model. I believe its main weaknesses lie in the need for a rough position indicator to disambiguate similar landmarks (though there is evidence from bee and ant studies that might support this; see particularly Gould 1986), and the need to encode landmarks as tuples of parameters that take on specific values. Mataric herself admits that her landmark nodes may be biologically unrealistic and that there is evidence of a more distributed representation for "place fields." In the next chapter I shall discuss other work with autonomous agents that goes some way toward meeting these objections. But first I discuss what I consider to be the most important implication of Mataric's work.

7.4 Mataric and Millikan: History of Use

In chapter 3, I discussed Millikan's (1984) proposal to ground the intentionality of internal representations through their history of use. I argued that Millikan's definition of proper function is the most radical attempt to infuse the pre-Darwinian notion of function based on design with the scientific legitimacy conferred by the theory of natural selection and that, unlike other philosophers, Millikan seemed to be clearly aware of the problems this entails. If intentionality is to be grounded in function, and function is to be grounded in natural selection, then an organ or trait or "intentional icon" must have a particular function not because we interpret it as having such by adopting a "design stance" but for objective reasons that can be derived from natural selection alone. Hence the need for a legitimizing functional history:

the function of the organ or trait is taken to depend on the historical role it played in the survival of the species that carries it. The functional component itself has survived only by playing that role in the creature's reproductive success. This contribution, and the way it was accomplished, define its proper function.

I have argued in previous chapters that the task of disentangling the contribution made by a hypothetical internal representation to the survival of a species whose behavior is supposed to depend on its use must be considered an impossible one. I have also implied that the problems I raised against Millikan's conception might be overcome if situated patterns of activity rather than internal representations were adopted as the natural kinds of a historical explanation. The crucial questions I raised were:

1. How can it ever be established, by looking at a functioning creature in the present, what its historically legitimized functional entities are?
2. How do we get around the problem of proving that its ecological niche, as it can be observed today, has been around long enough to constitute the determining factor?
3. How do we prove that the history of successive adaptations has not imposed its own logic and that the quirks of hitch-hiking genes and genetic drift have not skewed the results beyond any hope of functional decomposition?
4. How do we know that the "problem" posed by the environment has been correctly diagnosed?

We are looking for an evolutionary stamp of approval that will legitimize one explanatory entity rather than another; as Millikan makes clear, this stamp of approval can be conferred only retrospectively, by the fact that the creature carrying the trait has survived. I believe that Mataric's robot provides the outlines of a principled solution to the problems listed above. At first this might seem rather a heavy burden to place on such a primitive and simple artifact, but I hope to show that Mataric's robot can bear it.

I suggest that the retrospective stamp of approval we are looking for can be conferred only by higher levels of activity that depend for their operation on the behavioral traits we are seeking to legitimize. In Mataric's robot, the landmark detector and navigation layers rely on the structured, lower-level activity of wall following. If this were a naturally evolved organism, the fact that it displays landmark detection and navigational behavior that depends so crucially on the existence of that lower-level structured activity would constitute evidence that wall following must have been a stable element in the creature's behavioral repertoire for a considerable part of its evolutionary history. Any change in the wall-following behavior would have thrown off the higher levels completely. The use made of this dependable activity pattern to evolve a higher level of behavior implies a stable functional history and identifies it as a natural kind.

Whatever changes might have taken place in the environment, no matter how complicated the genetic mutations and recombinations that went into producing the low-level pattern, and irrespective of the neuronal structure subtending the two behaviors, if it is possible to establish navigation by landmarks on empirical grounds, and if it is possible to establish on the same grounds that the particular landmarks used by the creature come about only if the creature performs a certain type of structured low-level activity, which it does in fact reliably perform, then that low-level structured activity acquires the distinction of a natural kind, and it acquires that distinction purely on evolutionary grounds.

The obvious advantage of explanatory hypotheses that are justified in this way is that all the elements are open to empirical scrutiny. Low-level activity patterns can be observed and related to the environment. Comparative studies with related species as well as controlled changes in the environment can be used to establish the criteria and parameters at both levels. The dependence of one on the other can be investigated by artificially induced alterations in the low-level activity. This is very different from justifying a model whose explanatory entities are assumed to be internal to the creature on ethological and evolutionary grounds. The "meaning" of an explanatory entity identified in the way I have proposed need not be sought "in the creature's head," because the entity itself is not presumed to reside in its head. Nor does it depend on the observer's interpretation. Its "meaning" is defined by the use that is made of it by higher levels of activity.

At the end of one of her papers (Mataric 1991b), Mataric speculates on possible extensions to her robot. As a result of navigation by landmarks, the robot must produce a higher level of emergent activity. It may be possible to introduce yet another layer, which monitors this activity in terms of some dynamic feature that results from its interaction with the environment. She speculates that such a creature would "monitor the history of the agent's actions. Based on accumulated information it could form new correlations and rules over time, which could then be incorporated into the navigation substrate" (Mataric 1991b, p. 133). Mataric appears to have in mind a system that would evaluate and correct its own rules. I believe this to be wildly premature. The gap between such a system and the type of activity that Mataric's current robot is capable of performing seems too large to be bridged in a single step by a natural or artificial evolutionary process. In fact, I strongly suspect that even the step between wall following and landmark navigation is unrealistically large and that this accounts for the need to introduce the physical parameters I discussed earlier. (For a more gradual approach to a similar problem, which does not use such parameters, see Pfeifer and Verschure 1992.)

But I see no reason in principle why layers cannot continue to be grafted onto a functioning creature in the way that Mataric suggests. The important characteristics of the process are the emergence of a higher-level dynamic feature from the interaction between the robot's current level of activity and its environment, and the evolution of a sensing mechanism to track this feature. Each new layer will tend to be more abstract than the last, in the sense that it deals in "features" that are further and further removed from information that could be obtained by examining either the environment or the creature's neurophysiology. The notions of navigation and landmark can be taken in a much wider sense than that connected with traveling through a landscape. One may think of an infant as learning to navigate the space within its reach by the use of its hands and eyes, of a piano player as learning to navigate the keyboard by performing situated patterns of activity in the form of scales (see Sudnow 1978 for a somewhat irritating but nonetheless illuminating personal account), and of children as using the environment provided by speakers of their native language and their inborn dispositions to produce certain structured vocal patterns to learn to navigate the space of that language.

7.5 Conclusion

My aim in this chapter has been to use Brooks's and Mataric's work on autonomous robots as a kind of existence proof for an alternative mode of explanation. No claim is made for the biological validity of their choice of activity patterns, since I believe that their approach is still basically one of top-down design and therefore does not relieve us of the need to discover, through fieldwork and comparative studies, the particular natural kinds of human and animal behavior. But I believe they have shown the following:

1. Patterns of activity whose high-level structure cannot be reduced to a specific sequence of movements may emerge from the interactions between simple reflexes and the particular environment to which they are adapted.
2. Such patterns of activity can result in dynamic features with temporal extent that may correspond only very indirectly to "fea-

tures" in the world. They owe their characteristics to the interaction between the structure of the low-level activity and the nature of the creature's environment. But their reliable occurrence could encourage sensors to evolve that would be capable of monitoring them, thus providing information for the next level of activity.

3. This type of configuration, if found in a naturally occurring creature, would confer the status of a natural kind on the lower level of activity, since it would clearly establish a history of use for that activity in the creature's evolutionary past.

Chapter 8

An Examination of Alternative Conceptual Frameworks for Autonomous Agent Research

---

8.1 An Alternative Version of Mataric's Wall-Following Program

The descriptive framework I used in chapter 7 for my discussion of Mataric's robot is not the only formalization being proposed for autonomous agents. In this chapter I shall examine an alternative interpretation of Mataric's work by Koza (1992), and leading on from this, assess the comparative merits of various other approaches, such as Horswill's (1992) "implements relation" and Pfeifer and Vershure's (1992) paradigm of "distributed adaptive control." I shall conclude the chapter with an attempt to formulate some guidelines for this type of model building.

Koza (1992) takes Mataric's wall-following program as an example of subsumption architecture and asks if such a program could be evolved by genetic algorithm (GA). GAs are usually seen as a computational alternative to more conventional "hill-climbing" and optimization techniques, but in the context of situated robotics, the technique can serve as a generative mechanism whose operation is not that simple to reduce to formal terms. In what follows I shall be discussing Koza's use of GAs, which is characterized by the fact that he takes a classic approach to input-output coupling and uses computational entities as the basic building blocks of his models. This is not the only, or potentially the most promising, approach to using GAs for the generation of adaptive behavior. Husbands, Harvey, and Cliff have progressively extended the formal bounds of the paradigm and thereby heightened its ecological and evolutionary relevance (Husbands and Harvey 1992; Cliff, Husbands, and Harvey 1993; Husbands, Harvey, and Cliff 1993; Harvey, Husbands and Cliff 1994). I shall refer to their work at various points in my discussion to remind readers that my critique of Koza's program is not a critique of the application of GAs to the generation of adaptive behavior in general.

In their traditional form, GAs are based on a schematic view of evolution through natural selection. Random mutation, as well as gene splicing and recombination, are applied to some form of artificial "genotype," and the most promising individuals are selected from each generation by a "fitness function," to be subjected to another cycle of the same process. The run is terminated either after a fixed number of generations or when the performance of one of the individuals meets some preestablished criterion.

It is generally felt that the crossover mechanism borrowed from sexual reproduction enables GAs to outperform hill climbers and other optimization techniques, but as Mitchell, Forrest, and Holland (1992) point out, there is as yet no firm theoretical basis for this belief. If the fitness landscape is hierarchical (promising parts of solutions can be combined to produce better overall solutions), then crossover would appear to confer an advantage, and if a peak of fitness is surrounded by a relatively wide trough, which in turn is surrounded by areas of intermediate fitness, the intervening trough may be easier to cross by the leaps resulting from crossover than by the gradual steps of hill climbing. On the other hand, if two or more equally good but genetically incompatible partial solutions happen to evolve in the population, then crossover between them is likely to result in totally useless offspring.

Many of the limitations of conventional GAs are overcome by Harvey's (1992a, 1992b) species adaption genetic algorithms (SAGA), which introduce variable-length genotypes and replace the standard goal-seeking or problem-solving metaphor with an alternative conceptual framework of hill crawling by a convergent species. Harvey, like Brooks, takes an engineering approach and is prepared to investigate mechanisms of selection that do not necessarily conform to those in nature, while remaining open to any pointers that nature may provide. His genetic algorithms have been used successfully to generate neural-network controllers for simulated (and more recently, real), visually guided robots (Cliff, Husbands, and Harvey 1993; Harvey, Husbands, and Cliff 1993; Harvey, Husbands, and Cliff 1994; Husbands and Harvey 1992; Husbands, Harvey, and Cliff 1993).

For the purposes of this discussion, it is important to point out two main differences between GAs as a computational optimization technique and natural evolution as formalized in neo-Darwinism. The first, the notion of a fitness function, makes explicit the design view of natural selection against which I argued in chapter 6. Strictly speaking, nature applies only one fitness function: the number of copies of its genes that an individual is able to pass on to the next generation. Fitness functions turn artificial evolution by GA into a purposeful, goal-directed design process, whereas natural evolution has no goals. However, it should be possible, in theory, to do without fitness functions entirely and have creatures compete directly with each other within some "real" environment. The work of Husbands, Harvey, and Cliff, employing less explicit evaluation functions, constitutes a step in that direction and may be seen as a compromise between the exigencies of design and ecological verisimilitude.

The second important difference with natural selection is that GAs do not allow for ontogeny. (Husbands, Harvey, and Cliff are developing a new version of their system that will overcome this limitation.) The "genotypes" that are evolved by traditional GAs double up as phenotypes. Whether the basic building blocks are strings of code, bits of neural network, or some other computational device, it is the building blocks themselves that are mutated and recombined through crossover. This means, among other things, that the division of labor between genes and environment is simplified and distorted. In nature, genes by themselves cannot produce anything. Genetic and environmental factors are inextricably entwined in ontogeny. At each stage, further development can proceed only if the partly completed phenotype has developed appropriately up to that stage, the relevant genes are available, and environmental conditions fall within a certain range. The reason all these factors do tend to coincide at the right time and place is that the creature is a product of natural selection.

These differences do not detract from GAs as a developmental technique, but they do make it necessary to be careful when the process is invoked as an explanatory justification. As I shall attempt to show in my examination of Koza's program, genetic algorithms by themselves cannot confer scientific legitimacy on a model that has been developed by this process.

Koza's genotypes are LISP programs. His analysis of the "problem" solved by Mataric's robot is important and illuminating. He notes that the robot is capable of executing five primitive motor functions: moving forward by a set distance, moving backward by a set distance, turning right through 30 degrees, turning left through 30 degrees, and stopping. The robot has twelve sonar range finders that report the distance to the nearest wall and one sensor that reports the "stopped" condition. Regardless of which method is used to solve the wall-following problem (conventional AI, subsumption architecture, or genetic algorithms), the thirteen sensors can be viewed, says Koza, as the input to a computer program (as yet unwritten), which must process these inputs and cause the activation, in the right order, of the various primitive motor functions. So the required program can be seen as a "composition of the five available primitive motor functions and the 13 available sensors" (Koza 1992, p. 113).

Koza then analyzes Mataric's solution and concludes that her programs (STROLL, AVOID, ALIGN, and CORRECT) make use of nine LISP functions and a number of constants. This completes his list of "terminals" (sensor inputs and constants) and provides him with the basic strings of code to put into his gene pool. A collection of a thousand equal-length, random "programs" made up of these "genes" constituted the initial population. As a fitness function for wall following, Koza chose the number of "tiles" along the wall visited by the robot in four hundred time steps.

That criterion may seem obvious once it has been formulated, but its apparent simplicity disguises a number of crucial points. Fitness functions represent the most important design input into development by GA. They require the programmer to visualize objective consequences of the behavior whose evolution she is trying to encourage. They must also be susceptible to degrees of satisfaction, and better performance according to the fitness function must correspond to increasing skill in the desired behavior. But the definition of the behavior and of the fitness function are not necessarily identical. There may be all sorts of different ways of satisfying a particular fitness function.

A robot that never finds a wall will do poorly by Koza's criterion. A robot that finds a wall and stays put will do slightly better. A robot that bounces back and forth between walls will do better still, but it will waste a lot of time traveling between walls. The best strategy of all is to find a wall and stick to it while moving about continuously, thus visiting a wall-touching tile at every time step. Note that the choice of fitness function is crucial and requires considerable ingenuity, and that nothing comparable could ever occur in nature. In Koza's program, a run was terminated either when it had produced a computer program that touched all fifty-six tiles along the walls of the room or after 101 generations.

In fact, it took the genetic algorithm only fifty-seven generations to produce a perfect score of 56. The program that had evolved contained a large amount of useless code, but it could be simplified to a length comparable to Mataric's program by removing inconsequential subexpressions. Koza characterizes the result as follows: "The program consists of a composition of conditional statements which test various sensor inputs from the environment and invoke various given primitive motor functions of the robot in order to perform wall-following. In other words, the program is a program in the subsumption architecture" (Koza 1992, p. 118). This conclusion can be defended on the grounds that there is no hierarchical structure to the program and that it does not use an internal representation of the world to plan its actions. Its implementation of wall following is based on a decomposition by activity rather than by function. Apart from the four activity functions (move forward one foot, move backward 1.3 feet, turn left

30 degrees, and turn right 30 degrees), it employs only two special conditionals: IFTLE and PROGN2, which evaluate and compare inputs and return one of two possible results accordingly. It can thus be said that all decisions are made locally and that the overall behavior is due entirely to mutual suppression and inhibition of primitive activities.

In a more interesting sense, however, Koza's method has produced a program that does not conform to Brooks's original ideas, though Brooks (1992) himself appears to believe that it is an important step forward. One of the hallmarks of Brooks's approach is the practice of incrementally building up the capabilities of a robot through trial and error. Combinations of sensor readings and motor commands are welded into activity patterns through fine-tuning by studying the robot's interactions with the real world. Koza's program was not developed incrementally from viable low-level activity patterns in this way. It did not need to be, because the crucial parameters had already been provided by Mataric's prior implementation.

Koza stresses that his solution by GA has made use of no other information than that which is contained in a "basic formulation of the problem." He is at pains to point out that he has not used Mataric's STROLL, ALIGN, AVOID, and CORRECT behaviors or the ingenious combinations of sensor inputs that underlie those behaviors. It cannot be denied, however, that Koza had Mataric's successful implementation to work from. His formulation of the problem is indebted to that implementation for its choice of sensors, its choice of motor functions, its choice of "terminals," and its choice of LISP primitives to enter into the gene pool. Koza's program may contain no direct reference to Mataric's behavior modules, but it was Mataric's decision to implement wall following as an emergent activity resulting from STROLL, ALIGN, AVOID, and CORRECT in combination with a particular type of environment, which determined, to a large extent, the physical characteristics of the robot and its motor functions.

It is an open question whether, in the absence of Mataric's implementation, Koza could have come up with the right combination of ingredients to feed into his genetic algorithm. He has shown that once wall following has been implemented in Mataric's way, it is possible to use the primitives thrown up by that implementation to produce a more abstract formulation of the "problem," which can then be solved ostensibly without reference to Mataric's modules. But it should be clear that activity functions like "move forward 1 foot" and "move backward 1.3 feet" and constants like the edging distance of 1 foot are the result of fine-tuning a real robot with specific sensor characteristics and motor capabilities under certain well-defined constraints. Some of these constraints were imposed by the office environment, but the remainder are due to Mataric's conception of how wall following in this environment could be implemented—in other words, the particular nature of STROLL, AVOID, ALIGN, and CORRECT.

Koza's formulation of the "problem of wall following" should thus be seen as a restatement of Mataric's implementation of an autonomous agent that follows walls in a particular type of environment. The question is whether this restatement adds anything to our understanding, or whether, on the contrary, it threatens to obscure the real issues. A cursory examination of the code produced by Koza's genetic algorithm provides few clues as to how it solves the problem—beyond the fact that it does so in terms of the motor functions and conditionals already mentioned. There appears to be no recognizable structure to the solution, no way that it can be broken down into readily graspable constituents. Not only is this solution resistant to functional decomposition; it does not seem to lend itself to decomposition of any kind. This makes the program useless for the purposes of explanation. We cannot get a sense, from looking at the code, of what really makes this a wall-following creature in that particular environment.

STROLL, ALIGN, AVOID, and CORRECT do give us that sense. They make the wall-following behavior understandable as an emergent activity. It is unlikely that this particular configuration has its counterpart in naturally evolved organisms, but it is the *type* of explanation that is of interest here. Mataric set out with clear hypotheses concerning these various activity patterns and their interdependencies. By fine-tuning her robot, she was able to produce a model that exhibits precisely those activities and interdependencies. As a result, her low-level activities provide an explanation of wall following that makes it a highly illuminating natural kind. They enable us to visualize a reliably occurring entity that is neither a part of the robot nor a part of the world "out there" but comes into being only as the result of the robot's interactions with a specific type of environment. I showed in the previous chapter how this entity receives its stamp of approval through history of use. Landmark detection and navigation as implemented in Mataric's robot depend on the emergent, temporally extended structure of wall following. If these behaviors and their dependencies could be shown to occur reliably in a naturally evolved creature, wall following would make a convincing candidate for a natural kind. This permits us to envisage a type of explanation that provides a principled alternative to the traditional input-output model.

It may seem perverse that, after devoting the first six chapters of this book to arguments against the design stance, I am now recommending Mataric's model over Koza's on the grounds that it is the result of deliberate design. The explanation for this apparent paradox lies in the peculiar nature of the design process employed by Mataric. It is design aimed at producing prespecified activity patterns through interactive emergence. The constituent elements of the intended model are not functional parts but patterns of activity, which can result only from the interactions of an autonomous creature with a particular environment.

In the design stance I have been attacking, natural selection is invoked to confer scientific legitimacy on functionally derived internal representations or constituent parts, which serve as the natural kinds for computational explanations. Darwin's theory becomes essential in tying computational models to the rest of science. The scientific legitimacy of the activity patterns produced by Mataric's model does not depend on the theory of natural selection in this way.

If a behavioral model like Mataric's were used in scientific explanation, its patterns of activity would be derived from observations in the field. The nature of the hypotheses to be tested by the model would concern the taxonomy of the observed phenomena: how naturally occurring behavior should be carved up and how its various levels should be related to each other and to the environment. There is no claim that nature designed these activity patterns for a specific purpose or function. The activity evolved through genetic change and natural selection. We are able to observe it and make hypotheses relating the various levels of activity to each other and to the creature's environmental niche. A functioning model, incorporating these hypotheses, serves to confirm our choice of natural kinds in ways I have discussed in these last two chapters. R. Dawkins's (1986) hierarchical reductionism, based on analogies with machines, is thus replaced by what might be called construction through emergence, in which machines serve to produce behavioral models by interacting with their environment.

8.2 Horswill's Implements Relation

The design process practiced by Mataric and Brooks and various other researchers into autonomous systems is by definition tentative and laborious. "Automatic programming" by genetic algorithm represents one attempt to speed up that process. An entirely different approach is represented by Horswill's (1992) idea for an "implements relation."

The aim of Horswill's proposal is attractive and straightforward. As things stand, it is necessary to start more or less from scratch in every instance, working by trial and error to make the robot perform activity patterns that, prior to implementation, are merely hypotheses. The only way this can be done is through fine-tuning in situ. There are no laws or guidelines that specify the combination of sensors, motor reflexes, and environmental conditions that will produce a particular type of behavior, and there is no guarantee that the knowledge gained from one implementation can be transferred to others. It would be a great help if we had a comprehensive theoretical framework, a classificatory scheme that would allow us to identify differences and similarities—an "implements relation," which, given a specification of the desired behavior and the environment, would solve for the type of machine required. Horswill (1992) realizes there are major problems with this: "It seems difficult enough to completely understand individual systems, tasks and environments, much less to completely characterize the structure of the spaces of possible machines, tasks and environments. Moreover, notions such as 'activity' and 'habitat' are fuzzy at best. The notion of 'machinery' is somewhat better understood, but we still have nothing like an exhaustive taxonomy of it" (p. 59).

Horswill's first step in defining the implements relation is to introduce the notion of habitat constraints. Each constraint defines a class of habitats, and any particular habitat can be partially characterized in terms of the constraints it satisfies. Constraints, says Horswill, can play an important role in explaining a creature's activity, because an understanding of their nature illuminates the relationship between its habitat and the computations involved in guiding its activity. This is not a new idea, as Horswill admits. He mentions Marr's use of environmental constraints in defining the computational problems involved in low-level vision but claims that his own approach differs from Marr's in important respects. He does not mention the work of Gibson (1979) and his followers (Turvey and Kugler 1984; Turvey and Carello 1986), though in some ways Horswill's notion of a habitat constraint resembles Gibson's notion of an "affordance" more than Marr's computational definition.

Horswill gives two examples of what he means by habitat constraints. The first is the background texture constraint. An environment satisfies this constraint if there is a large band of spectral frequencies that have no energy in the markings of background surfaces, ensuring that "objects" that do have markings in those frequencies will stand out. His second example is the ground plane constraint, which is satisfied if all objects in the environment, including the creature itself, rest on the same planar surface. An environment of this type simplifies the problem of estimating distances to obstacles.

Both constraints have their origin in practical work with autonomous agents. Horswill and Brooks (1988) describe a robot that follows moving objects in real time using vision as its only input. The background texture constraint is used in the robot's "segmenter," while the ground plane constraint underpins the operation of its tracking system. Horswill and Brooks claim that tight coupling and the subsumption architecture have enabled them to solve two of the most intractable problems in computer vision: segmentation—the problem of isolating objects from their background in a two-dimensional projection—and motion analysis—keeping track of objects that move about in unpredictable ways.

In fact, Horswill and Brooks do not "solve" these problems as they have traditionally been formulated. It would be more correct to say that their implementation gets around them through being fine-tuned to perform specific activities in a given environment. The robot's segmenter does a poor job of finding the set of pixels that correspond to a particular object, and its motion detector is no better at keeping track of objects that move, but the performance of the two, in conjunction with some other modules, is adequate for the robot's needs. The various behavioral components compensate for each other's deficiencies. A principled distribution of the representation of the external world over a collection of independently functioning behavior modules makes the precision of each less critical, since the behaviors all converge on the object "out there." The external world serves as a constant corrective to deficiencies of the system itself.

This is very different from the relation between Marr's low-level vision modules, each of which had to deliver precise information in predefined, formal terms so that the system as a whole might "recover" a full-blown, three-dimensional representation of the object from its projection on the retina. Recovering a three-dimensional representation from a two-dimensional projection can be classed as a computational problem; building an autonomous agent that performs specific activity patterns in a specific environment is more of an engineering problem. It is likely that Marr would have dismissed Horswill and Brooks's "solution" as unprincipled and ad hoc. Marr insisted that it should be possible to define computational problems prior to devising algorithms for their solution. A computational theory, as Marr saw it, needs to be formulated in terms of *what* is being processed and *why*. This requires a commitment to specific internal representations. It is the internal representations, extracted by the application of carefully defined "primitives," that constitute the explanatory hypothesis in this type of theory. As Horswill (1992) himself admits: "Constraint descriptions do not formally define computational problems and so are incomplete in Marr's sense. Another, perhaps more important difference is that describing how constraints simplify a computation violates at least the letter of Marr's program of examining algorithmic issues only after having fixed a computational theory" (p. 63).

Informally, the strategy Horswill is trying to define seems self-evident. The background texture constraint may be used to distinguish a certain class of environments: those in which all objects stand out from their background because of differences in surface texture or color, or both. Knowing that the habitat of one's robot falls within this class of environments makes it possible to devise an algorithm for segmentation that has good chances of success. Similarly, the ground plane constraint picks out another (perhaps overlapping) class of environments, in which distance in a horizontal direction can be reliably correlated with vertical position in a retinal projection. By pointing the camera slightly down at a fixed angle and constructing an algorithm that causes the robot to hold the center of the object near the center of the frame, this sort of habitat may be exploited for tracking objects.

The problem is that these classes of habitat owe their status as classes to particular computational mechanisms. If the principled framework of Marr's theory of computation and representation is removed, then such classes seem arbitrary, defined in an ad hoc fashion as practical implementations are developed. Although their identity might seem self-evident, there is no objective theoretical basis for distinguishing them from other habitats, apart from the role they play in these implementations. Why single out habitats in which objects have different surface markings from their backgrounds, considering that this is unlikely to be a general or defining characteristic of any natural environment? Why concentrate on flat surfaces that define a very unnatural kind of "habitat," likely to be found only in man-made buildings? The answer is that we have developed systems that can cope with these conditions. Once we have developed such systems, we can go looking for the sorts of environment in which they might work. But in order for Horswill's implements relation to work, it should be possible to define the habitat and the desired behavior *prior to* any specification of a machine and *without reference to* specific computational mechanisms. I believe that such a definition is ruled out and that, in its absence, Horswill's proposal cannot provide a strategy for explanation. The following points may help to clarify the problem:

1. The "environment" of any but the most trivial behaviors cannot be equated with the environment described by Horswill in terms of his habitat constraints. It does not even exist separate from the behavior. As Mataric's robot shows, the combination of a particular set of low-level reflexes with a particular type of environment (or rather, with the aspects of that environment that are exploited and therefore given prominence by those low-level reflexes) will result in a new *Umwelt* for the higher levels of activ-

ity. This is an emergent environment of "affordances" (Gibson 1979) that can be described only in terms of features with temporal extent whose nature would have been difficult to predict without observing the activity patterns of a functioning creature.

2. It is not possible to provide a meaningful definition of an activity pattern in isolation, since activities are always defined in terms of other activities and their interactions with the environment. "Wall following" is merely a convenient description of an emergent behavior of Mataric's robot. In order to elevate it to a category of behavior, one would need to define it in formal terms. There are ways of doing this with reference to objective coordinate systems, but that would undermine the rationale of Mataric's solution. The specification of wall following, as implemented by Mataric, emerges from the actual performance. It is never exhaustive. Each performance contributes a little bit more to the specification. The definition of wall following consists in the history of wall following of different creatures. There is a family resemblance between different instances of wall following but no formal definition that pins it down precisely.

3. The machine term in Horswill's equation is even more problematic than the habitat and activity terms. It includes too many, mutually dependent factors. If Horswill is talking about a machine in computational terms—if he hopes to derive computational specifications from his three-place equation—that hope is clearly futile. The problem of implementing a particular activity in a given environment does not admit of a well-defined, canonical solution. It is not even a problem that can be stated in formal terms. A creature with a compliant hand does not have to solve the same problems in implementing "pick up block" as a creature with a rigid, centrally controlled hand. A creature with legs faces problems of a nature entirely different from those faced by a creature on wheels.

Horswill's proposal implies that the natural kinds for a description of behavior are to be sought in a classification of machines, tasks, and environments. It has been my contention that only the activity patterns that emerge from the interactions between autonomous creatures and their environments can provide fruitful explanatory entities. There is no formal rule for producing a particular pattern of situated activity in a particular type of environment. In view of the complexities involved and the impossibility of framing formal guidelines for specification, it would seem that our best hope lies in studying the activity patterns carved out by evolution.

The relations discovered in this way will not conform to a standard rule or pattern, but each will contribute to mapping out the space of possibilities. In Sloman's (1978) terms, this makes the science of emergent activity a historical, as opposed to an interpretative, science. It is concerned with mapping out the space of possibilities by defining and investigating particular instances rather than by discovering universal laws that could generate those instances.

Horswill's main interest is not in explanation but in engineering. However, his commitment to situated activity, tight coupling, and the subsumption architecture means that he too is constrained to a definition of possibilities in terms of particular instances. There are no rules for generating autonomous robots from formal specifications. His implements relation is a dream inspired by computational theory, and computational theory cannot provide the appropriate natural kinds for a definition of autonomous agents. But there are enough successful implementations in nature to save us from having to try out blindly every permutation of the factors involved.

8.3 A Robot That Learns from Emergent Activity

In my discussion of Mataric's work, I suggested that the need to introduce numeric parameters in the definition of landmarks might be considered a weakness of her system. I speculated that this flaw (if it is a flaw) might be a consequence of too large a gap between her levels of behavior. In passing, I mentioned the work of Pfeifer and Verschure (1992), implying that they avoided having to resort to numeric parameters because the levels of activity in their robot are more closely related.

Pfeifer and Verschure's robot is not a navigating robot in the true sense of the word. It cannot travel on command from its current location to some other location, as Mataric's robot does. It is incapable of building up a map in terms of specific landmarks defined by its own activity. But it does learn from its own activity patterns in a way that is different from, and perhaps more realistic than, the way in which Mataric's robot learns its landmarks.

I should mention that this system was developed in simulation rather than in a real robot, and the legitimacy of this approach is in dispute. Brooks (1991a), in particular, has made out a strong case that researchers who work in simulation are able to ignore the problems of sensor noise, slippage between actuators and the surfaces they work on, and the unpredictable contingencies of a dynamic, unplanned environment. In his view, these factors cannot be programmed into a simulation through the introduction of random perturbations. However, Harvey, Husbands, and Cliff (1993), as well as others, have argued that the introduction of noise in combination with a realistic simulation of the physics involved in movement and collisions can overcome these problems. Pfeifer and Verschure claim in a footnote to their paper that their code has now been tested in a real robot and has proved successful without modification.

The lowest level of their system consists of a set of autonomous reflexes along the lines of Mataric's STROLL, AVOID, ALIGN, and CORRECT. Pfeifer and Verschure call this the "value scheme" of the robot. The examples they give are: "Whenever a collision occurs, retract and turn in the other direction," and "Whenever a target is detected, turn toward it." It would seem that these low-level reflexes are quite crude in comparison with Mataric's. Wall following is not achieved by finely calibrated behaviors working from ingenious combinations of sensors; it results from a series of collisions followed by corrective movements.

Like Mataric's primitive behaviors, the low-level reflexes are implemented by hard-wired, tightly coupled sensor-feedback loops. They respond independently to selected environmental factors and result, in the "habitat" for which they have been designed, in patterns of emergent activity with a recognizable (but not formally definable) structure. As might be expected, the wall following that emerges from Pfeifer and Verschure's low-level reflexes lacks the precision and smoothness exhibited by Mataric's implementation. But the degree of structure resulting from this level is sufficient for the robot to move around in its environment without getting into trouble, and because of this it can provide a basis for further refinements.

In addition to the sensors used by these low-level behaviors, the robot has a range finder that is not implicated in the value scheme. The range finder is backed by a neural network, whose output neurons are connected to the motor command terminals of the low-level behaviors. The weights on these connections are updated following a Hebbian learning rule. If the neurons indicating a particular range-finder pattern are activated at the same time as those serving a particular motor command, then the connections between them are strengthened. Learning takes place simultaneously with performance, not in separate phases, as would be the case if the learning mechanism were back-propagation.

The result is that control of the collision-avoidance and target-approach behaviors gradually shifts from the collision detector and the target detector to the range finder. During the first one hundred time steps, twenty-nine avoidance movements are triggered by physical collisions. After six hundred time steps, this number has dropped to zero. "If the robot approaches an object from a certain direction and collides with it, the particular pattern in the range-finder will be learned via weight modification. . . . If at a later occasion the robot approaches the object from the same direction, a similar pattern will start to develop in the range-finder. Because of the similarity, at a certain point, this pattern will lead to sufficient activation in the avoidance layer to trigger the response: the robot has learned to anticipate obstacles" (Pfeifer and Verschure 1992, p. 26). It might be said that this is supervised learning without a human supervisor. The supervision is exercised by the activation of the robot's "value scheme" resulting from interactions with its environment. The robot is taught by its own activity patterns. It is able to monitor these, and detect their emergent structure, by means of the high-level sensing abilities conferred by the range finder and its associated neural network. But the network does not just monitor the structured patterns of "visual" input; it also (like Mataric's robot) monitors its own motor activity and correlates the two.

The difference from Mataric's robot is that Pfeifer and Verschure's robot does not apply numeric parameters to establish the correlation. There are no predefined criteria for landmark types, no minimum number of time steps during which the correlation must persist to qualify as a landmark, for the simple reason that Pfeifer and Verschure's robot does not learn specific landmarks. It learns repeated occurrences of correlated patterns of activation in its range-finder network and its motor command system. This does not give it information about specific environmental locations that might be converted into a map. The information stored in its neural connections as a result of Hebbian learning reflects general characteristics of the environment in which it learns, such as the fact that targets tend to be located behind holes in the wall.

As with Mataric's robot, it would be wrong to say that it stores these characteristics in terms of objective features of the world. "Whether a range finder pattern acts as an attractive or repellent force is not a function of the environment but of the system's 'interpretation' of this pattern due to its learning history. In an environment in which targets are always behind walls, the robot will develop wall-following behavior due to this regularity" (Pfeifer and Verschure 1992, p. 27). Without movement, no learning can take place. It is only by exercising and monitoring its motor commands at the same time as monitoring changes in range-finder patterns that the robot creates a "learning history" for itself. And if its movements were totally random, there would still be nothing to learn. The weights on the neural connections would not achieve significant biases as a result of the robot's exploration of its environment. But the interaction between a particular set of low-level reflexes and a particular type of environment results in movement with a recognizable temporal structure. This sets up the required correlations between the range-finder patterns and the patterns of motor commands. In a sense, the network has learned the associations between temporal patterns of movement and sensory input.

In an environment of the type used by Pfeifer and Verschure, where targets are placed behind gaps in walls, it will look as if the robot is following walls. What is more, it may seem as if the robot is actually searching for the target—as if it knows that the target is somewhere behind the wall, and all it needs to do is find a gap to reach it. In fact, the robot has simply learned an activity pattern. It has not learned an association between walls and targets as such; it has merely developed the ability to repeat certain activity patterns, which, interpreted as purposeful or goal-directed behavior, might create the impression that it has an internal representation of walls and targets and their relation in the world "out there."

The low-level reflexes have no temporal extent. The Hebbian learning adds a temporal dimension to the robot's behavior. This is due to the fact that the reflexes, in combination with a particular environment, produce activity that is structured in time, and the range-finder network is able to record temporal patterns of correlation.

Pfeifer and Verschure sum up their method in what they call the paradigm of Distributed Adaptive Control, which they recommend as a standard approach for building autonomous creatures:

1. Define the sensors and effectors of the robot, and specify the type of environment in which it is to function.
2. Define the "value scheme": the set of basic sensor-feedback loops or low-level behaviors.
3. Define a network architecture and a learning rule. These must provide an associative mechanism between the reflexes and the input from more sophisticated sensors.
4. Let the robot interact with the environment. Observe its behavior to see how a learned, higher level of activity emerges from the "training" of the network by the patterns of low-level activity emerging from interactions of its value scheme with certain features of its habitat.

Though basically sound, this prescription for building autonomous robots begs a number of questions. What criteria should one apply in "defining" the sensors and effectors, and how does one "specify" an environment that is not a simulation? Are Pfeifer and Verschure talking about formal definitions in Horswill's sense, or are they merely saying: "Choose an environment in which your robot has to function, and pick some likely sensors and effectors for that environment"? To what extent, and in what way, is the choice of sensors and effectors determined by a preconception about the desired emergent activity?

Even if the choice of hardware is to some degree arbitrary, the robot's "value scheme" clearly cannot be defined in isolation. The particular choice of low-level sensor-feedback loops will be determined by the robot's hardware and the nature of its environment but also by the type of activity the designer wishes to emerge from them. What methods may be used for achieving this? Do Pfeifer and Verschure, like Horswill, hope for some sort of implements relation, which will enable us to derive the value scheme from formal specifications, or can it be derived only by testing hypothetical permutations of sensors and effectors in the particular environment?

All of these questions finally lead back to a single question: What constitutes an adequate description of an autonomous agent and its activities? Item 4 of Pfeifer and Verschure's program seems to indicate that they concur with the conclusion I reached in the section on Horswill. Whether the aim of the exercise is engineering or explanation, adequate descriptions can emerge only from interactions between autonomous agents and their environments. The natural kinds of a science of behavior are emergent activity patterns. There are no competence theories to generate such patterns. A science of behavior is constrained to be a historical science, which delineates the space of possibilities in terms of exemplars. Artificially produced activity patterns can help to delineate this space of possibilities.

Pfeifer and Verschure's most important contribution is to have shown that a neural network that modifies its own weights according to a Hebbian learning rule can be "trained" by emergent activity. The network learns to "anticipate" recurring correlations between sensory input and motor commands, and gradually takes over control of the robot's behavior. The resulting activity is not very different in kind from the lower level it replaces. It does not deserve a distinctive classification, like Mataric's landmark detection and navigation levels, but it contributes a new strand to explanation in terms of emergent activity.

Note that the basic principles of Pfeifer and Verschure's model are the same as those of Mataric's. Low-level reflexes interacting with a particular environment result in emergent activity with a recognizable, though not formally definable, structure. The robot can function as a viable autonomous agent at this level. It does not need additional levels to get around. However, its structured activity creates opportunities for learning. It brings into existence a more abstract level of information that does not exist in the environment on its own, or in the robot's "value scheme," or in any possible representation of the environment by the robot. The addition of more sophisticated sensors attuned to this information then makes it possible for the robot to refine its behavior.

The performance of Mataric's robot seems more impressive than that of Pfeifer and Verschure's, since it is capable of constructing a cognitive map of its environment and using it to travel from one location to another. But it may be that our respect for this type of behavior is due to a lingering preference for explanations in terms of task domains. In nature, a creature is clearly not told to travel from its current location to another. Nor is it likely that it tells itself to do so. Of course, it does travel reliably from its feeding grounds to its nest, or from a specific beach on which it was spawned to a specific stretch of ocean where it will find plankton. But it is highly unlikely that it has any sense of where it is going when it sets out on its travels.

Jamon (1991) makes out a strong case that cognitive maps are not necessary to the explanation of homing behavior in mice, bees, salmon, and pigeons. He shows that the ability to detect environmental gradients (and in some cases an ability to tell compass directions), in combination with the natural structure of the environment, can give sufficient bias to a creature's movement to result in the same statistical percentage of returns as are found in nature.

Environmental gradients are a perfect example of information that becomes available through structured movement. Creatures perform patterns of activity that are specially adapted to bring them out. The temptation is to think of the generation of these movements, and the sensory processes attuned to gradients, as mechanisms for the construction of internal representations of the environment. This would lead us straight back to the problems of correspondence posed by Dretske (1988) and Millikan (1984), which I discussed in chapter 3.

Pfeifer and Verschure's robot provides an alternative and far more realistic model of the process. It does not extract information about the environment to enable it to steer its course. The changes in the weights of the range-finder network are not representations of walls or targets, or of the ways in which walls and targets are related. They record the experience of moving through a particular environment as a result of a particular set of low-level reflexes interacting with that environment. The "information" generated by the interaction between the robot's low-level activity and a structured environment is nowhere made explicit. The changed weights merely enable the robot to use its experience and navigate under control of its range finder. Information is not a separate entity; it is inextricably embedded in the various levels of behavior.

In order to get a clearer sense of these differences, it may be instructive to compare Pfeifer and Verschure's apparently successful implementation with a similar but less successful attempt by Dedieu and Mazer (1992). These authors make the point that the *behavior* of a well-adapted creature is in some sense a representation of its environment. They call this an "indirect" representation and claim that the goal of all sensory processing is to convert indirect representations into direct ones. On the strength of this analysis, they then propose a standard program for the robot builder:

1. Choose an environment and design a low-level control program. (It does not much matter of what sort.)
2. Get a robot, furnish it with a variety of sensors, and run the program in the environment.
3. Analyze the sensorimotor input provided by the sensors for topological dependencies (i.e., correlations) between independent input channels.
4. Express each discovered correlation as a new "channel" that transforms the previous channels' values into a new set of values.

The information transmitted by this new channel will be context dependent, in the sense of being structured by the sensorimotor history of the creature whose behavior resulted in the correlations. It will, say Dedieu and Mazer, provide a "representation" of the environment that is not subject to the symbol-grounding problem.

Note that the program for building robots set out by these authors is quite similar to that of Pfeifer and Verschure. Dedieu and Mazer's point 1 corresponds to Pfeifer and Verschure's points 1 and 2. Dedieu and Mazer's point 2 corresponds to Pfeifer and Verschure's point 4. Both pairs of authors are aware that the crux of the matter lies at the intersection between the robot's autonomous, low-level behavior and a more sophisticated sensory channel, which is not implicated in that behavior. They realize that the robot must be allowed to function autonomously in a specific environment, and it must monitor its own behavior, as well as its sensory input, to produce the results they are after. Where they disagree is in the way those results should be extracted and conceptualized.

Pfeifer and Verschure are interested in the activity patterns that emerge after the range-finder network has been trained by the low-level behavior and the sensory inputs. Dedieu and Mazer are interested in isolating information about the environment that is structured by the robot's low-level behavior and can therefore be said to be free from the symbol-grounding problem. Pfeifer and Verschure's explanatory model takes situated patterns of activity as its natural kinds; Dedieu and Mazer see activity as a means of extracting information.

As Dedieu and Mazer say themselves, it does not much matter what movements the robot performs, as long as it can correlate the patterns in those movements with the patterns in the input from its sensors. Dedieu and Mazer are interested in emergent information, not emergent activity, and they believe they can separate one from the other. This leads them into a crucial error in their method of experimentation. In order to keep things simple, they decide to restrict the movements of their robot to rotation around its own axis (though admittedly at varying speeds). The control of its movement is thus exercised entirely by the robot itself. There is no interaction with the environment involved in producing its low-level activity.

The robot monitors this rotational behavior at varying speeds and records the resulting input from its photosensors. Dedieu and Mazer then analyzed these two streams of data for significant correlations. They admit that the results were disappointing. At the end of their paper, they speculate that this approach may ultimately require the same amount of effort in preprocessing to bring out significant correlations as was expended on computational mechanisms to extract meaningful representations in classical AI. This remark shows how the mistake in their experimental approach is related to their basic premises, though it does not directly follow from them.

Dedieu and Mazer's declared aim was the extraction of "direct" representations from the "indirect" representations produced by a creature's movements in a particular environment. Clearly, for the creature's activity to be an indirect representation of the world, it has to result from *interactions* with that world. Simple rotation about its axis will not represent anything except the motor commands that make it happen, and no amount of preprocessing is going to remedy that fact.

A creature's movements, if they result from sensor-feedback loops that respond to specific environmental contingencies (proximity of obstacles, chemical gradients, alternations of light and darkness), will constitute a kind of representation of its environment. As I pointed out in my discussion of Mataric's robot, its low-level reflexes can be viewed as a transformation that maps the environment into structured patterns of activity. But this is a representation only from the point of view of an observer, who can describe the obstacles, measure the gradients, and locate the patterns of light and darkness. An observer is able to detect correlations between the structured path of the creature and the regularities in its environment, described in objective terms.

It is important to stress again that this representation is not in any sense located inside the creature, or even generated directly by internal structures of the creature. It emerges from the interactions of its low-level reflexes with the contingencies of the environment. The creature's path is a representation of the environment only to an observer. What

Dedieu and Mazer seem to be saying is that the object of all sensory processing is to convert this "indirect" representation contained in the creature's movements into an explicit representation that can be "used" by the creature itself. This is why they believe it is important for the creature to be able to discover correlations between the data from different sensors. Such correlations will reliably indicate the presence of certain objective features in the world. They will give the creature an objective view of the causes of its own movements and thus convert the indirect representation that might be available to an observer into a direct representation that is available to the creature itself.

The experimental error Dedieu and Mazer made is not difficult to remedy. A robot could be built that exhibits autonomous, low-level behavior modeled on that of Mataric's or Pfeifer and Verschure's robot. It could monitor this emergent behavior (which now can actually be described as a kind of representation of its environment) and correlate the data concerning its movements with inputs from its photosensors.

The question is, In what terms should the movements and sensor inputs be monitored and compared? Put in a different way, to what end are they being monitored and compared? The only answer Dedieu and Mazer can give is that their (or their robot's) purpose is to discover correlations between the data streams. No wonder they are puzzled by questions of preprocessing. We are back at Marr's question of *what* is being processed and *why*. As Marr pointed out, the purpose of the exercise will dictate its frame of reference and its units of measurement. Marr's own response was unequivocal: processing serves the purpose of building internal representations that "recover" the world of objects and their properties from an impoverished retinal projection.

Dedieu and Mazer clearly do not wish to go down that route. They believe it is possible to derive internal representations from correlations in sensor data without having to specify a task domain, that the descriptive framework required by an internal representation will somehow fall out of these correlations between the robot's motor signals and the signals from its sensors. What they do not realize is that this squeezes internal representation out of the system entirely. As Pfeifer and Verschure's robot shows, it is quite possible to correlate the motor commands involved in low-level behavior with input from more sophisticated sensors, as long as the correlation is performed inside a closed loop with the environment. Sensor-feedback loops do not require specifications of the data in terms of task domains or descriptive primitives. The "meaning" of the data is defined by the resultant behavior.

The weights in Pfeifer and Verschure's range-finder network have no other function apart from the role they play in an activity module.

It is not possible to specify any objective category of information that might be contained in those weights, nor do the signals that travel through the network contain such information. The behavior of the robot may be characterized by an observer in such terms as "wall following," "anticipation of collisions," and "searching for gaps in walls in order to reach the targets behind them." But if the aim of the exercise is to understand the underlying mechanism, such characterizations will be misleading, just as it was misleading to lump together the various behaviors of Lorenz's mother duck as parenting behavior. Dedieu and Mazer's fundamental mistake is that they are trying to describe the behavior of autonomous agents in terms of the wrong natural kinds. A true understanding requires a description in terms of sensor-feedback loops and emergent levels of situated activity and their interdependencies.

8.4 Delineating the Space of Possibilities

I have singled out the work of Koza, Horswill, Pfeifer and Verschure, and Dedieu and Mazer, because it helps to throw light on the insights provided by Mataric's robot and bring the essential principles into sharper focus. The conclusions I have drawn in this chapter and the previous one may be summed up as follows:

1. Autonomous robots can provide explanatory models of animal (and hopefully also human) behavior.

2. Computational mechanisms of various kinds, such as finite state machines, LISP programs, and connectionist networks, can be used (and may even be essential) in the construction of such models, but this does not make them computational models. They must be viewed as models of behavior, not models of "what goes on in the head."

3. There are no shortcuts to the construction of such models. Neither GAs nor some implements relation can obviate the need for clearly worked out hypotheses concerning the behaviors to be modeled and their interdependencies. Considering the problems of sensor noise, slippage between surfaces and actuators, and the unpredictable contingencies of a dynamic environment, it seems likely that a considerable amount of fine tuning will always be involved in producing the desired emergent behavior.

4. The resulting models may be seen as existence proofs. Each contributes to delineating further the space of possibilities. It is only by an accumulation of such natural kinds of behavior that the space of possibilities can be described. There can be no

generative rules for behavior, no competence theory from which particular instances may be derived. The science of behavior requires historical explanations, in the sense defined by Sloman (1978).

5. Fruitful hypotheses are most likely to come from observation of naturally evolved behavior, in its natural surroundings, supplemented by controlled experiments in the same natural habitat, and comparisons with the behavior of related species. Artificially built models serve to confirm the hypotheses of how such behavior is caused and may serve to bring out family resemblances between various types of behavioral interdependencies.

6. The basic explanatory mechanism employed in the construction of such robots and their use as models for naturally evolved behavior is that of interactive emergence. This may take various forms. A creature may have hard-wired sensor-feedback loops that produce reliable patterns of activity in the environment by which it was selected. These patterns of activity may provide an essential, emergent environment for even higher levels of activity, also hard-wired, which thus constitute an evolutionary "seal of approval" for the emergent activity at the lower level. Alternatively, the emergent low-level patterns of activity may serve as a crude but reliable template for behavior that is perfected through experience, as in Pfeifer and Verschure's robot. Once again, the presence of such mechanisms of learning, which depend on the interaction between lower levels of emergent activity and input from more sophisticated sensors, provides a legitimizing history of use for the lower levels of activity.

One of the main purposes of model building must be the discovery of such alternative mechanisms of interactive emergence.

Chapter 9

Models of Behavior Selection

9.1 Various Aspects of the Problem

One of the key problems in modeling autonomous creatures of any complexity is how choice between alternative activities should be managed. Brooks (1991a) calls this the macro level of design, as opposed to the micro level concerned with implementing particular behaviors. He identifies three different aspects of the problem:

1. The behavior or behaviors active at any particular moment should be appropriate to the creature's internal and external circumstances. (The creature should look for food when it is in need of sustenance and flee when it catches sight of a predator.)
2. Conflicts between different behaviors should be resolved in such a way that mutually contradictory behaviors are not active simultaneously, and switching between behaviors is effected smoothly and coherently. (The creature should not try to look for food and flee at the same time, or oscillate rapidly between the two behaviors, which would render them both useless.)
3. The overall behavior of the creature should serve what Brooks calls its "long-term goals." (In some cases it may need to take risks with predators in order to ensure that it finds enough food.)

Naturally evolved creatures seem to have few problems in managing these different aspects of behavior selection, though in some cases conflicts may result in displacement behavior inappropriate to their circumstances. As Brooks points out, ethology has struggled for many years to find adequate explanations for the mechanisms involved. He briefly refers to theories based on drive and motivation but goes on to take a straightforward engineering approach. The fundamental questions, Brooks decides, are whether behavior selection should be centralized or decentralized and whether conflict resolution should be fixed priority or dynamically reconfigurable. My conclusion in this chapter will be that situated activity requires by definition that the process be decentralized and dynamically reconfigurable. But the more important aim of the discussion will be to question whether these categories derived from Brooks's engineering approach provide the most illuminating description of the processes involved.

Stepping back from immediate considerations of engineering, it is possible to take at least three distinct views of a creature that has been "constructed" by nature so that the right choices will emerge from its interactions with the environment.

The first view corresponds roughly to traditional AI, top-down design, and the explanatory framework of "hierarchical reductionism" (R. Dawkins, 1986). It solves the problems of behavior selection by good management, proper planning, and strategic delegation of tasks. Correct decisions are made because high-level agents (Minsky 1987) foresee specific needs in achieving the creature's goals and call on lower-level agents at the correct time and place to perform the jobs for which they are designed.

The choice mechanism in this model is clearly located inside the creature. It is also a purposive model, in the sense that choice does not result from passive responses to environmental contingencies but serves to achieve the creature's goals. Goal-directed behavior is conceptualized in terms of internal representations (Miller, Galanter, and Pribram 1960). These natural kinds serve the purpose of turning the formal elements of a task description into functional elements in the decision-making process. The mechanism of choice is equated with programming devices like conditional loops and calls to subroutines. It may be centralized or decentralized, and it may be fixed priority or dynamically reconfigurable. What is distinctive about this model is that the creature is conceived as purposeful and that behavior choice is seen as the outcome of goal-directed mechanisms located inside it. Since much of this book has been concerned with a critique of the classical approach, I do not propose to say more about it in this chapter.

The second view of a creature constructed by nature to make the right choices might be called the economic model. Exemplified by such authors as McFarland (1985, 1989) and Houston (1991), it views the overall behavior of a creature as an optimization or maximization of some "currency" like fitness or "utility." Since this type of explanation has become an important element in autonomous creature research and the newly emerging discipline of artificial life, I shall discuss its strengths and weaknesses in greater detail before going on to my third and preferred model of decision making.

9.2 Economic Models of Choice Mechanisms in Artificial Life

Economic models stem from the notion of economic man, which was introduced into economics to account for human choices of behavior and consumption. Economic man is assumed to be a perfectly rational agent who contrives in all circumstances to maximize a notional quantity called utility. He will obtain a certain amount of utility from playing squash, a certain amount from attending movies, and even some from reading books. How much time and money he is prepared to spend on each will depend on the relative amounts of utility he derives from them, as well as on their respective costs.

It should be clear from this short explanation that utility can be defined only in terms of the creature's actual behavior. A person or animal cannot fail to maximize utility, because utility is simply that which is maximized by its behavior. Utility may be seen as a notional measure of the psychological value of goods, leisure, sensual gratification, social prestige, and all the other benefits on which people are prepared to spend their time and money. The only way in which the utility of playing an hour of squash can be compared with the utility of buying a record is by observing people's behavior. It is assumed that the behavior is the result of rational choice, and this makes it possible to introduce a common measure for comparing the two behaviors in economic terms. There is, of course, no suggestion that this quantity plays any causal role in the underlying mechanisms that subtend the behavior.

Economic theories are not concerned with underlying mechanisms, nor are they interested in the physical details of the environment or the creature's movements. There is no attempt at functional decomposition or causal descriptions of the activities involved. These theories merely formalize the observed allocation of time to various categories of behavior, such as "squash" and "movie attendance" in the case of humans, and "feeding," "parenting," "mating," or "fighting" in the case of other animals. The categories of behavior picked out by the theories clearly owe their status as categories to the economic perspective that the theories adopt.

It should also be clear that utility is a statistical measure. Jane may be prepared to spend twice as much money on an hour of squash as on a compact disk, whereas John prefers listening to music and has to be dragged onto the squash court. The relative utility of each behavior can be assessed only by taking an average over a large number of choices. Economic man is an abstraction, and for practical purposes he needs to be subdivided into socioeconomic classes, each with its own set of preferences and spending patterns and relative assignments of utility. This statistical nature of the concept also makes it an unlikely candidate for explanations of the mechanisms that subtend the behavior of an individual.

Economic models have made important contributions in behavioral ecology. They have played a part in formulating theories of territorial behavior, fight-or-flight strategies, and the variation of sex ratio in offspring, as well as many other phenomena. These theories may be seen as "explanations" of the behavioral patterns involved, in the sense that they account for the observed correlations between environmental factors and classes of behavior by applying a logical calculus like game theory. Computational models may be built that incorporate this logic and produce the desired correlations between input and output. The danger is that such models may then come to be seen as models of the underlying mechanisms that subtend the behavior.

The choice mechanism posited by economic models is notional but conceptually quite explicit: all alternative courses of action at each particular moment are evaluated with respect to a common currency. In the model as originally conceived by economic theorists, the evaluation is done by a rational agent who, consciously or unconsciously, endeavors to maximize utility. To convert this into a model that might be capable of physical implementation, utility needs to be reified, and a mechanism has to be posited that compares the quantities of utility associated with each choice of behavior. McFarland's (1989) solution to these design problems is hill climbing.

Hill climbing offers a powerful computational technique. Global, long-term aims of the system are achieved through large numbers of local, moment-to-moment adjustments, which do not seem to require any "knowledge" of the overall goal. The mechanism itself appears to hold out the promise of an explanation: "Natural selection has designed animals not to pursue a single goal, but to pursue a course of action which is optimal in relation to a large number of internal and external factors. . . . The result is that behaviour is directed, not by any goal-representation, but in a holistic manner which takes into account all (relevant) aspects of the animal's internal state, and of the (perceived) external situation" (McFarland 1989, p. 49). The picture McFarland is trying to convey is of a creature calibrated by natural selection and its own experience so that the appropriate behavior "emerges" from its internal mechanism. Such a creature has no need of internally represented goals as posited by classical AI. The calibration of its hill-climbing mechanism ensures that it always delivers the optimum response to the "inputs" presented by the external world and its own internal state. In a certain sense, this picture undoubtedly corresponds to reality. But what we would like is an explanation of how exactly that calibration is achieved. Hill climbing alone does not constitute an explanation. If the goal function and hill climbing are to serve as more than just abstract metaphors, the details of the mechanism need to be spelled out.

I have mentioned that economic models have become an important element in the newly emerging discipline of artificial life. In order to illustrate what I believe are the pitfalls of this approach, I shall discuss two systems that are intended as explanatory models of naturally occurring behavior in fish and insects.

Gabora and Colgan (1991) studied the incidence of exploratory behavior in banded killifish *(Fundulus diaphenous)* from two different lakes, one containing predators and the other not. In both populations, exploratory behavior tended to increase when the fish were exposed to a new environment, attaining a maximum after a certain amount of time and decreasing steadily from then on. However, the killifish from the lake without predators showed exploratory behavior that peaked sooner and was far more intense at its peak, though the total amount of time spent on exploration was greater in killifish from the environment containing predators.

Gabora and Colgan begin their analysis by assuming that natural selection tends to favor progressive differentiation into behavioral subsystems that are specialized to take care of "different aspects of survival," defined in terms of "ultimate causal goals," like "avoiding predators" and "obtaining energy." An explanation of the patterns of exploratory behavior should therefore be framed in terms of these functional subsystems, which compete for control over the creature's "behavioral final common path."

They propose a model in which exploratory behavior is the result of excitation by the subsystem concerned with obtaining energy and inhibition by the subsystem concerned with avoiding predators. Both excitation and inhibition are assumed to be at their peak on introduction to the new environment. Inhibition will tend to decrease faster, since predators would actively seek out the newly introduced fish, and thus their presence or absence will be established sooner than the presence or absence of prey. As a result, inhibition will be stronger than excitation at first, causing the fish to remain stationary. After a while its level will drop below that of excitation, which will decrease once the new environment has been explored. The fish will play safe at first, start to explore their new environment when they find out they are not likely to be attacked, and stop doing so once they have established the location and relative incidence of prey.

The computational implementation of this model is quite simple. It consists of a neural network with three units: an output unit that represents the amount of exploration and two hidden units that represent the excitatory subsystem of obtaining energy and the inhibitory subsystem of avoiding prey. The excitatory subsystem is linked by a positive weight to the output unit; the inhibitory subsystem is connected to it by a negative weight. Both subsystems receive negative feedback from the output unit. When activation of the output unit representing exploration exceeds a given threshold, this feedback decreases activation of the subsystems, and consequently their impact on the output is decreased as well. In addition, the activation of the inhibitory subsystem is reduced by a constant factor over time.

Gabora and Colgan are satisfied that their model reproduces the behavior they set out to explain. By varying the different factors and parameters of the model, they were able to reproduce the disparate patterns of behavior displayed by the killifish from the two lakes. Connectionism has made it possible to create models of this type, which do not contain explicit rules but from which the desired patterns of output seem to emerge. These models are nonrepresentational and embody empirical data derived from observations in the field. They therefore conform to most of the principles advocated by the disciplines of autonomous agent research and artificial life. However, as I indicated in my discussion of McFarland's proposal, I do not believe that a true explanation can be obtained from such economic models.

The natural kinds Gabora and Colgan used—"avoiding predators" and "obtaining energy"—are functional categories, not activity patterns. There is no reference to the physical parameters involved in these "behaviors," no analysis in terms of the creature's movements or its interactions with the environment. Yet the authors imply that these behaviors compete directly for control over the creature's skeletomusculature. This indicates that the killifish's "exploratory behavior" is seen as the outcome of an internal mechanism of choice rather than the statistical outcome of varying amounts of the two behaviors being executed at different times by the members of a killifish population.

"Avoiding predators" and "obtaining energy" thus become "agents" in Minsky's (1987) sense rather than "behaviors" in Brooks's (1986b) or Mataric's (1991a) sense. Gabora and Colgan's model is a traditional one implemented by a connectionist network, whose natural kinds are derived top down through functional analysis of the creature's behavior. The choice mechanism embodied in their neural network is not a realistic model of conflict resolution between activities, which must emerge from interaction with the environment, as well as from the actual mechanisms of skeletomuscular control.

Vonk, Putters, and Velthuis (1991) apply a similar technique of model building to sex ratio determination by female parasitic wasps. Like Gabora and Colgan, they place themselves in the camp of nonrepresentational, ethology-inspired research: "In order to explain the actual decisions of our wasps . . . we require systems which adapt to the environment without an explicit representation of the world, and which can achieve goals without a representation of these goals (i.e., without goal-directedness)" (Vonk, Putters, and Velthuis 1991, p. 485).

A female wasp can determine the sex of each offspring by either fertilizing an egg and thereby producing a female, or leaving it unfertilized and producing a male. In this way she is able to adjust the sex ratio of the first generation of offspring to the characteristics of the environment and ensure that the maximum number of copies of her genes will be passed on to the generation that succeeds it, a phenomenon called haplodiploidy. It is a genuine case of behavior linked to fitness rather than to survival value.

The wasps live on patches, each colonized by one or more females. Wasps belonging to a particular patch mate locally and randomly when they emerge. The inseminated females then migrate to a new patch to lay their eggs. Each egg is laid individually in a dead host, which will provide food for the larva when it emerges. The size of the host, determining the amount of food it will provide to the larva, is more critical for the proper development of females than for males. Of course, some hosts will be too small to provide sufficient nourishment for either sex.

Vonk, Putters, and Velthuis's model formalizes the female wasp's behavior, when faced with a host, as two choices: egg or no egg and fertilize or not. It assumes that both decisions are determined by the size of the host, as well as the outcome of the previous four egg-or-no-egg decisions. The theory is that if the female has not laid an egg for some time (if she rejected the last few hosts on the grounds that they were inadequate sources of food), then she will be more highly "motivated" to lay an egg on the present host.

The computational model Vonk, Putters, and Velthuis used is a three-layer, feed-forward neural network trained by back-propagation. The authors hasten to point out that their choice of learning mechanism carries no implications concerning the processes of biological learning or adaptation. They are interested only in the final result. Once it has been trained by this method, the neural network "provides a more realistic model of the principles of organization which real animals have acquired during evolution" (Vonk, Putters, and Velthuis 1991, p. 487).

The model has five input units, one representing host size and the others representing the most recent egg-or-no-egg decisions. There are two output units, representing the binary choices of egg or no egg and fertilize or not. Between input and output, there is a layer with two hidden units, each connected to all the input and all the output units. The network was trained on samples that were drawn randomly from a dataset of observed decisions by female wasps.

Like Gabora and Colgan's model of killifish behavior, Vonk, Putters, and Velthuis's model of parasitic wasp behavior is an economic model.

A neural network is trained using a statistical sample of "real" decisions, on the assumption that a system whose input-output patterns reflect the actuarial distribution of input-output patterns in a biological population must incorporate mechanisms that can serve as an explanatory model of the individual creatures. The mechanism of choice makes no reference to the physical activities involved in egg laying or fertilization. These activities are represented as binary digits. Presumably those digits should be seen as signals to egg-laying and fertilization modules or agents. The decision-making mechanism is thus divorced from the implementation of the activities themselves.

Economic models of this sort have their place in behavioral ecology, but it can be highly misleading to view them as explanatory models of the behavior of individual creatures. Connectionism does not provide a shortcut to explanation. It cannot absolve us from isolating genuine natural kinds of situated activity, which can be grounded through their underlying mechanisms and history of use.

9.3 Choice Mechanisms in Autonomous Agents

A number of attempts have been made to bridge the gap between the ecological insights afforded by an economic perspective and the paradigm of situated activity. Snaith and Holland (1991) propose a model in which the cost and benefit of different behaviors is converted into "stimulus strengths," which might correspond to concentrations of various activity-inducing hormones in naturally evolved creatures: "We emphasize that the robot or organism is not explicitly or implicitly computing the expected value of each behavior, but rather that the strengths of certain stimuli which are clearly available are good enough guides for a decision making strategy which approximates to choosing the behavior with the highest expected value to the organism" (p. 256). In Brooks's (1991a) terms, the mechanism Snaith and Holland propose is decentralized and dynamically reconfigurable. Conflict resolution is achieved not through one behavior's capturing a central "behavioral common path" but through the inhibitory, as well as excitatory, effects of the creature's "hormones." A hormone that induces one type of activity also inhibits execution of all the others. As the authors themselves admit, this assumes there is a simple, one-to-one correspondence between hormones or "stimuli" and uniquely defined categories of behavior.

Snaith and Holland do not specify the nature of these categories. They assume that the decision-making mechanism can be specified without reference to the activities between which it chooses. They point out that Brook's subsumption architecture is merely a special case of their own model, in which the behaviors are ranked according to priority, so that an active behavior does not send inhibitory signals to more important behaviors but completely inhibits the less important behaviors.

This analysis misses what is probably the most important point about decomposition by activity, as practiced by Brooks and his colleagues. The essence of Brooks's models is that they are autonomously functioning robots, which have been fine-tuned to a specific environment. Activities interact with each other as well as with the environment to produce the creature's behavior. Wall following in Mataric's robot cannot be traced to particular stimuli that turn it on and off. The actual pattern of behavior emerges from the movements of the calibrated robot in its environmental niche and cannot be placed into a one-to-one correspondence with internal stimuli. An explanation of why a particular architectural configuration works must make reference to the nature of the individual activities and the way they interact with each other and the creature's environment.

Such a creature cannot decide to execute one particular behavior rather than another, nor can a mechanism be identified inside the robot that is describable as the agent of choice. If it is possible to talk about choice at all, it can only be said to emerge from the totality of the behaviors and their interaction with the environment. The existence proofs Brooks and Mataric construct show that this is not just woolly holism. Behavioral choice can be implemented as an emergent phenomenon that requires an explanatory perspective radically different from that of computational and economic models.

The presumption behind Snaith and Holland's model is that the internal mechanism of a naturally evolved creature will have been calibrated by natural selection. The concentrations of the various hormones at any particular time will correspond to the "expected values" (in other words, the costs and benefits) of the activities they induce. Taken in the most general terms, this is merely a restatement of Darwin's notion of fitness. Whether the calibration is implemented through hormones or a neural mechanism, or a combination of both, creatures with the best "correspondences" will clearly pass on more copies of their genes. But as soon as an attempt is made to convert this general law into the specifications for a functional mechanism, we encounter all the problems I have described already. Natural selection does not define categories of behavior, and it does not sanction a teleological perspective. The design stance and Darwin's theory do not mix.

Subsumption architecture, in itself, is not a model of anything. It is certainly not a model of a decision-making mechanism. Subsumption architecture can result in choices being made if a robot has been fine-tuned in a particular environment, but to equate those choices with the mechanism of suppression and inhibition between the layers is to misinterpret the most important aspect of situated activity. In their search for formal relations and general principles of design, Brooks and his followers sometimes appear to fall into this error themselves.

The colleague of Brooks most closely associated with models of behavior selection is Pattie Maes (1991b, 1992). Her models are nonhierarchical, decentralized, and dynamically reconfigurable. Their basic structure is that of a "behavior network," whose nodes represent the different behaviors a creature is capable of performing. Between these nodes there are "conflictor," "successor," and predecessor' links, which transmit "spreading activation" in the way we have already encountered in Mataric's robot.

Every behavior has associated with it an "activation level," which is a real number. It also has a set of conditions that have to be met for the behavior to become "executable." Finally, it has a threshold. An executable behavior whose activation level exceeds its threshold becomes active. This means that a set of processes begin to run that "realize" the behavior. Only one behavior can be active at any particular time. After the behavior has been selected, its activation level is set to zero.

Behavior nodes are connected to each other by successor, predecessor, and conflictor links. An executable behavior spreads activation to its successors, promoting their execution and thus setting up routine sequences of behaviors, or "habits." Nonexecutable behaviors spread activation to their predecessors, encouraging their own conditions to become true. All behaviors decrease the activation level of their conflictors.

Sensory data are abstracted into a finite set of binary perceptual conditions, such as "obstacle within 1 foot," "person on the left," or "wall on the right." The occurrence of a perceptual condition increases the activation of the behaviors that have it on their condition lists.

The system also incorporates a set of "goals" or "motivations," whose activation increases with time but is diminished by the execution of related behaviors. Goals with high levels of activation increase the activation levels of the behaviors that help to fulfill them. Behaviors that fulfill goals are called "consummatory behaviors"; the remaining behaviors, called "appetitive behaviors," help to make the conditions of consummatory behaviors come true by spreading activation to their successors and by bringing the robot nearer to the goal.

Maes's latest model (Maes 1992) is able to improve its behavior selection through learning. In order to make this possible, weights have been introduced on the links. Every behavior module continuously monitors its list of conditions. When one of these changes state (passes from false to true or vice versa), the system ascribes that change to the module that was active in the previous time step. If there was no link between their nodes, a new link is set up. If the condition changed to true, it will be a predecessor link; if it changed from true to false, it will be a conflictor link. If a link already existed, its weight is changed.

To take an example, let us assume the creature was executing "follow wall" and that it suddenly found itself at a recharging station. All modules that have "at recharging station" as one of their conditions would then create a predecessor link to "follow wall." On the other hand, if "at recharging station" were suddenly to become false, and the most recently active module was "wander around," then those same modules would create a conflictor link to "wander around" for condition "at recharging station."

Successor links are established in a similar way but projected forward rather than backward. They are there to ensure that when a particular module is activated, other modules that have conditions that are likely to be satisfied by the execution of its behavior will tend to receive spreading activation. In learning, every module monitors the behaviors that become active after itself. Initially, this may occur quite independently of any connection between them. In that case a new link is created. If a link already existed, its weight is increased.

The weights are calculated by dividing the number of "successes" by the number of "trials." For a predecessor link, execution of the behavior at the receiving end of the link counts as a success for a particular condition if the condition became true following execution of the behavior at the origin of the link. Every execution of the receiving behavior counts as a trial. The weights on successor and conflictor links are calculated analogously.

The links and their weights establish internal connections between behaviors that are externally linked through perceptual conditions. This allows chains of appetitive behaviors to be set up, so that one appetitive behavior brings about the perceptual conditions for the execution of the next, leading eventually to a consummatory behavior that satisfies one of the creature's goals or motivations. If the creature learns that a chain of behavior modules A, B, and C leads to the fulfillment of motivation M_1, then activation will spread from C to B to A in proportion to the strength of M_1 and the values of the learned weights between the behaviors. If, in addition, it has learned that A, B, D, and E lead to fulfillment of M_2, then the "partial solution" A, B is applicable to both and will become stronger: the process is compositional. Knowledge gained in the context of one behavior can be applied in the context of another.

Clearly Maes's thinking is strongly influenced by the conceptual framework of ethology. Her model requires:

1. Well-defined behaviors similar to the fixed action patterns (FAPs) proposed by Lorenz (1935, 1937, 1939, 1952).
2. Well-defined perceptual conditions associated with each activity module. These resemble the notion of a "sign stimulus" in ethology, which serves to trigger an FAP, but Maes's model provides for more than one condition per behavior, and all conditions have to be satisfied before a behavior can "fire."
3. Fixed connections between consummatory behaviors and their related "motivations." The motivations in Maes's model may be equated with Lorenz's notion of "action-specific energy," in the sense that they tend to "fill up" with time, and are "emptied" by execution of their consummatory behavior.
4. An environment in which a given behavior will result with a reasonable degree of certainty in the occurrence of a particular set of perceptual conditions. Following walls will not always result in the recharging point's becoming visible to the robot, but if the probability of the correlation were no better than random, it would be impossible for successor and predecessor links to become established.

Innate sequences of behavior can be modeled in Maes's system by presetting the links between activity modules. A link of weight ½ will change far more quickly than a link of weight $^{5,000}/_{10,000}$, since one failure in the former case will alter the weight to ⅓, whereas in the latter it will change it to $^{5,000}/_{10,001}$. It is thus possible to predetermine the speed at which, and even the degree to which, correlations between behaviors can be altered.

Maes (1992) herself believes that her learning algorithm resembles operant conditioning: the creature learns that it has to perform a particular sequence of behaviors for some motivationally significant event to occur. But she also points out that the creature cannot learn completely new behaviors. It has to work with the "innate" patterns of behavior in its repertoire and learn how different sequences can help to achieve a particular result. In fact, Maes's model of learning has more in common with that proposed by Gardner and Gardner (1992) as an alternative to operant conditioning. Gardner and Gardner list various anomalies that have come to light in recent conditioning experiments. Key pecking in pigeons (which is assumed to be executed for a food reward) may be maintained even if food is delivered only when the pigeon *fails* to peck at the appropriate key. In a different experiment, pecking was observed to continue even when food was freely available. In still other experiments, fixed behavior patterns occurred that did not form part of the trained sequence and quite clearly hampered the creature's efforts in obtaining the reward.

Gardner and Gardner believe that all these instances of what the experimenters have called "misbehavior" point to the existence of innate behavior patterns that are evoked by particular environmental stimuli. Operant conditioning assumes that a standard reward may be used to reinforce and shape arbitrarily defined patterns of activity. The ethological view is that neither the form of fixed action patterns nor the innate releasing mechanism that connects them to particular sign stimuli can be changed. Gardner and Gardner point out that experimenters who use operant conditioning in many cases have unwittingly harnessed innate behaviors and natural sign stimuli to achieve their successes. Pecking in pigeons is natural prefeeding behavior that will be elicited by a moderately spaced delivery of food; it is not an arbitrary activity they learn to perform for the purpose of pressing levers. Clearly Maes's model so far has more in common with the ethological view proposed by Gardner and Gardner than with standard operant conditioning.

The Gardners' critique of operant conditioning does not stop there, however. They not only insist that behavior consists of predefined patterns of activity but also consider it a mistake to think of it as being executed for a reward. They reject all models that assign positive and negative values to behavioral consequences, requiring some internal mechanism that associates those consequences with particular acts, stores the associations, and weighs up the costs and benefits of each available choice at every moment in time: "The principle of response contingent reward and punishment is an intuitively attractive hypothesis that agrees with an everyday, common sense view of learning that has appealed to parents, teachers and animal trainers, moralists and psychologists for centuries. Nevertheless, for those who judge scientific merit on the basis of experimental operations rather than on the basis of intuition or common sense, a principle without any possibility of operational definition is also without any scientific merit" (Gardner and Gardner 1992, p. 406). What the Gardners are saying is that it is impossible to construct an experiment that would produce scientific evidence for a biological mechanism that would support the notion of operant conditioning. They claim that all experiments designed to reveal internal mechanisms involving contingent reward can also be explained by a far simpler alternative that does not involve the need for a behavioral consequence acting as a "cause" of the associated, prior behavior.

Maes's model contains specific goals or motivations attached to specific consummatory behaviors, in the way that Gardner and Gardner rule out for an explanatory model. However, her implementation makes clear that the creature does not perform the activities *in order to* achieve the goals or motivations. Motivations simply increase the activation level of their associated behavior modules, like action-specific energy in classical ethology. The achievement of a goal does not act as the sort of retrograde cause to which Gardner and Gardner object.

There is also no weighing up of costs and benefits at each moment in time. One behavior leads to another as a result of environmental contingencies and spreading activation within the network. Each consummatory behavior is already linked "innately" to its motivation, and the remaining links become established because the environmental contingencies resulting from one behavior create the perceptual conditions that trigger the next. Behavioral links are thus established on a principle of feed-forward rather than feedback, meeting one of Gardner and Gardner's main objections to operant conditioning. Motivations merely make certain paths through the behavior network more permeable than others, and thus increase the likelihood that certain sequences of behaviors will take place.

In a sense, Maes's model provides an existence proof of a mechanism that implements the response-contingent model to which Gardner and Gardner object. It is an improvement on other economic models, in that it links behaviors through perceptual conditions resulting from the creature's activity in a particular environment. However, Gardner and Gardner's criticism applies when it comes to experimental evidence for its natural kinds. "Motivations" are notional explanatory entities whose existence needs to be taken on trust. Ultimately they derive from economic categories like food, shelter, safety, and sex. Economic categories of this type cannot be imported into the underlying mechanism that subtends behavior. As will be seen in a later chapter, even the notion of action-specific energy to which I have compared Maes's motivations has now been abandoned in ethology. Teleological explanations cannot provide natural kinds for the mechanism of human and animal behavior.

9.4 Choice Mechanisms Involving Situated Activity

In Mataric's robot, low-level reflexes interact independently with the environment to produce the emergent behavior of wall following. It is possible to class the decision-making process as decentralized and dynamically reconfigurable, but this does not describe its most important features. Each of the robot's sensor-feedback loops is in continuous operation. The effect they have on its drive motors depends on contingencies in the environment. If it makes any sense to talk about a decision-making process that activates one reflex rather than another, that process clearly cannot be located inside the robot. To a large extent, it is the particular environment for which the robot was designed that serves as the choice mechanism between the various low-level reflexes.

This does not mean that the robot merely responds to its environment. Its own movement is as much responsible for the behavioral "choices" that result in wall following as is the structure of its environmental niche. If the robot did not move, the environmental contingencies that cause the low-level reflexes to come into play would not arise. At a higher level, it is only the particular structure of the robot's wall-following behavior, emerging from the interactions between its low-level reflexes and the environment, that allows it to make the behavioral "choices" involved in landmark navigation.

The agent does not choose, nor does the environment; the agent is constructed so that the right choices will emerge from the interactions between its movement and the environment. In the case of Mataric's robot, this choice mechanism was designed by trial and error. A set of hypotheses was framed concerning the combination of sensor-feedback loops that would result in the right movements at the right moments. These hypotheses were tested in a functioning robot, which was then fine-tuned in the particular environment until the correct decisions emerged. In a naturally evolved creature, if the right choices did not emerge at the right moments, the creature would not survive long enough to pass on copies of its genes.

It might be objected that Mataric's robot is a relatively simple creature. It has only one class of behaviors: those concerned with moving around in its particular world. A more realistic creature would have dozens of potentially conflicting classes of behavior. Perhaps the choices involved in wall following may be said to emerge from interactions between low-level reflexes and the environment, but surely the choices between "feeding" and "fighting," or "mating" and "parenting" are real choices that must be made by the creature itself if it is to survive?

The first answer to this objection is that there is as much conflict among STROLL, ALIGN, AVOID, and CORRECT as there is among "feeding," "parenting," "fighting," and "mating." The degree of conflict, if it can be defined at all, consists in the extent to which one activity rules out the other. Mataric's robot cannot both STROLL and AVOID at the same time. The explanation of why it does not try to do so must be sought in the particular implementation of the sensor-feedback loops and their fine-tuning to the environment.

The second answer to the objection concerns the status of behavioral classes. Part of the reason there appears to be a more genuine choice between fighting and parenting than between STROLL and AVOID is that the former seem to be more different in kind. However, it should always be remembered that such classes as feeding, parenting, fighting, and mating are descriptive categories that have no more compelling ontological status than any other way of carving up the totality of the creature's activities. We have seen already that a category like parenting may cause confusion rather than help in achieving a deeper understanding of the underlying mechanisms involved. One of the main arguments of this book has been that such intentionally defined descriptive categories are unlikely to pick out helpful natural kinds for behavior. The conviction that there is a genuine choice, which the creature itself has to make, between fighting and parenting, is largely due to the intentional flavor of these categories and the fact that we are convinced that *we* make such choices.

It is possible to view the totality of a creature's activities as one behavior—call it "gene transmission"—analogous to wall following in Mataric's robot. This overall behavior emerges from interactions between the creature's movement and its environment. One may say that the creature is "constructed" in such a way that the right choices are made under the appropriate circumstances, since otherwise its ancestors would not have been able to pass on copies of their genes. But it is not necessary to locate a choice mechanism inside the creature. From the point of view of the observer, who needs to carve up the totality of the behavior into descriptive categories in order to understand it, choices between various activities need to be made, but this does not imply that the creature itself makes those choices. Mataric's robot points to a way of carving up the behavior that allows for choices to emerge without the existence of a specific choice mechanism.

The emergence of choice in models like Mataric's robot is quite different from the emergence of choice in economic models, although, in both approaches, it is assumed that a biological creature will have been calibrated by natural selection so that the appropriate choices will emerge from moment to moment. In the economic model, choice emerges from an internal mechanism; it takes place inside the creature. The mechanism of emergence is invoked to explain the fact that the creature selects a particular category of behavior from a repertoire of behaviors defined in teleological terms. The notion of an input-output model implies that a choice mechanism must be located inside the creature, which implies categories of behavior that must be selected for a reason connected with the creature's "long-term goals." Models like Mataric's robot make no reference to purposes or goals. One may describe Mataric's robot as a wall-following robot, but it does not *intend* to follow walls; wall following is not a goal of the robot itself, not even an "emergent" goal. A model framed in terms of situated patterns of activity does not require hypothetical goals that need to be grounded by an appeal to fitness.

9.5 An Explanation of Behavior Selection That Does Not Invoke Goals, Plans, or Purposes

The traditional AI model sees choice as the outcome of a purposeful, goal-directed mechanism, implemented through classic programming devices acting on internal representations. The economic model views it as emerging from a neural network or dynamical system that has been calibrated by evolution to make the right choices in the proper circumstances. Both models incorporate a teleological perspective. The explanation of the mechanism of choice makes reference to a purpose. In the case of the traditional AI model, goals are represented inside the creature, and its behavior is directed toward the achievement of those goals. In the case of the economic model, purpose is introduced through the definition of behavioral categories. "Avoiding prey," "obtaining energy," "egg laying," and "fertilization" are purposeful behaviors. The choice among them may "emerge" through hill climbing, or constraint propagation, or as the result of the system's tendency to settle into a particular limit cycle, but the mechanism as a whole has already been characterized as purposeful by the model builder's choice of natural kinds.

One of the main arguments of this book has been that evolution does not sanction a teleological perspective. The internal representations of the traditional model and the intentional categories of the economic model cannot be grounded by appealing to fitness. Purpose imposes a folk psychological framework that leads to scientific deadlock. A scientific model of behavior must divest itself of references to purpose or goals and must discover natural kinds untainted by a teleological perspective.

This is not to deny that animals have complex internal mechanisms that require more intricate explanatory principles than the simple reflex arc. It is merely to deny that an explanation of the animal's behavior can be framed in terms of reified purposes. The conviction that complex behavior requires internally held goals and internally formulated plans of action is closely allied to the notion of an input-output model, which in turn derives from the conviction that a full explanation can be found "inside the creature's head."

Recent suggestions (van Gelder 1992; Beer 1995) that dynamical systems theory may provide a more appropriate conceptual framework for autonomous agents than computational theory have put forward an alternative to the traditional input-output model. In dynamical systems theory, creatures are assumed to be "dynamically coupled" to the environment. Input from the environment is seen not as directly altering the creature's internal state but as altering its parameters. This means there is no simple, reflex-like relation between specific inputs and specific outputs, but neither is there any need for an internal representation of the world.

The complex behavior of a dynamical system results from the fact that it obeys a "dynamical law" or "evolution equation." Behavior depends on the creature's perceptual and behavioral history. It may therefore be said to have a "memory" or "internal state," but this internal state does not necessarily represent anything, nor does its continuous evolution amount to computation. A change in the system's parameters, resulting from "perturbation" by the environment, changes the dynamical law of the system, not its representation of the world. A full explanation of the creature's behavior requires that the creature and its environment be conceptualized as a single, integrated system, in which each of the two dynamically coupled parts can alter what, prior to the coupling, were the parameters of the other part.

Dynamical systems theory is no more capable of providing us with the natural kinds of behavior than hill climbing or connectionism. What it does provide is a conceptual alternative to the Turing machine, showing that activity need not be cut up into logical or functional units derived from a formal task description. As Beer and van Gelder point out, one of the strongest arguments for the computational paradigm has always been that there was no alternative formalism that could account for the complexity of human and animal behavior. Dynamical systems theory provides such an alternative, and van Gelder makes out a strong case that Turing machines merely occupy a small region of the total space of possible systems that are conceivable in terms of this theory.

In order to conceptualize a creature's behavior in terms of dynamical systems theory, it is necessary to identify the key variables and parameters of the system and formalize their relation by a set of differential equations that together make up the system's dynamical law. Van Gelder and Beer each give a concrete example. Van Gelder's example is the traditional steam engine governor invented by James Watt; Beer's example concerns a model of a walking insect that was developed by his department. In both cases the mechanical or neural links that implement the behavior are relatively easy to grasp and relate to the behavior itself. The differential equations needed to describe the behavior of the arms on Watt's governor are in fact quite complex, but we can understand how the mechanism works by simply looking at it. Similarly, the coordination of legs and feet in a walking insect may involve all sorts of neural complexities, but the basic principle is easy to grasp. However, dynamical systems theory makes it possible to conceive of creatures with internal mechanisms of far greater complexity—including, perhaps, hormonal and neural mechanisms that might be classed as motivational or goal directed—without requiring the introduction of goals, plans, or reified "motivations" into the mechanism itself.

Such a creature "solves" Brooks's three problems of behavioral choice, but the explanation of how it does so need not involve a choice mechanism located inside the creature. As Nagel (1961) pointed out, a teleological explanation may be completely recast as an explanation that conceptualizes the creature as a dynamical system. The behavior active at any particular moment is appropriate to the creature's external and internal circumstances because the creature is dynamically coupled to its environment and its behavior conforms at all times to its evolution equation. Natural selection accounts for the coupling and the nature of the equation. It has seen to it that the creature does not switch wildly and ineffectually between different behaviors and that its overall behavior conforms to its "long-term goals." But of course the creature does not *have* any long-term goals. Nor do we need to invoke any to frame an explanation of its behavior. All that is required is an identification of the key parameters and variables and a formulation of the dynamical law that relates them in a principled way.

Dynamical systems theory itself does not provide a means of identifying the key parameters and variables. Van Gelder's and Beer's examples use entities of quite different conceptual types: angles, rotational velocities, and forces in one case, motor outputs in the other. I have indicated in my analysis of Mataric's robot what I believe to be the most promising natural kinds for an explanation of human and animal behavior. Situated patterns of activity that emerge from the creature's low-level interactions with its environment provide behavior-dependent variables and parameters for higher-level activities of increasing complexity. Such natural kinds can be grounded through history of use, if they are derived from careful observation in the field and prove capable of being modeled in a functioning robot. The burden of explanation shifts from formal task description and the generative structures implied by competence theories to the nature of the explanatory entities themselves and their interdependencies and dynamic coupling with the environment.

Chapter 10

A New Type of Model

My analysis in the previous three chapters of Mataric's robot and related work with autonomous agents points to the need for a new conception of models in scientific explanations of human and animal
behavior. In chapter 5, I pointed out that computational models are
unable to perform the role that machine-based models have historically performed in Western science. Analogies are in the first instance
holistic. Drawing an analogy requires no explicit understanding of
what underlies or causes the similarities; it merely requires an intuitive
leap in the dark proposing that similarities exist. (I shall have more to
say in chapter 16 about the mechanisms involved in intuitive leaps of
this kind.) The nature of the similarities is to a large extent established
by the very act of drawing the analogy. Analogies thus help to impose
a classificatory scheme. Once a holistic parallel has been posited, the
structure and causal relations of the model can be used to delineate the
structure and causal relations of the *explicandum*. The act of drawing
an analogy defines a new way of looking at things, bringing into focus
a new set of explanatory kinds. This accounts for much of the explanatory force of successful analogical models. It is the fact that the structural and causal relations are not clear from the start but become more
and more apparent as the analogy sinks in, that makes analogical models so fruitful.

Deliberately designed computational models are not productive in
this way. They require clearly defined parameters that delineate the
similarities between the model and the *explicandum* right from the start.
The model does not help to define the parameters, and it has no power
to reveal previously unsuspected causal and structural relations. These
need to have been defined before the model is ever built, since it is
built in terms of those parameters in an attempt to prove that certain
formally specified relations exist in the *explicandum* just as they do in
the model.

Models used as analogies tend to be productive of explanatory
kinds; deliberately designed models are not. They require that the

natural kinds be picked out and supported by some explanatory framework beyond the model itself. Functional decomposition, computational theory, and Darwin's theory of natural selection have traditionally been called upon to perform that role for the explanatory entities in computer-based models of the mind or brain. In chapters 3, 5, and 6, I examined the pitfalls of that approach—in particular, that internal representations derived from formal task descriptions cannot be "grounded" through natural selection and that hierarchical reductionism offers no hope of producing legitimate explanatory kinds for a psychological explanation "grounded" by natural selection. In the previous three chapters, I have tried to show that it *is* possible to tie situated patterns of activity into evolutionary theory through history of use.

Another question raised by deliberately designed models is what such models are meant to be models of. Are they intended as models of the creature's brain, or of some intermediate level that might be called its "mind," or are they merely abstract models of the interdependencies between formally defined classes of perceptual and behavioral events? Is the fact that the mechanism exhibits activity that mimics the behavior of the natural organism to be taken as evidence that its mechanism is structurally or generatively similar to the neural mechanism that subtends the naturally occurring behavior? Or should it be seen as no more than a simulation of the behavior itself? If the latter, should successful simulation be taken as evidence of anything inside the creature at all?

The answers to these questions have often been fudged by traditional AI. In defining the basic principles of his universal machine, Turing did not intend to model a mathematician's thought processes. His aim was to formalize the *tasks* involved in mathematical proof, just as the pioneers of mass production had formalized the tasks involved in manufacturing. It would not have occurred to the industrial psychologists who pioneered automation to claim that they were simulating the behavior of craftsmen, since they knew that the products they manufactured by their formal methods needed to be specially designed to fit the process.

In the same way, Turing was initially very much aware that a mathematician's mind does not construct proofs by running formal task descriptions. How, in fact, it does construct proofs seemed as much of a mystery to him as it remains to us (Hodges 1983). However, Turing himself came to believe that a computer-based simulation, once it became indistinguishable from the real thing, must be accepted as the real thing. His famous test for intelligence (Turing 1950) is based on a model of human dialogue that I shall question later in this book. It was conducted over a teletype and took no account of pragmatics. Convincing responses to questions involving logical and aesthetic judgment were considered sufficient evidence that the computational model based on formal task descriptions was an intelligent machine.

The formal task description had been imported into the creature's head. Turing's paper, among others (McCulloch and Pitts 1943; Minsky 1972; Shannon and McCarthy 1956), encouraged researchers in AI to see computation as an explanation of the underlying mechanism, not just as a method of formalizing its external manifestations or a technique for replicating those manifestations. To linguists, philosophers, and psychologists, the new formalism, with its unprecedented possibilities of implementation, appeared to offer a way out of the behaviorist straitjacket (Boden 1972; Chomsky 1957; Dennett 1969; Miller, Galanter, and Pribram 1960). Computation provided unprecedented power to model structure and process. For the first time, it allowed sensors and actuators to be linked in complex, temporally extended ways. The wealth of logical structure that was suddenly put at the disposal of researchers in AI seduced them into concentrating on computational formalisms rather than on the resulting behavior. Perception and activity were considered less important than the "intelligence module" in between. The inputs and outputs to the latter were conceptualized as internal representations, on the assumption that perceptual and motor modules would take care of the "interfaces" with the world, and transform its blooming and buzzing confusion into objects, properties, and events that could be handled by a mechanism based on formal task description.

Cognitive science saw this internal mechanism as an effective challenge to behaviorist prohibitions and simplifications. It accepted Turing's (1950) claim that computation in due course would provide a replicate of intelligence and that formal task description therefore provided a means of modeling the mind. Neither theoretical obstacles like the combinatorial explosion and the frame problem, nor the practical difficulties of producing systems that exhibited the flexibility of true intelligence, caused cognitive scientists to doubt this new way of modeling the mind. Such problems tended to have the opposite effect. Instead of questioning the basic assumptions underlying its claims to model building, AI developed more and more formal methods and descriptions. To counter accusations that its systems were merely ad hoc simulations of limited aspects of behavior under carefully controlled conditions, it pointed to competence theories, formal systems of internal representation, and Marr's insistence on a computational theory that underpins algorithmic and implementational solutions.

In order to defend the legitimacy of this way of model building, the models themselves had to become more and more abstract and divorced from details of "performance." As Lakoff (1980) remarked about Chomsky's continuing struggle to uphold his syntax module, the formal model can be maintained only by progressively refining its explanatory domain and increasingly distancing its generative output from the behavioral phenomena it was originally meant to explain.

10.2 *Models of Situated Activity*

The alternative view of model building I have begun to sketch out accepts the fact that no machine is ever likely to provide an adequate explanatory analogy for the human brain or mind. Machines will not produce "for free" the natural kinds of a psychological explanation. "Real" machines are too simple and limited in their functions, and the "virtual" machines of computer science merely import formal redescriptions of the surface phenomena into the explanatory model. The alternative view of model building accepts that computer-based models are purpose-built to mimic human or animal behavior and that they can only be models *of* behavior rather than models of brains or minds. This means that the natural kinds of such models need to be behavioral entities of some description or other and that they will have to come from (and derive their legitimacy from) a different source than the model itself.

My discussion of Mataric's robot introduced a new way of thinking about activity. Research with autonomous agents provides a principled framework for drawing a clear distinction between activity and movement. The difference does not lie in some mysterious intentional ingredient and does not require that the agent's behavior be directed toward some goal. It is simply due to the fact that a recognizable temporal structure emerges from the interactions of a number of low-level reflexes with a particular environment to which the reflexes are adapted. The fundamental principle involved is that of interactive emergence. It is important to stress again that the natural kinds of this type of model come into existence only as a result of the creature's situated activity. Their temporal structure cannot be expressed as a prespecified sequence of movements. They are not entities that can be reduced to events inside the creature's head, and they are not defined by classifying its environment. Interactive emergence provides a means of constructing models of behavioral interdependencies that become manifest only through the situated activity of an autonomous creature.

Such patterns of activity can result in dynamic features with temporal extent that correspond only indirectly to "features" in the world. They owe their characteristics to the interactions between the structure of the low-level activity and the nature of the creature's environment. In a naturally evolved creature, their reliable occurrence would tend to encourage the evolution of sensors capable of monitoring them, thus providing "information" for higher levels of activity. This type of configuration confers the status of a natural kind on the lower levels of activity, since it establishes a history of use for that activity in the creature's evolutionary past. Darwin's theory of natural selection can thus be harnessed to ground such explanatory entities.

Two components of an alternative scientific explanation are thus in place. We have the possibility in principle of explaining complex structured behavior at increasing levels of abstraction in terms of interactive emergence, and we have a principled means of grounding such behavior through a historical explanation using natural selection. However, the fact that natural selection might in principle be used to naturalize explanatory entities conceived in this way does not ensure that such entities are actually found in nature. The natural kinds for this type of model will have to come from a different source. What is required is an empirical discipline with the observational tools and descriptive framework to carve up naturally occurring behavior in a way that corresponds to the modeling capabilities of situated robotics. The science of ethology has recently been overshadowed by the explanatory successes of behavioral ecology. I have explained why these successes are unlikely to contribute to an explanation of the underlying mechanisms. The two disciplines are sometimes confused, but they are based on quite different approaches to the study of animal behavior, and properly understood, their aims are also different. In the next four chapters I shall attempt to identify the strengths and weaknesses of ethology and show how it accords with an explanation of animal behavior in terms of situated activity and interactive emergence.

Behavioral ecology treats development as a black box, in the same way that it treats the underlying mechanisms of the behavioral classes it identifies. As Maynard Smith (1995) puts it, "We can treat development as a black box because, if acquired characters are not inherited, novelty must start with mutation. To be sure, mutations, to be selected, must influence development, but how they do so hardly matters" (p. 30). An explanation of *human* behavior, however, if it is to be grounded by natural selection, cannot afford to ignore development in this way. As I shall argue in chapters 15 to 17, an evolutionary account of the emergence of intentionality requires that we open up Maynard Smith's black box. This does not mean that I shall try to reintroduce Lamarkian inheritance of acquired characteristics. I shall claim only that most of the species-typical activity patterns of newborn infants are adapted *for* development rather than for ultimate use by the mature individual, and therefore they can be identified and understood only by studying in detail how adult behavior emerges in a human context.

Most, if not all, of the behavioral classes that a behavioral ecologist might identify from studying adult human behavior are indelibly tainted by culture. It can no longer be said of humans that novelty is introduced only through mutation. On the other hand, it would be unrealistic (and explanatorily self-defeating) to deny that our behavior contains an important component that is shaped by natural selection. The natural environment of the human infant is a cultural environment consisting of man-made artifacts and adults who interpret their own and other people's behavior in intentional terms. An understanding of the way that our species-typical activity patterns may be grounded through natural selection requires that we take into account the exigencies of this environment, and this in turn makes it plain that most of our species-typical activity patterns are uniquely adapted to bootstrap the infant into an intentional world. How mutations influence development thus becomes of crucial importance to understanding what mutations are selected, and both are essential to an understanding of adult behavior.

That is why top-down analysis, in the style of either classical AI or behavioral ecology, cannot reveal the underlying mechanisms. Classical AI takes our intentional view of our own behavior and the symbols we use to describe it at face value and imports them into the explanatory mechanism. Behavioral ecology assumes that classes of behavior that can be linked directly to genetic factors may be isolated through statistical analyses of the behavior of adult human beings, in the same way that it has done for classes of animal behavior. My contention will be that only a historical explanation in terms of evolution and development can isolate the natural kinds that will give us an insight into the underlying mechanisms.

This type of explanation depends on identifying specific instances rather than formulating causal laws or generative rules. Fruitful hypotheses are most likely to come from observation of actual behavior in its natural surroundings, supplemented by controlled experiments conducted in the same natural environment, and comparisons with the behavior of related species. Artificial models serve to confirm hypotheses of how such behavior emerges, and they may serve to bring out family resemblances between various types of behavioral dependency. The resulting models can thus be seen as "existence proofs."

Each contributes to delineating further the space of possibilities. It is only by accumulating such natural kinds of behavior that the space of possibilities can be described. This alternative conception has always been latent in the notion of a computational model, but it has been obscured by precomputational uses of mechanical models in scientific explanation and by the imposition of a Cartesian framework that encourages explanations in terms of mechanisms inside the creature's head.

Chapter 11

Ethology: The Basic Concepts and "Orienting Attitudes"

11.1 Ethology and Autonomous Agent Research

Texts on ethology are often quoted in the literature of autonomous agent research. There is a feeling that the basic interests and approaches of the two disciplines coincide, although their ultimate aims may be quite different. It is possible to flag some of these underlying affinities without recourse to technical terms.

Ethologists hold that behavior should be studied in the creature's natural environment, not under laboratory conditions designed to elicit the desired responses. In autonomous agent research, there is a corresponding stress on producing robots that will operate in "natural environments," meaning, in this case, that the operational environment must not be altered to suit the robot's limitations. Both disciplines share an awareness of the importance of context, and of the way a creature interacts with its surroundings, and the role those surroundings can play in shaping the structure of its behavior. Finally both disciplines share an understanding that the overall behavior of a creature may be the result of the interplay of various activities, each operating independently, rather than of a central controlling mechanism. This leads, in autonomous agent research, to the principle of decomposition by activity, and, in ethology, to an emphasis on deriving explanatory concepts from the study of actual behavior patterns rather than imposing some overall theoretical framework on the diversity of behavior.

Hinde (1982) sums up what he calls the "orienting attitudes" of ethology as follows:

1. Start all analysis from a secure base of description.
2. View behavior in the context of the environment to which it has been adapted.
3. Analyze in great detail one type of behavior in one situation in one species and then compare with other behaviors, situations, and species.

As will become clear in the next three chapters, I believe that it is these orienting attitudes that constitute the most important legacy of the early work in ethology rather than the much-debated theoretical notions of fixed action pattern, sign stimulus, action-specific energy, and hierarchical organization introduced by Lorenz and Tinbergen. However, those orienting attitudes were able to establish themselves only because the concepts in question made it possible to think in a radically new way, and for that reason, if for no other, their strengths and weaknesses should be examined.

11.2 Lorenz's Compromise between Vitalistic and Mechanistic Explanations of Behavior

Ethology may be said to have started with von Uexkull (1934), but it was Lorenz (1935, 1937, 1939) who introduced the key concepts with which it is usually associated and which provided the framework for systematic description and analysis. These are the fixed action pattern (FAP) with its associated innate releasing mechanism (IRM), triggered by a specific sign stimulus and the action-specific energy that drives it.

FAPs are not simple reflexes or reflex chains. They differ from the former in that they may be complex, temporally extended patterns of activity, and they differ from the latter in that "if the excitation coordinated to an instinctive action is so slight that its full discharge, which alone has survival value for the species, cannot develop, the movement . . . occurs in a meaningless, incomplete form. There is every conceivable transition from the slightest incipient actions, termed 'intention movements,' as they betray the direction of an impending action, to the full, effective process" (Lorenz 1939, p. 245). In other words, if either the sign stimulus or the action-specific energy associated with an FAP is too weak, the FAP will not run its full course. Its initial components will appear in the same sequence as they appear in the full pattern, but the final components will be left out. This empirical observation constitutes an argument against the explanation of the activity pattern as a chain reflex, where the consequences of each component would provide the trigger for the succeeding component, causing the behavior to run to completion once it had begun.

An FAP is thus a temporally extended pattern of activity that can be seen as a behavioral unit, since it has "meaning" in survival terms only when it is performed in its entirety. It is fixed in the sense that given a sufficiently strong sign stimulus and action-specific energy for it to be performed in full, its components will always appear in the same sequence, and environmental contingencies will not affect that sequence. From the early papers it appears that Lorenz initially hoped that FAPs could be shown to be totally independent of environmental stimuli—in other words, that their "taxis," as well as the order of their components, was entirely determined by some internal mechanism, which might be equated with the more recent notion of a central pattern generator. However, even in the simplest FAPs like the egg-retrieval behavior of the mother goose (Lorenz and Tinbergen 1938), adjustments to the course of the behavior in response to environmental contingencies soon became apparent, and in order to accommodate these, the behavior was split into a motor component and an orienting component, operating simultaneously.

The final element in Lorenz's definition of an FAP is the assumption that it is innate. Lorenz believed that it was possible to draw a sharp distinction, conceptually as well as empirically, between behavior that is innate and behavior that is learned. Innate behavior, by Lorenz's definition, is not merely species typical. It corresponds in a fixed, unalterable way to the genetic blueprint that transmits it from one generation to the next. Innate behavior cannot be affected by environmental conditions during the creature's maturation; it will always appear in exactly the same form. According to Lorenz, it is possible to distinguish innate behavior from learned behavior by careful observation. Apart from the rigidity of the former and the greater plasticity of the latter, innate behavior tends to be triggered by simple, unambiguous stimuli that act like signs for the condition or object whose presence they signal, while learned behavior is initiated and guided by complex, "holistic" images:

> Let us suppose that two or more instinctive actions must be performed with the same object to secure their survival value. This unity in dealing with the object can be safeguarded in two ways. First, the releaser may be conceived objectively and appear identical in all of the subject's functional cycles. Secondly, the relatedness of different instinctive activities may be centered in the object, in which case the object has no subjective unity in the subject's world.
>
> The functional design of innate behavior patterns localizes the biologically necessary element of unity in the stimulus-emitting object, rather than in the acting subject. (Lorenz 1935, p. 87)

Lorenz's discovery that the "unity" of various elements of a creature's behavior in relation to a specific event or object may be explained with reference to the stimulus emitter rather than some form of internal representation has already been discussed in chapters 3 and 9. It was an important discovery, and it constitutes one of the main attractions of ethology to autonomous agent research. What is less apparent is why

Lorenz believed that only innate, as opposed to learned, behavior could be explained in this way. In fact, the rigidity of his distinction, and his insistence that FAPs must be innate, have proved a major stumbling block to a more general acceptance of ethology. This aspect of Lorenz's thinking is no longer taken very seriously by contemporary ethologists, but I believe it rewards examination.

Lorenz repeatedly expressed an intellectual debt to William McDougall. Like McDougall, Lorenz was intent on constructing a scientific theory of behavior that would provide an alternative to the mechanistic and reductionist tenets of behaviorism. Again like McDougall, he was struck by the appearance of purpose in human and animal behavior and felt that an adequate scientific theory should be able to account for this. McDougall had accepted that animal, as well as human, behavior really was purposeful. In his opinion, a satisfactory explanation needed to incorporate some principled notion of purpose. But as Boden (1972) points out, purposive explanations, unlike mechanistic ones, require a bottom stop. Certain actions must qualify as ends in themselves rather than be performed for the sake of further ends. McDougall's way of confronting this issue was to designate specific natural goals or instincts as basic units of theoretical analysis. The organism has these goals "naturally." They are part of its genetic inheritance. To the question, "Why does the animal seek this goal," the simple answer is: "Because it is in its nature to do so."

> For any one species the kinds of goals sought are characteristic and specific, and all members of the species seek those goals independently of example and of previous experience of attainment of them. (McDougall 1936, p. 458)

> Repeated observation of animals of the same species in similar situations enables us to define the goal. (Ibid., p. 416)

Lorenz's debt to these ideas will be obvious. They also make it clear why he clung so tenaciously, and in the face of much criticism, to the condition of innateness for FAPs. It is innateness that legitimizes certain goals in McDougall's scheme as the fundamental units of theoretical analysis. Innateness becomes a way of grounding purpose and goal directedness. In Lorenz's framework the FAP itself is turned into the end in itself. He insisted again and again that an FAP is not directed toward any goal; rather, *it* constitutes the end toward which the appetitive behavior that precedes it is directed. FAPs are the bottom stop of Lorenz's theory.

It has become difficult to understand properly the importance of such questions to Lorenz, because we approach the problem from a radically different perspective. Another, closely related and equally contentious, notion is that of action-specific energy. Again, it would seem that Lorenz inherited this idea from McDougall, who postulated a form of psychic or "hormic" energy to provide the motive power for his "instincts." The origin of this idea lies in the subjective impression that purposive activity is "caused" by a desire to attain some goal. "Does mental activity involve some form or forms of energy other than those recognized by the physical sciences?" McDougall (1932) asked. "In view of the purposive nature of human activity, the positive answer to this question seems inevitable. We must postulate some energy which conforms to laws not wholly identical with the laws of energy stated by the physical sciences.... We may call it hormic energy" (p. 51).

As Boden (1972) points out, the reason that "hormic" energy conformed to laws not wholly identical with the laws of the physical sciences was that it was assumed to act as a causal link between the desire-for-a-goal and the action-toward-a-goal: "The energy that activates the instinctive abilities is energy *towards;* directed energy; energy directed to a goal. Here we confront a very obscure problem; one which at present we cannot solve" (McDougall 1932, p. 50). Lorenz's ingenious solution to McDougall's problem was to split it into two components. He took over McDougall's notion of action-specific energy but did not require it to do all the work. Action-specific energy drives or pushes the creature to engage in a particular type of appetitive behavior. This behavior has evolved for the purpose of bringing the creature face to face with the appropriate sign stimulus that will trigger the IRM to release the FAP, which discharges the action-specific energy. The appetitive behavior that leads up to the release of the IRM is often described as "seeking out" or "searching for" the appropriate sign stimulus, but it is the activity that is assumed to be directed toward this goal, not the energy that drives it.

By separating out the notion of action-specific energy from goal directedness, Lorenz made it possible to conceptualize the energy as something that merely drives or pushes. It is thus no longer a matter of the energy's striving toward a goal; it is more a matter of the animal's being animated by a particular type of energy to engage in a particular type of activity that will tend to bring it face to face with the sign stimulus required to release the FAP, which constitutes its natural goal. This makes the energy involved seem far less mysterious. To the minds of the early ethologists, it closely resembled the notion of potential energy used in the physical sciences. Lorenz devised his famous cistern model to show that there was nothing mystical or unscientific about action-specific energy: it could be conceptualized as a kind of fluid that builds up pressure behind the IRM until the sign stimulus releases it. In fact, as will be discussed in the next chapter, the notion of action-specific energy has been thoroughly discredited. It has also become rather difficult to understand the need for it. We are far less worried by questions of "striving" and "spontaneity," and no longer believe that these folk psychological notions require causal correlatives in a scientific explanation of behavior. I have examined Lorenz's struggle with McDougall's problem in some detail because I believe it led to one of the most important contributions of ethology.

11.3 A Comparison of Lorenz's Solution with Explanations Proposed by Cybernetics and AI

To a large extent, the explanation of goal directedness, in Lorenz's solution, has been shifted from notions of purpose, energy, or drive onto the morphology of the creature's activity and its dependence on a particular ecological niche. Action-specific energy induces the creature to engage in appetitive behavior, which leads it to the sign stimulus that triggers the FAP, resulting in a discharge of that action-specific energy. The appetitive behavior is not rigid, like an FAP; it is sensitive to environmental contingencies. But it is activity of a type that will tend to bring the creature face to face with the appropriate sign stimulus, and the reason it will tend to do this is that it was selected for that effect. Its structure and direction may be seen as emergent phenomena, in the sense I described with reference to Mataric's robot. Although ethologists do not tend to draw this conclusion, it could be argued that there is no longer any need for a directive mechanism within the creature to explain its arrival at the goal.

The notion of the sign stimulus's releasing the IRM also removes the need for a generalized, task-oriented description of the goal. It is replaced by a simple lock-and-key mechanism that can be grounded through natural selection without recourse to correspondence theories. The creature does not go around comparing an internal representation of its goal with the sensory inputs it gets from the various objects it encounters. It does not have any sense of the remaining distance, or the alternative routes, to its stopping point. It merely stumbles about until it hits the right sign stimulus, and the reason its way of stumbling about tends to be successful is that it was selected for precisely this effect by natural selection.

The alternative, cybernetics-inspired solution to McDougall's problem was spelled out in detail by Boden (1972). Again, the notion of energy is separated from the explanation of goal directedness: "The notion of energy is related to the concept of instinct in that instincts, being action tendencies, mark certain changes in the animal's own body and in its relations with the material environment, and energy is required for any change to take place in the material world. But this is the familiar energy of the physical world, whether it be drawn from the impact of one inanimate mass upon another or from the phosphates and other molecules within a living body" (Boden 1972, pp. 287–288). There is nothing obscure about these forms of energy, and they can play no part in the explanation of purpose. The goal directedness of the instinct is explained by thinking of it "as a plan for achieving a particular goal, a plan in the service of which other—cognitive or executive—plans could be brought into play" (Boden 1972, p. 287). This explanation drew on the TOTE (Test-Operate-Test-Exit) model proposed by Miller, Galanter, and Pribram (1960), which in turn was based on the cybernetic concept of negative feedback. Purposive activity has ceased to be a "striving toward" a goal, which requires explanation in terms of energy-toward-a-goal. It has become a matter of the appropriate plans being called at the appropriate junctures by a higher-level plan to direct activity fueled by metabolically produced energy.

At first glance there might not seem to be much difference between the two solutions, since they basically agree on the need to divorce the explanation of goal directedness from its associations with energy. In Boden's solution, however, the burden of explanation is placed squarely on the controlling mechanism inside the creature and on a single explanatory device. Miller, Galanter, and Pribram's plans are hierarchies of control loops that at every level take the standard form of a TOTE unit. Negative feedback is used to explain the entire gamut of human and animal behavior, replacing the reflex arc as the standard unit of explanation: "The reflex is not the unit we should use as the element of behavior: the unit should be the feedback loop itself" (Miller, Galanter, and Pribram 1960, p. 27). Miller, Galanter, and Pribram resist any suggestion that the structure of a creature's behavior might be due to anything other than a plan. In a passage quoted by Hinde and Stevenson (1970) as well as Boden (1972), they note that occasionally a sequence of responses may appear to be integrated by an appropriate succession of environmental stimuli rather than an internal plan: "It is almost as if the Plan were not in the organism alone, but in the total constellation of organism and environment together. How far one is willing to extend the concept of a Plan beyond the boundaries of an organism seems to be a matter of metaphysical predilections. We shall try to confine our use of the term to Plans that either are, have been, or could be known to the organism, so that we shall not speak of concatenated behavior as part of a Plan even when it is highly adaptive" (Miller, Galanter, and Pribram 1960, p. 78). Clearly the integrity of the plan has to be preserved at all costs. Anomalies may need to be accounted for by extending the notion of hierarchical control to environmental contingencies as well, but if that threatens to unbalance the overall explanatory scheme, they are best left outside the framework of explanation altogether.

Hinde and Stevenson (1970), demonstrating a scrupulous adherence to the "orienting attitudes" of ethology, show that Miller, Galanter, and Pribram's TOTE loop cannot possibly account for the diversity of ways in which the adaptive consequences of creatures' actions are related to the actions themselves. Some behavior is triggered by, but not in any way guided by, the appearance and location of its goals. (The final strike behavior in the catching of prey in a large variety of animals clearly does not depend on negative feedback.) Other types of behavior result in an alteration of the initial stimulus, which in turn alters the behavior but in a way that cannot be described as negative feedback. (Woodlice tend to move more slowly as humidity increases, resulting in a concentration of these creatures in damp regions. However, it cannot be said that their behavior is internally controlled or centrally planned to achieve that goal. It is an emergent phenomenon, resulting from a direct response of the motor centers to environmental conditions.) Eating and drinking behavior in most animals is stopped not by any change in the environmental stimulus that drives the behavior but by new, "consummatory" stimuli that reduce the response to the eliciting stimulus even though it may still be present. Finally, execution of a particular piece of behavior may come to an end because some other type of behavior intervenes, not because the goal of the original behavior has been achieved.

In an earlier paper, Hinde (1957) pointed out how difficult it is to frame a satisfactory definition of goal, even if it is merely taken in the sense of "stopping condition." Such a definition assumes, he reminds us, that it is possible to distinguish the consequences of an act that contribute to its cessation from those that do not, and it is possible to distinguish, among all the different factors that may contribute to its cessation, those that should be classed as its goal from those which merely inhibit the act.

Hinde examines the examples of goals provided by Kortlandt (1955), whose paper he is discussing, and concludes:

> Basically, his method is to look for the other events correlated with the cessation of an activity, and then to designate one of these, chosen apparently arbitrarily, as the goal. He therefore groups "owning a nest," "alleviating hunger pangs" and "quiv-

ering" as goals, although cessation of the behavior is correlated in the first case with attaining a new situation not present before the behaviour was elicited, in the second, perhaps, with the removal of some of the eliciting factors, and in the third with nothing at all. Such a procedure cannot assist causal analysis. The mechanisms underlying behaviour are diverse, and a given pattern of behaviour may be brought to an end in many different ways. Nothing is gained by grouping all "causes of endings" under one heading. (Hinde 1957, pp. 117–118)

Hinde therefore rejects the use of goals as explanatory entities, even in the pared-down, cybernetic sense of goal as "stopping condition." The basic TOTE unit in Miller, Galanter, and Pribram's explanatory scheme is shown to be inadequate to the task of formalizing the different ways in which environmental factors may orient and terminate naturally occurring activity. Hinde and Stevenson's (1970) analysis of the activities they cite provides an object lesson in the ethological approach. Explanations are formulated to fit the observed patterns of behavior in relation to their natural environment, not in accordance with a formal theory of behavioral control based on a standard unit of explanation. This makes the activity pattern itself an important element in the explanatory hypothesis. Without reference to its detailed structure and the way that structure relates to the structure of the creature's ecological niche, the explanatory hypothesis cannot be framed.

In order to clarify further the differences between this approach and that of cybernetics, it may be useful to contrast Hinde and Stevenson's categorization of behavior with the classification provided by Rosenblueth, Wiener, and Bigelow (1943). This is a seminal paper in cybernetics and control theory. The authors are quite clear about their methodology and aims: "This essay has two goals. The first is to define the behaviouristic study of natural events and to classify behavior. The second is to stress the importance of the concept of purpose" (Rosenblueth, Wiener, and Bigelow 1943, p. 18). They set up an open-ended taxonomic hierarchy that is meant to serve as a comprehensive explanatory framework for all natural forms of behavior. At the very top of this hierarchy, they place a dichotomy between active behavior—behavior in which "the object is the source of the output energy involved"—and passive behavior—in which "all the energy in the output can be traced to the immediate input." Only active behavior is of interest in the present context. At the next level down, this category is subdivided into purposeless and purposeful behavior, defined in terms of goal directedness. Purposeful behavior is then split into feedback controlled (teleological) and nonfeedback controlled. Below this level, the subdivisions correspond to degrees of predictive power: whether the creature is able to take into account merely the location of its goal, or its direction and speed as well, or perhaps even its rate of acceleration, allowing it to execute adjustments of increasing mathematical complexity to its movements.

Rosenblueth, Wiener, and Bigelow's taxonomy is the taxonomy of engineering. It relies on a conceptualization of behavior in terms of an input-output model. The structure of the environment plays no part in the classification. It might be objected that the definitions of the various classes of behavior make explicit reference to the behavioral characteristics of a goal and that this clearly forms a part of the creature's environment, but the characteristics in question are derived from the abstractions of control theory, not from any attempt to understand the natural environment. There is no principled basis for dividing the world into creatures capable of constant movement and creatures capable of uniform acceleration, since it seems unlikely that natural selection would have resulted in such a clear-cut taxonomy.

Rosenblueth, Wiener, and Bigelow are not interested in the diverse and unpredictable contingencies of a natural environment. Environmental factors intrude into their classificatory scheme only as mathematical abstractions. The structure of activity is defined in terms of mathematical formulas, and it is assumed that the internal mechanism of the creature performs calculations corresponding to these formulas to produce the appropriate output from a given input, though the authors are keen to avoid references to the "intrinsic organization of the entity studied," which they say is the domain of the "alternative, functional method of study."

It is possible, of course, to describe the behavior of a cat pouncing on a mouse as "second-order predictive, feedback-driven, purposeful, active behavior" without implying that control of the behavior is implemented in the cat as an engineer would implement it from such a description. However, in that case the taxonomy would appear to have little explanatory purpose. Rosenblueth, Wiener, and Bigelow explicitly state that their aim is a classification of natural behavior, and not a prescriptive hierarchy for engineers.

So let us examine one of the activity patterns cited by Hinde and Stevenson (1970) in terms of the classification proposed by Rosenblueth, Wiener, and Bigelow. The behavior of woodlice that congregate in damp places would certainly have to be described as active and purposeful from their point of view, since purposeless behavior is characterized as random. With respect to damp places, the behavior of woodlice is not random; it slows down as the dampness increases. There is a principled explanatory relation between the behavior of woodlice and certain regions of the environment. Surprisingly enough, it must also be classed as feedback controlled, because the alternative is behavior "in which there are no signals from the goal that modify the activity of the object *in the course of the behavior.*" Since the behavior has been classed as purposeful, it must, by Rosenblueth, Wiener, and Bigelow's definition, necessarily have a goal, and that goal can only be the damp region in which the woodlouse's activity will eventually come to a stop. And clearly there are signals from this damp region that modify the woodlouse's activity while it is going on.

We already know that the classification we have just arrived at does not correspond to the facts. So what exactly has gone wrong? One side of the problem is that Rosenblueth, Wiener, and Bigelow have been too eager to claim all activity that does not appear to be random as purposeful. The other side is that purposeful activity has been equated with goal-directed activity. As a result, behavior with a recognizable tendency or structure is naturally assumed to be explicable in terms of goals. And if, in addition, the behavior is observed to change as it approaches this goal, rather than proceeding blindly like the strike behavior of the adder, then it must also be controlled by negative feedback from that goal.

Clearly a classificatory scheme based on abstract principles cannot capture the interactive complexities of natural behavior. The apparent purposiveness of the moisture-seeking woodlouse is an emergent phenomenon whose explanation is not helped by the notion of purpose and definitely does not require that of a goal, even though the behavior in question was almost certainly selected for its efficacy in depositing woodlice in regions where they would avoid the risk of drying out. An evolutionary story may be told in which damp regions figure as some sort of end of the activity, and the survival value of the behavior is described in terms of its efficacy to achieve that end. However, as we saw in chapter 6, it is safer to avoid the equation of goals with survival value in evolutionary explanations. The woodlouse's behavior was not *designed* to achieve that end; it emerged and proved advantageous— and we can see that the reason it proved advantageous is that it prevents woodlice from drying out. In order to understand this type of behavior, it is necessary to forget about goals and purposes and concentrate on the activity patterns themselves.

11.4 Intraspecies and Cross-Species Comparisons

Tinbergen (1951) discusses the nest-building behavior of the sparrowhawk and the long-tailed tit. Like most other birds, these species build their nests in a sitting position, depositing the material around them and shaping the cup by frequent scraping with their legs. But the sparrow-hawk works twigs into the nest wall by peculiar quivering movements, which are continued until the twig gets stuck, while the long-tailed tit builds its nest out of moss. Occasionally it will collect a beakful of spiders' webs, which it weaves over the rim of the nest cup, binding the moss together.

The quivering movements of the sparrow-hawk and the weaving movements of the long-tailed tit are very different, though they may be said to have the same function or purpose: to bind together the nesting material. A classification of the movements in terms of this purpose, though very tempting, provides neither an explanation of their evolutionary history nor a truly helpful description of the way that purpose is achieved. The historical and the functional explanation are in fact intertwined. Both behaviors, as Tinbergen points out, can have emerged only after the ancestors of the two birds had acquired the habit of building their nests from a seated position. This is the likely taxonomic link between the two species, and it accords with morphological evidence. It also plays an important part in the explanation of the activity patterns themselves.

The quivering movements of the sparrow-hawk will result in the twigs' becoming lodged in the nest wall only because of a number of convergent conditions. The quivering needs to be executed at the correct angle, which is ensured by the bird's position in the nest. The twigs need to have the right degree of stiffness and to be bent or forked so they will tend to get stuck. Given that degree of stiffness, the quivering needs to be vigorous enough to penetrate gaps in the nest, but not so vigorous as to destroy the part that is already in place. The goal of this activity is clearly an emergent phenomenon, and the nature of the activity as a whole could not possibly be described in terms of some abstract formalism. It depends on "passive compliance" in the nest, on a mechanism that causes the bird to release the twig once it has got stuck, on the weight of the bird and the availability of various nesting materials in its environment, as well as on the strength of the muscles in the bird's neck. Many of these elements must have evolved in tandem. They did not evolve for the purpose of producing a strong nest wall. Strong nest walls were the emergent product that gave birds in which all these elements were combined a selective advantage. The point is that the behavior can be properly explained only if the patterns of activity themselves are brought to the center of the explanatory framework.

Lorenz's descriptive terms provided a way of carving up the continuous stream of a creature's behavior. This allowed the isolation of temporally extended activity patterns and facilitated intraspecies and cross-species comparisons. It made it easier to relate similarities and differences in behavior to taxonomy based on morphology and to give a definitive answer where the evidence provided by morphological characters had been unclear: "Some structural characters are very superficial and lead to evidently artificial groupings. If there is a conflict between the evidence provided by morphological characters and that of behavior the taxonomist is increasingly inclined to give greater weight to the ethological evidence" (Mayr 1958, p. 345). Mayr gives examples of cases where a species, genus, or group of genera has been shifted from its traditional place in the zoological system to a new position as the result of the application of behavioral criteria. The revised classifications were subsequently confirmed by reevaluated or newly discovered morphological evidence.

We thus have a descriptive framework that, for all its faults and inadequacies (which will be discussed in the next chapter), isolates units of behavior that can be grounded in the theory of natural selection. We do not have a complete causal story to explain such behaviors—and it may ultimately prove impossible to frame such a story, if that means relating mechanistically specified causes and effects through the creature's neurophysiological substrate in a comprehensible way—but we have units whose evolutionary emergence and interdependencies may be traced. We have methods of relating these units to ecological niches and of understanding the relationships between them. As I argued in previous chapters, it has proved extremely difficult to do this for explanatory entities derived from cybernetic or computational formalisms or for internal representations derived through top-down analysis of folk psychological concepts.

Chapter 12

Critiques and Modifications of the Basic Concepts of Ethology

12.1 The Basic Concepts

The basic concepts introduced by ethology are the fixed action pattern, the innate releasing mechanism with its associated sign stimulus, action-specific energy, and the difference between appetitive and consummatory behavior. All of these notions have had to be modified, and at least one of them has effectively been discarded, since Lorenz and Tinbergen first defined them.

The fixed action pattern is a unit of behavior with a rigid motor component and—optionally—an orienting component to direct its course. It is "driven" by action-specific energy and set off by a particular sign stimulus, which triggers the associated innate releasing mechanism. The action-specific energy is "discharged" by the execution of the FAP. FAPs are species specific and "innate," in the sense that their development and final form in the individual cannot be altered by environmental conditions or by learning. In the absence of sufficient action-specific energy, the FAP may be executed in an incomplete form, but the sequence of components that *are* performed will always be the same.

The IRM works like a simple lock and key. Sign stimuli are uncomplicated features of the environment, such as a particular size, shape, or color, which, singly or in combinations, trigger the IRM. The contributions of compound sign stimuli are additive, and the components can be determined by straightforward experimentation. The animal is "blind" to all aspects of the environment apart from the relevant sign stimuli while it is engaged in a particular type of behavior. No two FAPs in a given species will have the same IRM.

FAPs are consummatory acts. They constitute the "goal" of the appetitive behavior that precedes them. While FAPs are fixed, appetitive behavior is susceptible to environmental contingencies and therefore will vary in its structure, sequence, and duration. It is driven by the same action-specific energy discharged in the FAP, and this results in a "striving toward" release of the IRM. Appetitive behavior can be modified by learning, whereas FAPs are genetically fixed.

Critiques of these concepts can be divided into three main phases. The first, launched by Hinde (1953, 1956, 1957), may be seen as an attempt to clean up the definitions of the concepts so that ethology might be put on a firmer scientific basis. The next critical onslaught came from comparative psychologists like Schneirla (1966) and Lehrman (1970), who were primarily concerned with Lorenz's definition of FAPs as innate. The third phase, exemplified by Barlow (1968), Fentress (1976), and Dewsbury (1978), questions the use of the word *fixed* in *fixed action pattern* on the basis of more precise recent measurements and tries to arrive at a more realistic alternative definition for patterns of species-typical behavior. In addition to these critiques, there have been moves to modify the "orienting attitudes" of ethology from within. These will be discussed more fully in the next chapter.

12.2 Appetitive and Consummatory Behavior

Hinde (1953) began by pointing out that although the distinction between consummatory and appetitive behavior had proved very useful, it was extremely difficult to formulate precise criteria separating the two. Using his own studies of the reproductive behavior of the great tit (*Parus major*), he examined the criteria that had generally been proposed and found that none stood up to rigorous observation and analysis. Hinde concluded that appetitive behavior may be as simple as the behavior involved in a consummatory act, and that, like an FAP, it can often be decomposed into a fixed locomotor pattern and an orienting or "taxis" component. He discovered that appetitive behavior—again like FAPs—may be released by a specific pattern of environmental stimuli, which plays no further part in directing it. Finally, he concluded that all the phenomena that had led Lorenz to associate an action-specific energy with a consummatory act also apply to the release of appetitive behavior and that appetitive behavior is not as readily modified by learning as had previously been supposed: "Of course consummatory acts are much less variable than most forms of appetitive behaviour, and the motor pattern is quite fixed, but even here variation occurs in the taxis component. Indeed from this point of view consummatory acts could be regarded as forms of appetitive behaviour in which only one motor pattern is possible. Further, in both appetitive behaviour and consummatory act, there may be learnt modifications in the releasing mechanism" (Hinde 1953, p. 194).

In Hinde's view, the main benefit of the distinction had been that it helped to diffuse controversy concerning the variability of inherited or "instinctive" behavior. It was felt that behavior that was variable and sensitive to environmental conditions could not be inherited. Genetically transmitted behavior had to be fixed, showing that it was totally determined by mechanisms inside the creature. The split into a variable and a rigid segment had allowed ethologists to concentrate on FAPs, leaving the variable part contained in the appetitive behavior until later. This strategy had, in Hinde's opinion, been amply justified by its successes, and he (1982) concluded that, for all its imprecisions, the distinction remains valuable, since it draws attention to the fact that species do have characteristic activity patterns.

From the point of view of situated activity and interactive emergence, it is not clear that the distinction between appetitive behavior and consummatory behavior is important. As I indicated in the previous chapter, one of Lorenz's main reasons for proposing the distinction was to provide a scientific basis for the notion of "purpose." Appetitive behavior was seen as a "searching for" the sign stimulus. It embodied a specific aim or intention on the part of the animal and eliminated the need for McDougall's "energy toward." I argued that the whole notion of energy or drive has become less important and that Lorenz's solution opens the way toward allowing the patterns of activity themselves to take on much of the explanatory burden. The most pressing need for the distinction thus appears to have dropped away.

As Hinde (1982) points out, the distinction between appetitive behavior and FAPs provided a means of carving up the continuous stream of the creature's activity. This in turn alerted ethologists to the importance of chaining: how one segment of behavior serves to put the creature into a stimulus situation that can trigger the next. But once the conceptual distinction has served that purpose, it ceases to be essential to the principle of segmentation. It is not necessary that appetitive behavior and consummatory acts should alternate with each other for behavior to be analyzed as a series of segments. In theory, one piece of appetitive behavior could lead to another piece of appetitive behavior, as Hinde (1953) claims it often does, and in the same way one consummatory act might lead to another by resulting in the appropriate sign stimulus.

The issue of rigidity, as opposed to stimulus dependence, takes on a different aspect if interactive emergence is accepted as a basic principle in the explanation of behavior. The strike behavior of an adder is fixed because there is insufficient time for the behavior to be oriented in the course of its execution. Stimulus-guided activity would be too cumbersome in that particular instance. The only effective mechanism is something along the lines of a central pattern generator, selected for its efficiency in catching prey (though, inevitably, the creature will miss on a certain number of occasions).

But simple activity patterns of this type are likely to be the exception. Most behavior is the result of continuous interaction with the environment and therefore will not display a rigid, predetermined form. As we saw earlier, this led early ethologists to conclude that the behavior cannot be inherited. The feeling has been that for behavior to be transmitted genetically, it must be totally determined by mechanisms inside the creature, leaving no room for variability. In fact, variability does not constitute an argument for or against the behavior's having been inherited. Variable (but recognizably structured) behavior may emerge from low-level reflexes that are quite rigid, as I showed in the chapters on autonomous robots, and rigid behavior can be learned, as drill sergeants and animal trainers know well.

It is possible to see appetitive behavior as a sort of default behavior that fills in the time between consummatory acts, where the nature of the default may be partly determined by the way the system's parameters are set at that particular time. The animal wanders about in an appropriately structured way. Its wandering about is well structured as a consequence of natural selection. It is an emergent phenomenon resulting from low-level interactions between the creature and its ecological niche. The nature of the low-level reflexes that are active at a particular time is affected by the system's parameters. These will be set in a certain way as the result of its internal and external history up to that point. Natural selection will have ensured that the way they are set causes the creature to interact with its environment in a particular way, which will result in emergent activity that tends to lead it to specific sign stimuli. The creature is always engaged in some default activity. FAPs are merely climactic events, where a central pattern generator takes over complete control of the animal's activity because there is not sufficient time for interaction.

12.3 Action-Specific Energy

Hinde (1956) next focused his critical attention on Lorenz's action-specific energy. Again, he starts by listing the explanatory successes of the concept. It had provided a consistent explanation of why the same response tends to be difficult to evoke twice in rapid succession and why there is a steady increase in responsiveness with the passing of time after the first performance. In the previous chapter, I argued that action-specific energy, in conjunction with the fixed action pattern, played a more important, liberating role in ethology. By detaching the notion of energy from that of purpose, it opened the way to a scientifically respectable explanation of purposive behavior. At least, so it seemed to the early ethologists. To them, action-specific energy was quite similar to potential energy in physics. Lorenz's well-known cistern model was designed to reinforce that interpretation. However, the apparent simplicity of his model, and its metaphorical appeal to potential energy, are in fact misleading.

The hydraulic model of drive plays a double explanatory role. It is meant to explain diminished response following a recent release, but also to serve as an analogy for what happens between the stimulus and the response. Action-specific energy both "impels" the action and gets "discharged" in it, and the two phenomena are conceptually linked. In practice, as Hinde (1956) reminds us, the reduction in responsiveness may be correlated with a variety of factors, including internal and external stimuli as well as conflicting behaviors. Lorenz's hydraulic model is much too simplistic to carry the explanatory burden that is placed on it.

The notions of push and discharge implied by the hydraulic analogy require the introduction of an innate releasing mechanism that acts as a block. This block needs to be removed by turning the "key" of the sign stimulus so that the action can take place. But the IRM tends to be used as a generic term in association with stimuli that "inhibit," "orient," and "stimulate" as well as "release" activity. Quite apart from this causal confusion, no one has ever been able to find any evidence of a neurophysiological mechanism that might act as a block. The hydraulic model has introduced explanatory entities that do not conform with experimental evidence and tend to obscure rather than explain observations. Hinde (1956) asked, "How is one to form a picture of an entity which, in addition to being 'discharged,' 'thwarted,' etc., may be 'satisfied' or 'unsatisfied,' is 'consumed by' movements which are 'fed' by it, which is 'obeyed' by the animal, may or may not be 'generalised,' has appetitive behaviour 'belonging' to it, may 'conflict' or 'compete' with other drives, and may even 'lack coordination' with the 'cognitive element'?" (p. 325).

As I have pointed out, scientific concern with energy, drive and impulse has receded into the background since the classic concepts of ethology were formulated. There is a clearer understanding that such notions derive from the subjective impression that purposive activity is "impelled" by a "desire" to reach some goal and that subjective descriptions of this kind may not provide the most helpful explanatory entities for behavior. Viewed from the perspective of autonomous agent research, an ethology without action-specific energy is more coherent. It no longer seems necessary to the explanation of appetitive behavior, which can be seen as default behavior produced by interactive emergence, or of consummatory acts, which do not require a special energy to drive them but are simply triggered by certain environmental conditions. Questions of "buildup" and "discharge" and "displacement activity" are more adequately conceptualized in terms of dynamical systems theory. The reasons for the conviction that action-specific energy is essential to bind these phenomena together lie buried in the long-forgotten controversy between vitalists and mechanists.

12.4 Species-Specific or Species-Typical Patterns of Behavior?

The same dispute lay behind Lorenz's insistence that FAPs should be viewed as innate. Lorenz saw the fixed action pattern as the bottom stop in a purposive explanation of behavior grounded through natural selection. It constituted the "goal" of appetitive behavior: an end in itself that was not performed for some further purpose. FAPs are the ultimate explanatory units of Lorenz's scheme.

To maintain the integrity of this scheme, Lorenz insisted, in the face of mounting criticism, that FAPs were not only innate but must be considered as fixed, in a double sense of the word: "fixed" in that they would always follow the same pattern, and "fixed" in that they could never be changed once they had matured in the individual. "Learned" behavior and "instinctive" behavior were for Lorenz totally different categories, easy to distinguish in practice and clearly separated in theory. Instinctive behavior could never be modified by learning, and neither could its innate releasing mechanism. To Lorenz, "instinctive," "innate," and "fixed," when applied to behavior, were more or less synonymous.

The picture that emerges is of a behavior pattern whose sequence, shape, and duration are wholly determined by some internal mechanism like a central pattern generator. The internal mechanism, or the neural structure that subtends it, is reproduced exactly in each individual from a genetic blueprint. This allows the behavior to be classed as "innate," in the sense of "exclusively determined by genetic factors," as well as "instinctive," in the sense of "spontaneous," or "directed from within." Lorenz and the early ethologists further believed that the integrity of their concept required a categorical rejection of any effects due to the creature's environment. Not only could learning play no part in determining the final form of the FAP; environmental factors must be assumed to have no effect on the maturation of the activity pattern either.

The objections Schneirla (1966) and Lehrman (1970) put forward to this drastic simplification of the process of ontogeny were sometimes dismissed by Lorenz as mere semantic quibbles. They were in fact much more than that. Schneirla had been impressed by the changes over time in the emergent organization of ant colonies and litters of domestic cats, and the ways in which such emergent organization affected the development of the young. He found that at each stage, the proper functioning of the unit as a whole, and its transformation into the next stage of organization, depended on the interaction of activity patterns performed by the individuals within the context of a species-typical environment. These behavioral interactions were mediated by the secretions of various pheromones, which in turn depended on the activity patterns of other individuals: "Hypotheses of specific pace-making agencies determining phase changes and durations in the cycle (as for example a strictly endogenous ovulation rhythm in the colony as the 'Zeitgeber') had to be abandoned. The queen's pattern of reproductive functions depends, as does that of worker behavior, upon a complex mosaic of changing functional conditions in the colony, and it centers on the stimulative and trophic properties of the brood and their developmental changes" (Schneirla 1966, p. 292).

These observations made Schneirla aware of the extreme complexity of the developmental process, and the diversity of endogenous and environmental factors that need to coincide to ensure the emergence of the appropriate structures at every stage of maturation. He rejected the blueprint model of genetic transmission and ontogeny. Ontogeny is a cumulative process in which each stage depends on the structure that has been built up in the previous stages, as well as the developmental medium pertaining at that time, and information contained in the genotype. These factors have all evolved together. Each stage of the process has been subjected to natural selection. The genetic material contains neither a comprehensive description of the final shape of the phenotype nor comprehensive instructions as to how that phenotype should be "built." As Lehrman (1970) puts it: "The interaction out of which the organism develops is *not* one, as is so often said, between heredity and environment. It is between *organism* and environment. And the organism is different at each different stage" (p. 20). This is particularly true for phenotypes that are activity patterns. Both Schneirla (1966) and Lehrman (1970) quote a striking example from research done by Kuo (1932), who studied the behavioral development of domestic chicks within the egg. On the basis of his observations, Kuo concluded that the pecking behavior chicks display immediately after hatching develops through a series of stages. Initially the head of the chick is supported on its thorax, causing it to be passively raised and lowered by the rhythmic beating of its heart. By day four or five, the movements have begun to occur actively in response to contact between the chick's head and thorax. On day six, following a shift in the embryo's position in the egg, active head turning occurs as a response to contact of the head with the yolk sac, which may be classed as external stimulation. The nervous impulses caused by these movements result in an opening and closing of the chick's beak, which only much later becomes independent of the head movements.

Schneirla and Lehrman object not only to the term *innate* but to *species specific* as a term used to describe activity patterns. As Lehrman (1970) shows, a genome arrived at by selective breeding in one environment may have quite different phenotypic characters in another environment, and an environmental change that has a profound influence on the developmental outcome of one genome may have no effect at all upon that of another. Genes do not determine the end result, even where a close correlation between the end result and genetic factors can be established. All that can be said about a particular behavioral character is that it typically occurs in that species when it both develops in and interacts with its natural environment.

"Species-typical" activity patterns are emergent phenomena in three senses of the word. They have emerged through natural selection, they emerge in the process of maturation and/or species-typical learning, and they emerge at the time of execution from interactions between the creature's lower-level activities and its species-typical environment. Within the conceptual framework of autonomous agent research, this makes better sense than the blueprint model espoused by early ethology. It sees natural selection as working on outcomes rather than achieving clearly defined functional results through a process akin to design. There is no genetic blueprint corresponding to the final form of an activity pattern, and there is no internal representation of the pattern within the fully grown creature. An adequate explanation of its behavior requires reference to the structure of its ecological niche, the morphology of its effectors and sensors, and the lower-level activities from which it emerges. It really becomes a species-typical activity pattern only when evolution gives it its seal of approval by making higher-level activities dependent on its existence.

12.5 How Fixed Is a Fixed Action Pattern?

Barlow's (1968) answer to that question may be summed up as: not very fixed at all. He is interested primarily in the neurophysiological structures and events that may be correlated with behavior and therefore believes it is important that the behavioral units posited by ethology should be precise: "If behavior studies are to have meaning to neurophysiologists, the models that result from the studies must be translatable into neurophysiological language. This means that the behavior must be quantified, yielding mathematical models that can be compared with the models produced by the neurophysiologists. There have been relatively few mathematical models generated by the ethologists" (Barlow 1968, p. 218).

From his observations of the courtship behavior of the cichlid fish *Etroplus maculatus* and a careful rereading of the classic texts, Barlow concludes that ethologists have tended to select examples that would confirm their hypotheses. Those who did conduct field studies tended to concentrate on animals showing behavior patterns that are exceptionally rigid, and much of the subsequent theorizing about FAPs "has been done in the absence of hard data" (Barlow 1968, p. 223). Barlow believes that the FAP, taken in its literal sense, is probably an extreme case within a spectrum of behavior extending, at the other extreme, to relatively unstructured movement.

He questions the universality of Lorenz and Tinbergen's separation of the FAP into a motor and an orienting component. He suggests that more studies of a greater variety of activities, under a wider variety of natural conditions and in a larger variety of animals, would reveal that in many cases the orientation and form of the FAP cannot be separated. Furthermore, he predicts that there must be a continuous spectrum from inseparability to the clear separability found by Lorenz in the greylag goose. Most FAPs, Barlow concludes, seem to consist of a core motor pattern that is itself continually modulated by the immediate environmental situation: "What is determined is not necessarily a precise expression of a movement, but rather a stipulated relation between the organism, its behavior, and key stimuli" (Barlow 1968, p. 225). Barlow does not provide an explanatory framework to support this "stipulated relation." I believe he is prevented from doing so by his insistence that there must be precise neurophysiological correlates for what in reality are emergent phenomena. On the one hand, Barlow is aware of the inappropriateness of the term *fixed* and the inadequacy of Lorenz and Tinbergen's clean separation between the rigid, "innate" motor component of an FAP and the orienting component that is sensitive to environmental contingencies. He realizes that what is important about FAPs is that they are species-typical units of behavior with a *recognizable* rather than a *fixed* temporal and spatial structure. But on the other hand, his search for neurophysiological correlates makes it necessary to achieve a mathematically precise description, which "must be translatable into neurophysiological language." This leads him to visualize a "C.N.S. [central nervous system] counterpart" of the FAP in which the orienting component, as well as the motor component, is somehow specified. The mathematical model of both the activity pattern and its neurophysiological counterpart can be only a statistical distribution about some mode. Barlow therefore suggests that the name *fixed action pattern* should be altered to *modal action pattern:* "This conveys the essential features of the phenomenon: there is a spatiotemporal pattern of coordinated movement, and the pattern clusters about some mode, making the behavior recognizable" (Barlow 1968, p. 230). Barlow is pessimistic about the prospects of an imminent breakthrough in the discovery of CNS correlates for the modal action patterns he proposes. If the arguments I have presented are accepted, it will be clear that his pessimism is fully justified. Barlow has loaded too much of the explanatory burden onto the neural mechanisms inside the creature.

The alternative explanation sees modal action patterns as emergent phenomena. This means that no mathematical formalism—not even a statistical distribution about some mode—is capable of capturing its spatiotemporal pattern. Of course, it may be possible to characterize wall following by Mataric's robot in terms of some mean distance maintained between the robot and the wall, but this clearly does not get us very far. In the first place, such a description does not amount to an exhaustive mathematical characterization of the behavior. It still requires reference to the structure of the creature's environment. Even more important, we happen to know that the robot does not contain a directive mechanism that uses such a parameter. Following Barlow's advice would lead us to the wrong conclusions about the subtending mechanism of the robot.

If, on the other hand, we see modal activity patterns as emergent phenomena, this allows us to introduce an entirely different explanatory framework. Decomposition by activity unproblematically explains variability due to environmental structure. It presumes that the nature of the creature's environment plays a continuous, inextricable part in shaping its behavior. There is no differentiation of the activity as a whole into a fixed and a variable component. Indeed, the explanation of why certain activity patterns appear fixed, in the sense of being easily recognizable, does not reduce to a formal representation or generative mechanism for those patterns inside the creature. It is the result of natural selection, and the fact that the creature's behavior has been shaped by and takes place in a particular ecological niche. The emergent pattern of activity will not have a correlate in the creature's nervous system, but it can be decomposed into simpler activities, which may themselves have neural correlates, or be further decomposable into even simpler activities. The synthesis of these activities, producing the emergent activity pattern, cannot be paralleled in a corresponding synthesis of their neurophysiological correlates or their mathematical characterizations. Interactive emergence means there exists no overall formal description of the high-level phenomenon, though its pattern will be clearly recognizable within the context of the creature's environment.

Over the past fifteen years, a new science has sprung up, which calls itself neuroethology and is based on the proposition articulated by Barlow: that the units of behavior isolated by ethology will ultimately be shown to have neurophysiological correlates (Camhi 1984; Hoyle 1984). It is not difficult to understand the attractions of the traditional concepts of ethology for scientists hoping to provide a purely neurophysiological explanation of behavior. As originally formulated, the fixed action pattern and its innate releasing mechanism, together with Lorenz's insistence on their innateness and immutability, point to an explanation in terms of functional mechanisms located entirely within the creature. However, as I have tried to show in this chapter, it is precisely these aspects of the classic framework that have had to be abandoned. Hinde (1982) remarks how few of the early hopes of a synthesis between ethology and neurophysiology have in fact been realized: "The view that it would be possible to isolate specific neural centres which controlled functionally related groups of activities proved naive. . . . Even with apparently stereotyped fixed action patterns, invariance in the movement does not necessarily involve invariance in the neural input" (p. 170).

It is probably no accident that the adherents of neuroethology tend to concentrate on the locomotory patterns and the approach and withdrawal behavior of primitive invertebrates. Even here, ongoing research by Beer and his colleagues (Beer, Chiel, and Sterling 1990; Beer 1995) into the replication by a robot of the various locomotory gaits of a six-legged insect indicates that the explanation is almost certainly far more complex than the "motor-tape" model proposed by most neuroethologists. If the arguments of this book are correct, neuroethology, as now conceived, has little hope of explaining any but the simplest types of behavior.

12.6 An Enduring Legacy

The most enduring legacy of the pioneers of ethology has been what Hinde (1982) called their orienting attitudes. They taught scientists who were interested in explaining behavior to start from a solid descriptive base, built up by detailed observation of specific patterns of activity in their natural environment. The classic concepts Lorenz formulated have not stood up to rigorous analytic scrutiny, and more precise empirical measurements have cast doubt on the legitimacy of his conceptual distinctions and defining terms. These concepts nevertheless enabled ethologists to dissect the continuous stream of an animal's behavior into identifiable units, the integrity of which could then be confirmed through intraspecies and cross-species comparisons.

From the point of view of autonomous agent research, the modifications and deletions that have had to be made since Lorenz introduced his concepts have resulted in a more coherent explanatory framework. There is no need for a hard and fast distinction between appetitive and consummatory behavior. Action-specific energy now appears to be merely a distraction from the important explanatory role played by activity patterns themselves. And patterns of activity, if they are viewed as emergent phenomena, cannot be either "fixed" or "innate," since they are neither expressions of some internal representation nor produced by a mechanism that is transmitted by a genetic blueprint.

Ethology does not provide a "causal" explanation of behavior in the mechanistic sense. Modern ethology often attempts to supplement the classic concepts with causal theories in terms of hormones, neural mechanisms, information transfer, or even "software," to provide that type of explanation. These explanatory strategies will be discussed more fully in the next chapter. It is worth pointing once again to the crucial role played by the activity pattern itself in Lorenz's original explanation of purposive activity. From the perspective of autonomous agent research, this, in addition to ethology's orienting attitudes, is its most important contribution. We can now see that the "push" provided by action-specific energy is in fact redundant to the explanation. What is important is the emergent structure of the appetitive behavior, which will lead the creature to the appropriate sign stimulus because it has been selected for its effectiveness in performing that service for the creature's ancestors.

It may be said that Lorenz's descriptive terms provide us with a "causal" explanation in Aristotle's sense of *aitia*. They make feasible a principled description of behavioral phenomena that indicates what constrained them to be the way they are. They give us a retrospective understanding of how the possibilities were restricted by the structures that were already in place, as well as the creature's ecological niche, so that its behavior turned out the way it did. They do not provide us with a generative formalism but facilitate exploration of the space of possibilities by discovering different manifestations and tracing them back through their evolutionary lineage in an environmental context.

A fundamental problem with this type of explanation is that it does not appear to address itself to the problem of how the various elements of behavior are actually deployed. What determines whether a creature engages in one type of behavior rather than another at a particular moment? What controls the proper sequencing and interleaving of the various behavioral units? What prevents a creature from starving to death because it cannot "decide" between mating and feeding and gets stuck in a loop where it keeps starting one and then the other without ever bringing them to fruition?

Chapter 13

Ethological Explanations of the Integration of Activity Patterns

---

13.1 Different Models of Integration

Hinde (1982) lists three different ways in which one might attempt to explain the integration of individual activity patterns into a larger, well-adapted, and apparently purposive structure. The integration may be ascribed to direct causal factors, as, for instance, when the various activities of the male canary that have been classed as sexual behavior are assumed to be "caused" by a unifying sex hormone. Alternatively, the integration may be explained in terms of some overall goal or plan toward which the various activities are directed. And finally, it may be seen as the result of simple chaining.

These models assume that a sharp dividing line can be drawn between endogenously caused integration and integration due to environmental contingencies. They either locate the integrating factors entirely within the creature (Hinde's first two alternatives, as well as the "economic" models I discussed in chapter 9), or they try for an interactive approach that is too simplistic (Hinde's final alternative of "chaining"). In the second form of explanation, the creature's perceptual and behavioral history plays no part. The integrative mechanism lacks a temporal dimension. Behavior is characterized as just one thing after another. As a result, the modeling of behavioral integration is reduced to a choice between simple Markov chains and some form of hierarchical structure.

In chapter 9, I pointed out that it is possible to adopt a radically different explanatory perspective, based on interactive emergence, natural selection, and dynamical systems theory. I here return to the subject not because I believe that explanation has been called into question by my discussion of ethology but because the notion of hierarchical structure has been the cause of much debate in this area. I shall argue in this chapter that it is a fundamentally alien concept, which has tended to obscure some of ethology's most important contributions.

As Baerends (1976) points out, Lorenz "denied the existence of superimposed mechanisms controlling the elements in groups, as had been asserted by McDougall (1923) in his theory of the hierarchy of instincts. In this Lorenzian view the occurrence of a particular activity was only dependent on the external stimulation and on the threshold for the release of that activity. Plasticity in behaviour should then be attributed to variation in one or both of these factors" (p. 726). But Lorenz's view did not prevail. Most of the integrative theories in ethology may be traced back to Tinbergen's (1951) reintroduction of hierarchies. The nodes of such hierarchies have stood for "behavior centers" (Tinbergen 1951), "motivations" (Baerends 1976), and "tasks" (R. Dawkins 1976b), while the links between them have symbolized "transfer of energy" (Tinbergen 1951), "inheritance of motivation" (Baerends 1976), "is boss of" (R. Dawkins 1976b), and "has a causal influence on" (Hinde 1982). At times it seems difficult to understand why the authors insist on forcing their ideas into the Procrustean bed of a hierarchy, but the concept appears to exert an irresistible attraction on scientists of otherwise very different persuasions.

13.2 Tinbergen's Hierarchy of Behavior Centers

An eagle begins its prey-catching behavior by circling high above the ground. When it catches sight of a vole, it switches to a different type of behavior that will bring it to within striking distance of its prey. Finally, it goes in for the kill, which is accomplished by yet another, highly stereotyped pattern of behavior. There appears to be some overall plan. The eagle does not perform the final FAP at the beginning of the sequence. Its swooping behavior always precedes the kill and comes after the initial circling behavior. Tinbergen's (1951) explanation of this apparent structure was to postulate what he called his hierarchy of "behavior centers."

He had observed that the initial activity involved in the general categories of behavior commonly displayed by animals, such as feeding, procreation, and defense of territory, was always of the diffuse, appetitive type, like the circling of the eagle. This became the pinnacle of his hierarchy and corresponded to the behavior center at the top. Tinbergen concluded that the activity involved must be "motivated" by a form of energy similar to Lorenz's action-specific energy but that it was, in a sense, specific to the entire category of behavior and could "flow" down the hierarchy to motivate the activity patterns below. Leading down from the top-level center, there were "paths" to conduct the energy to subordinate centers. Most of these paths were just that: conduits for the energy to flow down the hierarchy. Each of these conduits was "blocked" at its end by an IRM. The activity corresponding to the behavior center behind the block was prevented from being executed by this IRM. But at each level, one of the paths leading down to the level below was not a simple conduit; it corresponded to the next appetitive behavior in the sequence. This would be executed and would lead in due course to one of the blocks at the lower level being removed by an appropriate sign stimulus, "draining off" the energy from the previous appetitive behavior as it "discharged" through the new behavior.

At first sight, Tinbergen's model represents an advance (from the perspective of autonomous agent research) on that of Miller, Galanter, and Pribram (1960). It starts from the basic premise that natural selection imposed whatever purpose we may detect in the creature's behavior and that the creature itself does not act from a "knowledge" of that purpose. Tinbergen (1951) repeatedly warned against incorporating a behavior's survival value as the "goal" in a causal explanation: "There has been, and still is, a certain tendency to answer the causal question by merely pointing to the goal, end or purpose of behaviour, or of any life process. This tendency is, in my opinion, seriously hampering the progress of ethology" (p. 4). Goals, purposes, or internal representations play no part in this hierarchical model. Tinbergen locates the causal mechanism partly in the environment (the sign stimuli) and partly in the creature itself (the hierarchy of behavior centers). Most of the organization of the creature's behavior is located inside the creature. The environment has a facilitating rather than an organizing or directive function. It might be objected that apart from sign stimuli, Tinbergen also admits orienting stimuli, but these merely serve the purpose of keeping individual behaviors on course. They play no part in the sequential structuring of behavior, in the proper combination of activity patterns that gives the whole its purposeful appearance. The hierarchical structure of behavior centers ensures that the creature will perform the sort of activity that will bring it face to face with the appropriate sign stimulus to release the lower level of behavior.

Note, however, that Tinbergen gets away from the idea of a top-level "agent" calling appropriate "subagents" (Minsky 1987) or a high-level program calling appropriate subroutines. The creature does not "decide" what appetitive behavior to call next; in a sense, it is the environment that decides that. Natural selection has seen to it that by engaging in the higher level of appetitive behavior, the creature will eventually encounter the sign stimulus that releases one of the behaviors at the next level down. The previous activity will then cease, because the energy that has been driving it is drained off into the new activity. There is merely a generalized sort of push from above, applied by the energy or drive, through the predesigned system of conduits representing the control structure. Unfortunately, as Hinde (1956) conclusively demonstrated, it is this element of energy that makes the model scientifically untenable.

Tinbergen's model can be seen as an attempt to elevate the organizational principle Lorenz introduced to link appetitive and consummatory behavior to a more general explanation of behavioral choice. Lorenz's idea is simple: goal-directed activity is not intrinsically goal directed at all; it only appears to be goal directed because the animal is driven by action-specific energy to engage in a particular type of activity that brings it face to face with the appropriate sign stimulus. The explanation of apparent purpose is distributed between the push of the energy and the structure of the creature's activity pattern, which has been selected for its past performance in leading the creature's forebears to the sign stimulus. As I pointed out in the last chapter, it has become rather difficult to understand why Lorenz believed that action-specific energy was so important to his explanation of individual elements of behavior. But in Tinbergen's model the energy factor is essential. It provides the operational link between the successive levels of his hierarchy. Without the downward flow of energy, the appropriate activities cannot be released in the proper order. The explanation of sequential order as a manifestation of hierarchical structure depends crucially on the flow of energy, if Lorenz's interactive explanation without reference to "goals" is to be preserved.

As Hinde (1956) remarked, the model contains a curious mixture of analogical and quasi-physiological elements. At the time Tinbergen proposed it, he clearly believed that neurophysiological correlates would eventually be found for its behavior centers. He occasionally calls them "nervous centers" and tries to marshal ethological and physiological evidence to support the reduction: "First, the additive co-operation of sign stimuli releasing a reaction as a whole indicates that the afferent impulses are collected into one single 'container,' which acts in a purely quantitative way on the motor centre. Second, the configurational character of the motor response itself shows that the motor centre redispatches the stimuli and distributes them according to configurational principles. This 'container' is, in the terms of neurophysiology, a centre, or a system of centres" (Tinbergen 1951, p. 81). On the other hand, the centers correspond to descriptive categories of behavior, which are "motivated" by an elaboration of Lorenz's hydraulic model of "drive."

Hinde's main aim in his 1956 paper was to discredit the notion of action-specific energy and to show that by incorporating it into his hierarchical model, Tinbergen had fatally compromised its scientific credibility. His analysis cast serious doubts on the viability of Tinbergen's hierarchical view of behavior, but there have since been attempts to resurrect it by downplaying the association with action-specific energy. One way of doing this is to substitute a hierarchy of "motivations" for Tinbergen's hierarchy of behavior centers.

13.3 Baerends's Hierarchy of Motivations

At the beginning of this chapter, I quoted Baerends's (1976) comments on Lorenz, who had maintained that the overall structure of a creature's behavior could be explained entirely in terms of low-level phenomena. Baerends concluded that this was impossible. Like Tinbergen, he came to believe that a satisfactory explanation required some form of hierarchical structure. He was led to this conclusion by his study of the egg-laying and provisioning behavior of the digger wasp (*Ammophila pubescence*). This creature digs holes in the sand, deposits a single dead caterpillar in the hole, and then lays an egg on the caterpillar. When the larva has hatched, it is provided with one or two additional caterpillars. Finally, in the third phase of the behavior, the wasp adds between five and seven more caterpillars and seals off the nest.

Each phase begins with an inspection visit, and Baerends proved experimentally that the subsequent behavior of the wasp during that phase is totally determined by stimuli (size of larva and amount of food left in the nest) experienced during this initial visit. Only inspection visits without a caterpillar have the appropriate effect. Changes made prior to provisioning visits had no effect on the wasp's subsequent behavior. What is more, even if, prior to the final provisioning visit, the entire contents of the nest were removed, final closure still took place, proving that the activity is not in any sense directed by its goal or purpose.

Within a particular phase of the provisioning behavior, various activities occur. At the beginning of each phase, the nest needs to be reopened, and at the end of the phase it is closed. The caterpillars that are used for provisioning need to be hunted, killed, and dragged back to the nest. Depending on which of these activities the wasp is engaged in, it will respond in different ways to the same external stimulus. When a caterpillar is placed over the nest while it is being opened, the wasp will remove the caterpillar as though it were merely a clod of soil. If it is placed in the same position during hunting, the wasp will recognize the caterpillar as prey, sting it, and deposit it in the nest. During the act of closure, a caterpillar found near the nest will be used as a plug to seal it off.

Clearly the wasp's response to a given object depends on the activity in which the wasp is currently engaged. This shows that the wasp's behavior in relation to caterpillars is not determined by some centrally held internal representation of caterpillars (in which case it would "know" that caterpillars are a valuable source of food that should not be wasted, whatever it might be doing at the moment), but that, more likely, each one of its repertoire of responses is triggered by a simple releasing mechanism like Lorenz's IRM. The question is, What, at any particular moment, causes the firing of one releasing mechanism rather than another? A simple answer to this question might be that the wasp is currently engaged in digging behavior rather than hunting behavior, and that this means the IRM for clod removal will be triggered rather than the IRM for stinging. But does that constitute an explanation? Clearly Baerends believes it does not. He thinks his empirical observations require an intervening variable, which he calls the creature's "motivational state."

As Hinde (1982) points out, motivational states are posited to account for the fact that animals will behave differently under the same external circumstances at different times. But such intervening variables have little explanatory power if they merely describe the variability of one type of behavior. If, on the other hand, a single intervening variable can be used to account for variability in a number of different behaviors, then its use as an explanatory device becomes more economical than positing independent cause-effect links for each of the behaviors:

> If we merely observe that an animal ignores water at one time and drinks water at another, it does not add anything to say that it is "thirsty," because our only criterion for saying it is thirsty is that it drinks water. But if we note not only that it drinks water if water is offered, but also that it goes and looks in places where it has found water previously, is ready to drink adulterated water that it would normally reject, and so on, application of the word thirst implies that these several changes in behaviour can be explained in terms of a common factor. And if in addition we find that we can make the animal behave thus by treating it in a number of different ways—for instance by, depriving it of water, giving it dry food, or injecting it with strong salt solution, postulating the "intervening variable" of thirst will have even more explanatory power. (Hinde 1982, p. 48)

Baerends's reason for positing intervening variables is more complex. In his study of the digger wasp's egg-laying and provisioning behavior, he identified what he believed to be a number of distinct behavioral levels. At the lowest level, he located a set of classic FAPs, such as egg laying, excavating, carrying sand, seizing prey, stinging prey, carrying, and storing. At the next level up, Baerends identified four categories of behavior: digging, closing, hunting, and trans-porting. The fixed action patterns at the lowest level are, says Baerends, "controlled" by these four "subsystems," which are them-selves under the control of subsystems of a higher order (inspecting, founding, provisioning, final closing, and defending). Finally, those second-order control systems are under the overall control of still higher systems that correspond to the behavioral "phases" identified by Baerends in the wasp's egg-laying and provisioning behavior.

Of these four levels, only the lowest and highest appear to be firmly grounded in empirical data. As I mentioned earlier, the lowest level consists of standard FAPs, and its explanatory entities can therefore be identified and substantiated in the ways I described in the previous two chapters. The highest level also seems to have a firm, though rather different, empirical basis. Baerends divided the total sequence of egg-laying and provisioning into various phases, each of which be-gins with an inspection visit that determines the wasp's behavior dur-ing the remainder of that phase. In addition, there is a further reason for considering these phases as legitimate explanatory units. One of the most interesting aspects of the digger wasp's behavior is that it can interleave behavioral phases on various nests. In between two phases on one nest, it may perform different phases on some other nests, re-turning (as a rule) to take up correctly the work on the first nest at the point at which it was interrupted. A phase is thus a sequence of activi-ties, begun by an inspection visit that sets the parameters for that phase and terminated by closure of the nest. It qualifies for the status of a behavioral unit because the various phases of different nests may be interleaved.

The two intermediate levels in Baerends's hierarchy are an attempt to explain the way in which the different FAPs are deployed within any one phase. They are defined in terms of what Hinde (1982) calls "descriptions by consequence" (e.g., founding, provisioning, hunting, closing). Descriptions by consequence do not refer to particular pat-terns of activity but lump together all patterns that lead to the conse-quence specified in the description. They are intentional descriptions in the sense that the behavior is taken to be "about" some feature in the outside world, and they tend to lead to explanations in terms of the behavior's "survival value" rather than historical explanations or explanations in terms of immediate, physical causes.

I believe that Hinde's dichotomy between description by conse-quence and physical description is in fact unhelpful. It assumes that physical description is restricted to rigid patterns of activity or even specific sequences of muscle contractions (Hinde 1970). My analysis of Mataric's robot demonstrated that it is possible to pick out and describe patterns of activity that are not rigid or perfectly predictable. Such patterns emerge from the interactions between a creature and its environment, and for that reason their descriptions may require references to environmental features (e.g., *wall* following), but these references carry no implication of intentionality. Wall following may be said to be a consequence of the creature's low-level reflexes operating in a particular environment, but the explanation makes clear that this consequence plays no part in the subtending mechanism. As I argued, this sort of "consequence," if it were to be encountered in nature, would really be legitimized or verified only if it were shown that a higher level of behavior depended on it.

The explanatory units in Baerends's intermediate levels, however, are identified in terms of descriptions by consequence in Hinde's original sense. Intentional units are interposed between the behavioral phases and the FAPs to explain the correct sequencing of events. The question is whether they contribute to the explanation or, on the contrary, tend to introduce unhelpful conceptual complications. Let us examine the relation between the hierarchical structure and the actual sequence of activities in a particular phase.

Phase II of the system is shown to make use of INSPECTING and PROVISIONING at the next level down. INSPECTING in turn makes use of DIGGING and CLOSING, while PROVISIONING makes use of DIGGING, HUNTING, TRANSPORTING, and CLOSING. What this means in practice is that the wasp finds its way back to the nest (no behavioral entity is given for this), opens it by RAKING, EXCAVATING, and CARRYING AWAY clods of soil (all FAPs), somehow informs itself of the state of the nest (again, there is no behavioral entity in Baerends's analysis corresponding to this crucial part of the behavior), and closes it by SEARCHING FOR, TESTING, FIXING, and STAMPING DOWN clods of soil (also FAPs). This is what happens during INSPECTION. It is called INSPECTION to differentiate it from the activities that follow. The wasp now SEARCHES FOR, APPROACHES, TESTS, and SEIZES a caterpillar, which it then STINGS and MUNCHES (all FAPs). It CARRIES it to the nest, opens the nest in the same way as it did during the inspection visit, RETRIEVES the caterpillar, and STORES it (all FAPs). Finally, it closes the nest, again using the same series of FAPs as it did during the inspection visit.

The description I have just given is entirely framed in terms of low-level units of behavior, and it follows the actual sequence of events. It might be argued that no higher level of description is necessary. What differentiates an INSPECTION visit from a PROVISIONING visit is quite clear. In the second instance, the wasp is carrying a caterpillar; in the first, it is not. One can imagine how this might affect its behavior without dignifying the two sequences as a whole with different names and elevating them to behavioral subsystems. By interposing his descriptions by consequence, Baerends is forced to adopt classifications that lump together activities that are temporally dispersed. For instance, the first-order subsystem identified by the name "transporting" comprises the low-level activities CARRYING, RETRIEVING, and STORING. However, RETRIEVING and STORING do not occur in the same temporal sequence as CARRYING. After it arrives at the nest, the wasp needs to open it, performing at least three FAPs "controlled" by a different first-order behavior, before the activity of TRANSPORTING can be completed.

Baerends's hierarchy has abandoned the temporal coherence and straightforward, unitary control structure of Tinbergen's hierarchy. Second-order behaviors can use FAPs from the lowest level without having to pass through first-order behaviors. CLOSING of the nest (at the end of a particular phase) is a first-order behavior, while FINAL CLOSING (following completion of the entire provisioning sequence) is a second-order behavior. The main difference between them, in terms of actual activities, appears to be that FINAL CLOSING uses CLOSING, but also uses STAMPING, which, rather confusingly, is already used by CLOSING as well. Presumably this means that final closing involves more stamping than normal closing—a natural and sensible bit of activity that is made more mysterious by Baerends's hierarchy.

I believe that these problems arise from the incorporation of intentional categories and emergent patterns of activity in a single explanatory model. This confuses "control" and temporal sequencing, and it requires Baerends to postulate a hierarchy of "motivational states" corresponding to his first- and second-order behaviors. As an intervening variable, motivational state is currently a more respectable notion than energy or drive. It may be read simply as internal state, which, in dynamical systems terms, means that a creature's behavior will depend on its perceptual and behavioral history in a principled way.

A change in the system's parameters, resulting from a perturbation by the environment, will alter the dynamical equations of the system, causing it to behave differently for an indefinite period of time. Subsequent perturbations will in their turn cause further changes to the parameters, without necessarily undoing the effects of the first perturbations. This type of explanation includes a temporal dimension, which Baerend's model lacks. It does not equate internal states with intentional categories, and it does not assume that certain states control or call other, lower-level states or actual activity patterns.

Baerends's hierarchy of motivational states cannot describe the effects of successive environmental perturbations on a system's parameters. It implies a control structure of distinct motivational units that "call" each other, and it violates Hinde's strictures on introducing intervening variables. Rather than simplifying the explanation, it tends to increase the number of explanatory units and their interdependencies.

Tinbergen's hierarchy of behavior centers was an attempt to stretch the classic concepts of ethology to a more general integrative explanation, grounded in neurophysiology. It failed because it depended crucially on Lorenz's notion of action-specific energy, making it a hybrid between a realistic brain model and an analogical model of drive. Baerends's hierarchy of motivational states may be seen as a hybrid between ethology and computer science. His use of the terms *system* and *subsystem*, as well as his references to Miller, Galanter, and Pribram (1960) and Chomsky (1957), reveal the source of his ideas. Explanations in terms of energy or drive have been replaced by notions borrowed from control theory and AI, which, in my opinion, are basically incompatible with the explanatory framework laid down by classic ethology.

13.4 *Software Models*

One of the key papers in establishing this tendency was R. Dawkins (1976b). It is quoted not only by Baerends (1976) but also by Hinde (1982), who appears to believe that Dawkins's defense of hierarchical organization does much to diffuse his own, highly influential criticism of the concept in Hinde (1956).

R. Dawkins (1976b) begins by arguing the need for a level of explanation above that of neurophysiology and proposes that such a level should be called a "software explanation" of behavior: "I do not mean that animals work like computers. They may be very different. But just as the lowest level of explanation is not always the most appropriate for a computer, no more is it for an animal. Animals and computers are both so complex that something on the level of software explanation must be appropriate for both of them" (pp. 7–8). Stated in this way, the suggestion appears unobjectionable. It merely acknowledges the facts that neurophysiology may not be the most appropriate level for explanations of behavior and that an explanation at a higher level does not necessarily have to reduce to one at a lower level, and that this is true of both living creatures and computer programs. What it does not make clear is that, by adopting the term *software explanation*, Dawkins is buying into much more than a vague analogy. He reminds readers that ethology has shied away from general explanatory principles since the early models of motivation were shown to be too simplistic by Hinde, but he insists that the principle of hierarchical organization does not stand or fall with the scientific validity of energy models. To make his point, he then presents a variety of arguments for the principle in general.

The first is his familiar argument for hierarchical decomposition. Natural selection is compared to a designer. Effective design principles can be expected to "pervade the internal organization of animals down to the lowest level" (R. Dawkins 1976b, p. 15). One of the most effective design principles of all is to break down large tasks into a number of smaller subtasks. Not only does this make it easier to understand and assemble the larger task, it also ensures that if something goes wrong at a lower level, only the relevant subunit will need to be corrected. Finally, the principle allows multiple use of the same subtask for similar requirements. "The evolution of thermodynamically improbable assemblies proceeds more rapidly if there is a succession of intermediate stable sub-assemblies," says Dawkins. "Since the argument can be applied to the manufacture of each sub-assembly, it follows that highly complex systems which exist in the world are likely to have a hierarchical architecture . . . and nervous systems are probably not exceptional" (p. 16).

I have discussed Dawkins's arguments for hierarchical decomposition in chapter 6 and shall therefore not examine them in detail here. It is, of course, quite likely that natural selection opportunistically makes use of certain "subassemblies," which happen to be available as a result of previous selective processes. It might even be imagined that the same "subassembly" could turn up in a number of different places (whatever that might mean). But this is quite different from assuming that creatures are built according to the principles of good design.

In any case, what does Dawkins mean when he writes that "nervous systems are presumably not exceptional"? Is he arguing for a neurophysiologically based explanation after all? Is he suggesting that the structure of behavior can be explained, through the application of his principle of hierarchical reductionism, in terms of "design principles" applied to an evolving central nervous system? If that is his contention, it becomes difficult to see why he needs a software level at all. But as Dawkins himself has been at pains to point out, there is no straightforward, reductive correlation between behavior and neurophysiological structure. Nor are particular neural structures transmitted as pieces of good design by genotypes. Of course, some information about building neural structures *is* transmitted from a successful creature to its offspring, but the genetic material does not contain anything resembling a blueprint for the eventual connections between neurons. Brain development in the embryo and during early infancy is a very different process from building houses or assembling cars (see Johnson 1993a for some recent discoveries and conjectures).

Natural selection would not be able to affect Dawkins's "software" level of organization directly any more that it can directly select neural structures. If hierarchical organization is to be argued for on evolutionary grounds, it must be done in terms of natural selection working on outcomes—in other words, activity patterns. The argument would have to show how, for example, a particular sequence of activities organized along hierarchical principles might confer an advantage over a previously existing sequence of similar behavior linked through chaining. This might be accepted as "proof" that the hierarchical structure was a "better design" in this particular case. As far as I know, no actual examples of such organizational changes have ever been discovered, and it is difficult to conceive of a thought experiment to give the notion substance.

It is sometimes argued that a major advantage of hierarchical organization is the increased flexibility in deploying different elements of behavior. This is then equated with an ability to choose, so that a creature blessed with hierarchically structured "software" ceases to be tied to predetermined behavioral sequences, dictated by either a central pattern generator or environmental contingencies. It is debatable what "flexibility" and "choice" really mean in this context, but assuming that the argument is accepted, then it is most likely to be an argument against, rather than for, the emergence of hierarchical structure through natural selection. The ability to choose confers the ability to make mistakes. It puts the creature at the mercy of its first wrong "decision." Presumably its "inflexible" behavior prior to the introduction of hierarchical structure was reasonably well adapted. Any slight advantage conferred by an increase in flexibility is likely to be outweighed by the dangers of making mistakes.

This is not to deny that flexibility of response has in some way emerged in the course of evolution and emerges in the behavior of present-day creatures. It is merely to deny that a design argument for the organizational virtues of hierarchical structure can be supported by a straightforward appeal to natural selection. Contrary to R. Dawkins's (1976b) claims, hierarchical organization is very difficult to defend on evolutionary grounds. It is, of course, readily defended on logical grounds, and in the remainder of his paper, Dawkins concentrates on explaining the computational arguments in favor of hierarchies to his ethological audience.

The computational approach offers a far more convincing model than Tinbergen's hierarchy of behavior centers or Baerends's hierarchy of motivations: high-level programs that call subroutines when certain environmental parameters indicate that they are needed. There is no mystery in this sort of model about what determines the correct sequence of activities or what causes the current activity to stop. It is a simple matter of choice points. Control passes from the high-level program to the subprogram, and this means there can never be any conflicts.

This is the logical conclusion of Tinbergen's suggestion, once it has been accepted that Lorenz's action-specific energy should be eliminated from the picture. The explanation of behavioral control has been shifted entirely into the "creature's head." Environmental contingencies play a part at the choice points and in the form of orienting feedback, but the part they play can be explained only in terms of the entities manipulated by the program, which of course takes the form of a temporal sequence of formally defined instructions.

Nearly forty years of experience in AI have shown that such a control mechanism soon gets into trouble in the real world because of its lack of flexibility, the need to plan for all possible contingencies, the combinatorial explosion, the frame problem, and the problems of interfacing a formally defined planner, working with an internal representation of the world conceptualized as a task domain of objects, properties, and events, to effectors and receptors that need to deal with a noisy real world that clearly is not preregistered into objects, properties, and events.

All the suggestions that have been made to clean up Tinbergen's hierarchical model rely heavily on computational formalisms. From the point of view of autonomous agent research, this is a retrograde step, since it locates explanation squarely in the creature's head and imposes generative structure as the basic explanatory principle. These compromises negate most of the advantages of the ethological approach. Rather than give up the fundamental orienting attitudes identified by Hinde (1982), it seems better to relinquish Tinbergen's hierarchy and its elusive behavior centers. The alternative is to conceive of behavioral integration as the result of interactive emergence. The agent does not choose, and neither does the environment: the agent is constructed in such a way that the right choices will emerge from the interplay between its movements and its ecological niche. Behavioral integration is seen as the outcome of natural selection, which has ensured that the creature is integrated with its species-typical environment as a dynamically coupled system. The structure of its ecological niche plays a continuous, inextricable part in shaping its behavior. It might be said that the explanation of behavioral sequencing and integration lies at a level *below* that of the emergent activity patterns themselves. From the point of view of an observer, who needs to carve up the totality of the behavior into descriptive categories in order to explain it, choice points occur at the interstices between activity patterns. However, just as the activity patterns themselves are emergent phenomena, so are the changes from one activity to the next. Correct sequencing results from interactive emergence and depends on how the system's parameters are set by its perceptual and behavioral history.

A change in the creature's parameters, resulting from a "perturbation" by the environment, will alter the dynamic equations of the system, causing it to behave differently for an indefinite period of time. Subsequent perturbations will in their turn cause further changes to the parameters, without necessarily undoing the effects of the first perturbations. Baerends's wasp acts differently during an inspection visit and a provisioning visit because its internal parameters have been affected in the second case by the experience of carrying a caterpillar. Within a provisioning visit, its parameters will again be changed as it opens the hole, inserts the caterpillar, and closes the hole.

Such an explanation includes a temporal dimension, which hierarchical models lack. It does not equate internal states with intentional categories, and it does not assume that certain states control or call other, lower-level states or activity patterns.

Chapter 14

The Explanatory Relation between Ethology and Autonomous Agent Research

The most important of the syntheses attempted between ethology and other sciences have been the attempt to find a neurophysiological basis for the activity units singled out by classical ethology, the attempt to fuse ethological thinking and intentional explanation, and the various attempts to impose a standard software interpretation upon the diversity of its descriptive data. I have tried to show in the past three chapters why these syntheses have proved unsuccessful and why, in my opinion, they were bound to fail.

Ethology's orienting attitudes impose their own distinctive logic on explanation. Its emphasis on detailed analysis of specific activity patterns performed by particular species in their natural environment shifts attention from generative rules and formal task descriptions to problems of taxonomy. The variety of naturally occurring behavior, and its diverse relations to the structure of the environment, rule out a single, unifying explanatory device like the reflex or negative feedback loop. Explanations in terms of logical constructs or mathematical formalisms simply cannot account for the diversity of the descriptive data.

Before anything like a mechanistic causal explanation can be attempted, this wealth of data needs to be ordered and classified. Lorenz's requirement for "innate" units of behavior to serve as bottom stops for his explanatory scheme led to an interest in natural selection and comparative studies. It was discovered that the units of behavior isolated by ethological concepts could support, and in some cases even correct, zoological classification based on morphology. The temporal structure of a creature's activity patterns turned out to be recognizable and species typical in the same way as the physical structures of its body.

Lorenz's obsession with "innateness" did serve to promote intraspecies and cross-species comparisons, but it also had negative effects on ethology. An overly simplistic view of genetic transmission and ontogeny caused him to equate "innate" with "fixed" (both in the sense of totally determined by a genetic blueprint and immutable in its shape and structure), as well as with "endogenously generated." This led to a number of false starts. It tempted some ethologists to search for neurophysiological correlates of fixed action patterns or "behavior centers," and it tempted others to think in terms of "software" explanations involving "programs" or "systems."

Lorenz's definition of "innate" implied that an explanation of the behavior units discovered by ethology could be found entirely within the creature. It could be argued that this was a denial of ethology's most important contribution. It isolated the creature from its ecological niche and promoted explanations of behavior that did not require the structure of its natural environment to be taken into account.

The best corrective to these tendencies was provided by the critiques of comparative psychologists like Schneirla (1966) and Lehrman (1970), who demonstrated that no behavior is genetically fixed in the sense in which Lorenz wanted it to be. Species-typical activity patterns are emergent phenomena in three different senses of the word: they emerge in the species as a result of natural selection, in a maturing individual as the result of ontogeny, and every time they occur within the life of that individual as the result of interactions between the creature's low-level activities and its species-typical environment.

This means that there can be no straightforward neurophysiological correlate of the activity pattern, just as there is no genetic blueprint. Nor can one think of the unit of behavior as being represented in any way inside the creature. The explanation for its recognizable structure must not be sought in a generative mechanism that defines that structure; it is a consequence of the fact that the creature evolved, matured, and acts within a particular ecological niche, ensuring that its interactions with that niche display the structure in question.

Lehrman's and Schneirla's critiques brought to the surface certain fundamental implications of ethology that had been obscured by Lorenz's concern with old debates about energy and drive. If behavior is an emergent phenomenon in the three senses given above, it is unlikely that any universal laws (except those of natural selection and behavioral emergence) can be discovered to describe and explain it. The problem is not just one of finding a classification that will point to causal generalities; it is the fact that the causal explanation is likely to be unique to each particular case—or, at any rate, that the classes are likely to be too small and too many in number to make it worthwhile to approach the explanatory task in this way.

There is nothing new about this type of situation. It characterizes areas that are not susceptible to description in terms of formal rules, but only to what Marr (1982) called "Type 2" explanations. As Marr himself put it, in such cases the "problem" is "solved" by a large number of processes whose interaction is its simplest description. Marr believed this made explanation impossibly difficult. However, this is so only if one adopts his position that behavior is a "solution" to some "problem" set by the environment. As I have argued throughout this book, the natural environment does not set "problems," and evolution does not "solve" any. Explanation of behavior is not a matter of characterizing the appropriate "problem space"; it is a matter of describing the space of emergent phenomena by classifying and relating the actual instances produced by evolution from a historical point of view.

The burden of explanation shifts from formal task descriptions and the generative structures implied by competence theories to the nature of the explanatory entities themselves, and their interdependencies and dynamic coupling with the environment. Only by accumulating such natural kinds of behavior can the space of possibilities be described. Computational theory does not provide an explanatory framework for this type of description, but autonomous agent research is its natural ally. Artificially built models capable of diverse levels of situated activity within a specific environment may serve to confirm hypotheses about the interactive emergence of naturally occurring behavior and bring out family resemblances between different kinds of behavioral dependency. Such models are models of behavior, not attempts to model the brain or mind. There is no presumption that the computational devices used to implement the behavior bear any resemblance to mechanisms inside the creature whose behavior is being modeled. However, a deeper understanding of the behavioral dependencies may point to fruitful investigative strategies for the neural sciences.

At the end of the section on autonomous agent research, I conceded there were two outstanding problems with this approach. The first was the question of discovering naturally occurring patterns of activity that could give substance to my conjecture about natural kinds based on an analysis of Mataric's robot. Ethology provides us with the means to do this: the theoretical framework, the experimental techniques, and the orienting attitudes to isolate situated activity patterns and describe their relations to the creature's environment and to each other in historical terms. The remaining problem is how it is possible to explain the emergence of full-blown symbolic behavior from such a mundane explanatory base. I shall try to sketch out a tentative answer to this question in the chapters that follow.

Chapter 15

Species-Typical Activity Patterns of Human Infants

15.1 New Discoveries Resulting from an Ethological Approach

In the early 1970s, investigators started to report that very young infants, observed in their natural setting, perform activity patterns that are far more complex and far more varied than had previously been recognized. These investigators tended to be influenced by the "orienting attitudes" of ethology, as summed up by Hinde (1982) and discussed in chapter 11. They tried to observe infants' behavior in the context in which it naturally occurred, deferred analysis and theoretical speculation until they had built up a solid descriptive base, and examined in great detail a particular type of behavior rather than searching for evidence of a central law that might unify diverse behavioral phenomena.

Bateson (1975) provides a good example of how such a change in emphasis can render previously invisible (or in this case, inaudible) data perceptible to an observer. Her research centered on the acoustic analysis of infants' vocalizations during mother-infant interactions. She found that previous studies had concentrated almost exclusively on cries of distress and that the only research on expressions of contentment and pleasure had concluded that these did not occur at all before the age of three months. Bateson's own research uncovered a wealth of murmurs and coos that the mother clearly picked up and interpreted but previous investigators had apparently ignored. "The difference," she wrote, "seems to arise from a difference in sampling techniques, where Wasz-Hoekert et al. focused on describing an acoustic phenomenon and we are concerned with describing the acoustic aspects of an interpersonal process" (p. 109).

The same point is made by Trevarthen (1977) about the rich variety of facial expressions and expressive gestures displayed by very young infants, by Brazelton (1979) about an infant's species-typical responses to adult handling, and by Schaffer (1977b), Kaye (1979), Tronick, Als, and Adamson (1979), and Newson (1979) about the cues and temporal patterning involved in mother-infant turn taking. As Trevarthen (1977)

remarks; "Putting an accent on discrete problem-solving and task-per-
ceiving powers of infants, both problem and task being set by the experimenter, as well as emphasis on conditioning as a mechanism for
developmental change, have obscured the spontaneous, innate aspects
of infant behaviour" (pp. 227–228).

I shall argue with Trevarthen's use of the terms *spontaneous* and *innate*, which presage his conception of the young infant as a purposeful,
self-directed entity "regulated" and "unified" by inborn emotions. But
his comments on the importance of descriptive analysis and the obscuring effects of a problem-solving, task-oriented approach to behavioral explanation accord with my arguments in previous chapters.

All of the investigators I have mentioned made intensive use of film
or video and of the opportunities for microanalysis of the temporal
structure of activity that these media afford. They frequently remark
that, prior to the development of such techniques, detailed investigation of activity was virtually impossible. Trevarthen (1977) writes that
the actual movements of human beings—as opposed to the intentional
acts in terms of which we normally describe and perceive them—were
as difficult to observe before the invention of cinephotography as were
the planets before the invention of the telescope. He speculates that
this might be one of the reasons that psychology became a science of
perception and cognition rather than a science of activity patterns, gestures, and facial expressions.

The temporal patterning of behavior, and its importance in mother-
infant exchanges and the emergence of language and conceptual
thought, was not properly appreciated until quite recently. The explanatory entities of psychology tend to be static entities like beliefs, desires, memories, and mental states, whereas the new research suggests
that meaning emerges in dynamic interactions. As Tronick, Als, and
Adamson (1979) point out, "The message contained in a facial expression is not contained in a single facial configuration nor even in a
strung together series of such configurations. . . . Expressions are plastic transformations of the stimulus array. . . . They take a specific
amount of time to occur and to use stop-frame analysis would be to
forfeit information" (p. 354). Collis (1979) speaks of the need to compile
"dyadograms" of the temporally patterned interactions between mothers and their infants, and Newson (1979) makes the point that the behavior of newborn infants appears to be "pre-punctuated" and to
contain "structured episodes," which are highly organized as sequences of coordinated action.

Discovery of the important role temporal patterning plays thus required the orienting attitudes of ethology, as well as the development
of sophisticated analytical techniques based on film and video. These

revealed a large number of species-typical activity patterns that are either present at birth or mature during the first few months of life. Examples of such patterns are primitive reach-and-grasp (Trevarthen 1977; von Hofsten 1984; Fischer and Bidell 1991), the early lip and tongue movements that Trevarthen called "pre-speech" (Trevarthen 1977; Papousek and Papousek 1977), rhythmical stereotypes like supine kicking and hand waving (Thelen 1981), and burst-pause-burst in suckling (Kaye 1982).

The existence of such well-coordinated patterns of activity at a very early age, and the realization that these may disappear later, or become modified into more complex types of behavior, or serve as the context for the emergence of social interactions, prompted a reappraisal of many of the accepted views about inborn abilities and learning. It was realized that a rigid, stage-bound picture of development, such as had been proposed by Piaget (1952, 1954), could not adequately describe the processes that were being observed. Individual activity patterns had their own developmental profiles, and though their onsets and peaks might tend to occur at roughly the same ages for all children in a particular culture, this could not be ascribed to a rigid sequence of overall, unifying, internal equilibria. Some children follow idiosyncratic paths, and each mother-infant pair builds up its own repertoire of interactive patterns, substantially different from those of other mothers and infants (Schaffer 1977b; Bullowa 1979b; Kaye 1982; Fogel and Thelen 1987).

Adult skills and concepts do not spring up fully formed but emerge over time through a sequence of increasingly complex activity patterns. An ability like reaching-and-grasping, as "implemented" in human beings, cannot be explained in terms of a formally defined competence or a specific set of internal commands contingent on appropriate feedback signals. Only a historical explanation can make sense of the relation between analogous but not really homologous behaviors like the primitive reach-and-grasp of a two-month-old infant and the visually guided reaching of an adult human being. These behaviors are not manifestations of a single competence, but they can be related in a situated context through history of use (von Hofsten 1984; Fischer and Bidell 1991).

Early forms of behavior can and usually do have their own adaptive advantages. The rhythmical stereotypy of supine kicking, which is almost certainly an early manifestation of the swing-stance cycle in walking and may serve as a preparation in the sense of strengthening the muscles, also has expressive and communicative value. The mother tends to interpret variations in her infant's kicking as clues to internal state and responses to her own attempts at communication. Evolution has "hijacked" an early form of adult behavior for other purposes (Thelen 1981).

In many cases, it can be shown to be biologically advantageous to have an immature form of behavior at the early stages of development rather than the fully developed form. The infant's inability to distinguish separate words in his mother's vocalizations may allow him to treat her clauses as unitary utterances, equivalent to his own coos and murmurs, and thereby promotes the process of turn taking in early "dialogues," and provides a "scaffolding" for the later parsing of clauses into meaningful subunits (Bateson 1979; Hirsh-Pasek et al. 1987). Limited depth of field during the first months of life restricts the infant's resolution to objects at approximately twenty centimeters distance, and this, coupled with early fixation patterns, produces an *Umwelt* consisting predominantly of his mother's face, since she appears to be biologically primed to put herself into the optimum position (Turkewitz and Kenny 1993; Johnson 1993b). I shall discuss these dependencies in greater detail in a later section. At this point they are mentioned to indicate the limitations of a task-based approach that derives explanatory entities from functional decomposition of adult behavior.

Many of the early activity patterns that have been discovered recently appear to be typical to human beings. Burst-pause-burst in feeding does not occur even in the young of other phylogenetically advanced primates (Kaye 1982). Human infants display a large number of facial expressions (Charlesworth and Kreutzer 1973; Trevarthen 1977) and rhythmical stereotypes (Thelen 1981) that are absent in gorillas and chimpanzees. Face-to-face exchanges between mothers and infants, and the complex interaction of activity patterns from which these emerge, seem also to be unique to the human species.

On the other hand, many of these species-typical activity patterns disappear, become submerged, or disintegrate before the end of the first year. They are not functional components of adult behavior. Often their only reason for existence would appear to be that they enable other, more advanced forms of behavior to develop within the situated context they provide. This realization led the early researchers to formulate the notion of scaffolding (Bruner 1982; Newson 1979; Kaye 1982; Fischer and Bidell 1991).

There are a number of different ways in which one can think of scaffolding. One can apply it to the supportive framework, usually provided by an adult, that enables the child to perform activities of which he may not be capable on his own until somewhat later. Thus, infants will demonstrate the ability to "walk" if they are supported in the right way long before their leg muscles have developed sufficient strength to hold them up. This view of scaffolding stresses the intentional contribution of an adult. It sees the mother-infant dyad as two separate human beings, with the mother providing conscious support and guidance to enable her infant to learn new skills. The scaffolding continuously pushes the infant a little beyond his current capabilities, and it pushes him in the direction in which his mother wishes him to go. Scaffolding is then a pedagogical device, defined in terms of capabilities and tasks, and its nature and effect are presumed to be under the control of the adult. This is the concept of scaffolding as it was first introduced by Bruner.

A different, and for our purposes more interesting, view of scaffolding starts from the activity patterns themselves. It sees the mother-infant dyad as two tightly coupled dynamic systems (Fogel 1993). Recognizable patterns of behavior, which, however, are not preplanned or generated by internally represented rules, emerge from the continuous mutual adjustments between the two partners, much as wall following emerged from the continuous adjustments of Mataric's robot to its particular environment. The activity patterns, rather than the presumed intentions of the mother and the level of skill of the infant, become the natural kinds in this type of explanation. Scaffolding then takes on a meaning similar to the dynamic context provided by wall following for the emergence of landmarks and landmark navigation in Mataric's robot. Thus, the "dialogue" between a suckling infant and the mother who jiggles him whenever he pauses in feeding constitutes a recognizable interactive pattern that emerges from low-level reflexes and centrally generated rhythms and establishes a habit of turn taking on which later, face-to-face exchanges will be built. The "pragmatics" of meaningful communication, in this view, precede any explicit "content," and they are best conceptualized in terms of patterns of situated activity.

This notion of scaffolding stresses the importance of species-typical activity patterns, selected for their power to attract the attention of adults, deceive them into intentional interpretations, and establish the habit of turn taking, which is essential to human learning, rather than of inborn knowledge or innate cognitive structures. Movement subtended by a central pattern generator and/or simple reflexes requires no knowledge of the world and no a priori concepts of causation, space, time, objects, or their properties. Some of the species-typical activity patterns that newborn or very young infants are capable of performing may have no place in adult behavior. They may simply serve a bootstrapping role to launch the infant into an environment of adults who think in intentional terms and communicate through language and manipulate tools and artifacts. However, if the picture sketched

out in the previous two paragraphs is correct, then an adequate understanding of human thought can be achieved only through a historical
explanation in terms of interactive emergence that takes account of
these early activity patterns.

15.2 Different Interpretations of the Newly Discovered Capabilities of Young Infants

The discoveries described in the previous section have received at least
three fundamentally different interpretations. Cognitive psychologists
inspired by the ideas of Chomsky and Fodor have taken them as evidence for innate competences and/or mental structures embodying
knowledge of the world, which would contradict developmental theories like Piaget's (Baillargeon 1987; Diamond 1991; Spelke 1991). Hu-
manist psychologists like Bruner (1982) and Trevarthen (1993) see the
well-integrated behavior displayed by very young infants as evidence
of innate intentionality or incipient personhood of some sort.

Finally, most of the original investigators have concentrated on
building up a descriptive base of specific activity patterns, deferring
speculation as to central causes and internal structures until later.
However, their determination to study the infant's behavior in its natural setting has led to an understanding of the importance of mother-
infant interactions, and their use of film and video, coupled with
sophisticated analysis techniques, has revealed complexities of temporal patterning that had not been appreciated before. In addition, longi-
tudinal studies of specific behavior patterns have produced a deeper
understanding of the processes of maturation and the diverse parameters involved (Fogel and Thelen 1987; Camaioni 1993; Fischer and
Bidell 1991; Johnson 1993a; Turkewitz and Kenny 1993). These discoveries can be given an interpretation in terms of interactive emergence
and dynamical systems theory, which attaches far greater importance
to social and cultural factors than do the interpretations mentioned
above. I shall discuss briefly the strengths and weaknesses of the two
other interpretations, before concentrating on the approach that is central to this book.

Baillargeon (1987), Spelke (1991), and Diamond (1991) are concerned
with demonstrating that the concept of object permanence, and an understanding of the world as preregistered into unitary objects with
bounded extension, is an innate capacity in human beings. As I discussed in chapters 3 and 4, this question is of central concern to the
cognitive approach. Millikan's (1984) "biological" theory of intentionality stands or falls by a satisfactory explanation of the correspondence
between unitary objects-in-the-world and representations of objects in
the head. Much of AI vision research has focused on the problem of

extracting three-dimensional objects from a retinal projection containing no explicit information about their locations or boundaries. The problems of viewpoint dependence and size constancy have puzzled cognitive scientist and cognitive psychologist alike. Baillargeon, Spelke, and Diamond set out to refute Piaget's (1952, 1954) answer to these questions, which involved a gradual emergence of the notion of object permanence from sensorimotor experience. Their experiments are designed to show that infants at only three or four months of age already have the concept of object permanence and that sensorimotor experience is therefore not needed for its development.

Essentially, these investigators attempt to turn Piaget's theory on its head. They postulate that young infants have hidden cognitive abilities that they are unable to reveal because of insufficient skill in coordinating their actions. Not only is interactive activity and its attendant sensorimotor experience inessential to acquiring the concept of object permanence; according to these authors, the slow development of the child's ability to put together his actions actually *gets in the way* of demonstrating the presence of the concept at that early age. This, says Baillargeon (1987), explains the results of Piaget's own experiments and the numerous confirmations of his findings by subsequent researchers.

Baillargeon and Spelke get around the experimental problem they claim to have identified by an ingenious methodological ruse. They reason that if the infant possesses the concept of object permanence, he will be surprised by displays that violate that concept. Following habituation, infants are exposed to two different test events, the first of which accords with the concept, while the second is "impossible" under its constraints. If the infant looks longer at the second event, this is taken as evidence that it violates his expectations and that he does indeed possess the concept.

In a long and closely argued paper, Fischer and Bidell (1991) take issue with these experiments and question the conclusions drawn from them. These authors believe that researchers like Baillargeon and Spelke commit the fallacy I have previously discussed in relation to the experimental methods of behaviorism. Their experiments are specifically designed to produce responses that can be interpreted only in terms of the abstract principle whose operation the researchers are attempting to demonstrate. Or, as Fischer and Bidell (1991) put it, "The research questions in these studies are posed in a yes-or-no fashion that presupposes the meaning of the behaviors under study" (p. 219).

Fischer and Bidell contend that skills and concepts are not straightforward, one-off acquisitions; they take time to develop, the underlying mechanism that subtends the skill at a particular stage is related to the context in which it manifests itself, and a determined experimenter may rig the context in such a way that immature forms appear to give evidence of far more sophisticated "knowledge about the world" than is warranted by an examination of the behavior in its natural context. To back up their contention, they give various examples of the ways in which appropriate scaffolding may convert the coarse swipes of a two- or a five-month-old infant into apparently controlled, visually guided reaching for objects: "Arguments over the age of acquisition of a capacity are based on the notion that the child can be characterized as either having or not having some capacity regardless of the context. The concept of skill recasts this notion in terms of gradually emerging abilities that are context dependent" (Fischer and Bidell 1991, p. 232).

Fischer and Bidell's main purpose is to defend Piaget's conceptual framework. As will become clear in the course of this chapter, I believe there are serious problems with Piaget's stage-based approach and with his central concepts of assimilation and accommodation. However, like Fischer and Bidell, I also believe that Baillargeon, Spelke, and Diamond have misinterpreted Piaget's theoretical position. Piaget may be seen as a forerunner of the recent interest in dynamical systems theory. He saw organisms as self-regulating, autonomous, dynamic structures whose development should be conceptualized as a sequence of orderly transformations. The nature of the whole is preserved under perturbation by adaptive compensatory transformations of relations among the parts. Unfortunately, Piaget lacked the mathematics of evolution equations, limit cycles, and basins of attraction that is now available. Despite his interest in dynamic processes, his mathematics (set theory and mathematical logic) were essentially static. His notion of transformation is rule based, and his stages are conceptualized as formal structures, not as dynamic equilibria. This is what lays him open to criticism by cognitive psychologists like Baillargeon and Spelke, who assume that he shares their conceptual framework of mental structures and correspondence theories.

The approach adopted by Spelke, Baillargeon, and Diamond contravenes the orienting attitudes of ethology. They do not start from a descriptive base of naturally occurring behavior, which is modified in a controlled manner in its natural surroundings to isolate the crucial parameters and causal factors. They take as their starting point the abstract concept of object permanence, assume that it plays a central role in all object-related behavior, and try to evoke responses that will settle the question of whether that concept is already present in a three-month-old child. The experiments are set up in a way that acts as scaffolding for the desired manifestation of the cognitive skill. I shall argue in the next few chapters that the intentional faculty they believe to be innate (that of seeing the world in terms of permanent objects and properties and performing acts that are *about* those objects and properties) needs to be laboriously assembled within a cultural environment over the first months of life and that we are fortunate that this should be the case, because it is the *lack* of innate object permanence that ultimately enables us to act and think in flexible ways.

Jerome Bruner may be considered the progenitor of much of the research discussed in this chapter, since many of the early investigators drew their inspiration from working with him at Harvard. Bruner takes for granted that human action is intentional (in the psychological sense of "purposive"), and he defines this characteristic in terms that are instantly recognizable to a designer of AI planning systems: "An intention is present when an individual operates persistently toward achieving an end state, chooses among alternative means and/or routes to achieve that end state, persists in deploying means and corrects the deployment of means to get closer to the end state, and finally ceases the line of activity when specifiable features of the end state are achieved" (Bruner 1982, p. 313). He then goes on to say that much of this goal-directed planning happens below the threshold of consciousness and that the components of the resulting action will be organized in a hierarchical manner. These are all familiar AI notions. However, his experiments with young infants have shown that "the young infant will typically reveal a situation-related restlessness, a general activation before he is able fully to recognize means to an end, and indeed there is a body of data in the field of motivation that suggests that, under such conditions of activation, it may be necessary for the immature organism to learn what the end state is that terminates the diffuse intentionality (if I may use such a bizarre phrase as a synonym for activation)" (p. 315)

The problem is that activation and intentionality (in Bruner's psychological sense) are *not* synonymous and that "situation-related restlessness," or "general activation" is difficult to explain from a goal-directed perspective. Bruner would like to frame his explanation in terms of hierarchies of feedback loops. This requires that each activity has a well-defined goal or end state and can be formally represented as a task with clearly specified means for achieving that end state. His data on child development tell him that young infants merely display a "situation-related restlessness" and that they need to learn what end state will terminate that restlessness. In fact, it is difficult to conceive of any way in which they could possess the "knowledge," either conscious or unconscious, that there *is* such a thing as an end state that can terminate their restlessness. Bruner supports his notion of diffuse intentionality by appealing to the behavior of the mothers in his studies. Mothers clearly behave as if their infants are intentional beings:

"Either the mother is a victim of common sense and does not really understand action. . . . Or she is behaving appropriately toward an immature member of the species who does in fact operate along the lines of intentional action I originally proposed" (Bruner 1982, p. 317).

The answer I shall try to sketch out in this chapter is that the mothers frankly *do* deceive themselves when they conclude that their infants engage in intentional acts but that it is essential for the infants' psychological development that the mothers *should* deceive themselves in that way. Their infants' patterns of activity, and their own maternal responses, have been selected because they contribute to that deception, for it is only by treating their infants as intentional beings that the mothers can bootstrap them into a cultural world that depends on the illusion of intentionality. The child's conception of himself and his actions, his "beliefs and desires," his "goals," take shape from situated, interactive processes that his species-typical activity patterns enable him to enter into with his mother.

Diffuse intentionality makes little sense. To call an activity intentional implies that it is about something (philosophical sense) or that it is directed toward a clearly specifiable goal or end state (psychological sense). Diffuse activity, on the other hand, makes very good sense. The activities of young infants tend to be diffuse though intricately patterned. As Trevarthen (1979) points out, it is possible to detect facial expressions in newborn or very young infants that closely resemble the adult expressions of pleasure, surprise, confusion, and disgust, and well-coordinated movements of the head, trunk, and limbs may accompany such expressions. The sense in which these expressions and gestures are diffuse is precisely that they do not seem to be *about* anything. They are not focused on a particular object or toward a particular end but appear and disappear in a fleeting, evanescent way that rendered them almost invisible to conscious perception before the introduction of film and video.

Like Bruner, Trevarthen (1979) believes that infants are born with more than just a set of very convenient and suggestive activity patterns:

> It is often thought that the main cause of development in communication during infancy is the fabrication of structure by the mother. According to this view the infant's immature acts have rhythm and impulse, but are at the outset exceedingly simple in variety of form. The mother attributes intentions to these seemingly pointless movements, maintaining development by transfer of her intentions and understandings to the infant. This view of the development of communication neglects the regulation of de-

velopment from within the mind of the child and leaves the child's psychological growth unexplained. (p. 346)

Trevarthen assumes that development and psychological growth need to be directed processes and that complexity and variety of behavior can be explained only in terms of a purposeful directive agent. These notions derive, as Oyama (1993) has argued, from a deep-seated belief in Western culture that the specification of form must precede its actual emergence. In this view, it is not possible for an organism to settle into a particular configuration, or engage in a specific piece of behavior, if that form or behavior was not explicitly described either within the organism, or within the environment, or perhaps in some combination of the two. But as Oyama points out, there is no reason that the structure of a dynamical system needs to be prespecified in any form or shape. It simply emerges in the form that it does because of the coincidence of certain parameters and components, which in the past have tended to result in a viable system within a particular environment, and the possibility of whose emergence has thus been preserved by natural selection.

The processes of growth and development are not "directed from within the mind of the child," because there is no representation within the child of its developmental stages or the final result. The movements of young infants may be extremely varied and complex, and their variety and complexity may have come about through a selective process that ensures development proceeds appropriately, so that there is a "point" to such activity patterns in terms of the developmental processes that lead to an adult, but this does not mean that the child performs the activities for a purpose. To speak of a "regulation of development from within the mind of the child," as Trevarthen does, assigns a directive role to the child's mental structures and implies prior, internal specification of the direction that development will take.

Trevarthen's putative directive agents are more clearly defined than Bruner's "diffuse intentionality." He believes that the diverse emotions of which he has found evidence on the faces of very young infants are "intrinsically generated, central, regulating states of the brain that unify awareness and coordinate activity of a coherent, mentally active subject" (Trevarthen 1993, p. 48). For the past twenty years, Trevarthen has promoted this primary role for emotions in developmental psychology, seeking to establish that they shape experience rather than result from it, that they play a causal role in perception as well as action, and are not merely side effects or epiphenomena. Emotions, according to Trevarthen, protect the integrity of the body, guide perception, activity, and learning, and regulate social interaction with other people: "The evidence is clear that infants possess at birth, not only a coherent and differentiated emotional system that covers, in miniature, the full range observed in adults (as the hand of an infant, or foetus, has five fingers), but also the distinctions between 'person-related,' 'thing-related,' and 'body-related' functions of emotions" (Trevarthen 1993, p. 73).

The role of emotions in human behavior and development is a thorny subject in cognitive psychology, and I do not propose to enter into the details of this debate. In broad descriptive terms, there are at least four aspects or "components" to emotions. There are emotional expressions, some of them biologically determined and others imposed through cultural conventions (see Darwin 1872 and the various contributors to Ekman 1973a). There is the functional aspect by which emotions are credited with the regulation of behavior or alterations in the control structure of behavior (for a cognitive explanation, see Simon 1967 and Sloman 1990). There are "felt" emotions, which we know only through introspection. And finally there is folk psychological interpretation of emotions.

Clearly the details of the functional component are a matter of hypothesis and will depend on the explanatory framework that is adopted. Computational explanations tend to stress causal mechanisms like "interrupts" (Simon 1967; Sloman 1990). These are derived from programming techniques and a perceived need for a serial, hierarchically organized creature to have a way of responding to real-time emergencies rather than from any specific characteristic of emotions in their other aspects. Trevarthen, on the other hand, appears to rely heavily on emotional expressions as indicators of internal states, and even of the functional role they play in regulating an infant's behavior. As Darwin (1872) was the first to point out, the human species has inherited from its primate ancestors a basic set of expressions that signal fear, aggression, submission, and playful intent. These expressions seem also to be universally recognized by members of our species (Ekman 1973b). However, those observations do not imply that human infants are born with a fully specified spectrum of internal states corresponding to the universal expressions.

Such a conclusion does not even follow, as Ekman (1973b) and Trevarthen seem to believe, from the observation that basic expressions are given similar folk psychological interpretations in different cultures. Expressions may be read in a particular way without any basis in internal facts. We may be biologically primed to read infants' expressions as indicators of well-defined emotions and still not be born with the corresponding internal states. It might be that such a consistent reading actually helps to establish the underlying functional mechanism by providing the appropriate scaffolding.

The different aspects or components of emotions undoubtedly interact. Irrespective of the extent to which emotional dispositions are biologically inherited, there can be little doubt that varied contact with other people, reading novels, watching dramatic performances, and listening to music, among other things, sharpen emotional discrimination. A good writer or composer can provide moments of emotional discovery and reveal subtleties of emotional "form" (Langer 1942) that had not been "understood" before.

Clearly this process of emotional education begins in the mother-infant exchanges that take place during the first year. The mother continuously interprets her infant's behavior in terms of putative emotional states. She incorporates his activity patterns into interactive sequences that presume he is experiencing such states, and she attaches the folk psychological labels of her culture to her infant's expressions and gestures. Trevarthen would have us believe that the mother's interpretations correspond to a complex emotional structure already present in the child, but there is no a priori reason that this should be the case, and in some ways it seems more economical in evolutionary terms to do without "felt" emotions in human infants as well.

One of the major stumbling blocks to a better understanding of emotions may be the tendency to conceptualize them as states rather than as dynamic processes. I have already quoted Tronick, Als, and Adamson (1979) to the effect that emotional expressions cannot be understood as static facial configurations but must be seen as activity patterns that translate into dynamic transformations of the stimulus array. Similarly, felt emotions undoubtedly have temporal structure (Langer 1942; Clynes 1980, 1982), which accounts to some extent for the power of music to convey emotional subtleties that are difficult to convey in language. Minsky (1987) has suggested that emotions should be conceptualized as internal processes characterized by their "time patterns," but such a notion would probably be difficult to integrate into a traditional symbol-processing model of the mind. Recognition of the temporal structure of emotions accords quite well with a model in terms of interactively emergent activity, which accepts that emotions develop and change from moment to moment and that the labels we attach to them serve primarily as aids for articulation and scaffolding (see chapters 16 and 17).

The newly discovered complexity and diversity of activity patterns displayed by very young infants does not warrant positing the presence at this early age of mental structures or competences that can be derived by conceptual analysis from adult behavior described in folk psychological terms. Neither an inborn knowledge of object permanence, nor an innate intentionality, nor a set of biologically determined, highly differentiated regulatory emotions is warranted by the facts. Interpreters like Baillargeon, Spelke and Diamond, Bruner, and Trevarthen have put the cart of adult symbolic thinking and full-blown intentionality before the horse of species-typical, subcortically mediated activity patterns. The task of psychology must be not to explain these activity patterns in intentional terms but to explain how intentionality can emerge from such "mechanical" beginnings.

15.3 Species-Typical Activity Patterns, Mother-Infant Interaction, and Intentional Interpretation

All mammals are born with the activity pattern of sucking, but only human infants display the tendency to intersperse that activity with randomly distributed pauses. This appears to be a specifically human trait, which is not found even in the young of other primates. Human mothers, on their side, seem to be biologically primed to respond to these pauses by jiggling either the infant or whatever else they may happen to have in their hands. The strength of the urge is attested to by mothers themselves (Bateson 1979) and is demonstrated by Kaye's (1979, 1982) studies of their behavior.

The mothers believe that their jiggling encourages the infant to suck. In fact, jiggling *reduces* the likelihood of the beginning of a new burst, and it is only the *cessation* of jiggling that encourages the infant to resume sucking. The reason that the pauses in sucking are able to act as a trigger for jiggling is that the sucks themselves occur with rhythmic regularity that draws attention to the pauses. This regularity is probably best explained in terms of the interactional mechanics of sucking: the amount of milk that can be taken in by the infant in one suck, the muscle contractions of his mouth, and the mother's milk flow. The rhythm of sucking is an emergent pattern explicable in terms of two tightly coupled dynamical systems with physical components and parameters. It provides the temporal context for the more complex activity pattern of bursts and pauses.

Within each burst, the infant's sucking is rhythmical, but the duration of the bursts and pauses is random. It turns out that if the infant is left on the breast or bottle without jiggling, the likelihood of a new burst after ten seconds is about the same as it was after only three or four seconds. Clearly there is no need to postulate a mechanism that keeps track of the duration of bursts and pauses: the nervous system of the infant does not contain an internal representation of the pattern.

> One can represent the mechanisms involved in these so-called "interaction contingencies" as fairly simple stochastic processes with no awareness in the infant of any interaction with another person. However, this is not how a mother herself experiences the situation. She feels the infant was involved in feeding, then got lazy or dozed off or stopped paying attention to what he was doing, and had to be jostled back onto the job. Mothers are not aware that their jiggling actually lengthens the pause, that only jiggling and stopping is an effective way to hasten the next burst, or that they tend to shorten their jiggling over the first 2 weeks. They do feel, however, that their intervention is important, that they are doing something active and necessary to keep the infant sucking. Notice that in responding to a pause the mother is doing the same thing she does in response to pauses in adult conversation. When a partner stops talking, in the absence of certain floor-holding cues one feels obligated to say something. (Kaye 1982, p. 188)

What takes place between the mother and her infant at this early stage may be classed as communication, but a type of communication that breaks most of the rules. A standard way of defining communication after Shannon and Weaver (1949) is as a transmission of information that alters the state of the receiver. This tends to accord comfortably with an adaptive view of communicative behavior in lower animals, where intention movements are seen to confer advantages because they can be used to transmit clearly definable signals of courtship or threat. The content of the signal is linked to the change it brings about in the recipient, which induces the other creature to respond sexually or beat a retreat, thereby contributing to the survival of the sender's genes, and thus conferring selective advantage on the trait that is responsible.

The infant's pauses in sucking clearly do cause changes in the mother, since they induce her to start jiggling. What is not so clear is whether one can conceptualize those pauses as carriers of biologically specified "information," let alone how any such message might be linked to selective advantage for the infant. The infant needs no encouragement to drink (he will resume sucking when he "is ready"), and furthermore, jiggling does not have the effect that the mother believes it has. Conceptualizing burst-pause-burst and jiggling in terms of the transmission of information leads to the conclusion that a message is received that was never sent. It is not possible to establish a convincing explanatory link between the infant's activity, his mother's response, and a clear selective advantage in terms of milk intake.* Nonetheless, natural selection has seen to it that this species-typical activity pattern survived. Burst-pause-burst and jiggling clearly do confer some advantage on our species.

That advantage has nothing to do with feeding, but it is necessary that the mother believes that the interaction with her infant is about feeding. The biological advantage can, I suggest, arise only from the cooccurence of burst-pause-burst and jiggling with an intentional interpretation by the mother (that the baby is getting lazy and needs to be jostled back onto the job). Mothers would jiggle without folk psychological justification, since they are biologically primed to do so, but it is the intentional interpretation of their infant's and their own behavior that enables the interactive pattern of sucking and jiggling to play its bootstrapping role. It therefore appears that the infant's species-typical activity pattern is adapted to a natural environment of adults who think in intentional terms and that the advantages that have caused the activity pattern to survive have more to do with establishing the pragmatics of communication than with feeding.

Turn taking is not unique to human beings. One has only to observe the courting behavior or aggressive displays of certain birds and fishes to realize that it is an important feature of animal "communication." What makes human turn taking different from that of other animals is its flexibility and adaptiveness. The turn taking of other animals is an emergent aspect of specific action patterns triggered by specific cues. The components of the interaction are fixed, and the cues are action-specific sign stimuli. Turn taking, in these animals, is tied to a particular behavior like courting or mock fighting, and it cannot be generalized.

Human communication, on the other hand, requires underlying mechanisms with great flexibility. It must be capable of dealing with an unbounded range of subjects in an unlimited range of situations and of using a diversity of communicative media like sign language,

---

*It could be argued that short bouts of jiggling will encourage the infant to resume sucking more quickly than he would have done if the mother did not jiggle him at all and that therefore the action of jiggling followed by cessation can be given an adaptive rationale in terms of food intake. Remember, however, that we are trying to provide an adaptive explanation for the infant's pauses as well as the mother's response to them. Pausing does not increase the efficiency of feeding and is manifested only by human infants. This makes it difficult to ascribe to it a straightforward signaling function, in the way that behavioral ecologists have done for threat or courtship displays, and it would appear to rule out an adaptive explanation in terms of food intake for the emergence of the interactive pattern as a whole.

music, dance, and subtle details of expression, as well as vocal exchanges. We have inherited certain signals like smiling and eyebrow raising from our primate ancestors, but these become assimilated and elaborated into far more complex patterns of social interaction. Early communicative exchanges with adults provide the means for launching an infant into such flexible patterns of "dialogue." Human infants have to be bootstrapped into the world of meaning. Turn taking of the particular human variety is the mechanism that makes this possible.

Human turn taking requires two fundamental ingredients: a pattern of interaction that is not used to convey messages that are critical in a biological sense and a mother eager to interpret her infant's every move as meaningful, intentional, and responsive to herself. Turn taking in suckling fits that description. The mother tends to interpret her infant's pauses as signs that she must rouse him to renewed activity, but as we have seen, her interpretation has no biological basis. No discrete, biologically fixed messages are passed back and forth. A functional role in feeding is not the reason that the burst-pause-burst pattern of the baby, complemented by the mother's responsive jiggling, survived. These activity patterns survived because they resulted in interactively emergent turn taking that could serve as the context for subsequent communication.

By the age of six weeks, human infants and their mothers are communicating extensively face to face. The expressive elements the baby uses have become much more varied. They include coos, murmurs, smiles, frowns, and a variety of stereotyped activities like arm waving and kicking. The mother interprets these activities as indications of the infant's emotional state, of his "beliefs and desires," and of his responses to her own acts of mothering. In fact, as Kaye (1982) has pointed out, the infant's varied expressions and gestures are still randomly distributed in time. There is no predictable pattern to the partners' contributions in this interaction. One cannot anticipate the baby's behavior by assuming temporal entrainment or a framework of meaning. The crucial mechanism remains that of flexible turn taking, in which the infant's contributions are species-typical activity patterns well adapted to create an illusion in the mother that meaningful exchange is taking place.

It is the mother who contributes all the meaning. Whenever her infant does anything that can be interpreted as a turn in the "conversation," she will treat it as such. She fills in the gaps, pauses to allow her infant to respond, allows herself to be paced by him, but also subtly leads him on. She could not do this without the conviction that an actual dialogue is taking place, and that conviction depends on her intentional explanation of her infant's activity patterns and the

interactive turn taking with the infant that has already been established by feeding.

The mother-infant dialogue at this stage still has no specific content.
It cannot be conceptualized as a series of discrete messages with specific meanings that are being passed back and forth. But the pragmatics
of conversation that are being established are an important element in
the explanation of how meaning emerges for the infant. As Schaffer
(1977b) writes, turn taking of the nonspecific, flexible human variety is
eminently suited to a number of important developments that occur
over the next few months. It allows the infant to discover what sorts
of activity on his part will get responses from his mother. It allows
routine sequences of a predictable nature to be built up. And it provides a context of mutual expectations, which can be disrupted by the
infant around the age of four months, when another species-typical
activity pattern matures, and he begins to avoid eye contact with his
mother and to gaze at other objects in the world.

15.4 The Mechanics of Face-to-Face Contact

A satisfactory explanation of the interactive processes in these early
months would require a much fuller description of the activity patterns
of the mother and the child than is currently available. However, some
of the underlying mechanisms that maintain face-to-face contact and
mutual gaze have begun to be better understood. Earlier observers like
Bazelton (1979) and Bateson (1979) had realized the importance of the
infant's gaze, which tends to become locked on the face of the mother,
in sustaining her interest and encouraging her persistent attempts to
engage him in conversation. Some of these observers had further remarked that the mother tends to place herself not only in the line of
sight of her infant but also at a distance of approximately twenty to
twenty-five centimeters from his eyes, gently moving her face from
side to side to attract his attention (Papousek and Papousek 1977).

Johnson (1993b) provides a detailed neurological analysis of the way
that visual attention develops in human infants over the first few
months of life. His explanation of the changing patterns of eye movements in response to visual stimuli is framed entirely in terms of the
development of successive cortical layers. He identifies four distinct
neural pathways, which are sequentially activated as the infant's cortex matures over this period.

Newborn vision is mediated primarily by subcortical structures. If a
moving stimulus disappears from the temporal periphery of one eye,
both eyes will perform a saccade in that direction. The mechanism of
this early saccade is extremely simple. Once the eyes have locked on

to the moving stimulus, saccades of a specific amplitude continue to be performed each time the stimulus disappears from the field of vision. The interesting question, from our point of view, is why such an activity might confer adaptive advantage on a newborn. An infant at this age cannot use his vision to catch prey or avoid danger. He is helpless and totally dependent on his parents. One possible explanation might be that these early saccadic movements confer a communicative advantage. As Turkewitz and Kenny (1993) have pointed out, the young infant's environment and his restricted focal depth ensure that the mother's face is to all intents and purposes the only object that intrudes into his field of vision during these initial months. Crude accommodations to the mother's activities convey an impression of interest, even if they do not actually help in seeing better. They can be incorporated into an interactive pattern with the mother, which she is likely to interpret as intentional and purposeful. They may also provide a kind of scaffolding for more advanced levels of visual attention.

At the age of one month, the infant starts to display a mysterious excess of attention that has been called "obligatory gaze." His eyes may become locked on a specific point for as long as thirty minutes, sometimes causing the infant considerable distress. Johnson (1993b) speculates that an inhibitory mechanism in the lower areas of the cortex has begun to mature, so that peripheral stimuli have temporarily lost their power to distract the infant. Again, his explanation is framed entirely in neurophysiological and maturational terms, and it mentions only disadvantages to the infant. However, the resulting intent gaze can be highly stimulating to the mother. Brazelton (1979) has written of the "wide, soft and eager" look of an infant at that age, which "impels" a nurturing adult to respond. Mutual gaze is often cited in the literature as a crucial element in establishing face-to-face contact, and the onset of face-to-face communication is usually placed at around six weeks. Obligatory gaze can thus be seen as a highly adaptive stage in the development of visual attention. It strengthens the bond between mother and infant and reinforces the mother's conviction that she is dealing with a full human being.

Segments of smooth tracking become interleaved with peripheral tracking at between six and eight weeks. At the same time, there is a greatly increased sensitivity in the nasal area of the visual field. Johnson argues that these changes are caused by the fact that during the second and third months, layer 4 of the cortex becomes functionally mature, providing a cortical pathway to the middle temporal area, which is thought to be crucially involved in smooth tracking. The cortex gains control over eye movements, allowing the infant to detect stimuli in the nasal area, and the "externality effect" declines (infants become more able to attend to smaller features within larger frameworks).

From a behavioral and communicative point of view, it might be argued that having achieved eye contact through primitive saccades and obligatory gaze, the infant now becomes capable of attending to the mother's features and their changing expressions. This increases the illusion of intentional response. It makes the baby's reactions look more varied (his eye movements concentrating now on the mother's eyes, now on the movements of her mouth) and serves to draw him even more tightly into dialogues with the mother.

Between three and six months, smooth tracking becomes anticipatory tracking: the eyes have begun to move ahead to where the stimulus is likely to appear. Johnson (1993b) concludes that this is evidence of a "mechanism capable of computing the trajectory of a moving object." Such a description implies that the infant's cortex has acquired the ability to form dynamic representations of movement in the real world. Computing a trajectory means abstracting, from the present position and velocity of the image on the retina, a formal description of the movement of the corresponding object that allows extrapolation into the future. I have discussed the problems involved in this approach in chapter 11, where I argued against the classic attempt by Rosenblueth, Wiener, and Bigelow (1943) to provide a cybernetic basis for teleological explanations of purposeful behavior.

It seems more promising to examine the emergence of smooth and anticipatory tracking as integral parts of a developmental process. Smooth tracking gradually emerges within a framework of primitive saccadic movements performed in response to the mother's species-typical behavior. The way in which this system of subcortical reflexes might help to train the more sophisticated, cortically mediated activity of smooth tracking can be understood by analogy with Pfeifer and Verschure's (1992) learning robot, which I discussed in chapter 8. Pfeifer and Verschure's robot contained a neural network whose weights were modified according to a Hebbian learning rule, and this network was "trained" by emergent patterns of activity resulting from interactions of the robot with its environment, mediated by its primitive collision sensors. The network learned to "anticipate" recurring correlations between sensory input from a range finder and its own motor commands, allowing it gradually to take over control of the robot's behavior from the collision sensors.

It is possible to describe what happens in such a network as computation, but the interesting aspect of Pfeifer and Verschure's robot was its success in using the perceptual consequences of emergent behavior mediated by simple reflexes as the context for training a higher-level control mechanism. The network does not end up containing rules for evading obstacles or equations for performing specific types of movement; it contains information (if that is the right word) about movements in a specific environment performed by a robot with specific sensorimotor characteristics. This information is stored in the weights of the network and does not constitute an objective representation of the robot's environment; it ensures that the robot, with its particular sensorimotor characteristics, is directly attuned to that environment.

Analogously, the important elements in an explanation of the emergence of smooth, anticipatory tracking would be the primitive, subcortically mediated saccades of early infancy, coupled with a unique, species-typical environment. Due to the infant's limited depth of focus, this environment is composed almost entirely of gestures and expressions made by the mother. The cortical pathways that mediate adult visual attention are thus laid down under the influence of interactive movements, just like the weights in Pfeifer and Vershure's robot. The difference is that the mother introduces an intentional component into the system. Her responses are shaped by a conviction that the infant's eye movements, as well as her own, are *about* something and must be performed for a *purpose*. It could thus be said that patterns of intentional movement are built into adult patterns of visual attention by the early face-to-face contact between the mother and infant.

I have discussed Johnson's (1993b) neurological analysis of the maturation of attention in some detail because it brings out a number of important points. It demonstrates, first, that a close attention to the species-typical activity patterns of infants and their mothers, and their interactions in specifically human contexts, may provide insights concerning the "logic" of certain sequences of neural maturation. As Oyama (1993) says and Lehrman (1970) pointed out before her, a living organism, unlike a machine, needs to work at all stages of its development. It works in different ways and in different dynamic environments during the course of maturation. In the case of human beings, these ways are largely dictated by the need to involve adults in providing for an unusually helpless creature, and the environment is, from the very start, highly supportive and intentional.

A related point concerns the advantages that may be conferred by immaturity. As Turkewitz and Kenny (1993) complain, the use of the term *immature* to describe infant behavior tends to imply that it should be viewed as an imperfect version of the fully developed adult variety. However, an infant with fully developed foveating and focusing abilities would almost certainly be overwhelmed by his visual input, and what is just as important, his perceptual system would not be restricted to, and therefore incapable of being "trained" by, his mother's facial expressions and gestures. In a creature that needs to work at all stages of its development, immature forms of behavior are highly adaptive forms, which serve to provide emergent contexts for later forms.

My second motive for spending time on the mechanism of attention is to indicate the variety and complexity of the parameters involved and the way in which environmental and neurological factors need to be viewed within an interactive framework. Neurology by itself, as Marr (1982) long ago pointed out, cannot provide us with an understanding of *what* various pathways in the brain are actually doing. But neither can the sort of computational solutions to problems posed by the environment that Marr himself tended to advocate. Vision must be conceptualized as a collection of active processes, not in Marr's sense of successive stages that serve to construct internal representations of objects underdetermined by their retinal projections but in the sense that Mataric's and Pfeifer and Verschure's robots are conceived and built as collections of active processes.

The "information" that emerges from these processes is like the information that emerges from the low-level interactions of Mataric's and Pfeifer and Verschure's robots. It cannot be conceptualized in terms of objects, features, and events existing in a world out there, because it has largely been shaped by the system's own behavior, which depends on its sensorimotor characteristics and its developmental history.

This means that the environment becomes assimilated into the behavior of the mechanism at a very low level but in a way that is quite different from Piaget's (1954) concept of assimilation. Human eye movements are typically human because of certain species-typical activity patterns that appear as the cortex matures and because these activity patterns interact with a dynamic environment of purposive and intentional movements to provide a training context for the more advanced eye movements of adults. As Yarbus (1984) discovered, each human being has his own idiosyncratic style of scanning a scene, which is entirely subconscious. This may have quite a lot to do with the fact that each mother-infant dyad has its own idiosyncratic style of interacting and tends to develop its own favorite repetitive games (Kaye 1979; Papousek and Papousek 1977). The eye movements, in turn, play a crucial role in the pragmatics of adult communication, signaling intentions and contexts for meaning that cannot be gleaned from the spoken word alone.

15.5 Objects, Intentions, and Meanings

Around the age of four months, the infant displays a new, species-typical activity pattern. Having established intense, face-to-face contact with the mother, he begins to look away. This new activity is particularly noticeable to the mother because of its contrast to the pattern of turn taking and mutual gaze to which she has become accustomed. She interprets it as an intentional act, directed toward a specific object. As Collis (1979) and many others have pointed out, the infant does not in fact appear to gaze at anything in particular and certainly is not trying to inform his mother of a newly found interest in objects. It is *she* who will convert a particular object into the object of his attention by interpreting his gaze as interest in it.

The infant may perform a primitive reach-and-grasp gesture in the direction of the object; the mother will interpret this as an attempt to take hold of the object and intervene to complete the infant's action. She thereby incorporates the infant's rudimentary activity patterns into an action that is *about* an object. The mother provides the supportive framework or scaffolding in which the activity pattern acquires intentional significance.

With the aid of the dynamic scaffolding supplied by the mother, the infant thus performs intentional acts (acts directed toward objects and about objects) long before he is capable of intentional thought. Such acts do not require internal representations of the objects in question; in fact, I shall argue that the internal representations of adult thought are grounded in a long history of performances of such acts, from which the scaffolding is gradually removed.

Camaioni (1993) distinguishes three distinct levels of mother-infant-object interactions. Her interest is early mother-infant communication and how this develops into true "intentional communication" on the part of the child (Camaioni uses "intentional" in a psychological rather than a philosophical sense, to designate conscious purpose). Like most of the investigators whose work has been discussed in this chapter, she believes that initially the child is unaware of the signal value of his own activities: "The only partner with a goal in mind during early interaction is the parent, who imputes meaning to the baby's actions and vocalisations so that the baby begins to understand the significance of his actions/expressions for other people" (Camaioni 1993, p. 85). The object, brought into the primary mother-infant interaction, plays an important part in this shift to intentional communication, but the ability to coordinate attention to an object merely provides the scaffolding for the emergence of full-blown intentionality. Once the child begins to show a real interest in objects, he will try to use his mother's body as a tool to gain access to them, by, for instance, pushing her hand toward the object if it is out of reach. This is the most primitive level of mother-infant-object interaction. The infant looks at the object and the mother's hand but not at her face.

Next, says Camaioni, he will learn to use the mother as an agent for achieving his aims. An indication that this level has been achieved is that the infant's glance will move from the object to the mother's face rather than to her hand. Finally, as a sign of true intentionality, the infant learns to use objects, not for their own sake but to arouse the interest of his mother. He now sees the mother as an independent human being with her own mental states whose interests do not automatically coincide with his own. Camaioni believes that this type of communicative behavior requires a full-blown internal representation of the mother as an intentional agent.

Camaioni's categories of mother-infant-object interaction are important for an understanding of the infant's progressive integration into an intentional world. What is less certain is whether they can be used to support a conceptualization of the underlying mechanism in the way that she attempts to use them. Even at the end of their second year, children often appear to have little sense of their playmates as intentional beings (Eckerman 1993). On the other hand, infants who are quite a bit younger will display behavior (when the mother is requested by an investigator to look away from her child) that may be interpreted as attempts to recapture the mother's attention (Trevarthen 1984). To say that, around the age of ten or twelve months, the infant acquires an intentional representation of his mother that inspires and enables him to manipulate her attention seems to beg a lot of questions.

The problem stems, as Fogel (1993) argues, from a determination to conceptualize the mechanics of such exchanges in folk psychological terms. The child is seen as performing either one class of act or another, and these acts are presumed to be occasioned by specific desires or aims. The continuing interactive sequence is broken up into a series of discrete messages conveyed by intention movements, causing discrete changes of state in the recipient. Fogel argues that this is not a helpful description of what goes on between a mother and her infant—or, for that matter, between any two people interacting in a normal way.

His example is that of a child handing an object to his mother. In the discrete state view, the sequence can be described as follows: The infant holds out the object in his hand, signaling his desire to give it to the mother. The mother responds by holding out her hand, transmitting the message that she is ready to receive the object. If the infant correctly receives that message, he will drop the object into her hand. This description of the underlying mechanism is derived from a conceptual analysis of our folk psychological manner of describing such interactions.

Fogel claims that a careful analysis of the interactional sequence as captured on slow-motion video does not support such an interpretation. He points out, first, that both the mother and the infant are continuously moving toward the point of mutual contact with the object and that this point is not a predetermined location but is "dynamically constituted by the continuous co-regulated actions of the partners" (Fogel 1993, p. 10). In other words, the observed movements of mother and child are produced by interactive emergence. They result from low-level responses of two continuously active creatures, each of whose activities is adjusted from moment to moment to the position and movements of the other. This makes it impossible to determine, at any particular time, who is the "sender" and who the "receiver," and points to the need for an alternative model.

Fogel's other example is that of smiling. In the discrete state view, a smile conveys a specific message. The message is presumed to originate within the smiler, who uses her skill in controlling facial expressions, gaze direction, and body movements to fix the precise nature of the message she is trying to put across (a smile may be joyful, encouraging, cynical, or merely polite). The smiler's intention thus shapes the nature of a discrete intentional act and determines the message it transmits. From the point of view of the continuous process model that Fogel recommends, a smile emerges within an interactive context, and its nature may change at any point during its development. This is not just a matter of chopping up the interaction into even smaller discrete acts. It requires a radical change of perspective, in which the activities of the partners, rather than their presumed mental states and discrete intentional acts, become the natural kinds of the explanation.

Does Fogel's analysis contradict the notion of turn taking, which plays such an important part in the interactive explanation of psychological development? I believe that, on the contrary, it illuminates the role played by turn taking in bootstrapping the infant into meaning. Turn taking is not a prespecified pattern that can be traced to a mechanism contained within either of the partners engaged in communication. It is an emergent regularity, recognizable to an observer, just as wall following by Mataric's robot was an emergent, recognizable pattern that did not result from a prescriptive program inside the robot but from local adjustments mediated by its low-level reflexes.

In order that turn taking may serve as scaffolding for higher levels of behavior, the mother must see her interactions with the infant not only as composed of discrete turns, governed by formal rules, but she should also interpret these turns as intentional acts (in both the psychological sense of being inspired by conscious intentions, and the philosophical sense of being "about" events and objects in the world). Her contributions to the interaction are informed by an intentional perspective, and this provides her with the framework that enables her to fill in gaps, pace herself to the infant's activity patterns, and relate them to her own "meaningful" contributions.

The following quotations from different practitioners of the branch of sociology called ethnomethodology may help to clarify the nature of this process:

> Social meanings, then, and the social order which is produced by them, are the ongoing practical accomplishment of members achieved in situations of interaction. (Walsh 1970, p. 84)

> We notice that the apparent orderliness and coherency of the scenes of daily life are matters that members are continually and unavoidably engaged in recognising and making recognisable to each other. We notice that over the course of interaction members persuade and otherwise make evident to each other that events and actions directed toward them are coherent, consistent, planful, connected, and the like. (Zimmerman and Wieder 1971, p. 653)

In other words, even in adult interactions, people assign meanings to their ongoing interactive activities as they occur, deciding that they are performed in accordance with certain rules and that they indicate the occurrence, in both themselves and their partners, of certain well-defined mental states describable as beliefs and desires, which make them into acts that are intelligible and goal directed. This interpretation is essential to the maintenance of social interactions, and it clearly works on the level of folk psychology, but it becomes misleading if it is used as a model for the underlying mechanisms.

Human beings require a long apprenticeship to learn these techniques of interpretation, precisely because their underlying mechanisms do not operate naturally from beliefs and desires. Their mothers, having been inducted during their own infancy and childhood into this trick of interpreting their own and other people's behavior, provide the scaffolding for that apprenticeship. They are not aware of the detailed nature of their interactions with the infant, on the level that Fogel examines it, and it is to the advantage of the developmental process that they should be unaware of it, because this allows them to take the infant's turn taking seriously and to draw him into the plot of human interaction. It is only by partaking in intentional activity (at first heavily scaffolded) that we acquire the habits of intentional beings.

To return to Camaioni's analysis of intentional communication, it is clear that infants at a very young age display interactive patterns that a human observer will tend to interpret as attempts to attract the mother's attention. The mother will almost certainly treat them as attempts to attract her attention, and this is why they have survived. But it is quite different, as Camaioni herself would undoubtedly agree, to infer from this to the existence of a goal-directed, attention-seeking mechanism inside the three-month-old infant.

In the same way, later activity patterns involving objects may be interpreted in the terms that Camaioni uses, and the mother almost certainly does interpret them in those terms (taking the infant's glance from an object to her face as an indication that he is trying to draw her into a game, and assuming that his act of pointing at something outside a window is meant to capture her attention). But to conclude from this that a new underlying mechanism matures at that age that depends on an internal representation of the mother as an intentional being is almost certainly to make a category mistake. Infants at this age are unable to impose an intentional interpretation on their own and other people's actions because they lack the final, all-important ingredient of language, which will be discussed in the next chapter.

Human infants are biologically primed to perform certain activity patterns. These activity patterns have been selected for the advantages they confer on an exceptionally helpless young animal born into an environment of adults who think in intentional terms, use artifacts, and communicate through language. It is misleading to infer that the activity patterns embody knowledge about that world. They merely make it more likely that the infant will be drawn into patterned interactions with his mother and other adults. The activity patterns have been selected for their power to attract the attention of adults, to be interpreted as meaningful, and to promote the habit of turn taking that is essential to human communication.

Turn taking is an emergent phenomenon that itself serves as the scaffolding or dynamic context for more advanced patterns of behavior. It may be thought of as the cradle of meaning. It incorporates the infant's species-typical activity patterns into a structured exchange that can be interpreted as a series of discrete intentional acts and allows the mother to shape and direct that activity in accordance with her interpretation along those lines. Turn taking is initiated by burst-pause-burst in sucking, but it depends for its emergence on the mother's folk psychological stance. Eventually the infant himself learns to attach folk psychological labels to parts of his behavior that his mother points out to him, causing him to see it as a series of discrete acts bearing specific messages or meanings.

Chapter 16

Language and the Emergence of Intentionality

16.1 Standard Explanations of Intentionality

My aim is not to deny that human beings engage in conceptual thought. What I have argued against is the assumption that the mechanisms that subtend our public and mental behavior can be explained in terms of formal operations on symbolic structures whose relations and shapes may be derived by conceptual analysis from the folk psychological terms in which we naturally describe the surface phenomena. Human beings have minds, and they require an explanation. The explanations offered by cognitive science have tended to be redescriptions rather than explanations, and they have not succeeded in addressing the central problem of how mental phenomena can be naturalized.

Since Brentano, it has been accepted that the defining characteristic of mental phenomena is their intentionality. Thoughts, beliefs, human actions, as well as the linguistic and pictorial representations we compulsively produce, are *about* something. This aboutness distinguishes the mental from the (merely) physical. Brentano believed that it was an irreducible feature of mental phenomena and that therefore the mind should not be identified with the brain.

The strategy of traditional analytic philosophy has been to bracket the question of what intentionality really is and to examine instead the way in which people talk about mental phenomena. The problem of intentionality then becomes a question of describing the semantics of intentional idioms, which can be formalized and reduced to such expressions as "believes that P" or "desires that Q." Such idioms are "referentially opaque." Intentional relations depend on how their objects are specified (Oedipus wanted to marry Jocasta but did not want to marry his mother). The identity of a belief is tied to the object it is supposed to be about (the same belief cannot be about two different things). And the object of a belief does not have to exist (I can have beliefs about unicorns). Referential opacity provides a useful formal test for the intentionality of idioms. It separates intentional expressions from nonintentional ones. The question is whether it can help in explaining how intentional behavior works.

Quine (who can be held responsible for the strategy of "semantic ascent" described above) concluded that all intentional theories were necessarily bankrupt. (It should be clear that this includes "rational agent" economics, as well as cost-benefit theories in biology and "semantic token" theories in cognitive science.) He further concluded that this meant that the only acceptable theories about human and animal behavior had to be purely behavioristic or physiological theories. Unfortunately, such theories have so far failed to produce adequate explanations for the intelligent behavior of human beings, and it does not look as if they will enable us to bridge the gap between the physical sciences and the mental. Whenever a likely candidate is proposed, it can usually be shown that it derives its explanatory power from intentional terms that have inadvertently slipped into formulations of the theory as explanatory entities. (In earlier chapters I argued that this is the case with classic and connectionist representations in AI.) Quine's strategy of semantic ascent produced a useful test for intentional idioms, but it does not seem to have helped in providing an explanation.

There are a number of different stances one can take to intentionality:

> 1. It is possible to argue that the intentionality of linguistic and other representations is derived from some intrinsic quality of the mind. The "aboutness" that characterizes intentional phenomena is then seen as a result of the fact that such phenomena are produced and used by creatures with minds. This of course raises the question what it is about minds that makes them so different. One possible answer might be consciousness (Searle 1991). However, explanations of this type merely tend to transfer the problem to some other, equally mysterious phenomenon.

> 2. One can maintain that it is not only human phenomena that are about something but that, for instance, the beaver's tail splash contains information about danger (Millikan 1984), a ring around the moon contains information about a future change in the weather, and fossils contain information about life-forms that existed in the past. This is sometimes taken as a justification for positing that some concept of information underlies all instances of aboutness and that such a concept could unify mind, matter, and meaning in a single theory. (The work of Dretske 1986, 1988, which I discussed in chapter 3, may be seen as an elaboration of this strategy.) Shannon's mathematical theory of information (Shannon and Weaver 1949), and in particular Weaver's discus-

sion of its implications, contributed to the influence of this idea in cognitive science. However, Shannon himself made quite clear that his theory had nothing to say about content. It is an engineering tool that relates channel capacity and noise to the amount of redundancy required if a string of symbols with a known frequency distribution is to get across with a specified degree of accuracy.

As Millikan (1984) and many others have pointed out, information in the sense of content depends on a user and a particular context. The beaver's tail splash is "about" danger to other beavers only in certain situations (because it served the beavers' ancestors as a warning in such situations and contributed to their survival). A ring around the moon is probably "about" a change in the weather only to human beings, and fossils convey their full information only to trained paleontologists, who are able to interpret their "meaning." Information is not a universal explanatory category that can unite various forms of aboutness.

3. One can argue that intentional explanations using belief-desire ascriptions have been and continue to be "reliably and voluminously predictive" of human and animal behavior and that this justifies the "intentional stance" (Dennett 1978). The intentional stance picks out the "design specs" of an intentional creature. Minds are ultimately syntactic engines, and the final explanation will almost certainly have to be framed in causal-informational terms, but intentional descriptions pick out the relevant areas of competence. At the heart of this "ascriptionist" position lies the assumption of "good design," justified on the grounds of natural selection. I have spent much of this book arguing against the equation of evolutionary emergence with a notion of design.

4. One can argue, with Millikan (1984), that intentionality is proper function under normal conditions, bypassing all causal-informational accounts. Natural selection, according to this account, confers true intentionality. Intentionality does not reside in a mechanism in the creature's head; it is conferred by an entity's history of use. This position does not depend on the design stance needed by Dennett. Millikan's notion of proper function focuses on one of the crucial differences between function as derived from functional analysis informed by a design stance and function as grounded in natural selection. I have argued that it cannot be used to naturalize explanatory entities "in the head" (i.e., internal representations) but that it provides a strategy for identifying the natural kinds of emergent, situated activity. However, this is only a beginning in the explanation of human

intentionality. Millikan's aim was to show that language is just another biological category. I shall argue in this chapter that language is a separate cultural ingredient that must be added to the patterns of activity conferred on us by biology, though a considerable proportion of these species-typical activity patterns are specifically adapted to launch us into language use.

5. A fifth stance is exemplified by the language of thought hypothesis (Fodor 1976). The intentionality of linguistic entities, according to this position, is not derived from intrinsic properties of the minds that use them. On the contrary, minds derive their intentionality from the linguistic structures that are physically embodied in our brains. The intentionality of expressions in the language of thought is taken to be primary, and the intentionality of our public speech and other behavior is assumed to be derived from it. I have spent little time discussing this hypothesis because it leads to a serious explanatory impasse (Fodor 1980), and to the paradox that the basic constituents of all "knowledge" acquired through learning must already be contained in the system at birth. Fodor's position has nothing to say about context dependence, embodiment, or situated behavior, and although it depends on innate linguistic structures, it makes no real contact with Darwin's theory of natural selection. (Later in this chapter I shall discuss an attempt by Pinker and Bloom 1990 to provide an evolutionary rationale for the emergence of innate linguistic structures.)

This list of stances is not meant to be definitive or exhaustive but merely to give an idea of the variety of explanatory strategies that cognitive philosophers have proposed. There are two characteristics of these explanations to which I would like to draw attention: language plays an important part in many of them, but the actual processes of language acquisition are very rarely discussed. Often the central premises of these theories turn on questions of how much, or what aspect, or what form of language is innate and how much needs to be learned. However, little interest is shown in the evidence produced by developmental studies, which one might have thought would be the best way to shed some light on these matters.

In the previous chapter I suggested that the basic grounding for language acquisition and intentionality is laid before the infant uses his first word. I argued for a historical approach in terms of interactive emergence and scaffolding. In this chapter I shall try to sketch in the remaining ingredient of my explanation. It involves an alternative view of intentionality to those listed above: Intentionality, taken in the sense of "aboutness" which distinguishes mental from physical phenomena, needs to be learned, and it probably requires an interactive environment of cultural and linguistic artifacts to become established and to maintain itself.

Our intentional explanations of the behavior of other animals do not necessarily pick out the correct explanatory entities. The mother duck's behavior with respect to her duckling can be shown to be a conglomeration of independent activity patterns, each of which has its own, distinct, action-specific sign stimulus. The only reason these activity patterns converge on her duckling is that all those sign stimuli are situated on the duckling. Our intentional descriptions of animals can thus ascribe an aboutness to their actions that does not correspond to the operations of the underlying mechanisms. The mechanisms of the mother duck's behavior make no reference to the duckling, just as the mechanisms of wall following in Mataric's robot do not refer to walls, and the focusing mechanisms that cause a young infant's gaze to center on his mother's face are not about the mother. However, an adequate explanation of the behavior and thoughts of mature human beings *does* require a reference to the things they are about (real or counterfactual), because the underlying mechanisms that subtend this behavior have been affected by the objects, properties, and relations picked out by our language and culture.

In his latest book, Clark (1993), as part of his continuing project to reconcile folk psychology and connectionism, is forced to the following conclusions:

> Let us agree with Evans that the generality constraint requires that a being who is able to have the thought that John is happy must be exercising two distinct skills. One, the ability to think about John (and hence to have *other* John thoughts, e.g., "John is sad"). The other, the ability to think of happiness (and hence to have other happiness thoughts, e.g., "I am happy"). . . . But let us further insist that each of these abilities or skills may be sustained by a highly loosely-knit set of inner computational states. What welds the states together into a single skill is not the fact that they can be seen to share some common property visible in the vocabulary of physics or of neuroscience, or even of computational psychology. Instead, these several scientifically disunified inner states combine to constitute a single skill because their combined presence enables an agent successfully to negotiate some macro-level domain which interests us in virtue of the form of our daily human life. (pp. 202–203)

Note that Clark appears to conclude that the absence of a unifying property that can be characterized in the language of physics, neuroscience, or computational psychology rules out all hope of a scientific unification. My aim has been to show that we do have a scientific alternative to the deductive, probabilistic, and functional approaches that are often believed to exhaust science—that of historical explanations—and that in many cases this is the only explanatory strategy that can isolate appropriate natural kinds.

Clark's argument may be summed up as follows: Concepts do not correspond to specific internal states or structures. They must be equated with the ability to exercise a particular skill: the skill of deploying the concept in all relevant situations that do not lead to category mistakes. Internally, such a skill may be sustained by a variety of disjunct computational states that need to have nothing in common from the point of view of physics, neuroscience, or even computational psychology. They are held together purely by the fact that, together, they enable an agent to "negotiate some macro-level domain which interests us in virtue of our daily human life." Consequently, it is only from the point of view of folk psychology that they display their unity.

Clark compares mastery of a concept to being skillful at playing a game like golf. Being good at golf does not mean having a competence that can be identified with a mental structure corresponding to the entity "golf." The various skills that are required to play the game have nothing in common that allows us to posit an internal state or process that unites them. They are unified only by a public "macrolevel domain" that derives its structure from the "form of our daily life." The fact that there exists a public game of golf, which involves hitting a ball, first over long distances, then over progressively shorter distances, and finally into a little hole, makes golfers practice all these skills until they become "good at golf."

In the same way, being good at thinking about dogs and acting appropriately with respect to dogs (which is what having the concept "dog" amounts to) does not mean being good at manipulating some internal symbol that can be identified with the word "dog" or the various properties of dogs. The different skills involved in having thoughts about dogs do not share a common causal factor that may be found within the person who has mastered the concept. These skills are only *about* the concept because they converge on the public linguistic and cultural entity "dog," in the same way as the rearing skills of the mother duck were *about* her duckling only because they converged on the duckling "in the real world."

The convergence of duckling-related behavior came about because it produced reproductive advantage. Various activity patterns combined to produce emergent mothering, permitting more ducklings to survive. This established emergent mothering as a recognizable and stable behavior pattern. The opportunism of natural selection welded together the disjunct set of activities that we tend to describe in intentional terms. Such intentional description of the mother duck's behavior (that it is "about" the duckling) is applicable only because of its interactive nature and the fact that the various constituent activities are situated in a particular environment.

Similarly, intentional descriptions of thoughts about dogs are applicable because there exists a public entity "dog" on which all the subskills converge. However, in this case the entity is linguistic and cultural. The concept "dog" exists only in the artifacts produced by human beings and in linguistic expressions referring to dogs.

The question then becomes how all the subskills that are involved in the ability to grasp a particular concept *come* to converge on the linguistic and cultural entity "out there." Analysis of the public concept, and formal definitions that may be derived from it, cannot provide explanations of its use. Computational explanations involving the manipulation of symbols and subsymbols (including connectionist explanations that require analytically derived "features" and/or "properties" to be assigned to input terminals) cannot explain intentional use of a concept. Explanations will need to be couched in nonconceptual terms that can describe what it means to have a skill, particularly in relation to linguistic and cultural entities.

Clark's main purpose is to preserve an explanatory role for connectionist networks. He marshals evidence from the literature to show that networks are capable of "modularizing" themselves through a form of representational redescription and that it is possible to "shield" networks from the statistical vagaries of raw data, making it more likely for systematicity to emerge. Such explanatory devices continue to locate explanation "inside the creature's head," although Clark admits that "the space of words is doubtless one determinant of the particular constellation of cognitive skills we choose to focus on. We care about *whatever it takes* to come to know *enough* about *dogs* say, to count as understanding the word 'dog.' The question what determines the individuation of concepts (given that we cannot relate it to *inner facts*) is, however, a hard one, and I am aware that I have no fully adequate answer" (p. 205).

In the remainder of this chapter I shall address myself to that question and suggest that an adequate answer requires an abandonment of all attempts to seek explanatory principles or entities inside the creature's head, and a genuine commitment to the importance of developmental processes in determining the underlying mechanisms of intentional behavior.

16.2 A Species-Typical Vocal Environment for Language Acquisition

During the infant's first eight weeks of life, the sounds he produces are restricted to crying and "vegetative noises" like sucking, burping, and swallowing (Crystal 1987). There is nothing language specific about these noises, but the mother will respond to them from the start, interpreting her infant's utterances as indications of his emotional and physiological state. Between eight and twenty weeks, the infant starts to make cooing noises when he is quiet and alert (Bateson 1975, 1979). This elicits a softer tone of voice from the mother and heralds the beginning of turn taking during face-to-face contact. Toward the end of this period, the coos get strung together, but the resulting strings have no recognizable rhythm or intonational contour.

Between twenty and thirty weeks, a variety of consonant-and-vowel sequences begin to appear. These are frequently repeated. The child seems to try out different combinations of consonants and vowels, and there is some variation in pitch. The mother responds strongly to these developments. "Parents often imitate such syllabic vocalization," write Papousek and Papousek (1977), "using the pauses between individual bursts and thus giving the interaction the semblance of a dialogue, pleasing to both partners. However, below seven to nine months the syllabic sounds bear the character of incidental and passing products of the developing speech organs and do not represent any objects or situations" (p. 80).

Papousek and Papousek point out that the mother makes a clear distinction between her infant's "fundamental vowel-like sounds" (cooing and grizzling) and his more advanced "syllabic sounds." The first continue to be taken as signs of happiness or discomfort. In this role, "The more differentiated syllabic sounds cannot replace the fundamental vocalizations, although they may please the adults as signs of the prospective higher level of communication" (Papousek and Papousek 1977, p. 81). The syllabic sounds are not assumed to carry any messages at first, but by filling in the pauses between the infant's bursts with repetitions and imitations of his utterances, the parents give the interaction the semblance of a dialogue.

The beginnings of language as a vehicle of content are thus laid. Trevarthen (1977) places the origins of this specialization even earlier, by drawing attention to the small movements of the lips and tongue he has called "prespeech." Like Papousek and Papousek, he is at pains to point out that such movements occur at different times and appear to be manifestations of a different kind of state and are most certainly interpreted in a different way by the mother, as compared with signs of emotion or physiological state. Language as a vehicle for content appears to have a grounding in species-typical activity patterns entirely separate from the "oohs and aahs" of emotional expression. These species-typical activity patterns are exercised in an interactive context and incorporated into preverbal "dialogues," which serve to select and shape them further.

A subset of those consonant-and-vowel combinations with which the infant has experimented during the fourth and fifth months is retained and produced with greater frequency in the next stage, which is usually called the babbling stage. It tends to run from twenty-five to fifty weeks. Halfway through this period, variegated babbling emerges, in which the consonants and vowels are changed from one syllable to the next. The rhythm of the utterances begins to resemble that of adult speech, although the units of babbling appear to have no meaning. Most babbling consists of a small set of sounds very similar to those used in early language later on. Children thus have the physical ability to use the words of their native language long before they actually learn to utter words.

Between nine and eighteen months, variations in melody, rhythm, and stress become clearly recognizable in the child's vocal strings. Parents unhesitatingly attribute speech acts to their child, though his productions may at first contain no recognizable words. Games based on melodic sequences and particular syllables become established, producing proto-words associated with specific interactive situations. Children growing up in different language communities begin to sound more like adults in those communities than like each other.

In parallel with these developments in sound production (and in many cases prior to them), similar advances have been made by the infant in speech perception. Infants are able to make auditory discriminations at a very young age, and there is increasing evidence that some of these abilities are speech related. Researchers have established over the past twenty years that children between one and four months of age can perceive most of the phonetic distinctions that exist in human languages (Miller and Jusczyk 1989). These capacities require a subtending mechanism of surprising dynamic complexity, since there is no simple one-to-one relation between acoustic and phonetic segments. Speakers do not produce speech in well-defined phonetic atoms; the vocal gestures for a given segment will typically overlap those for the segments that precede and succeed it: "Given the sophisticated manner in which speech is perceived well before infants are able to consistently produce the sounds of speech, and certainly well before they are able to comprehend speech, the mechanisms underlying the perception of speech would seem to strongly reflect our biological heritage, and perhaps even our species-specific inheritance" (Miller and Jusczyk 1989, p. 117).

From a very young age (possibly from birth, or even before birth), infants seem to be attracted to the sound of their mother's voice. It is now realized that the style in which a mother is "biologically primed" to talk to her infant provides scaffolding for speech perception in a number of different ways. Her pitch, syntax, and pronunciation are all altered, resulting in a soothing but highly modulated, repetitive, almost ritualized form of speech. She closely monitors the infant's state and responses and adjusts her speech accordingly. As Kaye (1982) observed, the mother facilitates the infant's perception of her vocal utterances by her timing (slotting her phrases into the infant's pauses), by keeping him at the optimum level of arousal, and by continuously adjusting her contributions to maintain a balance between the infant's current perceptual abilities and what she would like him to be able to understand.

Between two and four months, infants begin to respond to the "meaning" of different tones of voice, and at around six months, certain utterances begin to be associated with specific situations. The mother's style of speaking changes in response to her infant's increasing perceptual and motor abilities. At around six months, the infant's more varied activities in relation to objects begin to elicit longer and more elaborate commentaries. The mother starts to ignore some of the baby's vowel-like utterances and to pay more attention to his syllabic babbling.

Hirsh-Pasek et al. (1987) showed that seven- to ten-month-old infants prefer samples of "motherese" in which pauses occur at clause boundaries to samples into which pauses have been randomly inserted. Adults speaking to children of this age tend to exaggerate the prosodic changes that naturally occur at a boundary: an extended pause, lengthening of the final syllable, rise or fall in pitch, and an increase in volume. By changing the locations of pauses in recordings of the mother, Hirsh-Pasek et al. revealed that the infant must have a sensitivity to some or all of the other cues that inform him where the "natural" boundaries should fall.

Clauses thus tend to be perceived as perceptual units, permitting them to serve as scaffolding for later grammatical parsing. They enable the infant to ignore false starts, "ums and ahs," and ungrammatical strings that do not sound like clauses. Such anomalies have often been cited as examples of the difficulties of extracting grammatical structure from spoken language, and therefore in support of theories positing innate grammatical structure. The fact that the infant is unable at this stage to attend to the fine structure within his mother's clauses works to his advantage. He treats her clauses as conversational equivalents to his own utterances, whether they be coos, syllabic strings, or the one- and two-word sentences he will begin to use a few months later. A premature ability to distinguish the syntactic or semantic details would make it difficult to attain the necessary proficiency in vocal exchanges and the intonational and rhythmic expertise required to distinguish and produce a variety of speech acts. The child's brain would be overwhelmed by detail and incapable of sustaining the interactive context out of which his language abilities will emerge.

Speech production and perception are thus made possible by a number of prelinguistic activity patterns that appear to be specifically adapted to serve as a potential vehicle for content. From the beginning, the vocal behavior that will eventually be appropriated for the production of contentful sentences is clearly differentiated from the vocal expressions of emotional and physiological state. A species-typical capacity to produce a variety of language-like sounds, which matures gradually during the first year and is spontaneously exercised by the infant, supplies the raw material from which the mother can shape primitive dialogues.

These species-typical activity patterns do not constitute anything like an innate ability to talk, nor can they be seen as evidence of an underlying grammatical competence. They provide the means for initiating and sustaining vocal interactions with the mother, which serve as scaffolding within which the infant can practice the ingredients of speech acts. Interactive timing, clause recognition and production, the rhythms, stresses, and intonations associated with commands, statements, and requests are all extensively practiced before the child learns his first words. What sustains and shapes this activity is the interactive context of mother-infant dialogue.

In order for speech acts to serve as vehicles of content, they must not be tied to specific contents. Language learning is literally a game. It is not serious in the sense that expressions of discomfort or need are serious. There are good reasons that mothers will attempt to engage their infants in "dialogue" only when the infants are in a quiet, moderately aroused state. An infant preoccupied with his own feelings will not be able to concentrate on the game. Speech acts are learned through interactive play, not through trying to express wishes or emotions that are of immediate concern. This clear separation between signals of immediate need and the interactive emergence of discursive language will eventually permit speech acts to be "about" things that are not present and even to contain counterfactuals.

Before the infant learns to comprehend and produce his first words, he has become surprisingly skilled at conducting conversations. He is able to interpret adult speech acts (distinguish questions, statements, and commands) and produce speech acts himself by varying the pitch, volume, and rhythm of his voice. He has become a master at turn taking, having learned to respond to adults' phrasing by using vocal and nonvocal cues. As a result, he can "follow" a conversation between two adults, even though he is not able to understand the explicit meaning of what is being said. He has learned a variety of ritualized games involving his mother, himself, and various objects. Finally, toward the end of the first year, he will have learned some words that stand for specific interactional contexts and games.

16.3 The Emergence of Concepts in Contentful Interaction

The use of recognizable linguistic forms begins with one-word sentences between the ages of twelve and eighteen months (the so-called holophrastic stage). The nature of the intended speech act is conveyed by prosody and gesture. "Dada?" with a rising intonation means, "Is that him?" "Dada" with a falling, triumphant intonation means, "See, I was right." "Da-da" with an insistent, level intonation means, "Pay attention to me." It is clear that much of the meaning of these speech acts is supplied by the context in which the child performs them and by the interpretative skills of the parents. Even when the child progresses to two-word sentences around the age of eighteen months, there may be uncertainty about their meaning, since they do not always lend themselves to clear grammatical analysis (Crystal 1987).

The first words the child uses tend to be names for the people who are closest to him, followed by designations for common activities, interactive situations, and daily routines ("bye-bye," "hello," "gone," "din-din"). Nelson (1974) draws attention to the fact that the outstanding characteristic of the child's earliest words is "their reference to objects and events that are perceived in dynamic relationships." She points out that the world of the young child is not a static one of well-defined objects, properties, and features; it is made up of complex dynamic events. Theories of concept formation that assume that concepts are constructed from combinations of primitive, static cues need to explain how the child extracts such cues from the dynamic perceptual array before reassembling them into an internal representation of the concept. Nelson calls this the "abstraction theory" of concept formation. As I discussed in chapter 4, it poses a number of serious problems for an understanding of how concepts are actually used in human interactions and thinking.

Classic abstraction theory posits that we detect similarities in objects, events, and situations and that this allows us to abstract from them the features they have in common. I drew attention in chapter 4 to the fact that this entails a notion of similarity that is context and viewpoint independent and based on hard-edged, predefined "atoms of meaning." Such meaning primitives prove difficult to pin down. No predefined, closed set of atomic features (even if one accepts "nonprojectable" ones) is ever likely to capture all of the metaphoric senses for a specific term that human beings are able to think up and grasp spontaneously. I further argued that abstraction models that take on board the centrality of metaphor in human thinking, such as Way's (1991) model of meaning hierarchies, are bound to run into problems with infinite regress, where the decision as to which context frame to apply in a particular situation will require an even higher-level mechanism, which in turn requires meta-knowledge about contexts, and so on.

Nelson (1974) cites experimental evidence showing that young children perform poorly at concept formation under experimental conditions that, from the point of view of the abstraction model, ought to be ideal. On the other hand, they are notoriously clever at attaining concepts under "natural" conditions, which impose almost insurmountable obstacles when viewed in terms of that model.* Early concept formation clearly requires a more dynamic and interactive explanation. As Nelson says, the feature representation of a concept is secondary to the grouping of instances and can be accomplished only after the grouping has already been done. What cognitive scientists call "systematicity" (the ability to wield the concept in all appropriate instances that do not involve category mistakes) is not the result of internalized atoms of meaning combined and transformed by syntactic rules; it is, as Clark (1993) suggested, the ability to act appropriately in a variety of contexts involving the object, property, or relation which the public concept picks out.

Bruner (1976) draws attention to the appearance of systematicity in early infant behavior:

---

*Recent evidence produced by language acquisition studies with pygmy or Bonobo chimpanzees *(Pan paniscus)* points to the same conclusion. Savage-Rumbaugh (1991) and Greenfield and Savage-Rumbaugh (1991) report that Bonobos that learn to use language tokens in the context of day-to-day activities learn much faster and are more likely to use such tokens as true symbols than if they have been explicitly trained in the meanings of the tokens. Savage-Rumbaugh calls this "observational learning," but from her reports it is clear that what is involved is active participation by the chimpanzee in shared, interactive, situated activities, on which the experimenters comment extensively in speech as well as use of the tokens available to the subjects.

> Much of the child's early mastery is achieved in oft-repeated tasks. The child spends most of his time doing a very limited number of things. There is endless time spent in reaching and taking and banging and looking, etc. But within any one of these restricted domains, there is a surprising amount of "systematicity." It consists of two forms of "playful" activity: in one, a single act (like banging) is applied to a wide range of objects. Everything on which the child can get his hands is banged. In the second type, the child directs to a single object all the motor routines of which he is capable—he takes hold of the object, bangs it, throws it on the floor, puts it in his mouth, puts it on top of his head, runs it through his entire repertoire. (p. 200)

We can see here the emergence of those loosely knit sets of activities that Clark (1993) identified as the ultimate explanation of the ability to wield concepts. Bruner believes that such early behavior provides evidence of some form of ingrained intentionality (or at least of the fact that the child's behavior is purposeful, which in turn implies that it is "about" aims and goals that may be identified with objects in the world). However, one could argue that the groupings Bruner describes are unified by nothing more than spatial or temporal contiguity, or both, and by the fact that the infant has only a limited repertoire of activity patterns and a limited set of objects to practice them on. These objects will tend to be specially designed toys characterized by their perceptual salience and interactive nature (brightly colored objects that produce noises when pushed or shaken or move in interesting ways at the slightest touch). The environment of the young infant is tailor-made for grasping, banging, and putting in the mouth. It provides a scaffolding of cultural artifacts that promotes the kinds of groupings to which Bruner draws attention.

I am not suggesting that the infant at this stage has a fully developed ability to wield concepts. True concepts can be manipulated, detached from their situated origin, and used in different combinations. It is a long way from the grounding that has just been described to proficient conceptual thinking. That is where language comes in.

The child learns that a word is consistently used by others in the context of one of his groupings. His eighteen-month-long training in "conversation" has made him receptive to linguistic units and given him a sense that these can be part of specific routines or games. He discovers that certain dynamic situations are reliably linked by his mother and other adults with particular words, and he begins to use these words himself to refer to the totality of the situation.

Holophrastic use of language acts as a bridge between concepts as loosely knit groups of activities and concepts as linguistic entities. Before syntax and combinatorial semantics emerge, it provides a holistic means of referring to entire situations, with all the activities that are habitually performed in them. The one-word sentence can act as a vehicle for content because the child and his parents have a shared experience of the situations and associated activities, which is brought into the well-established interactive context of speech acts. The child has long learned to sustain "meaningful" vocal interactions, in the sense that his contributions to these interactions have come to result in predictable responses from his parents, but up to now there has been no way of introducing meaning that went beyond the interactions themselves. One-word sentences provide the way to do this. They are vocal acts about something more than the act itself, but what they refer to is not an abstract concept defined in terms of some truth rule or a set of atomic features but a standard routine or a common situation the child has experienced as a grouping of his own and his parents' activity patterns.

One-word sentences, however, still impose severe limitations on the speaker's ability to refer to anything beyond the immediate context. Single-word commands and requests will not get you very far if you want to convey things *about* a routine or situation. In order to move beyond this stage in his speech, the child must learn to detach the linguistic object from the tight embrace of its grounding, so that it may be used combinatorially as an atom of meaning, with abstract markers for the relations into which it can enter. Language itself provides the scaffolding for this next stage of development. As Sinha (1988) argues, it is the acquisition of natural language, not the innate knowledge of some language of thought, that enables subjects to master discursive concepts and adopt intentional stances.

Around eighteen months, the child begins to use two-word sentences. He has now begun to attend to the internal structure of his own and other people's speech acts. These sentences do not always permit clear grammatical analysis. However, the existence of a public language with a grammatical structure enables the child to start making statements of fact, as opposed to merely performing vocal gestures as part of an interactive process. "Johnny hit," "There Daddy," "Kick ball," "Harry big": such utterances actually mean something that is not tied to the immediate needs or impulses of the child. They make sense because adults can use the structure of natural language, as well as the situational context, to disambiguate their meaning, enabling them to respond to the child's speech acts as propositional statements rather than mere signs of internal state. In this way, the grammatical structure of public language, once it begins to act as scaffolding for the utterances of the child, not only changes the syntactic character of his speech acts but also facilitates the breakthrough into content.

This explanation of linguistic competence as emergent from performance directly contradicts what is now the standard explanation in linguistics. Chomsky's conception of an innate language acquisition device (LAD) has dominated the field for the past thirty-five years. Public language is seen not as a resource or scaffolding that enables parents to bootstrap their children into propositional thought but as arising from inborn mental structures, out of which specific instances of performance are generated through rigidly defined transformation rules. Pinker and Bloom (1990) have argued (in my opinion correctly) that if the explanation of language is to depend on an innate structure of such coherence and complexity, then the emergence of that structure requires an evolutionary explanation. Unfortunately their paper then proceeds to turn the argument on its head. They take for granted that language is the product of an innate functional structure and point to its coherence and complexity as "evidence" for an evolutionary origin. As Lewontin (1990) makes clear in his commentary, this line of argument begs a number of important questions. In chapters 5 and 6, I argued that it would be difficult to provide a historical account in terms of differential fitness that would make sense of an evolutionary explanation for the LAD. Chomsky (1972) concedes that there is a problem but responds by arguing that the LAD could be a by-product of some other adaptive traits: "In studying the evolution of mind, we cannot guess to what extent there are physically possible alternatives to, say, transformational, generative grammar, for an organism meeting certain other physical conditions characteristic of humans. Conceivably, there are none—or very few—in which case talk about evolution of the language capacity is beside the point" (pp. 97–98).

The alternative I have sketched proposes that language competence does have a (partial) explanation in natural selection, in that we have certain species-typical activity patterns adapted for language acquisition but that the actual development of the competence can come about only through performance and requires the prior existence of a public language that can serve as scaffolding.

One standard argument against this type of explanation is that it would be impossible for children to extract the grammatical structure of their native language from the flawed and impoverished data available to them. I have tried to show that the interactive context provided by the parents, combined with certain species-typical perceptual abilities that seem to be adapted to speech comprehension, as well as extensive practice with speech acts before language acquisition begins, make this less of a stumbling block than has generally been assumed.

The other argument sometimes raised against the type of explanation I have put forward is the so-called chicken-and-egg problem: if a well-structured public language is required for a child to attain language competence, then how did well-structured public languages come about in the first place? All theories about the origin of language must necessarily be speculative, but Freyd (1983) shows that it is at least possible to imagine a scenario that weakens this line of attack.

Freyd argues, as I have done, that the structures evident in language do not necessarily derive from innate mental structure. They might be a property of language itself, and their explanation may lie in historical processes of transmission and elaboration. A better understanding of these processes, and of the sorts of structures that would facilitate and grow out of them, might be achieved by careful study of the situated, interactive properties of speech, which Freyd designates with the generic term "shareability."

Freyd suggests, for instance, that the apparently rulelike transformations that supporters of generative grammar have taken as evidence of deep linguistic structure may be the result of certain inherent difficulties in transmitting new ideas. Often the only way to get a totally new point across is to start from a structure that is already well known and transform it in a generally accepted, rulelike manner. Rules, like concepts, then become public resources for shared understanding rather than properties of internal mechanisms that constrain a person to think and act in certain ways.

16.4 A Nonregressive Explanation of Analogy and Metaphor

Language constitutes a continuously evolving public resource that we all maintain and share. But our personal concepts need to be grounded in the experience of concrete situations and the activities we habitually perform in them. Combinatorial rules and verbal definitions cannot replace the grounding in situated activity that underpins conceptual understanding. As Nelson (1974) says: "It is possible, of course, at a later time to teach a child a new concept through a verbal rule expressing its 'critical attributes' or simply by pointing at exemplars. Unless the child (or adult) identifies the essential functional core of the concept, however, and not just its descriptive features, he is likely to be badly misled about the true meaning of the concept to be learned" (p. 284). This recalls Kuhn's (1970) insight concerning the importance of doing paradigmatic experiments and working through paradigmatic problems for an understanding of the real meaning of explanatory concepts in science. When a new concept emerges, its understanding tends to involve a radically new way of seeing things. Often an already existing word may come to designate a totally different concept, and the only way this can be grasped is by working through exemplars.

In chapter 5, I pointed out that Kuhn's explanation foundered on the notion of similarity, just as Way's explanation of metaphor had done. After working enough exemplars, Kuhn suggested, the student of a new scientific paradigm will be able to view any future problem or situation as similar to the ones she has already encountered. But what determines this similarity? In what terms can it be described?

Kuhn realized that the similarity could not be characterized by rules or explicit features, but he continued to believe that it should be sought in the problem or in some internal representation of the problem. What is actually required is an explanation of the psychological mechanism that underlies the student's ability to see a similarity, and there is no a priori reason that this mechanism should involve similarities between problems as described by the theory. Any attempt to find criteria for similarity on the level of the scientific theory itself would be fruitless.

This is the difficulty that besets all attempts to characterize points of view or world models as task domains preregistered in terms of objects, properties, and features. As Hesse (1980) writes, if, before we can recognize repetition and similarity in nature, we need to adopt a particular point of view explicitly, then "a regressive problem would arise about how we even learn to apply the predicates in which we explicitly express our point of view" (p. 68).

The explanation of the genesis of concepts I sketched out in the previous section points to an escape from infinite regress. We can "see" similarities because the grounding of our concepts does not involve explicit features or context-independent "atoms of meaning" but groupings of situated activities. Things appear similar to us if they share the same or related perceptuomotor activity patterns. A new paradigm or concept can be acquired only by performing such patterns, allowing us to achieve a sense of its meaning by analogy with other concepts. Analogical thinking is grounded in such perceptuomotor commonality.

On the other hand, we need the public term that picks out the concept, and a description in terms of features, to make the analogy do work for us. As Hesse (1966) points out, similarity is established by the act of drawing an analogy, but once that holistic similarity has been grasped, the structural and causal relations of the model to which the analogy was drawn can be used to delineate the structural and causal relations of the concept we are trying to understand. Public language provides the scaffolding to articulate our concrete understanding.

It has often been observed that between two and three years of age, children tend to be very creative in their use of language. If the child does not have a word for what he wishes to convey, he will settle on a word that does form part of his vocabulary and use it in a way that resembles adult use of metaphor. This is called "overextension" by developmental psychologists. It is generally felt that overextension should not be equated with true metaphoric use. Most investigators agree that at that age children are totally incapable of *understanding* metaphors. In general, language comprehension precedes language production by some months, so it is argued that overextension cannot be a genuine use of metaphor.

Perhaps this reasoning obscures an important point, however. That production should lag behind comprehension in most areas of language seems natural. Language is not an inherent part of the behavioral repertoire of the child, in the way that some species-typical activity patterns are. The production of new words or more sophisticated syntactic rules can result only from extensive practice in interactive situations, and this necessarily requires understanding before production can begin. Most language learning is a matter of acquiring the interactive skills to navigate a public linguistic space.

The production of metaphor, on the other hand, can precede comprehension because it is not primarily a matter of applying linguistic concepts and rules, in the way that understanding other people's metaphors would need to be. As I have made clear, the all-important element in metaphor is context. In understanding a metaphor, the context needs to be grasped from the linguistic cues provided by the speaker's sentence. In producing a metaphor, it is available as past experience of situated activity patterns. The child wishes to convey a well-established grouping of perceptuomotor experiences. He finds that there is no word in his vocabulary associated with this particular grouping, but there is a word reliably associated with experiences that are similar. He therefore uses that word in an act of overextension, which is based on the same underlying mechanism as metaphoric use by adults.

Analogy and metaphor are grounded in a personal S-domain of non-conceptual content (Cussins 1990). Public language provides the labels we attach to the similarities we grasp holistically as similarities in activity patterns, and it gives us features to articulate those similarities and make sense of them. But any attempt to use concept labels or feature labels to describe the grounding and context that permits us to "see" those similarities in the first place will lead to infinite regress.

Task descriptions in terms of preregistered objects, properties, and features cannot explain analogical and metaphoric thinking. Mataric's (1992) robot is closer to metaphoric thinking than Way's (1991) elaborate system of concept masks and supertypes, because it contains a potential grounding for the concepts of "wall" and "landmark" in situated activity. What it lacks, of course, is the ability to learn to navigate the linguistic space provided by a public language in the way that it learns to navigate the physical space of its office environment.

Chapter 17
Situated Activity, Cultural Scaffolding, and Acts

17.1 The Elusive Act

The notion of an act—whether it be a physical act, a speech act, or an act of thought—lies at the heart of folk psychology. Once we articulate our situated, emergent behavior into separate acts, such acts have a beginning and an end. This raises the problem of how they arise. Something must *cause* the act; it cannot just begin spontaneously, and the cause needs to be related in some meaningful way to the act itself, as well as to its consequences.

Serious efforts have been made to base explanations of human behavior on detailed conceptual analyses of this notion of an act (for widely differing examples, see Danto 1973 and the various contributors to von Cranach and Harré 1982). The assumption behind those efforts has been that conceptual analysis can reveal functional constituents, which in turn will point to the underlying mechanisms. I shall argue in this chapter that the folk psychological notion of an act cannot provide natural kinds for an explanation of human activity and that the underlying mechanisms can be discovered only through a historical understanding of how we learn to perceive our behavior in terms of acts. This involves a process of articulation, which is mediated by language, culture, and interactive contact with adults.

17.2 Representational Redescription or Articulation?

In artificial intelligence, the folk psychological notion of an act is replaced by the notion of a program or procedure. Like an act, a procedure has a well-defined beginning and end. It is designed to accomplish a specific task. Formal definition of the task (usually a subtask of some other, more comprehensive task) must precede design of the procedure and will determine its form and "meaning." I have devoted much of this book to an investigation of the problems involved in subjecting the natural behavior of animals to this type of analysis, and I have argued that it is frequently impossible to identify a clear and plausible stopping condition and/or goal for segments of behavior that might be thought of as self-contained, formally specifiable procedures. Only under the tightly controlled conditions of behaviorist experiments do animals behave in ways that might be construed as acts. Their natural behavior is more fruitfully explained as arising from species-typical activity patterns whose interactions with the creature's ecological niche result in higher levels of emergent behavior of increasing abstraction and complexity.

In the previous two chapters, I have argued that human beings too are born with species-typical activity patterns and that these are adapted to a "natural" environment of purpose-built artifacts and adults who think in intentional terms. Such an intentional environment can serve as scaffolding to launch an infant into meaningful interactions and contentful speech. However, it might still be argued that an adequate explanation of full-blown intentional behavior by human adults requires some accommodation with the notion of a purposive act. Human adults make plans and decide on detailed courses of action to implement those plans. They are able to do so by viewing the alternatives as sequences of distinct acts, each designed to accomplish a subtask that prepares the way for the act that follows. How can one avoid taking into account this salient property of intentional behavior, and if one does take it into account, isn't the notion of a procedure the most promising conceptual tool we have for linking the spontaneous activity of young infants to such elaborately planned behavior of adults? One investigator who has taken that line is Annette Karmiloff-Smith.

Over the past fifteen years, Karmiloff-Smith has studied a variety of developmental processes in young children (Karmiloff-Smith 1990, 1991, 1992, 1993; Clark and Karmiloff-Smith 1991). Her results have led her to conclude that language learning, the acquisition of numeracy, and the increasing skills in drawing displayed by children between the ages of four and eleven all follow a common developmental pattern, which she ascribes to a spontaneous internal mechanism called representational redescription. This notion constitutes the most ambitious attempt made in recent years to square a developmental approach based on solid experimental data with a computational model of the underlying mechanisms.

The theory of representational redescription stands squarely in the cognitive tradition. Karmiloff-Smith (pers. comm.) has recently expressed reservations about her early enthusiasm for computational terms, but she remains committed to the notion of internal representations as causal structures and to a wholly endogenous explanation for the behavioral changes her studies have identified. On the other hand, she argues, as I have argued in this book, that human infants are born with species-typical activity patterns (what she calls "procedurally encoded knowledge") rather than explicit knowledge about the world (in her own terms, "the procedural knowledge is not accessible to the system as data"). She therefore rejects the conclusions drawn by such researchers as Baillargeon and Spelke, whose work I discussed in chapter 15. She is also at pains to point out that hers is not a stage-bound model, like Piaget's, and it does not involve conceptualizing the mind in terms of a standard sequence of predefined mathematical structures. Representational redescription is assumed to be domain specific, so that the process will occur at different times for different skills and will tend to have unique features for each skill.

The common pattern that Karmiloff-Smith has identified in various examples of skill acquisition may be described as the growing ability to break down a previously unified skill into separate components. The most frequently quoted example is that of children's drawing (Karmiloff-Smith 1990). Children between the ages of four and eleven were asked to draw a house and, subsequently, a house that does not exist. Karmiloff-Smith detected significant changes between the younger age group (aged four to six) and the somewhat older children (between eight and eleven) in their performance of the second task. The younger children could alter their standard drawing of a house by making changes in the relative size and shape of the elements. They were also able to leave out some of those elements if they normally occurred at the end of the drawing sequence. But they could not alter the relative position and orientation of the elements or delete elements that were executed in the middle of the drawing sequence. Nor were they able to combine elements from various conceptual categories in one drawing, as children of the older age group were able to do.

The theory of representational redescription proposes that this evidence should be explained in terms of the spontaneous and endogenous construction of increasingly explicit internal representations from what was initially a unified procedure. The growing ability to alter distinct elements of drawings, change their sequence, and replace them with elements from other drawings is equated with a progressive "availability as data" of parts of the procedure. This makes the encoded representations amenable to comparison, alteration, and substitution. Karmiloff-Smith has concluded that there are at least four clearly distinguishable levels of representation in the human mind, ranging from procedural representation at the first and lowest level, through two levels of representations that are explicit but not available to consciousness, to conscious representation in terms of a language that is "close enough to natural language for easy translation into stateable, communicable form" (Karmiloff-Smith 1993, p. 599):

> The model of representational redescription (the RR model for short) postulates that the mind stores multiple redescriptions of knowledge at different levels and in different types of representational format, which are increasingly explicit and accessible. At the initial level, I argue that representations are in the form of procedures for responding to and analysing stimuli in the external environment. . . .
>
> The redescriptions are abstractions in a higher level language and are open to potential intra- and inter-domain representational links, a process which enriches the system from within. (Karmiloff-Smith 1993, pp. 597–598).

One of Karmiloff-Smith's key arguments in support of her theory is her finding that articulation of a skill into separate components typically occurs *after* behavioral mastery has been achieved and that it may take place without any further "input of data." Karmiloff-Smith contrasts this empirical fact with the predictions of Piagetian and behaviorist theories, which would lead one to expect changes in internal organization following failure rather than success. However, the emergence of organizational change from a "stable state" of behavioral mastery does not necessarily imply that such a change is "endogenously driven." Stable organizational states may be perturbed by factors other than failure.

When the child begins to produce recognizable drawings, he is likely to receive a considerable amount of feedback from adults. They will tell him that what he is doing is drawing a house and reward him with praise if he produces one that meets their criteria but respond less favorably if the results are not up to scratch. They will almost certainly draw his attention to the individual elements of the houses he draws, pointing to the roof and calling it a roof, commenting on the number of windows, asking him why he drew the door in the center while in his own house it is situated on the right, and urging him to try to put it where it really is. These comments are most likely to increase after a basic level of behavioral mastery has been attained, for the simple reason that there is more for adults to comment on.

Karmiloff-Smith's insistence that representational redescription is "endogenously driven" puts her in the position of having to show that environmental and parental feedback of this sort plays no part in the process. It might be possible to prove experimentally that this is the case, but as far as I know such experimental evidence has not been produced. Karmiloff-Smith's contention is built on equating "environ-mentally affected" with "failure driven" rather than on isolating the child from all contact with the environment after behavioral mastery has been achieved, and showing that representational redescription still occurs in the normal way. Until evidence of that sort is produced, it seems more economical to describe the behavioral changes she has identified as a progressive articulation of activity patterns, which can be given an explanation quite similar to the articulation of concepts I described in the last chapter.

In my opinion Karmiloff-Smith conflates two distinct abilities, though she distinguishes between "explicit" and "available to con-sciousness." On the one hand there is the ability of a creature (possibly only human beings, but see recent studies by Savage-Rumbaugh 1991) to articulate consciously a piece of its own or another creature's behav-ior into distinct components. On the other hand, there is the ability to act in ways that might be interpreted as evidence of comparison, reordering and substitution of separate parts of the action. Karmiloff-Smith (1993) assumes that the latter requires formal operations acting on explicit representations of the various parts: "Information embed-ded in procedurally encoded representations is therefore not available to other operators in the cognitive system. Thus if two procedures con-tain some identical component parts, this potential inter-representa-tional commonality is not yet represented in the child's mind. A procedure *as a whole* is available to other operators; it is its component parts that are not accessible" (p. 597).

The use of a computational framework leads her to assume that commonality in behavior must arise from formal comparisons between internal representations of that behavior. I have argued in this book that a formal description of a sequence of behavior in terms of well-defined components is not essential to *knowing how* to act in similar circumstances, even if only parts of the normal sequence are called for. Mataric's robot does not contain internal representations of distinct components of its wall-following activity. It will act in a similar fashion on similar occasions because its low-level reflexes have been calibrated so that it responds appropriately to the contingencies of its office envi-ronment. From the point of view of an observer, the robot may seem to "have available" distinct components corresponding to walls and corners, but there are no explicit procedures held within the robot for staying close to walls and going around corners. It is true that its land-marks are identified in terms of correspondences between its own movements and its sensory inputs in response to specific features. However, the occurrence of such correspondences—and therefore the ultimate cause of the similarities—must be sought not in formal characteristics of behavioral components but in the fact that the robot's low-level reflexes have been calibrated to a particular environment. The components of the behavior are interactively emergent features, and the robot's ability to act similarly in similar conditions is a product of interactive emergence.

Where Karmiloff-Smith places the exploitation of similarity at the very top, assuming that it requires "explicit" if not conscious representation, I have argued that it must be placed at the very bottom, to account for analogical and metaphoric use of language (see chapters 4, 5, and 16). I do not dispute that articulation is itself an important element in our developmental processes. But whereas Karmiloff-Smith sees it as endogenously driven, I would argue that it is an interactive process mediated by language and cultural artifacts.

The requirements of a computational theory of representational redescription or "making explicit" were most fully worked out by David Marr (1982). Marr realized that such a notion implies a process of selection as well as a recovery of structure that is underdetermined by the data, and this in turn requires a set of "primitives"—elementary units of the type of information that needs to be made explicit. The primitives of a representation determine its "scope"—what can and what cannot be represented by the particular type of representation. Everything that cannot be "made explicit" in terms of these primitives will be lost in the descriptions that result.

Marr applied this notion to low-level vision, and the primitives he posited for the various levels of representation required by his theory were assumed to be the result of natural selection. They represented knowledge about the world that had become hard-wired into the human (and most likely also the animal) brain—reflections of certain immutable facts of nature, such as the continuity in intensity values across surfaces and the discontinuities that characterize object boundaries.

Karmiloff-Smith does not specify the primitives required by her theory. Clearly the primitives involved in the redescription of a child's procedure for drawing a house (so that it becomes explicit knowledge isolating components like the roof, the door, and the windows) cannot be of the hard-wired type that Marr proposed for low-level vision. The kinds of houses that children tend to draw have not been around long enough for their constituents to become hard-wired into our brains. Nor is it possible to imagine lower-level, endogenously generated primitives in terms of which drawing a window, drawing a roof, and drawing a door could be reliably differentiated. These are cultural entities, picked out by language and by the fact that children grow up in an environment containing houses and pictures of houses. What we are talking about is articulation rather than representational redescription: a growing ability to identify separate parts of one's own interactive performance and to deploy these elements independently.

Karmiloff-Smith locates her explanation of development wholly within the subject's head. The process of representational redescription is assumed to be endogenously driven, and the original procedures, as well as the various levels of representation that result, are all assumed to be internal to the creature. The achievement of greater flexibility that comes with mental development is explained entirely in terms of structural transformations over these internal elements, leaving no essential explanatory role for interactions with adults or the effects of a cultural environment. An explanation along these lines severely limits the way that adult behavior can be conceptualized. It imposes an atomic structure on activity, in the same way that the symbol-processing paradigm imposes an atomic structure on meaning, and this in turn necessitates the introduction of the notion of "planning." Purposive action becomes an internally generated sequence of predefined behavioral components, strung together by explicit choice points.

Agre and Chapman (1988) call this the "plan-as-program" view of behavior. It posits that extended sequences of activity are in some sense preplanned and that the plan is fully assembled inside the creature before activity begins. It may be conscious or unconscious, but in either case it is seen as a comprehensive internal representation of the required sequence of acts, which simply needs to be executed at the appropriate time and place. Since the description effectively dictates the performance, execution becomes a straightforward matter, depending only on certain predefined objective criteria.

Such a notion of plans does not correspond to the way that plans are used in everyday life. As Agre and Chapman point out, the most difficult part of using a plan tends to be the problem of deciding what plan and what part of it are relevant to a specific situation. The operational meanings of the terms used in a plan will depend on context, and the judgments required to apply the plan to actual situations are largely made in response to nonexplicit features that emerge from interactive processes as the action unfolds. I shall discuss these matters more fully in the next section and examine some real-life examples.

Skilled adult behavior is directed and flexible at the same time. A computational view of development along the lines Karmiloff-Smith proposed cannot produce mechanisms to explain this. No matter how small the "atoms of action" that result from representational redescription, the fact that they are prespecified and need to be explicitly combined into an overall plan before activity can begin severely limits the flexibility of the resulting behavior. It makes it difficult to conceive of a system capable of responding, in the way that we routinely respond, to the contingencies of a cultural and physical environment that is in continual flux. What is required is a view of development that imposes no limits on the potential flexibility and context sensitivity of behavior but also renders it susceptible to deliberate shaping. In the remainder of this chapter, I shall try to sketch out some of the ingredients of such a view.

17.3 Pointing, Naming, and Pedagogy

One of the most important and earliest ingredients in the child's mental development is the peculiarly human act of pointing. In chapter 15, I discussed the interactive emergence of object-related behavior around the age of six months. Bruner (1976) describes how pointing emerges naturally from the same context of mother-infant dialogue. Once reaching for an object has become a recognizable activity on the part of the child, the mother finds it difficult not to interpret this movement as a desire for the object. She will tend to pick up the object and hand it to the child. By eight or ten months, the infant's behavior has been modified by this response of the mother, and he begins to look at her face while reaching for the object.

A few months later, the pointing gesture becomes dissociated from the object entirely. The child may not even accept the object when the mother hands it to him. And finally, around thirteen months, the gesture is used extensively to draw attention to unfamiliar objects, objects in pictures, and even objects that are not currently in view. The child looks at the mother while performing the gesture and may even utter a "word." The movement of reaching has thus been converted into a general-purpose expression of interest.

As always, the mother adapts her behavior to take advantage of her infant's newly developed skill. She begins to engage him in "book reading," getting him to look at and point to the objects in pictures and involving him in new patterns of turn taking. (Bruner speculates that cultures without picture books must find appropriate substitutes.) The mother's responses to the vocal behavior of her child during these book-reading sessions can be divided into two clearly distinguishable categories. Normal coos and murmurs are treated as indicative of the child's emotional or physiological state, and the mother's responses are always addressed directly to the child, without referring to the book. However, if the child happens to make such noises while pointing at a picture in the book, then the utterance is treated as a label, and the child is praised for his efforts, while the correct name for the object is emphatically introduced by the mother. As the book-reading routine becomes better established, the mother tightens her criteria for the kind of sound that is acceptable as a label. Less precise vocalizations are progressively relegated to the category of mere "oohs and aahs."

Premack (1984), who has spent much of his working life trying to get chimpanzees to do the sorts of things that human beings do naturally, has come to the conclusion that what finally differentiates us from our nearest primate cousins is precisely this sort of pedagogy. He argues that the ability to observe the performance of a pupil, judge it according to some aesthetic standard, and demonstrate to the pupil how it ought to be done is a unique human characteristic, though chimpanzees may display some of the rudimentary elements of that skill. Premack points out that for the purposes of correcting a pupil's movements, pedagogy does not require speech: it is possible to move the pupil's arm into the right position or simply demonstrate how the movement ought to be performed. However, he then describes a highly revealing experiment by one of his students to draw attention to the limits of such "silent pedagogy."

Subjects were asked to watch a video recording of an agent performing a simple act, such as cutting an apple or washing a board. The experimenter demonstrated how to place stickers marked "agent," "instrument," and "recipient" on the television screen to identify the corresponding elements of the act. Subjects were then asked to perform this labeling task themselves, first on the videotape that had been used by the experimenter and, following that, on two videotapes of different acts. The experimenter nodded each time a label was stuck in the correct position but shifted the label when it was placed incorrectly. All subjects were trained until they had become proficient on each of the three training tapes. They were then asked to perform the same task on a video recording they had not seen before.

It was found that four-year-old children could not transfer the skill to new examples if they had been trained by this method ("silent pedagogy"). Adults, on the other hand, were able to do so without any trouble. A similar experiment was subsequently performed on a new group of subjects using speech as well as manual corrections. The children were told, in terms appropriate to the understanding of a four year old, what an agent, instrument, and recipient are, at the same time as they were shown how to place the stickers. On this occasion all children passed the transfer test, and they did so at about the same level of accuracy as adults following silent pedagogy.

Premack concludes that whereas silent pedagogy can teach children to understand events at a lower level of abstraction, only pedagogy using speech can take them to the level that is required to identify reliably the elements of an act. In the first experiment, the children learned to identify categories for persons, objects, and instruments, which can be distinguished on the basis of physical attributes alone. In the second experiment, they learned to identify the functional categories that characterize a human act. This understanding, Premack believes, is impossible to convey without the use of language.

Is it necessary to be able to identify the agent, instrument, and recipient of an act in order to perform one? The answer to that question depends on what is meant by "performing an act." As we have seen, even the earliest, species-typical activity patterns of newborns are interpreted as acts by their mothers. But the infant is not performing an act in the sense that his activity is about something or directed toward something. The notions of an agent, instrument, and recipient do not need to be invoked to explain such early behavior. Nor is it necessary for infants to be aware of these formal constituents in order that their species-typical activities be shaped into more sophisticated behavior through interactions with adults. Scaffolding requires that parents *treat* the infant's behavior as a sequence of acts and in this way structure the parent-infant dialogue along intentional lines, but there is no reason to assume that the child's behavior is generated as a sequence of acts. Learning to interact with adults, take part in vocal exchanges, perform "speech acts," acquire the all-important gesture of pointing, play intricate ritualistic games with the mother, and partake in "book reading" can all be explained without invoking a mechanism inside the infant's head that plans his actions in terms of agents, instruments, and recipients.

Scaffolding is a far more subtle and flexible instrument than moving the pupil's limbs in the required fashion or showing him how a specific movement ought to be performed (Premack's two methods of "silent pedagogy"). However, this flexibility has its limits. Adult human behavior takes many forms that cannot emerge from continuous interactive adjustments with other human beings. It is not possible to teach a person to drive a car in this way or inculcate the art of jazz improvisation on the piano. Mastering such activities requires the pupil to take over the task of scaffolding himself, and an intentional description in terms of agents, instruments, and recipients is eminently suited to that purpose. By the end of the second year, children tend to accompany any new or unusual activity with a running commentary on what they are doing. They have adopted their mothers' habit of drawing attention to their behavior in intentional terms. Eckerman (1993) describes the role played by such commentaries in the regulation of coordinated actions between various children: "Sometimes toddlers map their verbal utterances onto the non-verbal coordinated action in a redundant fashion, as when the child both imitates jumping off a box and describes her action as 'I am jumping.' At other times, they use language

in ways that seem to complement and regulate the non-verbal coordinated action, as when they ask for a turn of action ('My turn') before
performing their non-verbal turn" (pp. 129–130).

Eckerman suggests that coordinated play, which develops out of
simple imitative gestures strung together to form more extended sequences, may contribute to language development by providing a
structured context in which children can practice describing their own
behavior as constituent acts in the overall game. The fact that we can
learn to perform this feat opens up an entirely new class of *Merkwelten*
for human action and thought. It permits pedagogy in the sense of
verbal instruction, which Premack believes to be the differentiating
characteristic of human beings, and, what might be even more important, it enables us to tamper with our own scaffolding. Only a creature that can articulate and label its own emergent activity can be
taught to draw a house, or play professional tennis, or write music
in sonata form. Articulation and labeling open up the possibility of
"debugging" inappropriate or faulty parts of one's own behavior and
"reinternalizing" the results.

17.4 Catching Ourselves in the Act

An interesting example is given by Papert (1980). It occurs in a discussion about the advantages of teaching children to write programs in
Logo, but the example itself concerns juggling. Papert found that a
very common "bug" in the naturally emergent behavior of children
who tried to juggle with three or more balls is their tendency to track
the balls with their eyes. A juggler cannot afford to do this, because
there are usually at least two balls in the air, and both cannot be tracked
at the same time. The trick is to keep looking at only the top of the arc,
allowing gravity and the body's coordination to take care of the rest.
A modular description in terms of Logo-like procedures brought this
home to Papert's pupils and enabled them to learn cascade juggling in
half an hour, whereas usually it takes very much longer.

The Logo-like procedures into which Papert got his pupils to break
down the actions involved in cascade juggling closely resemble the
explicit results of representational redescription posited by Karmiloff-
Smith. A continuous activity is cut up into explicitly defined units,
so that these can be altered individually and their temporal sequence
transposed at will. The resulting subtasks may be conceptualized as
functionally self-contained procedures or acts—a conception to which
Logo is particularly well suited.

It is important to note two crucial differences between Papert's educational experiment and the assumptions made in the theory proposed
by Karmiloff-Smith. First, Papert does not imply that the modular

redescription that is used to facilitate learning occurs inside the child, and he certainly does not assume that it is created spontaneously or endogenously. The whole point of the exercise is to provide his pupils with an external aid that enables them to "debug" their own performance. Second, though Papert's book is about Logo programming and how it can help children to learn mathematics, this particular example does not result in a complete Logo procedure for cascade juggling. The movements required by the individual modules are not fully spelled out. It would be far too complex to provide detailed descriptions of what is required to implement the procedures TOSSLEFT and TOSSRIGHT, which involve judgments about the timing of throws, as well as the forces involved in getting the balls to describe slightly different arcs so they do not collide in mid-air, and the correct position of the receiving hand. "Since most people can perform these actions," writes Papert (1980), "we shall take TOSSLEFT and TOSSRIGHT as given and concentrate on how they can be combined to form a new procedure we shall call TO JUGGLE" (p. 107).

Papert's redescription is used by his pupils to scaffold their own movements. The judgments and arm displacements involved in executing the procedures are not made explicit in the external description, and there is no reason to assume that they are made explicit (at either a conscious or an unconscious level) inside the child, or that a formal task description underlies the performance of these constituent "acts." External task descriptions of this sort constitute a plan-as-resource (Agre and Chapman 1988), which the learner can rehearse as a running commentary on her movements rather than a plan-as-program that prescribes the action. The intentional description provides scaffolding to constrain emergent activity patterns and shape them into what may initially feel like "unnatural" forms of behavior.

This has long been known to trainers in professional sport. Sophisticated film and video techniques have made it possible to isolate minute bugs in highly skilled performances. The only way to remove these bugs is by articulating the professional's smooth, undifferentiated motion into sequential components, formulating an explicit description of the component that contains the bug in terms of positions and displacements of the relevant parts of the body, and consciously adjusting these elements until the movement is perfect. Once the bug has been removed by deliberate practice, the corrected piece of behavior can be reinserted into the complete swing or stroke, and the whole is then practiced further until the "joints" between the artificially imposed segments disappear.

Papert does not discuss what happens when a skill is "reinternalized" in this way. His assumption appears to be that the description that provides the most effective scaffolding for learning will also serve as the most helpful description for the underlying mechanisms that subtend the reintegrated performance. Two widely differing accounts of skill acquisition, one by Dreyfus and Dreyfus (1986b) and the other by Sudnow (1978), cast serious doubts on this assumption. Dreyfus and Dreyfus spent a number of years devising instruction programs for public agencies and private companies, analyzing the performance of students in such varied skills as piloting an airplane, driving a car, playing chess, and using a second language. Sudnow gives a detailed, ethnomethodologically inspired account of his own experiences in learning the art of modern jazz improvisation on a piano. Neither Dreyfus and Dreyfus nor Sudnow can be said to provide a satisfactory scientific explanation of skill acquisition. They make no claims that they have understood the underlying mechanisms of the processes they describe. However, their descriptive accounts provide valuable clues to the real nature of what is often called internalization. I shall use their empirical observations and try to support them with a coherent explanatory framework based on the notions I have developed in this book.

With most tasks that involve unfamiliar forms of behavior, the only way to get the novice going is to give her a set of objective, task-related facts and some simple rules that describe the desired performance in relation to those facts. This initial stage of learning corresponds to Premack's notion of pedagogy. It appears to be a uniquely human skill, for which we are prepared by species-typical activity patterns that are adapted to launch us into flexible dialogues with adults, using vehicles of content that are not dependent for their meaning on specific contexts (see chapter 16). Both the rules and the facts are context free. This is necessary because at this stage the novice has no experience to help her recognize context-dependent features. The description of the skill therefore corresponds closely to a task description in classical AI. Frequently it will have been derived from the observed behavior of an acknowledged expert, whose activities are articulated into a sequence of acts that are then formally described in terms of a notional task domain preregistered into objects, properties, and events.

In his initial attempts to master jazz improvisation, Sudnow tried to copy the sounds of piano players he had long admired by listening to their records. He found that it was extremely difficult to identify the precise notes and temporal values that were used. Even when he believed he had succeeded in making an exact transcription of the sounds on the records, it proved impossible to reproduce the experts' playing in a convincing way. The sounds did not provide sufficient scaffolding to guide his actions. They did not contain explicit rules that might enable him to get his hands moving across the keyboard. A more promising path into the skill was eventually suggested by an accomplished player, who advised him to practice a small number of simple scales and chord sequences that had the characteristic jazz sound he was after: "There were these three diminished scales to begin with, each identified by reference to a theoretic system that related its use to four of the twelve dominant chords, so in my thinking there was a 'cognitive map,' each scale named by a starting place, each related to its class of chords" (Sudnow 1978, p. 21).

The descriptive framework provided by a formal task domain helped Sudnow to identify rules and facts that could serve as scaffolding to get his movements going. He remarks that if you do not know what you are aiming for, it is impossible to get your hands moving with the proper timing and changes of dynamics. This parallels Papert's discovery with cascade juggling. Articulation into easily understandable acts with a beginning and an end and an explicit sequence of movements to get from one to the other is an essential first step in mastering activities that have no precedent in the learner's experience.

During the second phase identified by Dreyfus and Dreyfus, growing proficiency enables the learner to take account of more and more of such context-free facts. Her behavior becomes increasingly refined, because practice permits her to attend to more and more details of the explicit instructions. But simultaneously with this growing awareness of the features described in the explicit task description, another type of learning has also started to take place. By actually performing the activities, the student encounters "meaningful elements which neither the instructor nor the learner can define in terms of context-free features" (Dreyfus and Dreyfus 1986b, p. 22). A driver will begin to recognize the sound of the engine that heralds the need to shift from first to second gear, even though it has never been (and probably could not be) defined in her explicit instructions. An apprentice engraver will begin to recognize the angle at which his engraving tool would cease cutting into the metal and precipitate a slip, even though that angle cannot be explicitly specified, since it depends on the consistency of the metal and the properties of the cutting edge, as well as the pressure applied by the craftsman. Each skill brings out numerous emergent features of this kind. We have already encountered the phenomenon in our discussion of Mataric's robot: a structured activity pattern will result in reliable emergent correlations between the motor activities involved and the perceptual input deriving from interactions with a specific environment. These nonexplicit, context-dependent features now begin to contribute to the learner's performance. "I recall playing one day," writes Sudnow (1978), "and finding as I set out into a next course of notes, after a lift-off had occurred, that I was expressly aiming for the sound of those particular notes, that the sounds seemed to creep up into my fingers, that the depression of the keys realized a sound being prepared for on the way down" (p. 37). The scaffolding provided by the explicit task description has thus enabled the novice to start moving in approximately the right way, and this in turn has created a dynamically emergent *Merkwelt* associated with the performance of the movements that provides the context for more advanced learning. Sudnow (1978) makes quite clear that the "knowledge" derived from the dynamic *Merkwelt* that emerges from his interactions with the piano should not be confused with explicit, context-free musical knowledge: "As I found the next sounds coming up, as I set out into a course of notes, it was not as if I had learned about the keyboard so that looking down I could tell what a regarded note would sound like. I do not have that skill, nor do many musicians. I could tell because it was a next sound, because my hand was so engaged with the keyboard that it was given a setting of sounding places in its own configurations and potentialities" (p. 45). Put more simply, the situated activity of performing certain scales and chord sequences has enabled the player to become familiar with the attendant sounds and physical sensations and the correlations between them. One could say, paraphrasing Cussins (1990), that the player has constructed a map of the keyboard by walking across it by many different routes. A map of this sort is quite different from the "cognitive map" that allowed Sudnow to get moving in the first place. It is a map in terms of interactively emergent "landmarks," like those used by Mataric's robot. As with Mataric's robot, navigation of the keyboard gradually becomes not so much a matter of traveling from one chord and melody note to another but of slipping from the behavior specified by one "sounding" into the behavior specified by the next.

Sudnow can only "go for a sound" if there is a frequently traveled route linking his position on the keyboard to his "goal." He cannot tell what particular keys sound like if he observes the keyboard objectively, but he does know what they are going to sound like when they loom up as the next keys in his melodic line. The preceding melody gives them their sound. Because he has been playing for some time now, he has a large repertoire of pathways leading to each key on the piano, and thus a large number of approaches to define their sounds.

But Sudnow goes further. He insists that the same key, struck from different approaches and with different intent (leading to alternative melodic conclusions), will appear to have a slightly different sound, because, in producing it, he is "going for" that particular sound. Again there is a parallel with the activity of Mataric's robot, which will not follow a specific wall in precisely the same way on different occasions. A pianist's attack of a note depends on its context, on the melodic line and sequence of movements in which it occurs (which will affect the dynamics and sound profile of the note), just as the exact path of Mataric's robot depends on a particular approach and environmental contingencies like slippage. Both the F struck by the pianist and a specific instance of wall following by Mataric's robot are objectively recognizable and may be categorized by such labels as "middle F" and "left wall," but an objective classification along these lines does not provide the basis for an explanation of the sensorimotor mechanisms involved.

There is a crucial difference between the "middle F" used in the explicit notation that serves as part of the scaffolding in pedagogy and the "meaning" of this key as it emerges from interactive experience. Cussins's (1990) dream of "constructing" the explicit symbols required by a classic symbol-processing view of behavior out of "nonconceptual content" remains a dream. The "viewpoint-dependent content" that arises from traversing a structured world by a variety of routes cannot provide a grounding for the formal entities of a task description, because it cannot be translated into objective "atoms of meaning." It would be a category mistake to imagine that the pupil has now achieved a grounded ability to plan her activities as programs and run off explicit rules. Scaffolding remains scaffolding; it never becomes part of the underlying mechanisms that drive behavior. Interactive emergence cannot solve the "grounding problem" as formulated by Cussins and Harnad (see chapters 3 and 4), but it does provide the means for progressing to more expert levels of performance that could never be achieved by a creature whose every move needs to be specified in terms of context-free rules and choices.

17.5 Plans as Interactively Emergent Organizations of Activity

With complex skills that involve a large number of alternative actions and contingencies there comes a point when the amount of information that needs to be taken into account at every juncture grows overwhelming. According to Dreyfus and Dreyfus this precipitates phase three of the learning process, in which the learner starts to construct and use "plans." Dreyfus and Dreyfus have little to say about the nature of these plans, beyond the fact that they are "hierarchical procedures for decision-making" that restrict the number of context-free facts and situational elements the learner needs to take into account at any particular moment. Their choice of the term *hierarchical procedure* seems unfortunate. It is important to clearly differentiate these "plans" constructed by a relatively experienced practitioner of the skill from the explicitly formulated instructions that are given to a novice.

It is a category mistake to equate the objects, properties, and activity patterns that emerge from interactive practice with the objects, properties, and acts in terms of which a skill is formally described for the novice. Although the novice and skillful practitioner may use the same names, they are, in a sense, referring to different entities. The emergent concepts of the skilled practitioner are incapable of being systematically combined and logically manipulated as "atoms of meaning" in programs, and there is no way of constructing explicit "hierarchies of meaning" to relate them.

What interests us at this point is how such interactively emergent concepts might be used in something that could be called a plan, and not how public conceptual terms are combined to construct a task description. The debate between Lucy Suchman (1993) and Vera and Simon (1993) concerning the status of plans in explanations of complex behavior points to the difficulties of arriving at a clear understanding of this problem. Suchman (1987) has argued, from the perspective of ethnomethodology, that "plans as such neither determine the actual course of situated action nor adequately reconstruct it" (p. 72) and that "plans are constituent of practical action, but they are constituent as an artifact of our *reasoning about* action, not as the generative *mechanism* of the action" (p. 39). This leads Vera and Simon to accuse her of relegating plans to a position that makes them "epiphenomenal to action." Since Suchman has stated explicitly that she believes plans "do have a purpose" and are "brought to bear" on the organization of situated activity (Suchman 1993, p. 74). Vera and Simon's conclusion seems disingenuous. The trouble is that Suchman, as she readily admits, does not have a simple explanation of the way that plans and situated activity are related, whereas Vera and Simon (1993) are convinced that they *do* have such an explanation: "Again, we may perhaps be pardoned for thinking that there is extensive evidence in the literature today explicating these relations in symbol-processing terms" (p. 82).

I hope the reader has by now been convinced that there are serious problems with that approach. As Suchman says, plans do not determine action, and neither do they generate a course of action. But that does not mean that plans play no part in action. For a start, plans used as scaffolding clearly contribute to the action, even if they are not accorded complete control. But we are no longer talking here about plans as scaffolding. The plans constructed out of interactively emergent concepts are not the plans as resource that enable the novice to make her first moves, and neither are they the plans as programs posited by

Vera and Simon's symbol-processing view. Suchman's second phrase seems to rule out any alternative to these two conceptions. She appears to believe that plans can be conceptualized as either scaffolding ("an artifact of our reasoning about action") or the controlling mechanisms of our actions. I would like to suggest that there is a third way of conceptualizing the organization of complex human behavior, though the term *plan* might not be adequate to describe it.

In chapters 9 and 13, I discussed models of behavior selection in situated robotics and models of the integration of activity patterns in ethology. I came to the conclusion that choice points, as well as the acts that take a creature from one choice point to another, should be seen as emergent phenomena. The explanation of behavioral sequencing and integration lies at a level below that of the emergent activity patterns. From the point of view of an observer, who needs to carve up the totality of the behavior in order to understand it, choices appear to be made at the junctures between "acts." But this does not mean that the creature itself performs acts or decides between alternative acts. Notions of this kind are imports from intentional or teleological modes of explanation, which can only confuse matters by introducing explanatory entities where none are needed. Attempts to explain the organization of animal behavior in terms of plans involving explicit goals and choice points may be seen as a form of overkill or "overexplanation."

Human behavior *is* affected by the emergent concepts that result from our typically human patterns of interaction and language (see chapters 15 and 16). It is shaped, deflected, and integrated by such concepts in the sense that a person who has acquired a particular concept will be capable of acting in ways that she could not have acted before. But her actions are not internally specified in terms of the public definitions attached to these concepts, and neither are they directed toward goals that are internally defined by them. Once a concept has been truly understood—once it has become an interactively emergent concept that is "owned" by the subject rather than a mere label used in scaffolding—it is no longer connected to other concepts primarily at the level of syntactic relations and combinatorial semantics but at the level of activity patterns. The term can, of course, still be correctly deployed by the subject in public speech, but the private concept it connotes, the interactively emergent entity that plays a role in shaping behavior, should not be confused with the dictionary definition and the linguistic rules that define the public term.

A skilled performer using plans constructed out of interactively emergent concepts slips from an activity pattern associated with one concept (an activity that constitutes part of the concept's private meaning) into an activity associated with another concept, in the same way as Mataric's robot slips from the activity associated with one landmark into the activity associated with the next. The two concepts do not serve as the beginning and end of an act or the starting condition and stopping condition of a procedure. There is no need for a distinct natural kind to explain the role of concepts in skillful behavior. They simply constitute an ability to cope in various situations that are loosely designated by a public term.

This makes it necessary to think of the plans "constructed" through interactive experience not as hierarchies of procedures and concepts but as interactively emergent organizations of activity. We have arrived at the crucial difference between a conceptualization in terms of emergent activity and the traditional AI notion of planning based on programs and internal representations. The "plans" used by a competent performer are not imposed from above; they are constructed, or rather they emerge in situ, through the performance of structured but flexible sequences of activity. There is no need to "interpret" or "execute" such plans; they do not "call" subplans; there are no explicit decision points that require internal representations of conditions in the world. The activity patterns that occur during the performance of such a plan are appropriately related to each other and to the task at hand, as well as to the environment, because they emerged historically, and emerge each time the "plan" is performed, in an interactive, situated context.

The final two stages in Dreyfus and Dreyfus's analysis of skill acquisition are largely a matter of transferring more and more of the planning from explicit scaffolding to interactively emergent organizations of this type. Proficient practitioners (those who attain level 4) will experience extended periods of skilled behavior during which they are so deeply immersed in the task that only the relevant features of each situation become salient at precisely the right time, and the remaining facts and features recede into the background. "As events modify the salient features, plans, expectations, and even the relative salience of features will gradually change. No detached choice or deliberation occurs" (Dreyfus and Dreyfus 1986b, p. 28). In other words, the scaffolding of explicit task descriptions for these extended sequences of behavior has dropped away completely because it is no longer needed. The explicit features that were originally used to make decisions at choice points have been replaced by nonexplicit features that emerge from the interactive process itself and are therefore "available" only at the appropriate times and places. This can create problems when the skilled performer is asked by a novice to explain how exactly she performs the skill. The plan-as-resource that was used as scaffolding to learn the skill has been forgotten, and the plan-as-interactively-emergent-organization-of-activity is not amenable to explicit description in intentional terms. It is not the sort of entity that can be translated into clearly specified acts and conditions.

The difference between the proficient individual of level 4 and the true expert who achieves the fifth and final stage in the acquisition of a skill is just that the former still regularly encounters situations in which she needs to deliberate on her actions. Experts hardly ever need to leave the level of skilled performance at all. Sudnow discovers after a number of years that good notes are always to hand, right beneath his fingers; they never need to be strained for or searched for. His playing is borne along by the melodic and rhythmic structure of the tune, which takes hold of his entire body and informs all his movements. But, paradoxically, being taken over in this way appears to give him unexpected freedom and flexibility in his choice of notes: "To get the time into the fingers, hands, shoulders, everywhere, was to develop mobile ways with the terrain such that commitments to arrival times could be continuously altered and shifted about in the course of the negotiations, a steady beat to the song as a whole sustained all the while" (Sudnow 1978, p. 103).

Neither Dreyfus and Dreyfus (1986b) nor Sudnow (1978) provides a satisfactory scientific explanation of skill acquisition. Sudnow's language seems unnecessarily opaque, and Dreyfus and Dreyfus resort too often to such locutions as "it just happens." Their observations nevertheless provide valuable insights into some of the salient characteristics of complex human behavior, and these are difficult to square with a computational model based on explicit procedures and hierarchically organized plans. The alternative explanatory framework I have provided indicates how a developmental approach based on situated patterns of activity that are learned in situ with the aid of explicit scaffolding can account for behavior that is flexible and context sensitive but also susceptible to deliberate shaping.

It suggests that cultural artifacts like concepts, rules, plans, images, and models serve as scaffolding that enables us to organize our activities in ways that would otherwise be impossible. They allow us to perform the required sequences of movements, so that we can develop "concrete understanding" of what is involved in the performance of an unfamiliar skill. Concrete understanding is a matter of situated activity patterns that result in reliable sensorimotor correlations and extended "plans" that are constructed out of such patterns through interactive emergence in situated contexts. The words, rules, and plans of the scaffolding do not become causal entities in the underlying mechanism. As the practitioner becomes more skillful, there is less and less need to use the explicit instructions as a resource. Most of them are forgotten. But language provides unlimited possibilities for higher levels of scaffolding. Interactively emergent concepts that did not exist prior to the performance of a novel skill may be picked out by public terms that can be used in further scaffolding. That scaffolding can then be employed in pedagogy to instill concrete understanding of these new concepts, by getting the novice to behave in the appropriate manner. As Kuhn (1970) pointed out, the only way that unfamiliar concepts can be "internalized" is through working a large number of exemplars, but the only way that these exemplars can be meaningfully presented to the novice is by explicit definitions and logical scaffolding that includes the concept.

17.6 Cultural Scaffolding and Intentionality

Intentionality is not an intrinsic property of consciousness or an attribute conferred on us by an innate language of thought but something we need to acquire from interactive activity with adults who use language and artifacts. It involves the isolation of concepts in early speech and the articulation of our own and other people's emergent activity into acts. We need language to learn to do this, and we probably need other aspects of culture as well, such as tools, rule-governed play, and the implements and furniture of our daily lives.

Sinha (1988) speculates that our prolonged childhood may be an adaptation to a predominantly cultural environment, not in the hackneyed sense that it provides us with an extended period for learning but in the more interesting sense that certain features of childhood might have been selected by an environment of artifacts and tools. He hastens to add that he is not suggesting that human infants are born with *knowledge* about this specifically human environment. Rather, evolution has provided them with mechanisms that facilitate the process of *learning* about that environment. There certainly appear to be species-typical activity patterns (prelinguistic production of sound that serves no immediate communicative purpose but provides the vocal material for interactive language practice; early reaching that can be converted into the all-important gesture of pointing by an interactive context) that indicate a selective bias toward an environment of language and culture.

Intentional descriptions of our behavior cannot provide clues to the underlying mechanisms of that behavior, but they are essential to our ability to learn new skills. They allow us to articulate and debug our own and other people's emergent activity patterns. We need them to construct the scaffolding for our social interactions and extended projects. As Dennett (1984) put it in a slightly different context, an explanation of one's behavior in terms of acts, beliefs, and plans helps one to "keep one's eye on the ball and follow through," even if the swing is not actually caused by the belief or executed in accordance with the rules laid down in the plan.

Chapter 18

An Explanatory Framework That Reconciles Biology and Culture

18.1 Better the Devil You Know?

We have come a long way from the simple species-typical activity patterns of ethology and the even simpler, interactively emergent activity patterns performed by Mataric's robot. In this chapter I take the explanation even further, into the realms of human thought, but before I do so it might be a good idea to take stock. What guarantees that the elaborate explanatory structure I have built from such simple principles is more than a mildly interesting bit of storytelling? What ensures that my use of the terms *activity pattern, interactive emergence,* and *history of use,* when applied to adult human thought and behavior, is not just metaphorical speculation without any basis in fact? Perhaps the cognitive approach to explanation has its problems, but it can point to some very convincing simulations of high-level behavior in AI. Programs have been written that can play world-class chess, diagnose diseases, and plan and monitor all sorts of industrial processes, to name but a few of the many successful applications. Even if human beings do not perform these tasks in exactly the same way, at least the computational models provide a comprehensible description of the competences required at that level of abstraction.

"If something works, and you know how it works, e.g., you can specify which aspects of the design explain which aspects of its capabilities, and how a difference in the design would change those capabilities, then to that extent I claim that you have as deep an explanation as you can get in science. . . . Moreover, to the extent that something else works in the same way as an artifact (i.e., shares architecture or mechanisms or environment or some combination of those) then to that extent the same explanation is applicable to the other" (Aaron Sloman, personal communication, March 1995). My argument has been that the difficulty lies in this notion of "working in the same way." The AI systems I referred to are functional solutions to well-defined problems made up of programs that perform specific tasks. We know how they work and can specify "which aspects of their design explain which aspects of their capabilities," because we designed them in accordance with such functional principles. Although adult behavior may be conceptualized as a series of tasks or a collection of functions (and we routinely conceptualize it in these ways to "scaffold" our own behavior and respond to the behavior of others), it would be extremely surprising if we turned out to "work in the same way" as a system designed from functional principles. In fact, to talk of "working in the same way" is almost certainly to commit a category mistake. The underlying mechanisms of an AI simulation *do* "work." They accomplish specific jobs toward an overall end. Their functions and tasks have been derived from analyzing what is required to achieve that end. But the underlying mechanisms of a creature shaped by evolution and learning do not "work" in that sense, because they have not been put there for a specific purpose in conformance with an overall design. In the case of a simulation, the architecture and underlying mechanisms are those of an input-output device, and its "environment" is a task domain preregistered into objects, properties, and events. In the case of a human being, the "architecture" is that of a dynamic system, whose "environment" emerges interactively from the system's lower levels of activity and the culture in which the person is embedded. Analogies between the two that compare their architecture, internal mechanisms, and environment are therefore unlikely to be of help in an explanation of the mind, though they may provide excellent formal descriptions of certain aspects of human behavior.

The limitations of the traditional approach have become apparent over the years. It tends to work well for task domains that can be exhaustively described, but it quickly breaks down when the systems are extended to more general and more ambiguous domains, and it is notoriously poor at dealing with "natural" environments in real time. The "frame problem" and the threat of combinatorial explosion are "wired in" to the top-down approach based on task descriptions. One response to these problems is to put one's faith in complexity and computing power. This is a legitimate engineering approach and might actually remain the only way to achieve artificial intelligence of any power for many years to come. A different response is to accept that human intelligence is something quite different and that truly adaptive symbolic behavior will be achieved only by identifying the underlying mechanisms that enable a human being to learn and respond interactively within a cultural environment. I have argued that the principled way to do this is by adopting a historical approach based on species-typical activity patterns and interactive emergence.

The doubts expressed in the first paragraph of this chapter are not so easily dispelled, however. Behavior has a bad name in cognitive science. Is the new interpretation I have put on it by grounding it in ethology and situated robotics and stressing the importance of intentional scaffolding enough to overcome its damning associations with behaviorism? Isn't behavior by definition external to the creature? How can a behavior-based explanation refer to and explain human thought? In the absence of behavior-based models that can do clever things like play chess or diagnose diseases, why should this new explanatory framework be adopted in place of the currently more successful approach based on classical AI? Let me try to lay to rest the lingering ghost of behaviorism first.

18.2 Only a Better Theory of Behavior Can Lay to Rest the Ghost of Behaviorism

In 1959 Noam Chomsky published a review of B. F. Skinner's *Verbal Behavior* (Chomsky 1959) that is often cited as one of the opening shots in the "cognitive revolution." Chomsky's critique brings out the essential differences between the behaviorist and cognitive positions and should serve as a rigorous test of the scientific credentials of any behavior-based explanation. The purpose of Skinner's book, Chomsky observed, was to provide a functional analysis of verbal behavior by human beings and to identify its controlling variables. There are two main elements in Skinner's approach: a belief that the causes of behavior can be fully explained by observing and manipulating only the physical environment of the speaker and the assumption that all the essential variables of an explanation may be subsumed under the descriptive categories of "stimulus," "reinforcement," "deprivation," and "response," which have been given precise scientific meanings by Skinner's experiments with animals.

Most of Chomsky's article is devoted to a devastating analysis of this second assumption, based on extensive examples from Skinner's book. Chomsky argues, as I have in previous chapters, that what counts as a "stimulus" and what counts as a "response" in the context of Skinner's animal experiments depends to a large extent on his experimental design. The Skinner box presumes that an animal's behavior can be described in such terms, and it ensures that the subject's patterns of activity will be interpreted accordingly. Chomsky believes this procedure can be justified in behaviorist experiments with animals and that it has produced some valuable results. However, he then goes on to show that Skinner's extensions of his explanatory terms to an account of verbal behavior by human beings are either "meaningless" or "empty," or a disguised retreat into woolly mentalism:

No characterization of the notion *stimulus control* that is remotely related to the bar-pressing experiment (or that preserves the faintest objectivity) can be made to cover a set of examples like these. . . .

The way in which these terms are brought to bear on the actual data indicates that we must interpret them as mere paraphrases for the popular vocabulary commonly used to describe behavior and as having no particular connection with the homonymous expressions used in the description of laboratory experiments. . . .

What has been hoped for from the psychologist is some indication of how the causal and informal description of everyday behavior in the popular vocabulary can be explained or clarified in terms of notions developed in careful experiment and observation, or perhaps replaced in terms of a better scheme. A mere terminological revision, in which a term borrowed from the laboratory is used with the full vagueness of the ordinary vocabulary, is of no conceivable interest. (Chomsky 1959, pp. 554, 556, 558–559)

In other words, Chomsky accuses Skinner of redescribing rather than explaining verbal behavior, and of doing so in terms that derive a spurious aura of scientific rigor from his animal experiments, whereas in fact they serve mainly to obscure important distinctions. I believe this part of Chomsky's critique remains as pertinent today as it was in 1959. I also agree with much of what he says about Skinner's reliance on environmental stimuli to explain the complexity of human behavior.

Chomsky concedes that in the absence of independent neurological evidence, all a scientist can do is to observe the subject's behavior and try to "describe the function specifying the response in terms of the history of inputs. This is nothing more than the definition of the problem" (Chomsky 1959, p. 548). The point of contention, Chomsky argues, is not this one about the nature of the data but the extent to which the organism itself is assumed to contribute to the structure of its behavior. Skinner believes that the organism's contribution is negligible and that external factors consisting of current stimulation and the history of reinforcement are therefore sufficient for an explanation. Chomsky believes that the complexity of the behavior derives primarily from the internal structure of the creature. This means that although the scientist has to rely on observables for his data, his explanation will need to resort to hidden variables and cannot be framed entirely in terms of objective responses to objective stimuli: "If the contribution of the organism is complex, the only hope of predicting behavior even in a gross way will be through a very indirect program of research that begins by studying the detailed character of the behavior itself and the particular capacities of the organism involved" (Chomsky 1959, p. 549).

Chomsky ends his article by making a strong case for competence theories. Complex behavior cannot be explained as a succession of reflexes. It has a syntactic structure that must be imposed from within. He refers to another classic paper, by Lashley (1951), which concluded that the structure of such activities as piano playing, and in particular the verbal articulation of grammatical sentences, requires hierarchically organized internal mechanisms that prestructure the behavior at various levels of abstraction.

I have argued in this book that the contribution of the organism *is* complex and that it cannot be explained in terms of simple categories like stimulus, reinforcement, and response. Like Chomsky, I have concluded that an explanation must start from a detailed study of the activity itself rather than an assumption that all behavior can be forced into the straitjacket of a reflex arc or a TOTE unit. However, I have argued also that Chomsky's notion of a capacity or competence does not provide sufficient basis for an explanation, because the "syntax" of a creature's behavior cannot be divorced from its "performance" in a species-typical environment. There is no dispute that the organism contributes to the varied temporal structures of its activity patterns. But a true understanding of the underlying mechanisms that might account for those structures can be achieved only by studying how the animal's performance emerges in situ, and this goes for the verbal behavior of human beings as much as it does for the egg-rolling behavior of a greylag goose.

Speech is a continuously interactive, situated process. The complexity to which Lashley (1951) drew attention—that of serial order in production—is only one aspect of the richness and flexibility demonstrated by human beings in their routine verbal interactions. To separate it out and call it "syntax" may be to create an artificial problem (that of explaining a disembodied syntactic competence) and to leave the remainder, designated as "semantics" and "pragmatics," forever inexplicable.

Dynamical systems theory has made it possible to conceive of complex behavior as arising interactively from the structure of the environment in conjunction with the creature's internal dynamics. We no longer need hierarchically organized planning systems to explain intricate temporal structure. A natural creature's behavior does not need to be preplanned. It does not have to exist as an abstract internal representation in the creature's head before it is "executed." The complex structure can emerge as and when it happens from the dynamic coupling between the organism and its environment. As I have warned throughout this book, dynamical systems theory by itself cannot provide the natural kinds for an explanation, but it lays to rest the idea that complex behavior requires a computational explanation involving internal representations of the creature's activity that need to be prepared before they are "executed."

Chomsky decided that syntactic competence had to be largely innate. He based this conclusion on the complexity of the internal mechanism required, as well as on the surprising speed with which children appear to learn their first language. After reviewing the research literature of the past thirty years, Bruner (1990) concluded that three things have emerged to cast doubt on Chomsky's extreme rationalist position. Learning a first language has turned out to require far more experience and help from adults than Chomsky assumed. Practice with turn taking and the pragmatics of speech acts during prelinguistic mother-infant "dialogues" have been shown to play a crucial role in preparing the infant for the comprehension and production of his first grammatical sentences. And learning to attach meanings to spoken language cannot be divorced from situated contexts involving cultural artifacts and the child's own nonverbal activity in relation to such artifacts. In the previous three chapters, I have tried to show how an explanation in terms of species-typical activity patterns selected by a cultural environment of man-made objects and adults who respond to the infant's behavior in intentional terms might account for these findings.

The notions of activity pattern and situated emergence as used in this book can be applied to intentional as well as reflexive behavior, because they do not depend on assumptions concerning physical causes and effects. An activity pattern is not a specific movement or series of movements that is executed in response to an identifiable physical stimulus. It is a feature of the creature's behavior that has a recognizable temporal structure. (The notion of recognizable structure does not need to be "unpacked," since ultimately all of science depends on it.) The underlying mechanisms that make the activity possible might be extremely complex, but we do not need to understand them in order to identify the activity pattern itself. The activity pattern is an explanatory device that enables us to carve up a creature's ongoing behavior in a principled way. The justification for one particular way of carving up the behavior in preference to others comes not from "internal unities" provided by a neurophysiological or a computational explanation but from careful observation of the creature in its natural habitat, comparative studies with other individuals and species, and the concept of history of use.

An ethological and developmental perspective enables us to isolate such natural kinds of behavior in a principled way. Ultimate physical causes do not explain an activity pattern, in the sense that specific objectively defined features or events can be reliably correlated with its beginning and end. Rather, the underlying level of physical causes is likely to be better understood only after the key activity patterns that make up a creature's behavior have been identified in a principled way. The child's two-word sentence that emerges at the age of eighteen months is as much an activity pattern as the pattern of reach-and-grasp that can be identified much earlier, and both are essential for the emergence of more mature activity patterns. These later patterns develop only because the creature performs the earlier patterns in a situated context and thereby creates an interactive *Umwelt* from which the later patterns can emerge. Chomsky's strictures about the unwarranted extension to intentional behavior of terms that can be given precise scientific meanings only in a restricted experimental context do not apply.

I hope this has laid to rest any doubts about "hidden," or "lingering," or "disguised" behaviorism in the explanatory framework I have proposed. A more damning criticism of that framework might be that relatively few principled activity patterns have been identified in human behavior. What is to ensure that this type of explanation can be made to cover more than the restricted areas of infant activity I have cited? Although there is no conclusive answer, I shall try to show in the next section that recent discoveries and theoretical formulations in fields as diverse as cultural psychology, literary criticism, conversational analysis, ethnomethodology, and various branches of anthropology—disciplines that stress careful observation of intentional behavior in its "natural" environment—are far more readily explained by a situated, interactive, activity-based account than by an explanation derived from functional decomposition and symbol processing.

18.3 Telling Stories about Ourselves and the World

The great advantage of the perspective I have proposed is that it makes language and other cultural factors integral to the explanation without having to import "intentional icons" into the individual's head. The notions of scaffolding and interactive emergence dispel the need for reductive explanations in terms of internally manipulated "symbols," just as they dispel the need for reductive explanations in terms of objective physical states. There have been a number of recent attempts by philosophers and psychologists rooted in the cognitive tradition to come to terms with a view of culture as being constitutive of human thought rather than playing some reductive causal role. Among these attempts, I would class Dennett's (1991) notion of "heterophenomenology" and his "multiple drafts" model of consciousness (though Dennett himself might not agree), Sinha's (1988) attempt to reconcile the insights of semiotics with the cognitive notion of internal representation, Clark's (1993) project to provide a connectionist underpinning for concepts that do not correspond to specific internal states or structures but can be equated only with the ability to "negotiate some macro-level domain that interests us in virtue of our daily human life," and Bruner's (1990) efforts to rescue the cognitive revolution he himself helped to launch from what he now sees as the dead hand of computationalism.

What these very different books have in common is an acceptance that human beings live in a world of public meanings that are continuously being negotiated through situated and interactive processes of interpretation. Meaning does not issue fully specified from individual heads; it is constructed through interactions between people. What we say and what we do are inextricably bound up together, not in the sense that our behavior is verbally prepared in our heads as an intentional course of action or that it is planned in terms of some cognitively impenetrable "language of thought" that can be translated into action or verbal reports, or even that our reports about the causes of our actions should be taken as reliable indicators of the internal mechanisms that mediate those actions. Folk psychological descriptions are constitutive of our behavior because they help us make sense of our actions, and it is only by making sense of them that we can act and interact in human ways. The scaffolding of meaning provided by folk psychology is in continual flux. It is not a rigid structure that can be defined in terms of fixed relations between atoms of meaning, but its shared, public existence provides sufficient guidance to keep our actions and thoughts within meaningful bounds.

Dennett (1991) provides an exciting attempt to synthesize a functional and computational "explanation" of consciousness (he himself admits it can only be a sketch until more data are collected and better computational models are built) from a dizzying variety of ingredients. The book is packed full of suggestive examples from experimental psychology, and it demolishes a number of persistent myths that badly needed demolishing. I shall concentrate my discussion on Dennett because he is widely considered to be the main philosophical spokesman for cognitive science, because an examination of his current position will round off some of the central themes he floated in *Content and Consciousness* (1969) that have hovered over this book, and finally, because I believe that *Consciousness Explained* goes about as far as it is possible go in providing a computational explanation for the interactive aspects of language and culture. Dennett remains committed to the design stance (or, in an explanation of conscious phenomena, the intentional stance) and to an ultimate explanation in terms of computational entities and processes. But he takes on board a large number of insights from literary theory, anthropology, and ethnomethodology that most cognitive scientists prefer to ignore.

The main ingredients of Dennett's explanation are his substitution of a multiple drafts model for what he calls the Cartesian theater, his eclectic use of computational concepts and techniques, and a methodological approach to data collection for which he has coined the term *heterophenomenology*, which is meant to provide an objective, third-person way of reporting on mental phenomena that renders such reports legitimate data for science. Like Chomsky, Dennett makes the point that even though mental phenomena may not be observable and measurable, this does not rule them out for scientific study. What is needed is a neutral way of describing the data that makes no prior assumptions about the nature of consciousness. Heterophenomenology is Dennett's proposal for meeting that need.

Dennett introduces the notion by a roundabout way. He begins by drawing attention to the fact that psychologists employ principled methods in laboratory experiments to ensure that the verbal reports produced by their subjects are neutral in the sense that is required. Transcripts of the recorded procedures are made by people who do not have a vested interest in the outcome of the experiment. Various experimenters will agree on the interpretation to be put on the subject's reports, and the subjects themselves will be consulted as to the correctness of that interpretation. Dennett points out that all this activity of interpretation is possible only because the experimenters, as well as the subjects, adopt the intentional stance. They assume that the subjects' verbal reports can be interpreted as speech acts—propositions the subjects intended to assert—and that therefore these reports have an identifiable meaning:

> When doubts arise about whether the subject has said what he meant, or understood the problem, or knows the meanings of the words being used, we can ask for clarifications. Usually we can resolve the doubts. Ideally, the effect of these measures is to remove all likely sources of ambiguity and uncertainty from the experimental situation, so that *one* intentional interpretation of the text (including the button-pushings) has no plausible rivals. It has to be taken to be the sincere, reliable expression by a *single, unified subject* of that very subject's beliefs and opinions. (Dennett 1991, p. 77).

By "cleaning up" a folk psychological description of subjective experience, the experimenters and their subjects produce a "neutral" report of what those subjects believe to be going on in their minds. Note that even in the rigidly scaffolded situation of a laboratory experiment, Dennett admits that meanings often need to be negotiated. The subject's "speech acts"—or, to put it in a slightly different way, the range and nature of the interpretations that may be put on her verbal responses—are severely restricted by the methodology and apparatus of the experiment and the instructions the subject will have received from the experimenter. The experimental setup is in fact designed to elicit specific speech acts or impose a specific "meaningful" structure on the subject's ongoing activity. This is not to disparage all laboratory procedures in psychology. It is merely to point out that the important "data" for an explanation of everyday behavior may be hidden in what Dennett describes as the cleaning-up procedures: resolving doubts, removing likely sources of ambiguity, asking for clarifications so that one particular intentional interpretation can be established as the correct one.

Dennett then admits that the practice of interpreting verbal behavior as unambiguous reports of the subject's mental states is no guarantee that she *has* mental states. To establish that the world of mental states is nonetheless a fit object of scientific study, he draws analogies to literary criticism and anthropology. Dennett advocates accepting the authority of the subject's reports concerning her mental states in the same way that we accept the authority of an author's text concerning his fictional world: "This permits theorists to agree in detail about just what a subject's heterophenomenological world is, while offering entirely different accounts of how heterophenomenological worlds map onto events in the brain (or the soul, for that matter). The subject's heterophenomenological world will be a stable, intersubjectively confirmable theoretical posit, having the same metaphysical status as, say, Sherlock Holmes's London or the world according to Garp" (Dennett 1991, p. 81).

But will it? Sherlock Holmes's London is stable because it is *externally* represented in a series of stories. The stability of Sherlock Holmes's London derives entirely from the existence of these stories. Different readers undoubtedly have different mental images of the characters and events depicted in them, but to the extent that their interpretations agree, this is due to the external representations of those characters and events, which provide scaffolding for individual interpretations. To say that a subject's heterophenomenological world is stable in the same sense that Sherlock Holmes's London is stable implies that that world is external to the subject and fixed by the canonical text. It implies that the subject's heterophenomenological world just *is* that text. But it remains an open question, not only how the text "maps onto events in the brain" but also how it maps onto putative "mental states" or "mental processes," or whether it is meaningful to talk in such terms at all. "As in fiction," Dennett (1991) writes, "what the author (the apparent author) says goes. More precisely, what the apparent author says provides a text that, when interpreted according to the rules just mentioned, goes to stipulate the way a certain 'world' *is*" (p. 81).

The question is: what world? If the analogy with fiction is to hold, the answer to that question can only be *the world created by the text*. The texts of Conan Doyle's stories are the ultimate authority on *Sherlock Holmes's* London; they are certainly not an authority on late nineteenth-century London. We may gain information about London during that period from reading these stories, but that is purely fortuitous. Literary criticism provides no guarantees as to the veracity of that information, and it would be considered eccentric to take Conan Doyle's stories as *design specs* for nineteenth-century London—and this, ultimately, is what Dennett hopes the "cleaned-up" intentional reports made by subjects about their mental states will do for the brain.

Dennett's fictitious example from anthropology suffers from similar problems. He posits a group of anthropologists trying to make sense of the heterophenomenological world of a tribe that believes in a forest god called Feenoman. They interview members of the tribe and observe their behavior and try to put together a picture of the god: "Gradually a logical construct emerges: Feenoman the forest god, complete with a list of traits and habits and a biography. These agnostic scientists . . . have described, ordered, catalogued a part of the world constituted by the beliefs of the natives, and (if they have done their job of interpretation well) have compiled the *definitive* description of Feenoman" (Dennett 1991, p. 82). This is fine as long as the phrase "natives' beliefs" is used in an anthropological rather than a psychological sense—as an abstraction that collectively designates a body of rituals and verbal reports. There is no dispute that the anthropologists' picture of Feenoman helps them to catalog and make sense of the natives' practices. However, Dennett's next step is to ask what might be required for an empirical theory to vindicate subjects' beliefs in their own heterophenomenology. At this point Dennett starts to import the anthropologists' logical construct into the natives' heads. The "intentional object" becomes an intentional *icon* that may be used as an explanatory entity for the "beliefs" of individual natives. Dennett justifies this move by pointing out that one can sometimes discover the "real" person or event that acted as the "trigger" for a fictional character or religious belief. Perhaps Sherlock Holmes was based on someone Conan Doyle met in his club, and perhaps Feenoman originated in sightings of a real man in the forest who behaved in inexplicable ways. Both the author and the natives are likely to protest at this kind of explanation for their fictions, but, says Dennett, if the evidence is strong enough, we are likely to ignore their protests and accept the real characters and events as the ultimate causes of the fictions: "My suggestion, then, is that if we were to find real goings-on in people's brains that had *enough* of the 'defining' properties of the items that populate their heterophenomenological worlds, we could reasonably propose that we had discovered what they were *really* talking about—even if they initially resisted the identifications" (Dennett 1991, p. 85).

This is very confusing. The character of Sherlock Holmes may indeed have had its origins in a man who smoked a pipe in Conan Doyle's club, just as Feenoman worship may have been precipitated by sightings of Johnny Weissmuller in the forest. However, by no stretch of the imagination can the stories of Sherlock Holmes or Feenoman worship be *identified* with these events. There is no clear and simple correspondence between the precipitating "causes" and the fictional results. The creation of a work of fiction and the emergence of religious practices are complex, historical, and cultural processes, and they involve interactions with language and existing public narratives that are not well understood. "Real" events may contribute to setting off these processes, but to talk of "identification" is to simplify the relation between the precipitating cause and its fictional consequence beyond any explanatory use that it might have had as an analogy.

Dennett's notion of heterophenomenology fails on two counts. He is not able to make a convincing case that items in the texts produced by negotiation or abstraction point to mental states or processes that might serve as the natural kinds for an explanation of consciousness, and he is not able to make out a convincing case that it will ever be possible to link such items to neurophysiological explanations. Since Dennett's explanations are explanations in terms of internal states and processes, they crucially depend on such links.

In the main body of his book, Dennett effectively demolishes the notion of a Cartesian theater—a physical or temporal location in the brain where afferents come together and are "projected" as a coherent representation of the world that can be used by some internal mechanism to "plan" the overall system's actions. Dennett provides numerous examples from experimental psychology to show that our distinctions between perception, memory, and thinking are artificial ones. The mind should be conceptualized, he says, as a collection of "narrative fragments" that are continuously being revised, edited, reconstructed, and in many cases discarded before they can have any perceptible effect on behavior. Such narrative fragments emerge in the brain from a multiplicity of parallel "decisions," "discriminations," and "judgments," resulting in contentful "states" or "processes." There is no definitive version inside the brain of objective events and states of the world. Only when the brain is "probed," resulting in either a physical act or a speech act, does a unified interpretation emerge. "Probing this stream at various intervals produces different effects, precipitating different narratives—and these *are* narratives: single versions of a portion of 'the stream of consciousness' " (Dennett 1991, p. 135).

The question that arises is how the earlier "decisions," "discriminations," and "judgments" that produce the narrative fragments in the stream of consciousness can occur. As Dennett warned all those years ago, "*It makes no sense* to suppose that discrimination of stimuli *by their significance* can occur solely on the afferent side of the brain" (Dennett 1969, p. 74). One can ascribe content to a neural event, state, or structure only when it is a demonstrable link in a causal chain between the afferent and the efferent. Dennett has now argued that it also makes no sense to draw a clear internal distinction between the afferent and the efferent side of the brain. However, presumably he would still agree that the grounds for internal discriminations and judgments need to come from somewhere. An explanation in terms of internal discriminations and judgments, if it cannot depend on straightforward links between input and output, needs an endogenous meaning-producing mechanism along the lines of Marr's transformations based on representational primitives.

This is the old top-down–bottom-up dilemma. It is the inevitable consequence of adopting an explanation in terms of an input-output model that "takes in" sensory stimuli conceptualized as physical "features," or light waves, or "retinal maps" and that "outputs" meaningful speech acts and purposive behavior. Is the internal process directed toward the output? Does it consist of a sequence of transformations designed to extract meaning, to make explicit the sorts of "information" that will be required for the final "use"? If so, what could be the nature of those transformations, and how did they come to be "designed" so perfectly to produce the intentional results? (As I have argued repeatedly in this book, appeals to natural selection merely beg all sorts of questions.) If, on the other hand, the process of extracting meaning is not a directed process—if the "probe" that precipitates the speech act or the meaningful behavior is what causes the *real* narrative to take shape—then how does this happen, and how do the right sorts of brain states come to be available at the right time and place? Dennett appeals to a large number of computational techniques and concepts to answer these questions. I have discussed most of them already and shall not repeat my conclusions.

The problem of fitting an explanation into an input-output model is not ultimately solved by saying that there is no specific point at which input turns into output and that consciousness should not be construed as a homunculus or a spectator-initiator placed at such a point (however important that insight may be). It is the input-output model itself that causes the problems. Cognitive science inherited that model from behaviorism, and the result has been that, like behaviorism, it has tended to ignore and underrate behavior.

The distinction Dennett makes between the "narrative fragments" in the brain and the real narratives precipitated by "probes" is revealing. Dennett is aware that the syntax and semantics, and even the sounds, of language, as well as pictorial representations, play a crucial role in shaping our thoughts. He conceptualizes this by borrowing Dawkins's (1976a) notion of "memes" and importing these into the subject's head: "Thousands of memes, mostly borne by language, but also by wordless 'images' and other data structures, take up residence in an individual brain, shaping its tendencies and thereby turning it into a mind" (Dennett 1991, p. 263). These memes result in a "virtual von Neumann architecture" superimposed on the basically parallel, highly plastic neural architecture of the brain, and this accounts, according to Dennett, for our ability to think sequentially. There is no real evolutionary or neurophysiological explanation of why this might work with human brains but not with those of gorillas. Because he thinks in terms of a computational input-output model, Dennett conceives of adaptations for culture in architectural terms. But he admits that the "functionally important features" that distinguish an adult human mind will probably remain "invisible to neuroanatomical scrutiny" (p. 219), and he further admits that since there can be no formally specified "machine language" common to different brains, transmission of the "virtual machine" from one brain to another might be a problem. This implies, Dennett concedes, that bootstrapping an infant into meaning is a difficult process and must be highly situated and context sensitive. Public narrative plays an important role in getting meaning off the ground. It is useful as a method of instruction and "self-stimulation" that gets the memes into the head, and it can be thought of as a collection of culturally transmitted "tricks" that set up the virtual von Neumann machine inside an individual's brain.

In view of the problems and shortcomings of this input-output model, one often wonders why Dennett does not scrap the model and go for an explanation in terms of public narratives and situated behavior: "Just as spiders don't have to think, consciously or deliberately, about how to spin their webs, and just as beavers, unlike professional human engineers, do not consciously and deliberately plan the structures they build, we . . . do not consciously and deliberately figure out what narratives to tell and how to tell them. Our tales are spun, but for the most part we don't spin them; they spin us. Our human consciousness, and our narrative selfhood, is their product, not their source" (Dennett 1991, p. 418). In that case, shouldn't we be concentrating on the source rather than the product? If consciousness is the outcome of narratives that are not deliberately planned but that resemble the species-typical behavior of web-spinning spiders and dam-building beavers, shouldn't a study of consciousness begin by investigating these typically human activity patterns in their natural surroundings? What regularities, if any, do they exhibit? Can narratives be broken down into more basic activity patterns and taxonomized? Are there comparisons that can be made with the activity patterns of phylogenetically related animals? Is it possible to discover how patterns of narrative become established through maturation and learning? Instead of trying to justify functional components and internal representations of a fully fledged conscious mind by appeals to natural selection, wouldn't it be more logical to try to discover the underlying activity patterns that make it possible for a human infant to acquire this unique, unconscious ability to spin narratives about himself and the world? How exactly do narratives "spin us"? Or, to put it differently, how do our conscious selves become established as the result of participating in public dialogue that consists of coherent, intentional stories?

18.4 Why Narratives Remain Public Resources and Do Not Invade Our Minds

I have already discussed in chapters 15 to 17 what I believe to be the fundamental answers to these questions. Bruner (1990) provides further clues to how an explanation in terms of species-typical activity patterns and interactive emergence could be tied to recent discoveries and theories concerning the cultural and educational role played by narratives.

In every culture there are agreed-upon, canonical interpretations of behavior, and only deviations from such norms require intentional explanations. These serve to negotiate the meanings of such "breakdowns" and get us back onto the accepted tracks. The intentional explanations take the form of narratives. "Beliefs" and "desires" can be understood only in the context of such narratives, which in turn require the context of the "breakdowns" in situated behavior to be properly understood. It is the situated activity, and the deviations from the canonical forms of such activity, as well as the typically human skill of spinning narratives, that give meaning to intentional ascriptions. As Clark (1993) conjectured, concepts, beliefs, and desires cannot be equated with specific internal states but only with the "ability to negotiate some macro-level domain that interests us in virtue of our daily human life."

Even before they learn their first language, children have become adept at negotiating some of these domains. Language is not needed to learn to participate in the most basic forms of canonical behavior. But mothers tend to keep up a running commentary on what they themselves and their children are doing. The child thus learns to associate the intentional explanations provided by the mother with the canonical forms of behavior in their situated context. By the end of the second year, children themselves begin to accompany any new or unusual activity with their own running commentary (Eckerman 1993), and by the age of three or four, they have begun to justify deviations from the norm in terms of narratives involving intentional ascriptions. Bruner cites a series of studies (Nelson, 1989), showing that children around that age spend a lot of time soliloquizing about their own and other people's recent activities. The children are not simply reporting; they are trying to make sense of the way they themselves and other people have acted.

Bruner believes that an explanation of these findings requires that we assume that infants "come into the world already equipped with a primitive form of folk-psychology" (Bruner 1990, p. 73). He concedes that this might not be a full-blown theory of mind but merely "a set of predispositions to construe the social world in a particular way and to act upon our construals." He talks in terms of a "push" to construct narratives that determines the order in which infants acquire their first words and the order in which they master various grammatical forms. I have argued that an explanation can be given without recourse to such inborn forms of meaning or "diffuse intentionality"—an explanation framed entirely in terms of species-typical activity patterns adapted to a cultural environment and situated interactions with adults that lead to the interactive emergence of higher levels of behavior and thought.

We do not consciously plan our thoughts in the way that we plan our actions. Our thoughts occur to us, they slip into our minds, and we may even try to hold on to them or strain for them as we try to find the solution to a problem, but we do not, in the main, map out a train of thought before we embark on it. When we embark on a trip, we may rehearse mentally the route we intend to take. When we set out to construct a cabinet, we may plan the sequence of steps that are needed to fit together the various parts in the proper order. When we begin to write a book, we may think of chapter headings and use these to structure the development of our argument. But when we embark on an extended sequence of thoughts, we do not normally tell ourselves, "First I shall have this thought, and then I shall think that, and finally I shall conclude by thinking such and such." Thinking is something we just do, without first considering how we shall do it.

But although our thoughts are not consciously planned, they do have a structure. They follow plans in the sense I discussed in chapter 17: plans that cannot be conceptualized as programs or even as the explicit task descriptions used to scaffold unfamiliar actions but that depend on skilled activity patterns and concepts that have emerged from negotiating public domains. These emergent concepts are not explicitly represented inside the head. There is no need for a distinct natural kind to explain their role in thinking. They simply constitute an ability to cope in the various situations that are loosely designated by the public term. Our thinking is shaped, deflected, and integrated by such concepts in the sense that a person who has acquired them will be able to think in ways that she could not have thought before. But her thoughts are not logically structured in terms of the public definitions attached to these concepts, and neither are they directed toward goals internally specified in terms of them. The plans used by a competent thinker do not impose a structure that is predefined and separate from content. There is no need to "interpret" or "execute" such plans, and they do not call subplans. There are no explicit decision points that require internal representations of conditions in the world.

Experience in deploying the public narratives of one's culture is essential in acquiring the skills and concepts used in thinking. A child needs to practice extensively with his parents, with other children, and by himself in "patching up" discrepancies between acceptable forms of behavior and the emergently interactive behavior produced by himself and others to acquire these skills and concepts. Thinking is the result of such practice—an intentional skill that does not require intentional icons.

When Turing took mathematical proof as the paradigm for thinking, he chose a very specialized branch of thinking, in which the task description can easily be mistaken for the activity itself. Turing was initially very much aware that mathematicians do not develop new proofs in such an explicit, steplike fashion. He advised the reader of his seminal paper to picture mental states or "m-configurations" as notes that a mathematician might leave to himself—external scaffolding the mathematician could use to constrain and guide his own thinking. But some time around the beginning of the "cognitive revolution," Turing himself began to believe that a model based on formal task descriptions could be taken as an explanation of logical thinking. The task descriptions were imported into the mathematician's head, together with the Turing machine itself. And since the Turing machine could be used to run off any task that was describable as an effective procedure—since it had been shown to be a universal machine in this abstract sense—cognitive science decreed that it should be inserted even into the heads of nonmathematicians thinking about Sally's wedding or whether to apply for that lectureship in the *Times* educational supplement.

Explicit task descriptions need to be prepared before they can control a person's actions or thoughts. This introduces the notion that thought is given structure before it is actually executed, that it must exist in some predefined form prior to actually being thought. Planning then becomes the primary function, preceding both thought and action. This has been an enduring tendency in Western conceptions of form (Oyama 1993). We feel that structure cannot simply emerge, that it has to be specified before it actually happens. But intricate structure does continually emerge in nature without the need for an explicit plan, and it emerges also in our thoughts.

Unlike Dennett, I do not believe we are close to providing an explanation of consciousness, but like him, I believe that consciousness should be conceptualized as the outcome of "talking to ourselves" and "drawing pictures for ourselves." How and why this should lead to the phenomena we describe as "hearing ourselves think" and "having mental images" remains a mystery, but I am sure that it is not a matter of importing words and pictures into our heads. We do not have internal representations or brain states that are vehicles of folk psychologically defined content—or even "narrative fragments" that resemble real narratives but are *not* real narratives—inside our brains. These are the stuff of public scaffolding, and just as it is a mistake to believe that a professional pianist or a competent driver plans her activities in terms of the explicit features and acts that were used to scaffold her behavior when she first learned to play scales or shift gears, so it is a mistake to believe that a competent thinker does her thinking in terms of the explicit narratives and pictorial representations that helped to teach her to think. What has happened is that, in addition to doing the real work, the underlying nonrepresentational mechanisms also produce mental echoes and mental after-images of the scaffolding—or something like that.

The real challenge to cognitive science today is to provide a convincing model for an explanation along these lines. I believe that the explanatory framework I have set out in this book has a greater likelihood of meeting that challenge than any other computational solution proposed to date.

References

Agre, P. E., and Chapman, D. (1988). *What Are Plans For?* MIT AI memo 1050.

Baerends, G. P. (1976). "The Functional Organisation of Behaviour." *Animal Behaviour* 24:726–738.

Baillargeon, R. (1987). "Object Permanence in 3½ and 4½ Month-Old Infants." *Developmental Psychology* 23, no. 5:655–664.

Ballard, D. H. (1989), "Reference Frames for Animate Vision." In *Proceedings of the International Joint Conference on Artificial Intelligence. IJCAI-89,* 1635–1641.

Barlow, G. W. (1968). "Ethological Units of Behaviour." In D. Ingle (ed.), *The Central Nervous System and Fish Behaviour,* 217–232. Chicago: University of Chicago Press.

Barlow, R. B. (1990). "What the Brain Tells the Eye." *Scientific American* (April):66–71.

Barlow, R. B., Powers, M. K., and Krass, L. (1988). "Vision and Mating Behaviour in Limulus." In J. Atema et al. (eds.), *Sensory Biology of Aquatic Animals,* 419–434. New York: Springer-Verlag.

Bateson, M. C. (1975). "Mother-Infant Exchanges: The Epigenesis of Conversational Interaction." In D. Aaronson and R. W. Rieber (eds.), *Developmental Psycholinguistics and Communication Disorders,* 101–113. New York: New York Academy of Sciences.

Bateson, M. C. (1979). "The Epigenesis of Conversational Interaction: A Personal Account of Research Development." In Bullowa (1979a), 63–78.

Beer, R. D. (1995). "A Dynamical Systems Perspective on Agent-Environment Interaction." *Artificial Intelligence* 72:173–215.

Beer, R. D., Chiel, H. J., and Sterling, L. S. (1990). "A Biological Perspective on Autonomous Agent Design." In Maes (ed.) (1991a), 169–186.

Boden, M. A. (1962) "The Paradox of Explanation." *Proceedings of the Aristotelian Society,* n.s., 159–178. Reprinted in M. A. Boden (1981). *Minds and Mechanisms.* Ithaca, NY: Cornell University Press.

Boden, M. A. (1972). *Purposive Explanation in Psychology.* Cambridge, MA: Harvard University Press.

Boden, M. A. (1988). *Computer Models of Mind: Computational Approaches in Theoretical Psychology.* Cambridge: Cambridge University Press.

Boden, M. A. (1989). *Artificial Intelligence in Psychology: Interdisciplinary Essays.* Cambridge, MA: The MIT Press.

Boden, M. A. (ed.). (1990). *The Philosophy of Artificial Intelligence.* London: Oxford University Press.

Boden, M. A. (1994). *Piaget.* 2d ed. London: Fontana.

Boorse, C. (1976). "Wright on Functions." *Philosophical Review* 85:70–86. Reprinted in E. Sober (ed.), *Conceptual Issues in Evolutionary Biology.* Cambridge, MA: The MIT Press.

Brazelton, T. B. (1979). "Evidence of Communication during Neonatal Behavioral Assessment." In Bullowa (1979a), 79–88.

Brody, N. (1988). *Personality: In Search of Individuality.* San Diego: Academic Press.

Brooks, R. A. (1981). "Symbolic Reasoning Among 3-D Models and 2-D Images." *Artificial Intelligence* 17, no. 1–3:285–347.

Brooks, R. A. (1986a). "A Robust Layered Control System for a Mobile Robot." *IEEE Journal of Robotics and Automation RA-2,* 14–23.

Brooks, R. A. (1986b). Achieving Artificial Intelligence through Building Robots. MIT A. I. Memo 899.

Brooks, R. A. (1991a). "Challenges for Complete Creature Architectures." In Myer and Wilson (1991), 434–443.

Brooks, R. A. (1991b). "Intelligence Without Representations." *Artificial Intelligence* 47:139–159.

Brooks, R. A. (1992). "Artificial Life and Real Robots." In Varela and Bourgine (1992), 3–10.

Brooks, R. A., and Stein, L. A. (1993). Building Brains for Bodies. MIT Artificial Intelligence Laboratory Memo 1439.

Bruner, J. S. (1951) "Personality Dynamics and the Process of Perceiving." In R. R. Blake and G. V. Ramsey (eds.), *Perception: An Approach to Personality,* 121–147. New York: Ronald Press.

Bruner, J. S. (1976). "On Prelinguistic Prerequisites of Speech." In R. N. Campbell and R. T. Smith (eds.), *Recent Advances in the Psychology of Language: Language Development and Mother-Child Interaction,* 199–214. London: Plenum Press.

Bruner, J. S. (1982). "The Organisation of Action and the Nature of Adult-Infant Transaction." In M. von Cranach and R. Harré (eds.), *The Analysis of Action,* 313–328. Cambridge: Cambridge University Press.

Bruner, J. S. (1990). *Acts of Meaning.* Cambridge, MA: Harvard University Press.

Bullowa, M. (ed.) (1979a). *Before Speech: The Beginning of Interpersonal Communication,* Cambridge: Cambridge University Press.

Bullowa, M. (1979b). "Pre-linguistic Communication: A Field for Scientific Research." In Bullowa (1979a), 1–62.

Camaioni, L. (1993). "The Development of Intentional Communication." In Nadel and Camaioni (1993), 82–96.

Camhi, J. M. (1984). *Neuroethology: Nerve Cells and the Natural Behaviour of Animals.* Sunderland, MA: Sinhauser Associates.

Cartwright, B. A., and Collett, T. S. (1987). "Landmark Maps for Honeybees." *Biological Cybernetics* 57:85–93.

Carey, S., and Gelman, R. (eds.). (1991). *The Epigenesis of Mind: Essays on Biology and Cognition.* Hillsdale, NJ: Lawrence Erlbaum.

Chapman, D., and Agre, P. E. (1987). "Abstract Reasoning as Emergent from Concrete Activity." In M. P. Georgeff and A. L. Lansky (eds.), *Reasoning About Actions and Plans,* 411–424. Los Angeles: Morgan-Kauffman.

Charlesworth, W. R., and Kreuzer, M. A. (1973). "Facial Expressions of Infants and Children." In Ekman (1973a), 91–168.

Chevalier-Skolnikoff, S. (1973). "Facial Expressions of Emotion in Nonhuman Primates." In Ekman (1973a), 11–90.

Chomsky, N. (1957). *Syntactic Structures.* The Hague: Mouton.

Chomsky, N. (1959). "A Review of B. F. Skinner's *Verbal Behavior.*" In J. A. Fodor and J. J. Katz (eds.), *The Structure of Language: Readings in the Philosophy of Language,* 547–578. Englewood Cliffs, NJ: Prentice-Hall.

Chomsky, N. (1965). *Aspects of the Theory of Syntax.* Cambridge, MA: The MIT Press.

Chomsky, N. (1972). *Language and Mind.* Harcourt, Brace & World.

Chomsky, N. (1980). "Rules and Representations." *Behavioral and Brain Sciences* 3:1–61.

Churchland, P. M. (1989). *A Neurocomputational Perspective: The Nature of Mind and the Structure of Science.* Cambridge, MA: The MIT Press.

Clark, A. (1989). *Microcognition: Philosophy, Cognitive Science and Parallel Distributed Processing.* Cambridge, MA: The MIT Press.

Clark, A. (1990). "Connectionism, Competence and Explanation." In Boden (1990), 281–308.

Clark, A. (1993). *Associative Engines: Connectionism, Concepts and Representational Change.* Cambridge, MA: The MIT Press.

Clark, A., and Karmiloff-Smith, A. (1991). *The Cognizer's Innards: A Psychological and Philosophical Perspective on the Development of Thought.* CSRP 193, University of Sussex.

Cliff, D. T. (1990). *Computational Neuroethology: A Provisional Manifesto.* CSRP 162, University of Sussex.

Cliff, D. T. (1991). Neural Networks for Visual Tracking in an Artificial Fly. CSRP 206, University of Sussex.

Cliff, D. T., Husbands, P., and Harvey, I. (1993). "Evolving Visually Guided Robots." In J. A. Meyer, H. Roitblat, and S. Wilson (eds.), *Proceedings of the Second International Conference on Simulation of Adaptive Behaviour.* Cambridge, MA: The MIT Press.

Cliff, D. T., Husbands, P., Meyer, J.-A., and Wilson, S. W. (eds.). (1994). *From Animals to Animats 3: Proceedings of the Third International Conference on Simulation of Adaptive Behavior.* Cambridge, MA: The MIT Press.

Clynes, M. (1980). "The Communication of Emotion: The Theory of Sentics." In R. Plutchik and H. Kellerman (eds.), *Emotion: Theory, Research and Experience,* 1:271–304. New York: Academic Press.

Clynes, M. (1982). *Music, Mind and Brain: The Neurophysiology of Music.* New York: Plenum Press.

Collett, T. S., and Cartwright, B. A. (1983). "Eidetic Images in Insects: Their Role in Navigation." *Trends in Neuroscience* 6:101–105.

Collis, G. M. (1979). "Describing the Structure of Social Interaction in Infancy." In Bullowa (1979a), 111–130.

Condon, W. S. (1979). "Neonatal Entrainment and Enculturation." In Bullowa (1979a), 131–148.

Crick, F. (1989). "The Recent Excitement about Neural Networks." *Nature* 337:129–132.

Cummins, R. (1975). "Functional Analysis." *Journal of Philosophy* 72, no. 20:741–764. Reprinted in E. Sober (ed.), *Conceptual Issues in Evolutionary Biology.* Cambridge, MA: The MIT Press.

Crystal, D. (ed.). (1987). *The Cambridge Encyclopaedia of Language.* London: Guild Publishing.

Cussins, A. (1990). "The Connectionist Construction of Concepts." In Boden (1990), 368–440.

Danto, A. C. (1973). *Analytical Philosophy of Action.* Cambridge: Cambridge University Press.

Darwin, C. (1872). *The Expression of Emotion in Man and Animals.* London: Methuen.

Dawkins, M. S. (1986). *Unravelling Animal Behaviour.* Harlow, Essex: Longman.

Dawkins, R. (1976a). *The Selfish Gene.* Oxford: Oxford University Press.

Dawkins, R. (1976b). "Hierarchical Organisation: A Candidate Principle for Ethology." In P. P. G. Bateson and R. A. Hinde (eds.), *Growing Points in Ethology,* 7–54. Cambridge: Cambridge University Press.

Dawkins, R. (1986). *The Blind Watchmaker.* Harmondsworth: Penguin.

Dedieu, E., and Mazer, E. (1992). "An Approach to Sensorimotor Relevance." In Varela and Bourgine (1992), 88–95.

De Groot, A. D. (1966). "Perception and Memory Versus Thought: Some Old Ideas and Recent Findings." In B. Kleinmutz (ed.), *Problem Solving*. New York: Wiley.

Dennett, D. C. (1969). *Content and Consciousness*. London: Routledge and Kegan Paul.

Dennett, D. C. (1978). *The Intentional Stance*. Cambridge, MA: The MIT Press.

Dennett, D. C. (1981). *Brainstorms*. Brighton: Harvester Press.

Dennett, D. C. (1983). "Intentional Systems in Cognitive Ethology: The Panglossian Paradigm Defended." *Behavioral and Brain Sciences* 6:343–390.

Dennett, D. C. (1984). *Elbow Room: The Varieties of Free Will Worth Wanting*. Cambridge, MA: The MIT Press.

Dennett, D. C. (1988). "The Evolution of Consciousness." Jacobsen Lecture, Tufts University, Center for Cognitive Studies, Circulating Manuscript CCM 88-1.

Dennett, D. C. (1991). *Consciousness Explained*. London: Allen Lane, Penguin Press.

Dewsbury, D. A. (1978). "What Is (Was?) the Fixed Action Pattern?" *Animal Behaviour* 26, no. 1:310–311.

Diamond, A. (1991). "Neurophysiological Insights into the Meaning of Object Concept Development." In Carey and Gelman (1991), 67–110.

Dretske, F. (1986). "Misrepresentation." In R. J. Bogdan (ed.), *Belief, Content and Function*. Oxford: Clarendon Press.

Dretske, F. (1988). *Explaining Behavior: Reasons in a World of Causes*. Cambridge, MA: The MIT Press.

Dreyfus, H. L., and Dreyfus, S. C. (1986a). "Making a Mind Versus Modelling the Brain: Artificial Intelligence Back at a Branch-Point." In Boden (1990), 309–333.

Dreyfus, H. L., and Dreyfus, S. C. (1986b). *Mind over Machine: The Power of Human Intuition and Expertise in the Era of the Computer*. New York: Free Press.

Eckerman, C. O. (1993). "Imitation and Toddlers' Achievement of Coordinated Action with Others." In Nadel and Camaioni (1993), 116–138.

Ekman, P. (ed.) (1973a). *Darwin and Facial Expression: A Century of Research in Review*. New York: Academic Press.

Ekman, P. (1973b). "Cross-Cultural Studies of Facial Expression." In Ekman (1973a), 169–222.

Ericsson, K. A., and Simon, H. A. (1980). "Verbal Reports as Data." *Psychological Review* 87, no. 3:215–251.

Fentress, J. C. (1976). "Dynamic Boundaries of Patterned Behaviour: Interaction and Self-Organisation." In P. P. G. Bateson and R. A. Hinde (eds.), *Growing Points in Ethology*, 135–170. Cambridge: Cambridge University Press.

Fischer, K. W., and Bidell, T. (1991). "Constraining Nativist Inferences about Cognitive Capacities." In Carey and Gelman (1991), 199–235.

Fodor, J. A. (1976). *The Language of Thought*. Hassocks: Harvester Press.

Fodor, J. A. (1978a). "Propositional Attitudes." *Monist* 61, no. 4:501–524.

Fodor, J. A. (1978b). "Tom Swift and His Procedural Grandmother." *Cognition* 6:229–247.

Fodor, J. A. (1980). "Methodological Solipsism Considered as a Research Strategy in Cognitive Psychology." *Behavioral and Brain Sciences* 3:63–110.

Fodor, J. A., and Pylyshyn, Z. (1988). "Connectionism and Cognitive Architecture." *Cognition* 28:71.

Fogel, A. (1985). "Coordinative Structures in the Development of Expressive Behaviour in Early Infancy." In G. Zivin (ed.), *The Development of Expressive Behaviour: Biology-Environment Interactions*, 249–267. Orlando: Academic Press.

Fogel, A. (1993) "Two Principles of Communication: Co—Regulation and Framing." In Nadel and Camaioni (1993), 9–22.

Fogel, A., and Thelen, E. (1987). "Development of Early Expressive and Communicative Action: Reinterpreting the Evidence from a Dynamic Systems Perspective." *Developmental Psychology* 23, no. 6:747–761.

Foster, T. C., Castro, C. A., and McNaughton, B. L. (1989). "Spatial Selectivity of Rat Hippocampal Neurons: Dependence on Preparedness for Movement." *Science*, June 30, 1589–1584.

Freyd, J. J. (1983). "Shareability: The Social Psychology of Epistemology." *Cognitive Science* 7:191–210.

Gabora, L. M., and Colgan, P. W. (1991). "A Model of the Mechanisms Underlying Exploratory Behaviour." In Meyer and Wilson (1991), 475–484.

Gardner, R. A., and Gardner, B. T. (1992). "Feedforward: The Ethological Basis of Animal Learning." In Varela and Bourgine (1992), 399–410.

Gibson, J. J. (1979). *The Ecological Approach to Visual Perception.* Boston: Houghton Mifflin.

Gould, J. L. (1986). "Landmark Maps for Honeybees." *Biological Cybernetics* 57:85–93.

Gould, J. L., and Marler, P. (1984). "Ethology and the Natural History of Learning." In P. Marler and H. S. Terrace (eds.), *The Biology of Learning,* 47–74. Berlin: Springer-Verlag.

Gould, S. J., and Lewontin, R. C. (1978). "The Spandrels of San Marco and the Panglossian Paradigm: A Critique of the Adaptionist Programme." *Proceedings of the Royal Society of London* 205:581–598. Reprinted in E. Sober (ed.), *Conceptual Issues in Evolutionary Biology.* Cambridge, MA: The MIT Press.

Greenfield, P. M., and Savage-Rumbaugh, E. S. (1991). "Imitation, Grammatical Developments and the Invention of Protogrammar by an Ape." In N. A. Krasnegor, D. M. Rumbaugh, R. L. Sciefelbusch, and M. Studdert-Kennedy (eds.), *Biological and Behavioral Determinants of Language Development.* Hillsdale, NJ: Lawrence Erlbaum Associates.

Grossberg, S., and Todorovic, D. (1988). "Neural Dynamics of 1-D and 2-D Brightness Perception: A Unified Model of Classical and Recent Phenomena." *Perception and Psychophysics* 43:241–277.

Guzman, A. (1969) "Decomposition of a Visual Scene into Three-Dimensional Bodies." In A. Grasselli (ed.), *Automatic Interpretation and Classification of Images,* 243–276 New York: Academic Press.

Halliday, M. A. K. (1979). "One Child's Protolanguage." In Bullowa (1979a), 171–190.

Harnad, S. (1987). *Categorical Perception: The Groundwork of Cognition.* New York: Cambridge University Press.

Harnad, S. (1990). "The Symbol Grounding Problem." *Physica D* 42:335–346.

Harvey, I. (1992a). "The SAGA Cross: The Mechanics of Crossover for Variable-Length Genetic Algorithms." In R. Manner and B. Manderick (eds.), *Parallel Problem Solving from Nature,* 2:269–278. Amsterdam: Elsevier.

Harvey, I. (1992b). "Species Adaption Genetic Algorithms: A Basis for a Continuing SAGA." In Varela and Bourgine (1992), 346–354.

Harvey, I. Husbands, P., and Cliff, D. T. (1993). "Issues in Evolutionary Robotics." In J.-A. Meyer, H. Roitblat, and S. Wilson (eds.), *Proceedings of the Second Conference on Simulation of Adaptive Behavior.* Cambridge, MA: The MIT Press.

Harvey, I., Husbands, P., and Cliff, D. T. (1994). *Seeing the Light: Artificial Evolution, Real Vision.* Cognitive Science Research Paper 317. Brighton: University of Sussex.

Heil, J. (1981). "Does Cognitive Psychology Rest on a Mistake?" *Mind* 90:321–342.

Hendriks-Jansen, H. J. (1990). Stage Three: A Critique of Marr's Theory of Vision. Master's thesis, School of Cognitive and Computing Sciences, The University of Sussex.

Heritage, J. (1984). *Garfinkel and Ethnomethodology*. Cambridge: Polity Press.

Hesse, M. B. (1966). *Models and Analogies in Science*. Notre Dame, IN: University of Notre Dame Press.

Hesse, M. B. (1980). *Revolutions and Reconstructions in the Philosophy of Science*. Brighton: Harvester Press.

Hinde, R. A. (1953). "Appetitive Behaviour, Consummatory Act, and the Hierarchical Organisation of Behaviour—with Special Reference to the Great Tit *(Parus major)*." *Behaviour* 5:189–224.

Hinde, R. A. (1956). "Ethological Models and the Concept of Drive." *Science* 6:321–331.

Hinde, R. A. (1957). "Consequences and Goals: Some Issues Raised by Dr Kortlandt's Paper on Aspects and Prospects of the Concept of Instinct." *British Journal of Animal Behaviour* 5:116–118.

Hinde, R. A. (1970). *Animal Behaviour: A Synthesis of Ethology and Comparative Psychology*. New York: McGraw-Hill.

Hinde, R. A. (1982). *Ethology: Its Nature and Relations with Other Sciences*. Oxford: Oxford University Press.

Hinde, R. A., and Stevenson, J. G. (1970). "Goals and Response Control." In L. R. Aronson (ed.), *Development and Evolution of Behavior*, 216–237. San Francisco: W. H. Freeman.

Hinton, G. E. (1981). "Shape Representations in Parallel Systems." *Proceedings of the Seventh Joint Conference on Artificial Intelligence*. Vancouver, 1088–1096.

Hirsh-Pasek, K., Jusczyk, P. W., Wright Cassidy, K., Druss, B., and Kennedy, C. (1987). "Clauses Are Perceptual Units of Young Infants." *Cognition* 26:269–286.

Hodges, A. (1983). *Alan Turing: The Enigma*. London: Burnet Books.

Hofstadter, D. (1980). *Gödel, Escher, Bach: An Eternal Golden Braid*. Harmondsworth: Penguin.

Hofstadter, D. (1985). "Waking Up from the Boolean Dream." In D. Hofstadter, *Metamagical Themas: Questing for the Essence of Mind and Pattern*. Harmondsworth: Penguin Books.

Horswill, I. (1992). "Characterising Adaption by Constraint." In Varela and Bourgine (1992), 58–63.

Horswill, I., and Brooks, R. A. (1988). "Situated Vision in a Dynamic World: Chasing Objects." Conference of the American Association for Artificial Intelligence, *AAAI-88*, pp. 796–800.

Houston, A. I. (1991). "Matching, Maximizing and Meliorization as Alternative Descriptions of Behaviour." In Meyer and Wilson (1991), 498–509.

Hoyle, G. (1984). "The Scope of Neuroethology." *Behavioral and Brain Sciences* 7:367–412.

Husbands, P., and Harvey, I. (1992). "Evolution Versus Design: Controlling Autonomous Robots." In *Integrating Perception, Planning and Action, Proceedings of the Third Annual Conference on Artificial Intelligence, Simulation and Planning*, 139–146. New York: IEEE Press.

Husbands, P., Harvey, I., and Cliff, D. T. (1993). "An Evolutionary Approach to AI." In A. Sloman et al. (eds.), *Prospects for Artificial Intelligence*, 61–70. Amsterdam: IOS Press.

Jamon, M. (1991). "The Contribution of Quatitative Models to the Long Distance Orientation Problems." In Meyer and Wilson (1991), 160–168.

Johnson, M. H. (ed.). (1993a). *Brain Development and Cognition: A Reader*. Oxford: Blackwell.

Johnson, M. H. (1993b). "Constraints on Cortical Plasticity." In Johnson (1993a), 703–721.

Johnson-Laird, P. N. (1978). "What's Wrong with Grandma's Guide to Procedural Semantics: A Reply to Jerry Fodor." *Cognition* 6:262–271.

Karmiloff-Smith, A. (1990). "Constraints on Representational Change: Evidence from Children's Drawing." *Cognition* 34:57–83.

Karmiloff-Smith, A. (1991). "Beyond Modularity: Innate Constraints and Developmental Change." In Carey and Gelman (1991), 171–197.

Karmiloff-Smith, A. (1992). *Beyond Modularity: A Developmental Perspective on Cognitive Change.* London: The MIT Press.

Karmiloff-Smith, A. (1993). "Self-Organisation and Cognitive Change." In Johnson (1993a), 592–618.

Kaye, K. (1979). "Thickening Thin Data: The Maternal Role in Developing Communication and Language." In Bullowa (1979a), 191–206.

Kaye, K. (1982). "Organism, Apprentice and Person." In E. Z. Tronick (ed.), *Social Interchange in Infancy*, 183–196. Baltimore: University Park Press.

Kortlandt, A. (1955). "Aspects and Prospects of the Concept of Instinct." *Archives Néerlandaises de Zoologie* 11:155–284 (cited by Hinde [1957]).

Kosslyn, S. (1975). "Information Representation in Visual Images." *Cognitive Psychology* 7:341–370.

Koza, J. R. (1992). "Evolution of Subsumption Using Genetic Programming." In Varela and Bourgine (1992), 110–122.

Kuo, Z.-Y. (1932). "Ontogeny of Embryonic Behaviour in Aves II. The Mechanical Factors in the Various Stages Leading to Hatching." *Journal of Comparative Psychology* 13, 245–272.

Kuhn, T. S. (1970). *The Structure of Scientific Revolutions.* 2d ed. Chicago: University of Chicago Press.

Lakoff, G. (1980). "Whatever Happened to Deep Structure?" *Behavioral and Brain Sciences* 3:22–23.

Land, E. H. (1977). "The Retinex Theory of Vision." *Scientific American* 237:108–128.

Land, E. H. (1986). "Recent Advances in Retinex Theory." *Vision Research* 26, no. 1:7–21.

Langer, S. (1942). *Philosophy in a New Key: A Study in the Symbolism of Reason, Rite and Art.* New York: Mentor Books.

Lashley, K. (1951). "The Problem of Serial Order in Behavior." In L. A. Jefress (ed.), *Hixon Symposium on Cerebral Mechanisms in Behavior.* New York: John Wiley.

Lehrman, D. S. (1970). "Semantic and Conceptual Issues in the Nature-Nurture Problem." In L. Aronson (ed.), *Development and Evolution of Behavior*, 17–52. San Francisco: W. H. Freeman.

Lewontin, R. C. (1980). "Adaption." From the *Encyclopaedia Einaudi.* Reprinted in E. Sober (ed.), *Conceptual Issues in Evolutionary Biology*, 234–251. Cambridge, MA: The MIT Press.

Lewontin, R. C. (1990). "How Much Did the Brain Have to Change for Speech?" *Behavioral and Brain Sciences* 13:740–741.

Lorenz, K. (1935). "Companionship in Bird Life." In Schiller and Lashley (1957), 83–128.

Lorenz, K. (1937). "The Nature of Instinct: The Conception of Instinctive Behaviour." In Schiller and Lashley (1957), 129–175.

Lorenz, K. (1939). "Comparative Study of Behaviour." In Schiller and Lashley (1957), 239–263.

Lorenz, K. (1952). "The Past Twelve Years in the Comparative Study of Behaviour." In Schiller and Lashley (1957), 288–310.

Lorenz, K., and Tinbergen, N. (1938). "Taxis and Instinct: Taxis and Instinctive Action in the Egg-Retrieving Behaviour of the Greylag Goose." In Schiller and Lashley (1957), 176–208.

McClelland, J. L., and Rumelhart, D. (eds.) (1986). *Parallel Distributed Processing.* Cambridge, MA: The MIT Press.

McCulloch, W. S., and Pitts, W. (1943). "A Logical Calculus of Ideas Immanent in Nervous Activity." *Bulletin of Mathematical Biophysics* 5:115–133.

McDougall, W. (1932). *The Energies of Men: A Study of the Fundamentals of Dynamic Psychology.* London: Methuen.

McDougall, W. (1936). *An Introduction to Social Psychology.* London: Methuen.

McFarland, D. (1985). *Animal Behaviour: Psychology, Ethology and Evolution.* London: Pitman Publishing.

McFarland, D. (1989). "Goals, No-Goals and Own Goals." In Montefiore and Noble (1989), 39–57.

Maes, P. (ed.). (1991a). *Designing Autonomous Agents: Theory and Practice from Biology to Engineering and Back.* Cambridge, MA: The MIT Press.

Maes, P. (1991b). "A Bottom-Up Mechanism for Behaviour Selection in an Artificial Creature." In Meyer and Wilson (1991), 238–246.

Maes, P. (1992). "Learning Behaviour Networks from Experience." In Varela and Bourgine (1992), 48–57.

Marr, D. (1977). "Artificial Intelligence—A Personal View." *Artificial Intelligence* 9:37–48.

Marr, D. (1982). *Vision.* New York: Freeman and Co.

Mataric, M. J. (1991a). "Navigating with a Rat Brain: A Neurobiologically Inspired Model for Robot Spatial Representation." In Meyer and Wilson (1991), 169–175.

Mataric, M. J. (1991b). "Behavioural Synergy Without Explicit Integration." In *Proceedings AAAI Spring Symposium on Integrated Intelligent Architectures,* Stanford University, *Sigart Bulletin* 2, no. 4:130–133.

Mataric, M. J. (1992). "Integration of Representation into Goal-Driven Behavior-Based Robots." *IEEE Transactions on Robotics and Automation* 8, no. 3:304–312.

Mataric, M. J., and Brooks, R. A. (1990). "Learning a Distributed Map Representation Based on Navigation Behaviors." In *Proceedings of 1990 USA Japan Symposium on Flexible Automation,* Kyoto, Japan, 499–506.

Maynard Smith, J. (1978). "Optimization Theory in Evolution." *Annual Review of Ecology and Systematics* 9:31–56.

Maynard Smith, J. (1995). "Darwinism Evolving by David J. Depew and Bruce H. Weber." *New York Review of Books* 42, no. 4:28–30.

Mayr, E. (1958). "Behaviour and Systematics." In A. Roe and G. G. Simpson (eds.), *Behaviour and Evolution,* 341–362. New Haven: Yale University Press.

Meehl, P. E. (1954). *Clinical Versus Statistical Prediction.* Minneapolis: University of Minnesota Press.

Meyer, J. A., and Wilson, S. W. (eds.). (1991). *From Animals to Animats: Proceedings of the First International Conference on Simulation of Adaptive Behavior:* Cambridge, MA: The MIT Press.

Miller, G. A., Galanter, E., and Pribram, K. H. (1960). *Plans and the Structure of Behavior.* New York: Holt, Rinehart and Winston.

Miller, J. L., and Jusczyk, P. W. (1989). "Seeking the Neurobiological Bases of Speech Perception." *Cognition* 33:111–137.

Millikan, R. (1984). *Language, Thought and Other Biological Categories: New Foundations for Realism.* Cambridge, MA: The MIT Press.

Millikan, R. (1986). "Thoughts Without Laws; Cognitive Science Without Content." *Philosophical Review* 95, no. 1:47–80.

Millikan, R. (1989). "Biosemantics." *Journal of Philosophy* 86, no. 6:281–297.

Minsky, M. (1972). *Computation: Finite and Infinite Machines.* London: Prentice-Hall International.

Minsky, M. (1987). *The Society of Mind.* London: Picador.

Minsky, M., and Papert, S. (1969). *Perceptrons: An Introduction to Computational Geometry* (exp. ed., 1988). Cambridge, MA: The MIT Press.

Mitchell, M., Forrest, S., and Holland, J. H. (1992). "The Royal Road for Genetic Algorithms: Fitness Landscapes and G. A. Performance." In Varela and Bourgine (1992), 245–254.

Montefiore, A., and Noble, N. (eds.) (1989). *Goals, No-Goals and Own Goals.* London: Unwin Hyman.

Nadel, J., and Camaioni, L. (eds.) (1993). *New Perspectives in Early Communicative Development.* London: Routledge.

Nagel, E. (1961). *The Structure of Science: Problems in the Logic of Scientific Explanation.* London: Routledge and Kegan Paul.

Nelson, K. (1974). "Concept, Word and Sentence: Interrelations in Acquisition and Development." *Psychological Review* 81, no. 4:267–285.

Nelson, K. (ed.). (1989). *Narratives from the Crib.* Cambridge, MA: Harvard University Press.

Newell, A. (1973). "You Can't Play Twenty Questions with Nature and Win." In W. G. Chase (ed.), *Visual Information Processing,* 283–308. New York: Academic Press.

Newell, A. (1980). "Physical Symbol Systems." *Cognitive Science* 4:135–183.

Newell, A., and Simon, H. A. (1961). "GPS—A Program That Simulates Human Thought." In H. Billing (ed.), *Lerende Automaten.* Munich: Oldenbourg, 109–124. Reprinted in E. A. Feigenbaum and J. Feldman (eds.), *Computers and Thought,* 109–133. New York: McGraw-Hill, 1963.

Newell, A., and Simon, H. A. (1972). *Human Problem Solving.* Englewood Cliffs, NJ: Prentice-Hall.

Newell, A., and Simon, H. A. (1976). "Computer Science as Empirical Inquiry: Symbols and Search." *Communications of the ACM* 19, no. 3:113–126.

Newson, J. (1979). "The Growth of Shared Understandings between Infant and Caregiver." In Bullowa (1979a), 207–222.

Nisbett, R. E., and Wilson, T. D. (1977). "Telling More Than We Can Know: Verbal Reports on Mental Processes." *Psychological Review* 84, no. 3:231–259.

O'Keefe, J. (1989). "Computations the Hippocampus Might Perform." In L. Nadel et al. (eds.), *Neural Connections, Mental Computation.* Cambridge, MA: The MIT Press.

Oyama, S. (1993). "The Problem of Change." In Johnson (1993a), 19–30.

Papert, S. (1980). *Mindstorms: Children, Computers and Powerful Ideas.* Brighton: Harvester Press.

Papousek, H., and Papousek, M. (1977). "Mothering and the Cognitive Head-Start: Psychobiological Considerations." In Schaffer (1977a), 63–85.

Pfeifer, R., and Verschure, P. (1992). "Distributive Adaptive Control: A Paradigm for Designing Autonomous Agents." In Varela and Bourgine (1992), 21–30.

Piaget, J. (1952). *The Origins of Intelligence in the Child.* London: Routledge and Kegan Paul.

Piaget, J. (1954). *The Construction of Reality in the Child.* New York: Basic Books.

Pinker, S., and Bloom, P. (1990). "Natural Language and Natural Selection." *Behaviour and Brain Sciences* 13:707–784.

Popper, K. (1963). *Conjectures and Refutations: The Growth of Scientific Knowledge.* London: Routledge and Kegan Paul.

Premack, D. (1984). "Pedagogy and Aesthetics as Sources of Culture." In M. Gazzaniga (ed.), *Handbook of Cognitive Neuroscience,* 15–35. New York: Plenum Press.

Pylyshyn, Z. (1984). *Computation and Cognition.* Cambridge, MA: The MIT Press.

Rosenblueth, A., Wiener, N., and Bigelow, J. (1943). "Behaviour, Purpose and Teleology." *Philosophy of Science* 10:18–24.

Rumelhart, D. E., Smolensky, P., McLelland, J. L., and Hinton, G. E. (1986). "Schemata and Sequential Processes in PDP Models." In McClelland and Rumelhart (1987), 2:7–57.

Savage-Rumbaugh, E. S. (1991). "Language Learning in the Bonobo: How and Why They Learn." In N. A. Krasnegor, D. M. Rumbaugh, R. L. Schiefelbush, and M. Studdert-Kennedy (eds.), *Biological and Behavioral Determinants of Language Development.* Hillsdale, NJ: Lawrence Erlbaum Associates.

Schaffer, H. R. (ed.). (1977a). *Studies in Mother-Infant Interaction: Proceedings of Loch Lomond Symposium.* New York: Academic Press.

Schaffer, H. R. (1977b). "Early Interactive Development." In Schaffer (1977a), 3–18.

Schiller, C. H. (1949). "Innate Motor Action as a Basis of Learning: Manipulative Patterns in the Chimpanzee." In Schiller and Lashley (1957), 239–263.

Schiller, C. H., and Lashley, K. S. (eds.). (1957). *Instinctive Behaviour: The Development of a Modern Concept.* New York: International University Press.

Schneirla, T. C.(1966). "Behavioural Development and Comparative Psychology." *Quarterly Review of Biology* 41:283–302.

Searle, J. (1980). "Minds, Brains, and Programs." *Behavioral and Brain Sciences* 3:417–457.

Searle, J. (1991). "Consciousness, Explanatory Inversion and Cognitive Science." *Behavioral and Brain Sciences* 13:585–642.

Sejnowski, T. J., Koch, C., and Churchland, P. S. (1988). "Computational Neuroscience." *Science* 241:1299–1306.

Shanon, B. (1988). "Semantic Representation of Meaning: A Critique." *Psychological Bulletin* 104, no. 1:70–83.

Shannon, C. E., and McCarthy, J. (eds.). (1956). *Automata Studies.* London: Oxford University Press.

Shannon, C. E., and Weaver, W. (1949). *The Mathematical Theory of Communication.* Urbana: University of Illinois Press.

Sinha, C. (1988). *Language and Representation.* Hemel-Hempstead: Harvester-Wheatsheaf.

Simon, H. A. (1967). "Motivational and Emotional Controls of Cognition." *Psychological Review* 74, no. 1:29–39.

Sloman, A. (1978). *The Computer Revolution in Philosophy.* Hassocks, Sussex: Harvester Press.

Sloman, A. (1990), "Motives, Mechanisms, and Emotions." In Boden (1990), 231–247.

Sloman, A. (1993). "The Mind as a Control System." In C. Hookway and D. Peterson (eds.), *Philosophy and the Cognitive Sciences: Proceedings of the 1992 Royal Institute of Philosophy Conference.* Cambridge: Cambridge University Press.

Smolensky, P. (1988). "On the Proper Treatment of Connectionism." *Behavioral and Brain Sciences* 11:1–74.

Snaith, M., and Holland, O. (1991). "An Investigation of Two Mediated Strategies Suitable for Behavioural Control in Animals and Animats." In Meyer and Wilson (1991), 255–262.

Spelke, E. S. (1991). "Physical Knowledge in Infancy: Reflections on Piaget's Theory." In Carey and Gelman (1991), 133–169.

Springer, S., and Deutch, G. (1981). *Left Brain, Right Brain.* New York: W. H. Freeman.

Sterelny, K. (1990). *The Representational Theory of Mind.* Oxford: Basil Blackwell.

Storms, M. D., and Nisbett, R. J. (1970). "Insomnia and the Attribution Process." *Journal of Personality and Social Psychology* 16:319–328.

Suchman, L. A. (1987). *Plans and Situated Actions: The Problem of Human-Machine Communication.* New York: Cambridge University Press.

Suchman, L. A. (1993). "Response to Vera and Simon's Situated Action: A Symbolic Interpretation." *Cognitive Science* 17:71–75.

Sudnow, D. (1978). *Ways of the Hand: The Organisation of Improvised Conduct.* London: Routledge and Kegan Paul.

Thelen, E. (1981). "Rhythmical Behaviour in Infancy: An Ethological Perspective." *Developmental Psychology* 17, no. 3:237–257.

Thelen, E. (1982). "Newborn Stepping: An Explanation for a 'Disappearing' Reflex." *Developmental Psychology* 18, no. 5:760–775.

Thelen, E. (1985). "Expression as Action: A Motor Perspective of the Transition from Spontaneous to Instrumental Behaviours." In G. Zivin (ed.), *The Development of Expressive Behaviour: Biology Environment Interactions,* 221–248. Orlando: Academic Press.

Thelen, E. (1993). "Self-Organisation in Developmental Processes: Can Systems Approaches Work?" In Johnson (1993a), 555–591.

Tinbergen, N. (1951). *The Study of Instinct.* Oxford: Clarendon Press.

Trevarthen, C. (1977). "Descriptive Analyses of Infant Communicative Behaviour." In Schaffer (1977a), 227–270.

Trevarthen, C. (1979). "Communication and Cooperation in Early Infancy: A Description of Primary Intersubjectivity." In Bullowa (1977a), 321–348.

Trevarthen, C. (1984). "Emotions in Infancy: Regulators of Contact and Relationships with Persons." In K. Scherer and P. Ekman (eds.), *Approaches to Emotion.* Hillsdale, NJ: Laurence Erlbaum.

Trevarthen, C. (1987). "Infancy, Mind In." In R. L. Gregory (ed.), *The Oxford Companion to the Mind,* 362–368. Oxford: Oxford University Press.

Trevarthen, C. (1993). "The Function of Emotions in Early Infant Communication and Development." In Nadel and Camaioni (1993), 48–81.

Tronick, E., Als, E., and Adamson, L. (1979). "Structure of Early Face-to-Face Communicative Interactions." In Bullowa (1979a), 349–372.

Turing, A. (1936). "On Computable Numbers, with an Application to the Entscheidungsproblem." *Proceedings of the London Mathematical Society* 42:230–265.

Turing, A. (1950). "Computing Machinery and Intelligence." *Mind* 59:433–460.

Turkewitz, G., and Kenny, P. A. (1993). "Limitations on Input as a Basis for Neural Organisation and Perceptual Development: A Preliminary Theoretical Statement." In Johnson (1993a), 510–522.

Turvey, M. T., and Kugler, P. N. (1984). "An Ecological Approach to Perception and Action." In H. T. A. Whiting (ed.), *Human Motor Actions—Bernstein Reassessed.* Amsterdam: Elsevier.

Turvey, M. T., and Carello, C. (1986). "The Ecological Approach to Perceiving-Acting: A Pictorial Essay." *Acta Psychologica* 63:133–155.

Ullman, S. (1980). "Against Direct Perception." *Behavioral and Brain Sciences* 3:373–416.

Ullman, S. (1984). "Visual Routines." *Cognition* 18:97–159.

Van Gelder, T. (1992). "What Might Cognition Be If Not Computation?" *Indiana University Cognitive Science Research Report* 75.

Varela, F., and Bourgine, P. (eds.). (1992). *Toward a Practice of Autonomous Systems: Proceedings of the First European Conference on Artificial Life.* Cambridge: MA: The MIT Press.

Vera, H. A., and Simon, H. A. (1993). "Situated Action: A Symbolic Interpretation." *Cognitive Science* 17, no. 1:7–48, 77–87, 117–133.

Von Cranach, M., and Harré, R. (eds.) (1982). *The Analysis of Action.* Cambridge Cambridge University Press.

Von Hofsten, C. (1984). "Developmental Changes in the Organisation of Prereaching Movements." *Developmental Psychology* 20, no. 3:378–388.

Von Uexkull, J. (1934). "A Stroll Through the Worlds of Animals and Men." In Schiller and Lashley (1957), 5–82.

Vonk, M., Putters, P., and Velthuis, B.-J. (1991). "The Causal Analysis of an Adaptive System: Sex Ratio Decisions as Observed in a Parasitic Wasp and Simulated by a Network Model." In Meyer and Wilson (1991), 285–291.

Walsh, D. (1970). "Sociology and the Social World." In P. Worsley (ed.), *Modern Sociology: Introductory Readings*, 79–91. Harmondsworth: Penguin Books.

Waltz, D. (1972). Generating Semantic Descriptions from Drawings of Scenes with Shadows. MIT Artificial Intelligence Laboratory.

Way, E. C. (1991). *Knowledge Representation and Metaphor*. Dordrecht: Kluwer Academic Press.

Webb, B. (1993). "Modeling Biological Behaviour, or Dumb Animals and Stupid Robots." In *Proceedings of ECAL 93*, 1090–1103.

Webb, B. (1994). "Robotic Experiments in Cricket Phonotaxis." In Cliff, Husbands, Meyer, and Wilson (1994), 45–54.

Webb, B., and Smithers, T. (1992). "The Connection between AI and Biology in the Study of Behaviour." In Varela and Bourgine (1992), 421–428.

Wilkes, K. (1989). "Explanation–How Not to Miss the Point." In A. Montefiore and D. Noble (eds.), *Goals, No Goals and Own Goals*, 194–210. London: Unwin Hyman.

Winston, P. H. (1975). "Learning Structural Descriptions from Examples." In P. H. Winston (ed.), *The Psychology of Computer Vision*, 157–210. New York: McGraw-Hill.

Wright, L. (1973). "Functions." *Philosophical Review* 82:139–168. Reprinted in E. Sober (ed.), *Conceptual Issues in Evolutionary Biology*. Cambridge, MA: The MIT Press.

Yarbus, A. L. (1984). *Eye Movement and Vision*. New York: Plenum Press.

Zimbardo, P. G. (1969). *The Cognitive Control of Motivation: The Consequences of Choice and Dissonance*. Glenview, IL: Scott, Forseman.

Zimmerman, D. H., and Wieder, D. L. (1971). "Ethnomethodology and the Problem of Order." In P. Worsley (ed.), *Modern Sociology: Introductory Readings*, 651–657. Harmondsworth: Penguin Books.

Index